# The European debt crisis

Manchester University Press

European Policy Research Unit Series

Series Editors: *Simon Bulmer, Peter Humphreys, Andrew Geddes* and *Dimitris Papadimitriou*

The European Policy Research Unit Series aims to provide advanced textbooks and thematic studies of key public policy issues in Europe. They concentrate, in particular, on comparing patterns of national policy content, but pay due attention to the European Union dimension. The thematic studies are guided by the character of the policy issue under examination.

The European Policy Research Unit (EPRU) was set up in 1989 within the University of Manchester's Department of Government to promote research on European politics and public policy. The series is part of EPRU's effort to facilitate intellectual exchange and substantive debate on the key policy issues confronting the European states and the European Union.

# The European debt crisis

## The Greek case

*Costas Simitis*

Translated from the Greek by P. Douzina-Stiakaki
Revised by Ewan Munro

*Στου Μιχάλη Κωττάκη*

*Κ. Σιμίτης*

*9/12/2014*

## Manchester University Press

Manchester and New York

distributed in the United States exclusively
by Palgrave Macmillan

First English-language edition published in 2014 by Manchester University Press
Oxford Road, Manchester M13 9NR, UK

Published by Manchester University Press
Oxford Road, Manchester M13 9NR, UK
and Room 400, 175 Fifth Avenue, New York, NY 10010, USA
www.manchesteruniversitypress.co.uk

Distributed exclusively in the USA by
Palgrave Macmillan, 175 Fifth Avenue, New York,
NY 10010, USA

Distributed exclusively in Canada by
UBC Press, University of British Columbia, 2029 West Mall,
Vancouver, BC, Canada V6T 1Z2

British Library Cataloguing-in-Publication Data
A catalogue record for this book is available from the British Library

Library of Congress Cataloging-in-Publication Data applied for

ISBN  978 0 7190 9579 5   hardback

ISBN  978 0 7190 9578 8   paperback

First published 2014

Typeset in Sabon by R. J. Footring Ltd, Derby, UK
Printed in Great Britain
by Bell & Bain Ltd, Glasgow

# Contents

## Part IV  Coalition government, private sector involvement and the second Memorandum

## Part V  Elections of 6 May and 17 June 2012

## Part VI  The future of Greece and the European Union

# Preface

In September 2009 international public opinion appeared contented that the global financial crisis, which had begun in 2007, had been successfully dealt with. The measures that had been taken by the developed world – the drastic lowering of interest rates, unprecedented support for banks with public money and International Monetary Fund support for certain countries – had managed to avert a general economic collapse. Newspapers reported good news: stock prices were on the rise again; liquidity was returning to the markets; banks had regained access to capital; sovereign borrowing costs had shrunk spectacularly.[1]

In September 2009, the G-20 Summit at Pittsburgh, USA, also confirmed that the response to the 2007 crisis had been successful. It was noted that positive rates of economic growth had returned.[2] The European Council of 10–11 December 2009 was also optimistic. It stated that 'the economic situation is beginning to stabilise and confidence is growing. We predict a weak recovery for 2010 and a return to higher rates of growth in 2011.'[3]

But there were also some critical voices, pointing out that the aftermath of the 2007 crisis was not so rosy.[4] Experience, they maintained, shows that financial crises open up deep wounds. When sovereign debt grows beyond certain levels, restrictive policies become necessary. Growth does return but at a much lower rate than before and the risk of long-term stagnation is great. However, a widespread feeling that the crisis was over prevailed and with it came the conviction that stability and growth would soon follow. What failed to be predicted was the extent to which a sovereign debt crisis would create serious problems for the functioning of the European Union (EU).

By mid-October 2009, commentators appeared increasingly concerned 'that the fear of debt shall replace the existing fear of crisis'.[5] Projections of the fiscal performance of member states revealed that in many countries budget deficits would far exceed the 3% limit stipulated by EU treaties and, in many cases, would reach between 5% and 10% of gross domestic product (GDP). Such deficits, under the recession fuelled by the crisis, would lead to a fast rise in sovereign debt. Certain economists maintained that governments should react swiftly with public spending cuts. However, the then dominant view within the Union held that it was too early to implement a common strategy for curbing debt. Every country would, therefore, have to show prudence and strive for economic stability independently, using whatever 'national' means it had at its disposal.

In this climate of doubt and indecision the news that Greece's deficit for 2009 had reached 12% of GDP turned everyone's attention on Athens. European public opinion felt that Greece had squandered European funds and goodwill and, as such, did not belong in the Eurozone. Greece was an example that proved how mismanagement leads to crisis. Greece's predicament, it was thought, was exceptional, not the result of the Eurozone's own design.

As the crisis unfolded, it became apparent that other Eurozone countries displayed identical symptoms to those of Greece, albeit to a different degree. Portugal, Ireland, Spain and even Italy were described as countries in danger. From being a strictly Greek problem, the debt crisis now turned into a problem for the Eurozone and the EU as a whole. The attempts to deal with it raised the need to restructure European institutions. The task of reform, however, still remains incomplete, despite the efforts that have been made in this direction.

This book traces the development of the debt crisis in the Eurozone from the moment it manifested itself in Greece to June 2013, when European leaders began to seek a broader and permanent solution for its economic governance.

Special thanks are due to Dimitris Papadimitriou and John Spraos for their valuable support in preparing the English edition of the book. I wish to thank also Ewan Munro for his editorial assistance with the manuscript.

### Notes

1 See M. Wolf, 'Economie', *Le Monde*, 8 September 2009; P. A. Delhommais, 'La crise de 1929 n'aura pas lieu', *Le Monde*, 6/7 September 2009.
2 See 'Economie', *Le Monde*, 27/28 September 2009.
3 European Council, 10/11 December 2009, 'Conclusions', p. 3.
4 See J. Pisani-Ferry, '*Economie*', *Le Monde*, 29 September 2009.
5 J. Pisani-Ferry, 'La peur de la dette', 'Economie', *Le Monde*, 27 October 2009. See also M. Wolf, 'La dette ce fardeau soutenable', 'Economie', *Le Monde*, 1 December 2009.

# The main Greek political parties

**New Democracy**, also known by its initials ND, is the main conservative party. It was founded after the fall of the military dictatorship by the former and in 1974 acting Prime Minister Konstantinos Karamanlis. It governed the country 1974–81 (Prime Ministers Konstantinos Karamanlis and George Rallis), 1990–93 (Prime Minister Konstantinos Mitsotakis) and 2004–09 (Prime Minister Kostas Karamanlis, nephew of the founder).

The **Panhellenic Socialist Movement**, known by its initials PASOK, was founded after the fall of the military dictatorship by Andreas Papandreou in September 1974. In 1981 it became the first social democratic party to win a majority in Parliament. It governed the country 1981–89 (Prime Minister Andreas Papandreou), 1993–96 (Prime Minister Andreas Papandreou), 1996–2004 (Prime Minister Costas Simitis) and 2009–11 (Prime Minister George Papandreou, son of the founder).

The **Coalition of the Radical Left Unified Social Front**, known by its acronym SYRIZA, is a left-wing party representing various groups with different left ideologies, critical of or hostile to Greece's membership of the European Union. In parliamentary elections up to 2012 the party won around 5% of the vote. In the June 2012 elections it increased its share to just under 22% of votes polled and became the main opposition party.

**Democratic Left**, known by its initials DIMAR, was founded on 27 June 2010 by a group that disagreed with the anti-European policy of SYRIZA. Its political position is thus socialist and pro-European. In the June 2012 elections it won 17 seats out of 300, with 6.3% of the vote.

The **Popular Orthodox Rally**, LAOS, was a radical right-wing nationalist and populist party represented in Parliament in 2007 and 2009. In the 2012 elections it was out-distanced by two other radical right-wing parties, the Golden Dawn and the Independent Greeks, which were far more aggressive. It failed to secure any seats in Parliament and was largely abandoned.

# Abbreviations

| | |
|---|---|
| AMECO | annual macroeconomic database |
| CDS | credit default swap |
| DIMAR | Democratic Left |
| EBA | European Banking Authority |
| ECB | European Central Bank |
| Ecofin | Economic and Financial Affairs Council |
| EFSF | European Financial Stability Facility |
| EIOPA | European Insurance and Occupational Pensions Authority |
| ELA | Emergency Liquidity Assistance |
| EMU | Economic and Monetary Union |
| ESM | European Stability Mechanism |
| ESMA | European Securities and Markets Authority |
| ESRB | European Systemic Risk Board |
| EU | European Union |
| Eurogroup | finance ministers of the Eurozone |
| Eurostat | Statistical Office of the European Communities |
| *FAZ* | *Frankfurter Allgemeine Zeitung* |
| GDP | gross domestic product |
| Grexit | Greek exit (from the euro) |
| *IHT* | *International Herald Tribune* |
| IIF | Institute for International Finance |
| IMF | International Monetary Fund |
| IOU | I owe you (formal acknowledgement of debt) |
| LAOS | Popular Orthodox Rally |
| OECD | Organisation for Economic Co-operation and Development |
| PASOK | Panhellenic Socialist Movement |
| PSI | private sector involvement |
| SDR | special drawing rights |
| SGP | Stability and Growth Plan |
| SYRIZA | Coalition of the Radical Left |
| VAT | value added tax |

# Part I
# How we arrived at the first Memorandum

# 1

# Was Greece ready for the euro?[1]

The argument widely advanced across Europe was that the cause of the Greek debt crisis lay in the absence of the prerequisites to participate in the single-currency project. Greece was not ready.

From the mid-1990s Greece had launched an intense effort to satisfy the convergence criteria. All available financial tools were used: fiscal policy, monetary policy, taxation and redistribution, and the privatisation of banks and public sector companies. However calculated, the state deficit was reduced by 10 percentage points, from 12.5% of gross domestic product (GDP) in 1993, to 2.5% by 1999, the year in which assessment to gauge Greece's suitability for participation in the Eurozone was undertaken. Progress towards meeting the other criteria for nominal convergence (rate of inflation, long-term interest rates, public debt and exchange rates) was equally positive. The European Council's decision taken at Santa Maria da Feira in June 2000 to include Greece was based on detailed scrutiny of the performance of the Greek economy, by the European Commission, the European Central Bank and the Economic and Financial Committee. It is worth noting that, despite the tight fiscal and monetary policy at the time, absolutely necessary in order to reduce the state deficit and the rate of inflation, the rate of growth in GDP in Greece had begun to improve. From a negative rate in 1993, it grew to an annual 4% by the end of the 1990s, and this continued until 2007. Private investment and an influx of foreign capital in Greece did much to fuel this growth. This was made possible only by the falling inflation rates and interest rates, now at single figures after two double-digit decades.

## The supposed tampering with the 1999 Greek statistics

Those who maintain that Greece should not have been admitted to the Economic and Monetary Union (EMU) usually present the argument that the country tampered with its economic figures in order to satisfy the convergence criteria.

The New Democracy[2] administration elected in 2004, four years after the data for Greece's admission had been approved, faced the unfortunate demand

3

to change the way in which defence expenditures were recorded, in order to lighten the fiscal burden for the period over which it was to govern. The desire to present balanced books led to a restructuring of the recording of payments. Expenditure on defence equipment, previously recorded at the point of receipt, was retroactively registered at the date of purchase. Thus the expenses were reallocated to previous budgets. The transfer of part of the deficit to the previous government allowed New Democracy to reduce the expenditure recorded during its own administration. This restructuring of payments made more capital available for immediate expenditure while Greece remained inside the 3% budget deficit cap prescribed by the Union. This change in the recording methodology increased the level of deficits prior to 2004. The change in the structure of Greek accounting fuelled the defamation of Greece across the continent. Other figures were also questioned, including those related to the deficits of the public services and social security system, as well as transactions between the state and public sector companies. The latter differences were known and they were being examined in cooperation with Eurostat (the Statistical Office of the European Communities). They were not the result of false reporting of data. In any case, the decisive factor affecting the new assessments was the scale of the deficit accrued through military expenditure.

The mantra that 'Greece was admitted to the Eurozone on falsified figures' received global coverage. It was unfortunately adopted by many politicians inside the Eurozone, and is still widely propagated today. *This charge, however, ignores the facts.*[3] Even with the change in recording methodology and with the revised figures, the state deficit for the decisive year (1999) is 3.1% of GDP, up from 2.5%. To be exact, it is 3.07% according to Eurostat figures from the annual macroeconomic database (AMECO). This deficit remains lower than the corresponding revised deficits of other 'first wave' countries which were evaluated on data for 1997. Figures on AMECO's website clearly indicate that other member states entered the Eurozone with deficits higher than 3.1% of GDP. Spain's and France's deficits were 3.3% of GDP, while Portugal's was 3.4%.

As in the case of Greece, the deficit figures of the other countries emerged only after repeated reappraisals of government expenditure by Eurostat. However, the slanderous charge of 'creative accounting' was reserved for Greece alone.[4] Only Greece was continually discussed in such terms in global media coverage and political discourse, despite the challenges and irregularities both Spain and Portugal presented. It was in Greece alone that the government of the day systematically blamed its predecessor for deceiving and misleading the European Union (EU) and international public opinion.[5]

Responsibility for what happened rests surely on the shoulders of the New Democracy administration of the period in question. However, responsibility also lies with Eurostat and the EU, which adapted the fiscal data received from the new Greek government. Accusations of a lack of due diligence are justified when one considers that the input of neither the Bank of Greece nor of the previous Minister of Finance was sought. What happened next was completely illogical. In 2006 Eurostat deemed that the correct method for recording expenditure on military equipment was when taking delivery of it,[6] as Greece had done prior to 2004. From 2005 onwards all member states not already recording expenditure in this fashion, including Greece for the period after 2004, were obliged to do so. However, despite this decision, Eurostat did not proceed to adjust Greece's deficit for 1999 to reflect this. The prior correction of the deficit at 3.07% of GDP was held, and not adjusted in line with the change in policy. The insignificant 0.07% of GDP deviation from the Treaty limit, uncritically imposed on the Eurozone, was thus pounced upon to discredit a monumental effort at fiscal adjustment in Greece.[7]

Recently, new efforts to slander Greece have been propagated; these concern a routine currency swap transaction between the Greek Ministry of Finance and the Goldman Sachs bank at the end of 2001. This transaction is not distinct from hundreds of others undertaken by other countries in the same period. While other member states' activities are framed in the discourse of public debt management, the actions of Athens are vilified as reckless and malign. Greece exchanged bonds denominated in yen for those in euro denomination, in order to mitigate exchange rate risks. The euro is its currency, and the country also participates – through the European Central Bank – in determining its value. All the euro countries were seeking to convert their debts into euros at the time. Greece was once again subjected to pejorative claims, with accusations that the government was manipulating the figures to satisfy membership criteria. As was the case with reconstruction of accounting methodology discussed above, despite such practices occurring across the continent, it was Greece that made front-page news and dominated political discourse. No significance whatsoever was attached to the fact that these transactions were undertaken in 2001, two years after Greece was assessed for compliance with the convergence criteria and a whole year after the decision to admit Greece was taken by the European Council at Santa Maria da Feira. Nor is it mentioned that, according to the European Statistical Service, the 2001 swap was in full accordance with the Union regulations for that period.[8]

## The real tampering with statistical data in 2009

On 4 October 2009, elections were to be held to elect a new Parliament. On 30 September 2009 the New Democracy administration of the day sent in-complete tables of data to Eurostat, missing all data for 2008 and 2009. It was obvious that the government did not wish to reveal data which would highlight its own shortcomings. On 2 October a new communication to Eurostat was sent, which claimed that the budget deficit was estimated at 6% of GDP. This calculation did not bear any relation to the figures produced by the various departments of the Statistical Service. An analysis of the correspond-ing data indicates a deficit of 12.5% of GDP, more than twice that claimed by New Democracy. This was the deficit that the new government, led by the Panhellenic Socialist Movement (PASOK), informed Eurostat of. In further revision of the figures by Eurostat the deficit for 2009 was determined to be 15.4%. While New Democracy contested the 15.4% figure for the 2009 deficit, it did not counter claims that it had overseen the deficit's rise to 12.5% of GDP, despite its prior assessment of 6%. This development rekindled discourse over the 'false' data for 2004, and offered further ammunition to those seeking to question the credibility of Greek statistics. In both 2004 and 2009 it was the same attitude of the conservatives that provoked the problem. What was expedient and beneficial for the party determined how the country would execute its commitments.

### The excessive level of Greek sovereign debt

*The second argument used by the Eurozone to explain the causes of the Greek problem was the external level of Greek sovereign debt.* When Greece became a member of the EMU, its sovereign debt was much higher than the maximum 60% of GDP prescribed by the Eurozone. In 1999 it stood at 93.3%. In 1997, when they were deemed fit for Eurozone membership, both Italy and Belgium had a level of sovereign debt exceeding 100% of GDP.[9] By the end of 2003 Greek sovereign debt had reached €168 billion, 97.4% of GDP. Under the oversight of the New Democracy administration, this trend continued.[10]

### The excessive budget deficit

From 2004 onwards, Greece was under almost continual fiscal supervision, in accordance with the Treaties, because of its failure to adhere to the 3% cap. Supervision was overseen by the European Commission. The objective was to closely monitor all developments and provide advice on how best to conform to EU rules. This supervision should have flagged up the warning signs and the failures in terms of compliance much sooner than it did. If these worrying trends had been highlighted at this juncture, the crisis would have been unlikely to reach the magnitude it did. However, in the case of Greece there proved to be a measure of 'friendly' collaboration between the European Commission and the conservative government, particularly during the pre-election periods of 2007 and 2009. The European Commission failed to show either the objectivity or the diligence it should have. Had it intervened in time, the Greek sovereign debt problem would not have led to the major crisis that followed. However, it would still have posed challenges for the Eurozone as a whole.

The reasons for the current sovereign debt crisis in Europe are not confined to the fiscal deficits and the high levels of sovereign debt of certain countries. It was the fact that Greece was the first country to fall into trouble that led to the prevailing view that the crisis was fiscal.[11] Spain, which did not have deficits exceeding the limit of 3% of GDP and whose sovereign debt in 2006 was just 31% of its GDP, also finds itself in crisis today. The reason for the challenges currently faced by Spain lies in the explosive, unsustainable growth of the construction industry. The subsequent collapse of real estate prices, the realisation of the high levels of toxic debt on the balance sheets of Spanish banks, and the drastic fall in competitiveness owing to the inflation brought about by the real estate 'bubble' were the cause of Spain's economic demise. The state's intervention to save the banks and to limit the effects of the crisis became inevitable.

Similarly in Ireland, annual government deficits did not exceed 3% of GDP, and sovereign debt fluctuated at acceptable levels. Irish banks, however, lent without due diligence or consideration. Upon the realisation that the banks had accrued balance sheets they did not have the capital to honour, the state intervened and took on their loans in order to save the banking system. Sovereign debt increased dramatically as a result, to 120% of GDP.

## The main causes of the crisis[12]

There is a much more serious reason for the explosion of sovereign debt in the countries of the Union's Periphery aside from the incompetence of their governments.[13] This reason is endogenous to the single-currency area created by the EMU. It is *the level of divergence in terms of growth rates between the North and the South, the reduced competitiveness of the peripheral countries, and the large deficits in their balance of payments.* The South buys high-quality and technologically advanced industrial products from the North. It also buys agricultural products, such as flowers or meat, which, owing to technological developments, are produced more cheaply in Germany or the Netherlands. The North buys considerably less from the South. As a result, structural trading deficits emerge, to the benefit of the Core and the cost of the Periphery. During the period 2000–07, Greece's annual trade deficit was 8.4% on average and Portugal's 9.4%, while Germany's surplus was 3.2% and that of the Netherlands 5.4%. To cover these deficits the peripheral countries have been obliged to borrow. Once the crisis fuelled an increase in the cost of borrowing in the private sector, states were obliged to step in and borrow themselves, so as to avoid a lack of liquidity and the suffocation of the market. This movement from private to public debt occurred in Greece without due care or diligence. Those responsible never stopped to think what limits they should set to avoid future problems.

The minimum interest rate on loans set by the European Central Bank (ECB), which applies to all states, irrespective of national rates of inflation, compounded negative developments. The ECB interest rate was based upon, and suited to, the German model of low rates of growth and inflation. However, the ECB interest rate was too high for many states. It prolonged the recession. For Greece, the same ECB interest rate was low, due to Greece's higher level of inflation, which fluctuated around the level of the interest rate.

In addition, it was much lower than the interest rate prevailing before Greece's entrance to the EMU. The consequence was a high demand for credit and a flourish in economic activity fuelled by the increased availability of credit, which drove higher rates of growth and a fall in levels of unemployment. Foreign banks, particularly the German and French ones, saw an opportunity for profit. They made credit both widely available and easily accessible. As money supply in the economy increased, salaries, which had been curtailed in order to achieve entry into the EMU, grew exponentially. During the period 2000–09, Greece saw the largest relative increase in salaries across the Eurozone. The effects on the Greek economy's competitiveness were negative. It fell after 2005, and worsened drastically from 2007 onwards. The immediate result was a rise in imports, a fall in exports and a continual widening of the current account deficit.

But within the Eurozone, finding funds to finance this deficit no longer presented the problem it had done in the time of the drachma. The foreign banks made credit easily available.[14] The supposed stability and security of the single currency led banks to presume that no default was possible. They were not concerned about a possible economic crisis. They considered all Eurozone nations to be equally creditworthy. Between 2001 and 2007 the Greek state borrowed at an interest rate *only 0.2% or 0.3% higher than that of the German state.*

But after 2004 the Greek government also relaxed. Despite the steady rise in the current account deficit, they did not foresee any danger. Stabilising measures were deemed superfluous. The climate in the foreign capital markets changed from 2007 on, when sovereign debt began to grow. Interest rates took off and by 2009 they exceeded 5%. At such an interest rate, the debt was no longer sustainable given the prevailing economic conditions in Greece.[15]

The continual budget deficits and growing sovereign debt meant that *Greece was spending more than it produced.* The deficit had to be contained; budgets had to have a surplus to reduce debt and, above all, to permit investment and improve productivity and competitiveness. However, the process of adjustment needs time. The restructuring of economic activity to reverse structural deficits cannot be achieved overnight. Holistic and pragmatic planning of the necessary steps is required, with regard to both time scales and targets. The governments of the South, however, avoided this choice because they did not want to incur the political cost. They preferred to borrow to cover the loss of capital that the lack of competitiveness produced.

Opinion in Greece, both inside the New Democracy government and on the part of the wider public, held that entrance into the EMU was the end game. Lax adherence to the Maastricht criteria with regard to the deficit merely indicated the economy's stability and maturity. It was widely believed that additional measures were unnecessary. Recommendations by the European Commission regarding structural reform aroused strong reactions. New Democracy continually exceeded criteria on deficit limits, in order to fund its system of political patronage, safe in the knowledge that severe financial penalties from the European Commission were highly improbable. It paid little attention to the fact that the Maastricht criteria for deficits and debt levels (which Greece did not adhere to) were designed to aid in the operation and stability of a single-currency area, and to promote convergence in terms of competitiveness. Diligent and concerted effort was vital. A member state which did not care would find itself in serious difficulties.

This development had not been foreseen by the creators of the EMU. They believed that the free movement of capital and the single market would ensure investment in the peripheral countries, thanks to their lower cost of labour, and thus convergence with developed countries would gradually follow. They ignored the fact that the process of convergence cannot be achieved in a narrow time frame. Furthermore, overcoming disparity in levels of growth cannot be achieved by limiting attention to economic concerns. Shortcomings in other sectors, such as administration and education, need to be addressed, where changes need time. Delays in convergence could have been countered by the creation of an EU mechanism to finance weaker countries at a very low interest rate to cover the deficits in their trading accounts. But this was superfluous, according to the economic theory that had inspired the formation of the Eurozone. This theory held that the correction of the imbalances in the trading accounts would come about automatically. If an acceptable limit to the trade deficit were exceeded, this would lead banks to limit the credit that permitted import activity. The resultant negative trickle down would restrict purchasing power, driving wage restraint and a subsequent return to competitiveness, and a gradual economic recovery. This theoretical scheme was not borne out by events. The banks continued to provide public and private credit, even when any reasoned economic assessment would have questioned the sustainability of such a trajectory. 'The self-adjustment of the market proved to be a chimera in the financial markets.'[16] When their money dried up, states were obliged to visit the international bond market to cover the shortfall and this downward spiral drove the accumulation of an enormous sovereign debt.

*The Treaties do not provide for the transfer of funds from the wealthier states to the weaker ones.* The rules for subsidising states and activities are strictly determined, and very specific with regard to actions that may be financed. The framework does not allow for the gulf between the North and the South to be addressed through fiscal transfers.

In the USA and in the Federal Republic of Germany, a transfer of funds from the central government to those federal states that are struggling in terms of growth or liquidity is made to redress any imbalance. This is a solution that has been discussed within the framework of the EU. According to calculations made in 2010, across the entire EU the average tax receipt per capita was €7,146. Seven countries collected taxes below the average and they would have been entitled to fiscal transfers from the Core, had such a mechanism to promote convergence been established. For this mechanism to be established, the following contributions would have had to be made: Finland, €3,500 per resident, France €940 and Germany approximately only €100, because the (former) East Germany is still behind Western Germany.[17] The total figure required to action such a transfer would have amounted to approximately €200 billion annually. This is an exceptionally large amount. Furthermore, without conditionality attached to the transfer, there was no guarantee it would not merely sustain undesirable structural conditions in the Periphery. It would entrench a structural divide between the North which produced and the South which consumed, as is the case within Italy, and maintain a relationship of dependency. The notion of a new federal organisation, with competency in the field of taxation and the power to oversee fiscal transfers to the Periphery, is not acceptable to most member states. They deem the existing system of support for the poorer areas, with structural programmes and special subsidies, to be less expensive and more effective. Under this system, in 2009 Germany paid €6,358 million, the largest sum for inter community aid, and Greece received €3,121 million, the second largest sum received by any member state.[18]

The existence of the single currency concealed the acute differences in economic health between states for a time. The result was that countries with weaker economic foundations could borrow at approximately the same interest rate as the developed and mature economies of the Core. When the interest rate gradually began to differ between states, a clear example of which was the gulf that developed between the rates available to Germany and Greece, it became clear that *the banks of the strong countries had overextended loans to the weaker countries.* The risk of exposure became increasingly apparent. Awareness of such exposure could cause a banking crisis in the developed countries, principally in Germany and France, and act as a catalyst to a loss of confidence the continent over. In order to mitigate losses and the risk of a loss of liquidity, liability was transferred from private balance sheets to national public ones, and then to the Union. The EU was required to step into the breach to prevent insolvency either in the banking sector or in public finances; this, however, contravened the regulatory framework of the Union.

Aside from the loss of competitiveness, the countries of the Periphery are also afflicted by failings in terms of *administration, efficiency and accountability of their services, and human capital with regard to expertise and experience.* While the Union's regulatory framework is applied in the Periphery, it is hampered by delays, and rarely achieves its aims. For example, until recently, the Greek Statistical Service constituted part of the Ministry of Finance, from which it took its orders. When it began operating as an independent authority, as required by the EU, there were disagreements within its board of directors about how data would be presented.

These institutional challenges were seized upon by some to argue that Greece, and perhaps other peripheral countries as well, should not have become members of the EMU. However, the EMU is not merely a collective of developed countries with common interests and goals. It is in the modus operandi of the EU to promote convergence and cooperation across member states in varying stages of development. The EU seeks to promote progress across the continent and drive economic and political cooperation. It should, therefore, account for the needs of both the mature and developed economies, and those less mature, in its planning. It should at all times be acutely sensitive to disparity, and the consequences this has for the structural needs of varied economies. While the more developed nations do benefit greatly from the strength of their export and financial sectors they must also share their proportion of the costs of integration.

When the EMU was established, many observers in the UK and the USA deemed that the project was doomed to failure. They claimed that a *monetary union presupposes a political union*, and a central authority with expanded competency was required to oversee such a project. The lack of such an authority would impede the Union's ability to act. Throughout the crisis they repeated these arguments. Europe is facing difficulties because the political elites forced the adoption of a single currency prematurely, on the basis of political rather than economic considerations.[19] They called the EMU a 'Euro-salad'. They predicted that, in the event of a crisis in one EMU member state, the loss of ability to devalue the currency would have negative ramifications. The member state would be obliged to effect an internal devaluation through a reduction of salaries and purchasing power. This, in turn, would result in a degradation of quality of life and an acute recession, which would only keep making the situation worse.

Developments have vindicated these predictions in part. The EMU was beneficial for all its members in the early years. The peripheral countries achieved high levels of growth, their borrowing costs fell significantly and they began to converge with the developed countries. The crisis that broke out in 2007 showed that claims of convergence were premature. The full ramifications of the loss of control over monetary policy were not realised; neither were any preparations made to counter such risks. The leadership of the EMU ignored the inevitable expansion of deficits, and was not conscious of the debt crisis this expansion would entail. In spite of this, implementing EMU, even while basic details were yet to be settled, was the right step to take. If the member states had postponed the decision on monetary union until after arranging the details of a political and economic union, the outcome would have been negative. Sooner or later, under the pressure of an economic crisis, there would have been competitive devaluations, restrictions on the single market and a retreat from the realisation of the joint enterprise.[20]

Initially, the members of EMU greeted the financial crisis and the recession which had already emerged from the end of 2007 with denial. On 12 and 13 September 2008, two days before the US bank Lehman Brothers collapsed, the finance ministers of the Eurozone and the representatives of the ECB met to discuss if – and to what extent – there was a crisis, and what measures should be taken. Denial continued to prevail. The ministers decided that the data showing a fall in economic activity in the EU did not justify the view that there was a crisis. They also agreed that there was no need for a European intervention plan. Following that, over the next month of negotiations and statements, a 'cacophony' of opinions emerged. Common agreement on how to deal with the banking crisis was realised only at the summit of the Eurozone nations and the UK held on 12 October 2008.

This experience made the members of the EMU more cautious. However, a year later, as the Greek crisis arose, the European Commission and the Core members of the Union refused to see that developments in Greece were not exclusively the product of mismanagement and incompetence on the part of the national government. They would not accept that the imbalances between the peripheral countries and the central nucleus, as well as the reckless provision of credit, had contributed significantly to the position in which Greece now found itself. It was only at the end of 2009 that the EMU began to realise that disparity in levels of competitiveness across the Union, the unsustainable levels of debt accrued in the Periphery and the insecurity caused by the financial crisis were driving ominous developments across the Eurozone. The increasing realisation that the fallout could affect the banking sectors and national economies of all the member states aroused anxiety.

The immediate reaction of the leadership was, once again, to defend the regulatory and institutional framework of the EMU. Developments were framed in terms of failure to adhere to the Maastricht criteria. Responsibility was understood to rest with the profligate governments: those nations participating in the EMU that had failed to satisfy the prerequisites for membership and the undisciplined governments that did not adhere to prescribed limits on deficit and debt. The single market, the single currency, the freedom of movement of capital and, more generally, the creation of a European economic area were not responsible. Any discourse that contested this understanding of cause was absent from official analysis and policy.[21]

### The obligation for solidarity

The EU and the EMU, in their current form, constitute an enormous investment in ideas, capital and labour, which not one of the members of the Eurozone is in a position to ignore or sacrifice without incurring an enormous cost for itself. The results of a break-up or dissolution are impossible to calculate. They would be exceptionally negative, even for those who think the EMU does not serve their economic interests. Across all member states, the ramifications for both political influence and their economic potential would be severe. 'It would be a giant blow to the wider European project, which has ensured peace and democracy to a continent with a tragic history.'[22] For this reason, it is in the vital interest of the members of the EMU to cooperate, to foresee challenges and to implement a coherent structural framework to redress the failings that have become so apparent throughout the crisis. Solidarity is vital.[23]

Solidarity, however, is a term that certain countries of the Union do not like at all. They consider that it implies an obligation to show support for others, a commitment which burdens them. They oppose the use of such language and the policy it implies. The situation, however, demands mutual action and support. The extent of cooperation is not merely determined by the legal texts but also by conditions on the ground, the relations that have been forged and the risks that arise. In an entity where there are continual interactive efforts between its members, both the strongest as well as the weakest have an interest in maintaining and strengthening it. At the same time, however, the degree of solidarity can be understood to bear a strong relation to adherence to the common rules and contributions to the collective effort. If one member refuses to adhere to all that has been agreed to in common, this gives the other members of the group the right to refuse their solidarity.

## Notes

1   The text of this chapter is based on an article by C. Simitis and Y. Stournaras published on the *Guardian*'s website, www.guardian.co.uk, 26 April 2012, on the *24 Ore* website, www.ilsole24ore.com, 29 April 2012, and in *Suddeutsche Zeitung*, 9 May 2012.

2   See 'The main Greek political parties', p. ix.

3   Nikos Christodoulakis, 'Griechenland hat nie betrogen', *Wirtschaft* online, 25 September 2013, www.spiegel.de/wirtschaft/soziales/euro-beitritt-griechenlands-ex-finanzminister-christodoulakis-ueber-bilanztricks-a-923492.html.

4   'Kreativ, vor allem in der Buchfuhrung' ['Creative, especially in accounting'], *FAZ*, 18 November 2011.

5   In April 2011, seven years after the revision of figures, the New Democracy spokesman, on the occasion of a conflict over the responsibilities of the New Democracy government, stated that 'the policy of revising the figures was catastrophic for the country'. Party cadres also repeated that 'it has been proved that the revision of figures was a historical mistake'. See *Kathimerini*, 22 April 2011; *Ethnos*, 22 April 2011.

6   Eurostat news release 31/2006, 9 March 2006.

7   Eurostat has stopped publishing Greece's fiscal deficit from 1995 to 1999 inclusive in its tables of the EU countries' fiscal deficits. In the columns where the relevant data should appear there are question marks instead. See Eurostat, Tables, graphs and maps (TGM) update, 14 January 2003. These question marks prove that Eurostat does not recognise the data submitted by New Democracy in 2004 as genuine. For more details see http://epp.eurostat.ec.europa.eu.

8   See Walter Rademacher, 'There is no problem with the Greek swaps', *Ta Nea* online, 4 February 2011; Eurostat, Information note on Greece, 24 February 2010. The chief of Eurostat, W. Rademacher, in an interview published in the Belgian newspaper *Le Soir*, 15 July 2013, refers to the swaps. But he mentions the swaps undertaken by the New Democracy administration in 2005 and 2008 that were not announced, as prescribed by Eurostat. This was not the case for the swap of 2001.

9   Belgium 122.5% of GDP, Italy 117.4% of GDP. European Commission, General government data, spring 2012.

10  See Chapter 2, note 8, p. 21.

11  M. Wolf, 'The toxic legacy of the Greek crisis', *Financial Times*, ft.com, 19 June 2013.

12  For an analysis of the causes of the European debt crisis, the financial assistance programmes for Greece, Ireland and Portugal, and their assessment see Jean Pisani-Ferry, André Sapir and Guntram Wolff, *EU–IMF Assistance to the Euro-Area Countries: An Early Assessment*, Bruegel, May 2013. The story of the crisis is narrated by Gavin Hewitt, *The Lost Continent*, Hodder and Stoughton, 2013.

13  For an analysis of the systemic deficiencies of the EMU see J. Pisani-Fery, *The Known Unknowns and Unknowns Unknowns of the EMU*, Policy Contribution 2012/18, Bruegel, October 2012; Z. Darvas, *The Euro Crisis: Ten Roots, But Fewer Solutions*, Policy Contribution 2012/12, Bruegel, October 2012.

14  Wolf, 'The toxic legacy': 'By deciding that the crisis was largely fiscal, policy makers could ignore the truth that the underlying cause of the disarray was irresponsible cross-border lending for which suppliers of credit are surely as responsible as users.'

15  For the role of the single minimum interest rate on borrowing in Europe see F. W. Scharpf, *Monetary Union, Fiscal Crisis and the Preemption of Democracy*, Max Plank Institute for the Study of Societies, 2011.

16  According to P. Bofinger the developments in Ireland and Spain show that a large part of the Eurozone's problems are not due to the institutional context of the EMU but 'to the general blindness and lack of restraint which spread globally over the years 2000–2007, to the banks and other factors of the financial markets.' See P. Bofinger, *Zurück zur D. Mark*, Droemer, 2012, pp. 52, 56.

17  See 'Dossier', *Le Monde*, 9 February 2010.

18  *Der Spiegel*, issue 31, 2011, p. 66. In the opinion of the German Central Bank (Bundesbank), Germany has abandoned the policy of not transferring funds, and in various ways supports other countries of the Union. This policy – it underlines – is wrong.

19  P. Krugman, 'A hunt for culprits in Eurocrisis', *IHT*, 21 February 2010; *IHT*, 31 July 2012; *IHT*, 25–26 August 2012.

20  See M. Monti, 'Entretien avec P. Krugman', *Le Monde*, 18 June 2013.

21  The differences in economic efficiency between the different member states were attributed to the malfunctioning of the single market. Attention was thus placed on 'a new strategy for the single market'. See Mario Monti, *A New Strategy for the Single Market*, European Commission, 9 May 2010.

22  P. Krugman, 'Crash of the bumblebee', *New York Times*, nytimes.com, 30 July 2012.

23  J. Delors, 'Fear not, we will get there', *Notre Europe*, 27 June 2013: 'Solidarity in particular involves cohesion policy, which must maintain its deeper meaning.' Solidarity is not realised by bargaining in the Councils, 'when all the governments get together, with each one trying to take home a bit more than the others'. See also J. Habermas, *Im Sog der Technokratie*, Suhrkamp Verlag, 2013, p. 82.

# 2

# New Democracy's criminal indifference

By the end of 2003, Greece's international standing had risen drastically compared with the preceding decade and the efforts made to actively participate in European developments had gained international recognition. Greece was a member of the EMU and the introduction of the euro had been accomplished without difficulty. The Greek presidency of 2003 had succeeded in maintaining European unity over the Iraq crisis. The completion of negotiations over the accession of new states – including Cyprus – into the Union, as well as the agreement over a new agricultural policy and the completion of the European Constitution all contributed to Greece's growing political capital.

In March 2004 the new New Democracy government took charge of a country which was very different from that of its recent past, a country with potential and new infrastructure, ready to maintain its high levels of growth.[1] It took charge of a country which still had 70% of the 3rd European Structural Fund Programmes for Greece at its disposal, the largest growth programme ever in the history of Greece. It had means that the 1996 PASOK government could not have dreamt of. It had opportunities and capital that the country had not possessed ever before in its history.

The project of bringing Greece up to par with its major European counterparts had not, of course, been completed. There is no 'end' date to a project of modernisation. Nor is there some magical policy matrix that can solve all matters once and for all. Reform is an ongoing and incremental process.[2] There were still many challenges and shortcomings that remained unresolved. Regardless of who took the reins of power after the 2004 elections, further work was required to stabilise the economy, and structural change was still needed to modernise the country. Greece could not afford to have the luxury of resting on its laurels and taking a break; there was no time to take a step back and admire the progress made.

New Democracy, however, did not appear aware of the need for continued and coherent efforts. This is evident from its electioneering leading up to the 2004 contest. New Democracy promised that it would give everything that PASOK could not. So it was hardly surprising that the change of government in 2004 signified the beginning of a period when adherence to EU restrictions, macroeconomic rules and obligations and due diligence was relegated to mere window-dressing. The new administration reverted to traditional methods of selective political patronage of its support base. Characteristic of this regression were the measures taken to support farmers through a €500 million subsidy, in direct contravention of EU regulations, for which the Greek state was condemned by the European Court. The €3,000 indemnity for victims of the forest fires of August 2007 in Elia (in the West Peloponnese) was granted to anyone who showed up and merely stated that they had been a victim. This was indicative of the spirit of the times. Partisan competition and electioneering fuelled the cultivation of an ethos of abundance that bore no relationship to reality. The country refused to accept that there were limits to its possibilities. According to the ethos of this new era, restrictive structural reforms constituted efforts to bring back 'austerity', a 'condemned' and 'hated' practice from the time prior to EMU membership.

New Democracy advanced 'mild adjustment' as its mantra for reform. This meant limited action, but a framework for discourse designed to appease those afraid the country would not adhere to its European obligations. The government had no intention of dealing with the large problems that arose from social changes; instead, it sought to service the needs of its power base. In this sense it tallied with the aspirations of voters who sought reforms that would benefit them, such as early pensions, special taxation settlements, a reduction of their dues to social security funds and, of course, appointments to the public sector.

The institution of the ASEP (Supreme Council for the Selection of Personnel) by the PASOK government had been a significant step (ending appointments to the public sector on the basis of patronage). Before the 2004 election New Democracy promised to abolish it, as the party's supporters had demanded. After the election it retreated partially from its prior position; however, it still dismissed part of the institution and opened once again (slightly more covertly) public sector appointments on the basis of a personal interview. Appointments are estimated to have exceeded 150,000.

As time went on, it became increasingly apparent that government believed its own claims that the market served as an 'automatic pilot' charting the correct course. It remained perplexed, motionless and unresponsive when faced with challenges. It hesitated to become involved in the resolution of social conflicts. It lacked a long-term vision and so met problems on an opportunistic basis with ad hoc responses. It governed on the basis of the naïve belief problems would resolve themselves. All that was needed was the occasional friendly pat on the back, broad smiles and reassuring affirmations.

Tax evasion, one of the country's major problems, ceased to be of concern in public opinion. In order to limit its inevitable political decline, the government followed Silvio Berlusconi's government in Italy, requesting the tax authorities not to pressure citizens to pay their taxes. It also followed the example of the

French President, Nicolas Sarkozy, by abolishing inheritance tax. This was a welcome reform for the majority of citizens, a reform, however, that enhanced social inequality and limited public revenue at a time of capital shortfalls.

Greece was not drastically affected by the slump in economic activity in the EU. In 2008, the recession in the Eurozone was greater than that in Greece. Government cadres claimed that Greece's relative resilience was due to New Democracy's economic policy. The Minister of Finance for the period asserted that 'the growth dynamic which has been created over the last five years, as the result of a series of significant reforms, has enhanced the resistance of the Greek economy to the recessionary wave sweeping the other European economies.'[3]

More pragmatic observers urged caution. They pointed out that in a peripheral country the crisis would manifest itself only after some delay. The rise in deficits and debts could lead to risky and malign conditions, especially with regard to Greece. The long-term aversion to reform of the economy, and public administration, posed a major hazard. 'The problems for the Greek economy are only just beginning.'[4]

From 2006 onwards, pragmatic analysis highlighted an increasing loss of direction and control of the trajectory of the Greek economy. However, growth fuelled by consumption underwrote government policy, with the inevitable consequences this had for levels of borrowing.[5] As has been widely noted,[6] New Democracy remained in a state of denial as to the true state of the Greek economy and dismissed calls for necessary reforms. The New Democracy administration continued to increase hand-outs, contributing to the continual rise in deficits and debt, and its own demise. It is indicative of this reckless trend in spending that the total public sector payroll rose by €124 billion over the five-year period 2004–09. In the eight-year period 1996–2003 under the PASOK administration the rise had been only €9.61 billion.[7]

The equilibrium achieved by the PASOK government was thus reversed in one administration. The interest paid by the country while under PASOK fluctuated around €8–10 billion per annum. At the same time, however, the level of growth was adding approximately €10–15 billion each year. The growth in GDP ensured sufficient revenue to service the interest. Debt actually fell from 104.4% of GDP in 1999 to 98.3% by 2003. Debt thus kept falling as a percentage of GDP. The market viewed the Greek economy positively. Greek rates of interest on borrowing were only marginally higher than those available to Germany.

This situation, however, worsened dramatically; this was most pronounced during 2008–09. The country's growth stagnated. New funds to pay off sovereign debt did not exist. Between the end of 2003 and 2009, debt, as a percentage of GDP, rose by 34%.[8] The country was obliged to borrow exponentially more. This prompted a response from the markets, driving a continual hike in interest rates, which in turn contributed to the alarming trend of growing debt and deficit. The vicious circle was provoked in no small part by the nonchalance and indecision of New Democracy. An excessive budget deficit combined with credit fuelled excessive private consumption and provoked the continual rise in the negative balance of payments. Excessive borrowing inevitably followed to deal with this balance of payments deficit. The country was led blindly down a path of relentless and ominous debt.[9]

The Greek Court of Audit's report for 2009, published in 2012,[10] details the deterioration in fiscal management. Borrowing suited to Greece's needs, and within the country's means, would have amounted to €40.5 billion. However, Greece borrowed €105 billion – an unprecedented and reckless trend. Over the period 1990–2007, the mean public expenditure accounted for 44.6% of GDP. By 2008 the figure had reached 48.3%, rising to 52% the subsequent year. These figures constitute post-Junta records.[11]

The difference in the scale of investments made, and level of consumption enjoyed, is indicative of the trajectory of the Greek economy. After 2004 investment in Greece fell dramatically, and by 2009 had fallen by 27%. Consumption, however, grew by 40% over the same period. Policy was directed towards immediate gratification, with minimal to nonexistent consideration of the long-term ramifications.

The underlying causes of this downward spiral rest with the structural problems of the Greek economy and society: the continual decline in competitiveness; the malfunctioning of state administration and the rise in public spending; the mismanagement and poor organisation of the goods and services markets; the lack of flexibility in the labour market and the political system of patronage that underwrote it. These all contributed to the difficulty Greece experienced in adjusting to international developments, and sustained the gulf in terms of development between the nation and its Core counterparts. Political patronage and the scope of trade union influence inhibited any genuine chance of modernisation, jeopardised the possibility of convergence with the Core and was intrinsically resistant to the structural reform vital to prepare Greece for the changing nature of its economic environment, in the single market and the Eurozone. Decisive intervention was required to overcome these shortcomings. It was not forthcoming.[12] The New Democracy administration lacked the political will or courage to implement inevitably unpopular but vital reforms.

Indicative of this absence of courage was the administration's response to the downturn in the automobile sector. Despite the financial challenges becoming increasingly apparent, the government looked to support the ailing automobile retail industry, as this provided a significant support base. Turnover in the industry had fallen dramatically owing to the crisis. New Democracy took measures to subsidise the purchase of cars, under the pretext of sustaining employment in the increasingly unprofitable sector. Moreover, instead of urging wage restraint and a radical reduction in public expenses, it increased salaries, pensions and allowances, contributing a further €8.5 billion to state expenditure. This was done to placate its support base and mitigate the political cost of public protests and populist dissent. In 2009, public revenue fell a further €2.3 billion, compounding an already increasingly unhealthy budget situation.[13]

At the beginning of September 2009, of primary concern to the ruling party were discussions of prospective elections. The party leadership favoured early elections, while the support base did not see the value in calling elections two years before they were mandatory. As for matters of substantive and vital reform, in the face of the shifting global economic environment, the government paid little more than lip service. The desire to hold early elections can be understood in primarily political and partisan terms. An election would provide the opportunity to rekindle and focus on partisan division, and relegate once again the more pressing and unpopular need for structural reform. The calling of an election might have led to a short-term loss of power, but would afford New Democracy the opportunity to pass the controversial and inevitably unpopular reforms to PASOK, which would rapidly suffer in terms of popular support, and permit an expedient return to power for New Democracy with immunity from the political costs reform would entail. Moves to call early elections were purely tactical, so that PASOK might pay these political costs, and New Democracy might rapidly return to power.

Abroad it was recognised that the problems in Greece were becoming increasingly acute. Instead of borrowing from the market, Greek banks were obliged seek the ECB's support in the form of loans, provided at a special 1% interest rate. Fluctuations in the interest rate available to Greece on the bond markets were marking a clear and ominous trend. The markets were considering Greece an increasingly risky investment, and rates of interest reflected this. At the same time, state expenditure was growing without a corresponding rise in revenue. The budget deficit continued to spiral out of control. All indicators highlighted an alarming and exponential deterioration in the state of Greek finances.

In late December 2008 in my speech to Parliament[14] concerning the budget for the following year I made public my increasing concern:

> It is a common secret in the circles of the European Commission that Greece is not adhering to the directives of the EMU; in addition oversight and supervision are proving insufficient.... It would be good for Greece – they believe – to be forced to the International Monetary Fund (IMF) for further recourse, so that the monitoring of the Greek economy will fall under its responsibility and oversight, and not that of the European Commission.

This speech of mine provoked an angry response from the government; I was decried as a danger by New Democracy, and accused of hyperbole by PASOK.

The problem was also raised by the International Monetary Fund (IMF).[15] Attention was drawn to the increasing number of indicators mentioned above, and it was noted that the condition of the Greek economy could deteriorate rapidly. It therefore deemed it necessary to develop and implement further oversight and a coherent policy aimed at stabilisation.[16] It observed, however, that the Greek government did not accept this analysis nor did it fully recognise the gravity of the situation in which it now found itself; it considered the consequences of the crisis to be limited, owing to the unique nature of the Greek economy, largely based as it is upon small to medium-sized enterprises.

It was not clear where Greek public opinion stood. The citizens could discern that there were difficulties, but they were not in a position to ascertain their extent. The positions of the government and the opposition were highly contradictory. The New Democracy administration highlighted that while 'the harshest crisis of the last 80 years' had had 'acute consequences for our country ... the consequences of the economic crisis are much smaller than in other European countries'.[17] The fault was placed at the feet of previous administrations, in that the problem was said to be primarily due to the fact that the country 'is encumbered by the enormous sovereign debt bequeathed to us from the past'. The Prime Minister, Kostas Karamanlis, in his speech to the Thessaloniki International Exhibition, in September 2009, proposed the curtailing of public expenditure and reducing the deficit through limited reform. In comparison with the conditions of the Memorandum of Understanding underpinning the Greek bailout, and later reform imposed by PASOK, these proposals were negligible and clearly insufficient. He proposed restricting state appointments and freezing pensions, allowances and salaries in the public sector for 2010, as well as limitations on overtime. Karamanlis did not present an analysis of the causes, nor a comprehensive or coherent plan to address the situation. He limited himself to the usual rhetoric, the lists of limited actions, the repetition of prior promises and generic warnings (e.g. 'very severe scrutiny of public expenses'). The vague nature of these promises was such that everything remained possible, but nothing received concrete commitment. This was designed to ensure that New Democracy could continue to take action on the basis of possible political costs to the party. He proposed, for example, 'opening up those closed professions deemed critical for the Greek economy'. 'Critical' was presumably to receive definition at a later date, when it could be determined how this might affect the fortunes of New Democracy.

Notes

1   Over the previous eight- year period (1996–2004), the Greek economy grew at an average rate of 3.5% of GDP, five times greater than the 0.7% which was the average for the period 1991–93 and significantly above the EU average.
2   R. Hermann writes: 'Costas Simitis' government (1996–2004) showed that Greece is capable of effecting reforms. The successor government of Kostas Karamanlis rapidly wasted the successes of the former.' R. Hermann, 'Fessel Klientelismus', *FAZ*, 24 August 2012.
3   *Kathimerini*, 6 September 2009, special edition, Thessaloniki International Exhibition. See also P. Tsimas, *The Diary of the Crisis*, Metechmio, 2011, p. 93ff.
4   T. Yannitsis, D. Chionis, Y. Stournaras and G. Chardouvelis, *To Vima*, 20 September 2009, pp. A29ff.

5  Tsimas, *The Diary of the Crisis*, p. 100.
6  See: N. Christodoulakis, *Can the Titanic Be Saved? From the Memorandum Back to Growth*, Polis Editions, 2011, pp. 27ff.; P. Mandravelis, in T. Theodoropoulos, P. Mandravelis, P. Markaris and V. Papavasiliou, *Below Zero: Four Comments on the Crisis*, Oceanida, 2010, pp. 143ff. In his book *The Cold Civil War, the People, the Events that Destroyed the Country*, Patakis, 2012, Y. Pretenteris describes the development of the crisis in Greece from 2009 to 2012.
7  European Commission, General data, spring 2012.
8  In 2004 New Democracy took over sovereign debt at 97.4% of GDP, and left it in 2009 at 129.4% of GDP. In other words it rose over approximately six years by 32 percentage points of GDP. In 1993 PASOK took over sovereign debt at 99.2% of GDP, and by the end of 2003 it had *reduced* it to 97.4% of GDP. In amounts of billions, we have the following picture: in 2004 New Democracy took over sovereign debt amounting to €168 billion and left it at €299.7 billion; that is, over approximately five and a half years it increased it by some €130 billion. In 1996, the PASOK government took over a sovereign debt at €97.8 billion and left it in 2003 at €168 billion. It increased it by €70.2 billion. However, PASOK reduced debt as a percentage of GDP, and therefore facilitated and did not burden the following government. Of the €299 billion, €24 billion of the 2009 deficit was a primary deficit, that is, it did not include payment of interest and redemption of bonds maturing. The claim that Greece borrowed after 2004 in order to pay the interest on previous loans distorts the real picture. New Democracy borrowed to cover needs *apart* from interest.
9  Christodoulakis, *Can the Titanic Be Saved?*, p. 39.
10 See *Kathimerini*, 22 March 2012.
11 See table 1, *Borrowing of the Greek Government and Economy*.
12 V. Ziras, *Kathimerini*, 27 September 2009: 'The global crisis is not responsible for the sombre state of the Greek economy. The crisis simply absorbed all the vitality left from entry into the EMU, it unstitched the last fibres of the carpet under which the deficits and debt had been swept, it put an end to the artificial euphoria created by the euro and low interest rates.'
13 Tsimas, *The Diary of the Crisis*, p. 122.
14 *Parliamentary Proceedings*, 18 December 2008.
15 *Greece: 2009 Article IV Consultation*, Country Report No. 9/244, IMF, 2009.
16 This view was also shared by the Organisation for Economic Co-operation and Development (OECD), which noted that up till then stabilisation had been based on temporary measures and did not effectively bring under control the expansion of public expenses. See *Economic Surveys: Greece*, OECD, 2009.
17 C. Chadjidakis, *Kathimerini*, 6 September 2009, special edition, Thessaloniki International Exhibition, p. 8.

# PASOK's opportunistic optimism

New Democracy's electioneering during the campaign was as selective as it was cynical. It portrayed itself as the honest party, omitting any mention of its own enormous responsibility and the challenges faced by Greece. The opposition, PASOK, in turn placed responsibility on the shoulders of the ruling party. However, the opposition did not provide a comprehensive or complete analysis of what had led the Greek economy into crisis. PASOK's campaign was equally riddled with vague claims and generalities. The country was 'on the brink', the budget 'was off target as never before'. Propaganda and political opportunism dominated the discourse. PASOK sought to distinguish itself from the policies of New Democracy. A vote for PASOK would be a vote for change; PASOK would not be afflicted by the same difficulties and shortcomings as the current administration. It would ensure 'economic growth, stability, cohesion'.[1]

How this was to be achieved was not articulated. A comprehensive plan to deal with the crisis did not exist. The practice of traditional partisan politics continued; the campaign was dominated by slogans and promises for popular measures, while pledges of the previous years were rehashed and repackaged. The economic manifesto of PASOK promised: *income support*, with rises above the level of inflation and an extra solidarity allowance; measures to protect those who had taken out loans; the *freezing of public utility company bills* for a year; *enhanced economic activity*, with an increase in public investment of 4% of GDP from the first budget and speeding up of the public investment programme; an *injection of liquidity into the market*; the *protection and enhancement of employment and support of the unemployed*, with unemployment benefit to be increased gradually to 70% of the minimum wage; the *cleaning up of public finances and a 'war on squander'*. The preamble of the programme stated: 'We shall immediately put into effect a 100-day Plan', through which 'we shall thus create the framework for the following necessary step towards green growth, through a radical change of the ways in which we produce wealth'. The mantra regularly propagated by the leader of PASOK, George Papandreou, was 'there is money'. This announcement was not qualified by any conditions or reservations.[2] Expenditure was to be funded by previously evaded tax. 'We shall find it from uncollected tax receipts amounting to €31 billion.' It should be noted that the 'uncollected taxes' referred to were those of companies that had gone bankrupt, of publicly owned companies and of people who could no longer be located. Inevitably these tax receipts were not collected by the new PASOK administration, after its electoral success. The conviction that 'there was money' meant that no preparation or planning was made with regard to Greece's principal problem, the need both to fund and to reverse the exponential growth in the deficit. This problem was no secret: it had been noted in the reports of a range of international organisations, in the commentary of the foreign media and by certain sections within PASOK.[3]

Prime Minister G. Papandreou's programme statement in Parliament on 16 October 2009 was a repetition of his pre-election promises. There was no indication of substantive developments in terms of policy, nor of careful and considered assessment of the situation. No reference was made to a coherent stabilisation policy, wage restraint, or broader cuts in public expenditure. On the contrary, the public was reassured there would be 'no negative surprises'. The only reference to the situation was the admission that 'The deficit must be scaled down, in order to start reducing our sovereign debt'. The Prime Minister's promises went no further than to say: 'All wasteful spending in the Ministries must be cut down, and my own office will be the first to set an example'. The government's basic aim was to 'bring the country back to the centre of international developments, both inside and outside the framework of the European Union. From now on Greece will be present at the discussions of all large global matters.' At the end of another speech he called on his audience 'to write the new pages of the history of this country together'.[4] Not even two years had passed and reality proved to be completely different. Greece had lost its international standing, its credibility and the ability to play any role whatsoever in European and international developments. Once again, at the beginning of a critical period for the country, its leadership exhibited a lamentable combination of denial and indecision. It refused to acknowledge the reality of the situation in which it now found itself, it did nothing to remedy the worsening economic health of the nation, it made no effort to instigate an open and frank debate on the challenges faced, and it stumbled blindly on without direction or consideration.

## Notes

1  PASOK party leaflet, 1 October 2009.
2  See pre-election speech in Kozani, 10 September 2009, Pasokweb TV, Press conference at the 74th Thessaloniki International Exhibition, 13 September 2009.
3  According to PASOK's *Economy Sector Information Bulletin*, 28 May 2009, 'the financial crisis has had a larger effect on the Greek state's cost of borrowing … Greece's borrowing costs are higher than those of other Eurozone countries'.
4  Speech at Thessaloniki International Exhibition, 13 September 2009.

# 4

# Being in denial

In the October 2009 elections PASOK secured a resounding victory over New Democracy.[1] The result scuppered New Democracy's plan for an expedient return to power. The result of these elections was instrumental in the admission and revelation of the true scope of Greece's financial woes. On 21 October the Minister of Finance informed the European Commission that at the end of 2009 the deficit would reach 12.5% of GDP, in excess of two times the figure claimed by the previous government (6%).[2] Further revisions followed,[3] till a figure for the deficit of 15.4% of GDP was finalised.[4] During these revisions it also emerged that sovereign debt, by 2009, exceeded the 91.4% of GDP published as part of the December 2008 budget under New Democracy. Rather, sovereign debt stood at 126.8% of GDP, owing to major liabilities in Greek public services that had been overlooked.

These revisions fuelled a barrage of negative commentaries concerning Greek manipulation of data, and led international public opinion to the conclusion that Greece had systematically falsified its data. The immediate result was that the country's credit rating was downgraded. In successive decisions, the international rating agencies downgraded Greece by one or more points. The markets also reacted. The interest rates available to Greece rose dramatically. At the beginning of November, the state borrowed €7 billion through the issue of new fifteen-year bonds. The interest rate was 5.385%, 1.42% higher than the average European interest rate.

At the meeting of the Eurogroup[5] on 19 October, the members sent an ultimatum demanding the new Greek administration take measures in the 2010 budget to begin reducing the deficit. The President of the Group, Prime Minister of Luxembourg Jean Claude Juncker, concluded: 'The party is over for Greece.'[6] Greece attempted to offer reassurances. It affirmed that the necessary measures were already being taken. Despite that, however, the Minister of Finance, George Papaconstantinou, issued a press release to the Greek media, after the Eurogroup meeting, stating that the commitments that had been made (by PASOK) to the people were non-negotiable. Consequently, the €2.5 billion in benefits which had been promised by the party prior to the elections would still be honoured. Commentators observed that the government needed to take a clear position with regard to the economy. It could not continue to cater to populist demands.

Greece had been under a regime of external fiscal supervision from 2004; in 2007 it was once again granted its economic independence, because in 2006 it had succeeded in reducing its deficit to less than 3% of GDP. Later scrutiny by Eurostat proved this move premature. Actually, the deficit for 2006 had been nearly twice that stipulated by the Treaties: it was running at 5.7% for the year in question. Subsequently external supervision was once again introduced. The Commissioner responsible for this oversight was Joaquin Almunía, the very Commissioner who, in 2004, had approved the revision of figures by New Democracy. Almunía's supervision of Greece was a rather unintrusive affair.[7] The Commissioner did not even voice a protest when, on 30 September 2009, the New Democracy government submitted Eurostat figures where data for the years 2008 and 2009 were omitted so as to ensure that the level of deficit would not and could not become a salient issue in the upcoming elections, to be held on 4 October.[8]

As it began to emerge that the Greek problem was of central concern to the whole of the EMU, many member states drew attention to the joint responsibility that should have been shouldered by the Commission, which had failed to act with due diligence in its supervision. Almunía announced on 11 November 2009, at a time when the problem was already grave, that, as of February 2010, Greece was to be subjected to a special regime allowing the European Commission the right to request specific measures for the reduction of the deficit.

The fact that the state of the economy was made public after the elections gave rise to extensive discussions over whether the leading figures in New Democracy and PASOK were aware of the realities or not.[9] The debate, however, did not focus on the more salient point that awareness of the state of finances should have been a mandatory responsibility. Ignorance cannot be a defence. All the necessary information was readily available – the reports of the Bank of Greece as well as the statistics of the EU, the IMF and the Organisation for Economic Co-operation and Development (OECD) all detailed the dire state of Greek accounts. The Bank of Greece had already drawn attention to the increasingly concerning developments, as had the European Commission, as well as many economists and journalists. If the leadership of either of the main parties were lacking knowledge, then their ignorance highlights an alarming level of apathy and incompetence.

At the end of November 2009 the European Commission requested that a list of specific measures for the reduction of the deficit be drawn up. 'The measures shall be described in detail, the time schedule for implementation shall be clearly set and the fiscal benefit sought shall be determined.'[10] A much clearer expression of the lack of faith in Greece's ability to redress its own shortcomings would be hard to find.

The government asserted that the 2010 budget would satisfy demands for drastic and immediate action. It was submitted in December 2009. However, it did not contain any significant reforms. It made provision for a limited reduction of expenses and an increase in revenue. In essence, the budget was little more than window-dressing, as a cursory reading would suggest. Most of the proposed reforms were impossible to implement.

The government was indecisive. It recognised the need to reduce the deficit and to check the debt, but was averse to reneging on its election promises, and afraid of the political costs of such action. The budget that was supposed to mark the beginning of efforts to significantly reduce the deficit contained a package of €2.6 billion in income support for the least affluent members of Greek society. Under EU pressure the government limited the level of income support contained in the budget, partially abandoning prior reassurances to the electorate.

Courageous and unpopular action was absolutely vital. Precedents did exist, in the form of undertakings PASOK made in 1985 and 1993 to overcome economic instability through a systematic reduction in state expenses and the mandatory promotion of wage restraint. Regrettably, the PASOK of 2009 did not have the political courage or conviction of its predecessors. Internal party strife and positioning afflicted it. The reforms designed to promote stability and satisfy the convergence criteria during the period 1996–2003 had proved painful and unpopular. The new leadership of PASOK offered in 2004 repeated public apologies for the scope of the pain felt and mistakes made in this previous period. By once again implementing a painful programme of reform, the party would be reneging on repeated promises made to the electorate. PASOK was overly sensitive to the possible ramifications such a programme might have for its credibility in light of these promises, and feared any future efforts at innovative reform or policy would be put on public trial. The desire to distance the party from past reforms meant that none of the economic staff of the Ministry of Finance during the period 1996–2003 was called upon. The Prime Minister regularly sought input from American economists, with limited experience in European affairs.

The government's continual quest for a reform package that would resolve the economic woes of the nation, but without prompting widespread dissent and a populist backlash, resulted in wide-reaching inertia. By the end of 2009 government expenditure had reached a record high of 53.2% of GDP,[11] while revenue had fallen to levels not seen since 1996, at just 37.8% of GDP. Such a gulf between the two figures had not been recorded for the previous two decades. Borrowing could no longer provide a solution in its own right. Even if sufficient credit could be acquired, the exponential trajectory of the sovereign debt and the balance of payments would guarantee the continual deterioration of the health of Greek finances. The inevitable recession, the ever-growing costs of borrowing and the servicing of existing debt, expansions in health care and the social security system, and the deficits on the books of public corporations would ensure sovereign debt in excess of sustainable levels. The inertia was inexcusable.

Public opinion reacted intensely. It was incomprehensible: how could the state be spending approximately €30 billion over and above the revenue it collected? The realisation that 'things have been left completely to chance, with no planning and no checks',[12] that the coffers were empty, that 'the state of the finances indicated that the state had collapsed'[13] was increasingly widespread. The conclusion for a large section of public opinion was apparent. Immediate and decisive intervention on a grand scale was necessary. Policy was needed that would convince Greece's partners that the nation had recognised the dimension of the problems and had begun to reform the structural causes. Borrowing from the international markets on sustainable terms, which could halt the exponential deterioration of the situation, could be acquired only if such action were taken.

Public opinion began to question the causes of this increased expenditure. 'Where did the money go?' Answers were not forthcoming. The debate on the substantial squandering of funds was avoided through references to changes in the budget, which were hardly enlightening. New Democracy offered no explanation as to why 52,000 people were hired for training programmes, even though there was no EU funding for this. Nor did they explain why Greece had to borrow €2.2 billion for armaments programmes.

At the Ecofin meeting held on 2 December 2009, the ministers of finance noted that Greece had not acted on repeated recommendations: 'Greek public finances have worsened beyond what could have been expected as a result of the economic downturn. New measures for the new budget consist mainly of revenue enhancing measures ... [many of which are] temporary, and [do not contain] permanent measures on the expenditure side as called for by the Council.'[14] However, coverage in the Greek media was reassuring: 'A first yes from Brussels'. At the same time the press noted that 'despite the agreement and the temporary breathing space the ministers of finance [have] achieved, the balance remains fragile.' 'The agreement consists of an expressed commitment by Greece to take the measures designated and to accept an extremely suffocating European supervision framework.' 'If it does not succeed in this effort, then [Greece] must proceed to new measures to reduce the deficit.'[15] The difficulties highlighted by the Council were not the only ones. The private sector of the economy was in a very poor state: 'We are not competitive. We sell fewer goods and services than we consume. We do this either by selling assets, companies, shares, plots of land, or by borrowing. Consequently, the rise in external debt is explosive.'[16] These were facts that contributed massively to the loss of international confidence in Greece, and the doubts over whether it could meet its commitments.

The Greek crisis drew into sharp focus a broader weakness that affected the EU. The EU had no provisions in place to mitigate or counter the risks of contagion from an economic crisis. The Treaties had no framework for a collective response to major economic challenges inside any given member state. Every state must manage on its own, and was alone responsible for its own liabilities. The other states were not obliged to help it. Nor was there any provision for some common support mechanism of the type provided by the IMF. The member states of the Union were also members of the IMF. Although recourse to it was not expressly forbidden, it was not possible in practice. It would show the EU up as incapable of protecting itself in times of crisis, and its currency would appear vulnerable. The German Chancellor had expressly stated: 'Whatever happens in one member state concerns all the others too. A common currency entails common responsibility.'[17] However, this common responsibility lacked substance. There was no established institutional framework for responding to a crisis; there was no extraordinary lending mechanism, or designated lender of last resort.

The Greek crisis marked the first crisis in credibility of a member state of the Union. Its members appeared unprepared and averse to major legislative reform. The principle of 'intergovernmental cooperation' imposed, after all, extensive cooperation and debate was required if there were to be any major reform of the framework of the Union. A quick fix was not possible. There were unprecedented questions that required an answer before any action could be taken. Should aid be granted, would the framework for supervision, already written into the Treaties for cases when the member state's deficit exceeded 3%, suffice? Or was a far stricter and intrusive form required? To what extent would the member state retain its independence in managing its economic matters? Prior to the Greek crisis, efforts to formulate a new regulatory framework had not been effective. Discourse within the Union had for quite some time revolved around some notion of common 'economic governance', but the discussion was limited to vague aspirations, and no concrete action had been taken. The immediacy of the Greek problem, therefore, required a solution from within the existing framework. However, any response faced structural challenges in the current *acquis communautaire*, and risked setting a dangerous precedent.

The problem was discussed at the European Council in Brussels on 10–11 December 2009. The leaders of the member states were not eager to effect substantive changes in the management or functioning of the Union. They reaffirmed previous decisions concerning the need to apply community regulations to guarantee economic stability and the reduction of the fiscal deficit. Regulations, applicable within the existing framework, were already in place in case of violation of the deficit cap. Aversion to reform led to further reassertion of the principles of individual member state responsibility, and the refutation of any Union-wide obligation to provide assistance. In private discussions the political elite within the EU underlined the need for Greece to freeze salaries, and drew attention to the risks further negative market reactions would pose for Greece's ability to finance its debt.

At the summit, the Greek Prime Minister rejected the proposals: 'The salary earners will not be the ones to pay for this; we shall not impose cuts or a pay freeze.' He argued that these measures were unacceptable, as the Greek economy was not 'on the brink of catastrophe'.[18] A few short months later, developments would prove these assertions to be a fallacy. In April 2010, the Prime Minister himself would acknowledge that Greece was in danger of going bankrupt without EU support. It is obvious that in December 2009 the government was in a state of utter confusion. It was of the view that the heightening of the crisis that month was due to international speculators. According to Greek media coverage of the summit, the Prime Minister was justifiably assertive in ensuring that Greece would not become subservient to Union directives.

However, subsequent events indicated that the government recognised the limitation to the options available to it. Three days later the government announced 'a full frontal attack' and an 'SOS package of 30 measures'. This was a plan 'to be carried out over a four-year period, providing for a series of revolutionary changes in the state and the broader public sector, aiming at radically reorganising the country', and the gradual reduction of the deficit below 3% by the end of the four-year period.[19] On 16 December, at a presentation on the state of the Greek economy to foreign institutional investors, the Minister of Finance asserted there would be a faster reduction in the deficit than that which had been announced. These statements indicated a complete u-turn on the part of the government, and suggested the country would be complying completely with the EU directives.

Certain commentators, along with economic and political elites, remained sceptical of Greek statements of intent. They once again viewed these statements as riddled with rhetoric over substance. References to the need to undertake some vague notion of a necessary 'social dialogue' obscured the fact that the government was actually 'rejecting the change in course for the Greek economy'.[20] It was obvious that there existed within government competing beliefs on the need for reform. Official press releases and statements made by the administration were contradictory. Some wanted drastic and expedient reform to be implemented, while others decried such measures as unnecessary. Some spoke of a 'radical reorganisation' and others complained of excessive foreign pressure on Greece. Such severe foreign intervention threatened to leave the nation politically impotent. Greece was being forced into a straitjacket, imposing harsh conditions in exchange for financial help, should the country ask for it.

The Prime Minister rejected calls for forceful changes in policy: 'mild measures' and 'institutional changes' would suffice. His reluctance to drive through decisive reform has been noted by those he consulted with during the period. It has been noted that he had no intention of implementing a tough austerity programme.[21] Furthermore, in certain sections of PASOK, it was held that such a programme would not be commensurate with the party's ideology.

Under such circumstances the markets grew increasingly anxious. The interest rate on Greek debt grew, Greek bonds lost their value and 'credit default swap' (CDS) agreements covering a possible Greek default were more expensive than comparable policies for Egypt, Kazakhstan, Vietnam or Bulgaria. Greece's credit rating was downgraded by the most influential credit rating agency (Moody's), even though its bonds remained eligible as collateral with the ECB. The perennial warnings once again appeared in both the domestic and the international media; the coming weeks would be critical for the Greek economy.

The initial borrowing target for 2009 that had been set at the beginning of September, by the Greek government, was €40 billion. Towards the end of the month it was revised up a further €20 billion, or approximately 8% of GDP, a disconcertingly rapid and significant revision.[22] Media observation drew attention to the fact that the level of that year's borrowing was unprecedented for Greece. Public opinion questioned why PASOK had not prepared and immediately introduced a plan to deal with the deep crisis the country found itself in, rather than wasting three months on little more than rhetoric. The party was subjected to severe criticism. Even camps friendly to the government felt that PASOK had 'managed to create a climate of uncertainty, mainly through its inability to present a cohesive and complete plan for the economy'.[23] They considered it absolutely necessary that the government formulate a long-term strategy in the form of a 10-year plan, which should set as a target the reduction of debt to 80% of GDP over the next decade, and determine the measures required to achieve it (social security structure, taxation, expenditure).[24]

The administration concealed the policy vacuum with discourse concerning the corruption prevalent in the country. The Prime Minister asserted that 'corruption is widespread in the public services'. 'Our political system gives rise to nepotism and unbridled squandering.' To remedy tax evasion he presented new regulations that his government would introduce, including reforms to ensure 'medical expenses will be deductible from income', and public sector appointments 'will be [made] ... on the basis of tough examinations'.[25] However, both these measures had been in force for years. The ASEP (the Supreme Council for the Selection of Personnel), for example, had been established in 1995. An American journalist praised the Greek leader for his 'straight talking'[26] concerning the deficit and the economic situation. However, was this straight talking from the Prime Minister, or was this merely misdirection and deflection of the substantive challenges at hand?

On 20 November 2009, the discovery that 150 doctors in the high-class Kolonaki area of Athens had evaded their income tax was presented as a symbolic break with the past. In truth, what was presented as a major breakthrough was negligible in the grander scheme. No figures were ever provided on what tax had been recovered following the public ridicule of these doctors. In any case, it certainly made no difference to the health of Greece's finances. The country's problem was the billions in shortfall in its balance of payments, and accountability and transparency in expenditure, not millions or thousands of euros which had be recouped from a few health-care professionals.

According to data from the Ministry of Finance's Department of Public Debt that appeared in the press at the beginning of 2010, the state had to redeem bonds to the value of €31 billion maturing in 2010, and €117 billion maturing over the subsequent four years. It would also have to pay approximately €13 billion in interest alone in 2010, a figure that would only rise over the coming years. It had to cover the deficit in the balance of payments for the same year, which was to reach approximately €25 billion. Furthermore, it also had to source approximately €5 billion in further savings to achieve the reduction of the deficit from 15.5% to 10.4% for that year, as per the agreement it had reached with the EU.[27] These sums were astronomical, given Greece's state of finances. They dwarfed tax receipts and had to derive almost entirely from new loans. Loans, however, would result in further rises in both deficit and debt. Greece was caught in a relentless downward spiral. Indeed, according to IMF data, debt, which in 2009 stood at 127% of GDP, would reach 143% of GDP in 2010 and 166% in 2011. Financial commentators abroad described Greece's problems as 'extreme'. They could see only two possibilities: either the country would default, or else it would face years of struggle with little to show for it. They did not, though, consider default a viable solution. 'The Eurozone would be faced with such economic problems that the recession of 2009 would look like a party in comparison. Therefore the only possible way out was the position that Greece will struggle and finally overcome the difficulties.'[28] This would be possible only with the help of the EU. Inevitably the country would have to surrender the reins of its economy to the European authorities.

Because of its indecision, the government lost valuable time. The interest rate the market required to finance Greek bonds fluctuated around 4.5%, on 10-year bonds, following the 2009 election. By the end of the year it had reached 5.8%. The rise in figures for one-year treasury bills was comparable. Owing to the combination of the lack of preparation and indecision in the face of the rapidly shifting economic environment, the government lost the opportunity to borrow at sustainable levels and maintain any meaningful economic independence. This would have enabled it to negotiate from a better position with the Union. The greatest offence was this indecision, and the doubts and loss of faith in the government it fuelled the world over. It did not manage to curtail the reactions of the markets, which inevitably responded far quicker than the government was able to, exacerbating already challenging circumstances, and further limiting the already constrained avenues available.

## Notes

1 PASOK won the elections with 43.92% of the vote and acquired 160 seats. New Democracy won 33.48% of the vote and 91 seats.
2 The report of the Committee for the Credibility of Fiscal Data of January 2010, p. 29, states: 'On 2nd Oct. 2009 new notification was sent [to Eurostat]. In this notification the general government deficit for 2009 was estimated at €14.360 billion

or 6% of GDP. Finally on 21st October, a third notification was sent to Eurostat, where the deficit for 2009 is estimated at €30.102 billion, or 12.5% of GDP. The revision of the notification of 2nd October ... was due to the fact that the data ... did not correspond to the data that had been sent to the National Statistical Service of Greece, by various departments and services. What changed in the notification of 21st October is that the actual data of the various departments and services were recorded.... The data ... of 2nd October ... did not incorporate the great deterioration of fiscal figures which had occurred between January and the end of August 2009.'

3  Eurostat's revision of 15 November 2011. With the various revisions, the data not only for the deficits but also for the macroeconomic figures changed from year to year. The data are mentioned in the text as they were presented during the period under discussion, though sometimes they were changed later. Thus they can differ from period to period.

4  New Democracy doubted the size of the deficit. A parliamentary committee which examined the matter in the spring of 2012 deemed that there was no tampering with the data by the then PASOK government.

5  The Eurogroup is the Council of the ministers of finance of the 17 member states of the Eurozone. Ecofin is the Council of the ministers of finance of the (then) 27 members of the EU.

6  *Ta Nea*, 20 October 2011.

7  Information and statements by J. Almounía that Greek deficits over the period 2005–08 fluctuated around 3% of GDP and that Greek data were 'credit worthy' owing to the 'spirit of cooperation prevailing over recent years between Greek and Community services' were published in Greek newspapers. See for example *To Vima*, 5 October 2005, *Kathimerini*, 23 February 2006, *Kathimerini*, 9 March 2007, *To Vima*, 26 February 2009. However, according to Eurostat's data, the deficit in 2005 was 5.5% of GDP, 5.7% in 2006, 6.5% in 2007 and 9.8% in 2008. In the memorandum he sent to the parliamentary committee which in March 2012 examined the fiscal figures for 2009, Almounía stated that the European Commission had warned the Eurogroup in July 2009 'that the execution of the budget over the period January–March 2009 shows a significant deviation from targets'. He also noted that 'the N.D. [New Democracy] government had repeatedly announced that it intended to take measures.... In many cases, however, the measures had a limited field of application and a low degree of execution.' The question is why Almounía did not proceed with the necessary actions with regard to the Greek government. He did not do so because he obviously wished to avoid notification of the data.

8  A report from Brussels in *Kathimerini*, 15 September 2009, stated that the Union 'is expected to grant Greece more time, most probably up to the end of 2011, provided the Greek side takes measures that the Commission finds convincing'. This is indicative. The crisis did not wait for 2011. It had arrived, dramatically, in 2009 already.

9  See D. Mitropoulos, 'How the deficit sank us', *Ta Nea*, 17–18 March 2012.

10  Vasilis Zeras, *Economiki Kathimerini*, 29 November 2009, p. 3.

11  During the period of preparation for the 2004 Olympic Games it fluctuated around 45% of GDP, despite increased expenses. Average expenses from 1990 to 2007 were around 44.6% of GDP.

12  Ghikas Chardouvelis, *Kathimerini*, special edition, 26 November 2009.

13 Kostas Kallitisis, *Kathimerini*, 20 November 2009.
14 Council of the European Union, 16838/09, Presse 352, pp. 10ff.
15 *Ta Nea*, 2 December 2009.
16 Ghikas Chardouvelis, 'Financial crisis and the economy', talk to the Greek Society of Banking Law and Law of the Capital Market, 11 December 2009, p. 5.
17 See *Le Monde*, 14 January 2011.
18 *Kathimerini*, 12 December 2009.
19 *Ta Nea*, 15 December 2009.
20 *Kathimerini*, 15 December 2009.
21 See P. Papadopoulos, *To Vima*, 9 October 2011.
22 *Kathimerini*, 12 September 2009.
23 *Ta Nea*, 28–29 November 2009.
24 Yannis Stournaras, *Ta Nea*, 28–29 November 2009.
25 'Interview with Manfred Estel and Mathieu Von Rohr', *Der Spiegel*, 22 February 2010.
26 S. Daley, 'Greek leader finds balm for deficit: straight talk', *New York Times*, 16 June 2010.
27 Data mentioned in *Greece: Fourth Review*, Country Report No. 11/73, IMF, July 2011.
28 See M. Wolf, *Imerisia*, 21 January 2010.

# 5

# Ineffective solutions

On 15 January 2010, the government published a new Stability and Growth Plan (SGP, 2009–13). This was designed to allay mounting concerns and counter the fallout from continual uncertainty. The plan sought to reduce the deficit – estimated at 12.7% of GDP – to 8.7% in 2010, and to conform to the Maastricht deficit cap of 3% of GDP by the end of 2012. At the same time the plan introduced austerity measures to rectify the gulf in the balance of payments, including a rise in value added tax (VAT), the freezing of appointments in the public sector, along with cuts in allowances available to existing public sector employees. It also promised systematic efforts to eradicate tax evasion. The Stability and Growth Plan was an effort to 'present the government's medium-term strategy for the reduction of the deficit in a more credible way than the budget which had been drawn up in 40 days'. It was the road map for dealing with the crisis.

The government believed that the reforms proposed constituted a comprehensive and satisfactory programme to reverse the trajectory of Greece's fortunes. All that was needed was a little time to convince those in doubt. The climate and criticism that the Prime Minister had experienced during the World Economic Forum at Davos in February 2010 contributed to this increasingly decisive stand on the reduction of the deficit. At the Forum, various global players had expressed in no uncertain terms the dangers posed by Greece's refusal to recognise its exceptionally critical condition. It was at Davos, according to official sources, that the die was cast in favour of a policy of austerity. However, the form this u-turn in economic policy took again failed to convince Greece's sceptics. Athens' international standing had fallen so dramatically it now commanded less respect than Egypt or Bulgaria. The Greek interest rate on the international bond markets now exceeded 6%, and credibility was proving a currency as hard to come by as the credit that underscored its demise. This credibility was not restored by acting in response to pressure at Davos. The plan was not positively received abroad. International opinion was summarised by the head of a European think-tank: 'Even the most cursory glance at the official Hellenic Stability and Growth Plan seems to justify the lack of faith on the part of financial markets. The figures in the document suggest that a substantial part of the projected revenue increases are unlikely to materialise and the hard choices and unavoidable cuts have been postponed.'[1]

At the beginning of January 2010, Greece borrowed €8 billion through the sale of five-year bonds at an interest rate of 6.22%. This was an alarmingly high rate of interest, warning that Greece was rapidly losing the ability to borrow at sustainable levels. At the beginning of February, it became increasingly apparent just how anxious the markets were becoming, and how this was far more than merely a Hellenic concern. The headline on the front page of the French newspaper *Le Monde* on 6 February read: 'The financial markets are attacking the euro, and threatening recovery.' On the same day, the American newspaper *International Herald Tribune* – the global edition of the *New York Times* – also carried an equally alarming analysis on its front page: 'The Euro is involved in a serious political trial'; 'The cost of borrowing is putting pressure on Europe's weak links'. The assessment of the gravity of the situation was comparable in the two reports. The stock markets in Greece, Portugal and Spain had fallen sharply over the previous days. A comparable movement the other way increased both the cost of the CDS policies for these member states, and the interest rates available to them on the markets. Rates for Greece rose to 6.7%. The danger of a Greek default appeared on the horizon, even though it remained 'extremely unlikely' that the rest of the Eurozone nations would permit this. The increasingly alarming market reactions put pressure on key European nations to find ways of helping Greece. However, the perennial indecision and division within the Union continued to act as an impediment to action.

Events over the following days led to intense negotiations between European nations over 'how to help Greece to deal with its mountain of debt'. These negotiations, however, did not solely focus on Greece, but looked to address some of the wider pressing issues concerning the overall functioning of the Union. The problem of individual liability had already been tabled at the European Council held in December. The Treaties clearly stipulated that every member state is responsible for its liabilities alone. The creation of the Eurozone, however, instituted such ties between its members that the fate of one now affected the fate of all. The requirement for solidarity, apparent in such times of crisis, had no provision within the Treaties. The long-term stability of the euro, one of the strongest currencies in the world, could not be put at risk by structural flaws stemming from this individual liability. This would inevitably lead to the contagion of crisis.

Regulatory frameworks in place stipulating solidarity existed only to a limited degree. They entailed community support plans and subsidies to the weaker countries. But they did not provide for support comparable to that which exists in federal states such as the USA or Germany. A comprehensive mechanism for collective support to rebalance disparity in economic performance was required. However, it should be constructed in such a fashion that it did not merely serve the needs of the Core nations of the Union.

In these Core nations it was not widely accepted that the Greek crisis raised the matter of EU solidarity. For them, the broader structure of the EMU was not at fault here; rather, Greece's failure to adhere to the regulatory framework and to provide correct and complete economic data was the root cause. Athens presented false data and did not stick to its commitments with regard to the deficit and debt. If its behaviour went unchecked and without consequences, a dangerous precedent would be set, and other struggling member states could expect to offload their sovereign debt without ramifications.

Greece did indeed infringe the regulations for both gathering and providing economic data, as well as those for levels of deficit and debt, particularly over the period 2007–09. But the organs of the Union did not exercise the super-vision they were bound to.[2] The European Commission remained indifferent to the deficits and debt had been allowed to grow to alarming levels. It did not intervene in time to prevent the crisis. The Union also bears responsibility for not paying closer attention to, and directing further efforts to redress, the levels of disparity between the North and the South.

During negotiations at the beginning of February 2010, the possible par-ticipation of the IMF in the solution was discussed. The Union had already sought assistance from the IMF in cases of members that were not part of the Eurozone, such as Lithuania (2008) and Hungary (2008). The IMF had both the capital at its disposal, as well as the experience and expertise in the field of economic management in times of crisis. However, the ECB and the European Commission considered the intervention of the IMF in the case of Greece, a member of the Eurozone, both humiliating and an eventuality to be avoided. One prime minister publicly asserted that since Europeans were seeking to improve their coordination and strengthen their ability to take coherent and collective action, a policy that was to be directed from Washington was highly undesirable.[3]

Furthermore, there was a widely held fear that estimates of the country's rate of growth, the size of its deficits and debt were inexact. A grand plan for European recovery without new scrutiny of these figures would run the risk of being an entirely futile effort. Further action would be required if it emerged at a later date that the scale of the challenge was far greater than the official figures suggested. Indeed, financial analysts deemed that the Stability and Growth Plan announced by Athens in January 2010 was exceptionally ambitious with regard to forecasts for growth and the reduction in deficits. It was therefore very difficult to construct any plan for recovery on the basis of the figures it contained.

The increasingly prevalent view, most notably in France, was that major intervention in Greece was required. It would counter the risk of contagion to Portugal, Spain or any other nations with worrying levels of debt. The crisis provided the opportunity to 'proceed to real economic governance', as opposed to just the rhetoric of such a notion that existed before. The solution proposed was an 'IMF plan without funding' to be imposed on Greece. The belief was that a statement of intent indicating that 'the Europeans will not let Greece fail' would suffice 'to discourage the markets from harmful speculation. It was very possible that in such a case financial support would not even be needed for Greece.'[4]

On 11 February 2010 an (informal) EU summit was to take place. The President of the European Council, Herman Van Rompuy, was to propose a plan 'for a European strategy for growth and employment'. Events changed the agenda. The Greek crisis became the central issue.[5] Media coverage, various statements from ministers of finance and broader analysis in the financial sector had cultivated a debate heavily focused on how significant aid towards Greece would be.

After months of debate and argument, experts from the Commission, the ECB and the major nations of the Union prepared a plan for the 'salvation' of Greece. The plan had been constructed following intense negotiations between France and Germany, over the few days before the Council was held. Germany accepted European involvement, despite earlier assertions that the Treaties did not allow any intervention by the Union whatsoever. Public opinion demanded decisive action at the summit to check the crisis in the countries of the South, and that the Union take control of events.

The efforts of the heads of state and government of the Eurozone on 11 February did not meet expectations.[6] The Greek proverb 'the mountain was in labour and gave birth to a mouse' is apt. The Eurozone summit limited itself to a statement of support:

> We fully support the efforts of the Greek government to do whatever is necessary, including additional measures that will ensure that the ambitious targets contained in the Stability and Growth Plan for 2010 and the following years will be achieved.

It was an unfortunately typical statement from the Eurozone summit, lacking in substance and providing no coherent programme or solution. There was no discussion of specific reforms, an aid package, or extraordinary measures to check the expansion of the crisis. It was, however, emphatic in confirming that Greece would have to follow the recommendations of the European Commission and the ECB, along with any additional measures arising from 'the IMF's expert appraisal'.

The question posed after the meeting was whether Greece had requested something more, or whether the Greek government had brought any fresh proposals of its own. Unfortunately, this had not been the case. In a press conference he gave on the eve of the Council meeting, the Greek Prime Minister said:

> We have not asked for financial support. We are working according to the stability plan which the Commission approved.... We need the psychological

and political support of Europe. We want it to say: Yes, Greece is credible, we guarantee that her plan is realistic.[7]

So the summit gave exactly what it was asked to, a political guarantee. The summit announced that Greece would now be under the triadic supervision of the EU, the ECB and the IMF ('the Troika'). With regard to the IMF, at the aforementioned press conference the Prime Minister had stated: 'We have not requested the IMF's assistance. It is legally possible for us to do so, but we have not chosen this solution at this point in time.'

The reaction of the international media to this decision was negative. It deemed that 'the much awaited plan to help Greece is an unclear prescription of intentions and not a plan to save her economy'.[8] The guarantees of European support given to Greece did not assuage anxiety, but rather rekindled fears concerning the sale of Greek bonds on the international markets at low prices, and further rises in the country's borrowing rates; that is what happened.

The Ecofin Council of February 16 focused on the situation regarding government deficit and debt in Greece. It gave notice to Greece to correct its excessive deficit by 2012.[9] The government's behaviour did not contribute to a climate of confidence. It was marked by a series of small tactical retreats, to pacify criticism and demonstrate good will. At the beginning of February the Prime Minister announced additional fiscal measures to reduce the deficit. Immediately afterwards, during discussions over European approval of the Stability and Growth Plan that same month, Athens committed itself to a plan of structural reform. The Stability and Growth Plan was approved only after this commitment to reform was made. The government then announced a 'new package of measures' on 3 March. Such action did not inspire confidence in public opinion across the Union, and certainly did little to assuage anxiety in the markets. It demonstrated that events were driving political action and not the other way round. In Brussels, in an effort to justify the piecemeal nature of the reforms put in place to counter the crisis, the Minister of Finance, George Papaconstantinou, asserted that 'the government is trying to change the course of the *Titanic*, and this cannot be done in a day'.[10]

After a period of relative calm, anxiety over whether Greece was in a position to fulfil its commitments began growing again. In April and May 2010 it would have to redeem €20 billion of debt. The markets considered it highly unlikely that Greece would be able to come up with such a sum. At the same time indications were growing of an extended recession, which would render the creation of surpluses to service repayment of debts impossible. In 2009 GDP shrank by 2%, and according to forecasts it was expected to shrink by a further 4% in 2010, which it did. On 4 March the government borrowed a further €5 billion through the issue of 10-year bonds. The interest rate was 'only' 6.37%, whereas forecasts in the international media had predicted that it would reach 7%. However, this still marked a significant increase on the previous interest rate, and did not allow the country any breathing space. It indicated that continued borrowing on international markets was unsustain-able. Discussions concerning the need for financial assistance to the country flared up again. The matter proved divisive as both Greece and Germany held conflicting opinions on what remedy should be sought.

The Greek government questioned Union recommendations and disputed mandatory prescriptions. It believed it would be able to resolve its crisis with support from elsewhere. It repeatedly referred to the possibility of borrowing from China. The Minister of Finance had announced a trip to China to discuss matters of funding. The trip, however, did not take place. The Prime Minister's adviser, the American Nobel Laureate Professor Joseph Stiglitz, criticised the Union, and made calls in private discussions for Greece to leave the Eurozone. Such a drastic measure would at least allow the devaluation of its new currency in an effort to solve crisis, following a policy similar to that of Argentina.[11] Public discussion returned once again to a possible IMF-directed reform package. The Minister of Finance observed that 'if we had had recourse to the IMF it would have subjected us to the same measures, but it would have given us €30 billion.' Prime Minister George Papandreou also commented: 'Why don't we have recourse to the IMF? We are already taking the IMF measures, without the advantages that derive from this.'[12] The country carried on without a comprehensive or coherent plan to deal with the crisis. It was believed at this point that the acquisition a €30 billion package from the IMF would have been sufficient. As later developments showed, however, the country needed more than €200 billion, an amount neither the IMF nor the EU would grant in isolation of the other. A full grasp of the scale of the problem, or any insight as to a possible solution, appeared to elude the country's leadership.

For those commenting on Greek political action, it was unclear whether the remarks concerning an IMF solution were motivated by a desire to indicate decisiveness on the part of the government, or were directed at the EMU to suggest Greece had options elsewhere. The Greek government had been in contact with the now former head of the IMF, Dominique Strauss-Kahn. Discussions concerning the possibility of IMF intervention had taken place. In an interview on French television, Strauss-Kahn himself mentioned that Papandreou had requested the intervention of the IMF in December 2010. The chief of the IMF had, however, advised him to come to an agreement with European leaders because they 'will not accept the unilateral intervention of the IMF in a country of the Eurozone, under any circumstances'.[13]

The reason why discourse, not merely in Germany but across the Union, was so divided over a possible package of financial assistance for Greece stemmed from the fear of the precedent it might set, and concern over ramifications for the EMU as a whole. What would be the consequences if one member state of the Eurozone were to default on its debt? Would it be mandatory for that country to leave the EMU? Could it pull out of the Eurozone before the default and establish a new currency for itself? Was it possible to provide a mechanism for orderly default? Would the restructuring of the debt be the right course to take? Could it solve the crisis once and for all?

There followed intense negotiations once again. A compromise began to emerge on 10 March, after a nine-hour meeting of the representatives of the ministries of finance. The next day, however, at the Ecofin meeting, the matter was deferred to the next summit, at the end of March, to be resolved then. The political problem remained the most significant hurdle, and that was a matter for the heads of state. The legal challenge of bypassing the Treaties had been solved. Funding would be provided on a bilateral basis in the form of loans from member states of the EMU directly to Greece. In this way it would not contravene the *acquis communautaire*, nor risk setting a precedent with wide-reaching consequences.

At the Ecofin meeting Germany refused to entertain any mutual political solution, premised on the argument that over the last few years Germany had made radical modernising reforms in employment regulation and social policy. As such, it would be unfair for Germany to bear the costs of its southern partners' failure to implement comparable programmes of reform. The Germans had already undertaken painful structural reform programmes. They were not, therefore, willing to pay the bill for countries that did not comply with the rules of the Union and modernise to ensure the stability of their own economies. The German Chancellor encapsulated the prevailing public opinion in Germany in a statement to the Bundestag a few days after the Ecofin meeting; the Eurozone should have the ability to exclude one of its members if it repeatedly failed to fulfil the prerequisites imposed by the Stability and Growth Plan.

After the March Ecofin meeting, confusion again prevailed. Greece, as the Prime Minister made apparent in discussions with one after another of his European counterparts, was not requesting financial aid but was asking for tangible support from the Union.[14] Community sources explained that this support would consist of approval of the establishment of a mechanism to ensure the fiscal stability of the Eurozone. The call to activate the mechanism, in the event it was needed, would have to be made by the member state in need of support. If Greece wished to avail itself of this, it could do so whenever it deemed it necessary.

All the while, Greece was sending out conflicting signals. As noted above, it was claiming no immediate financial assistance was necessary, but at the same time calls were made for immediate support. The Minister of Finance requested 'immediate initiatives', warning that if swift action were not taken 'the only solution, the only possible solution, would be the IMF'.[15] The Prime Minister, during a visit to Budapest, noted that 'we are talking to the IMF and they told us that they would not ask for any more measures than what we have already taken'.[16] A few days later a Greek newspaper published an article indicating 'the plan for Greece to seek recourse to the IMF is ready in every detail, should the government wish to do so'.[17] The funding available to Greece through the

IMF was US$15 billion, at an interest rate of approximately 3.25%, which was significantly lower than the rate proposed in discussions within the EU and the ECB. However, would this amount be enough? A range of figures were banded around in political and public discourse in Greece: €20 billion to service debts maturing over the next two months, €53 billion for the coming year, over €100 billion to repay maturing bonds over the coming years. The characteristic confusion continued to prevail, and led the leadership of Greece, and more specifically the Minister of Finance, to naïvely believe the country could easily borrow on the international markets, at sustainable interest rates, provided the EU offered guarantees on Greek debt. So no coherent plan was required on the part of the Union, but only an immediate statement of support. After that, Greece would be able to direct its own efforts at reform and recovery.

Greece had the support of France. France maintained that this was more than a matter of reckless behaviour on the part of a lone member state. This was a far more salient debate concerning how the Eurozone should respond should one of its members find itself in need of assistance. The matter concerned how the Eurozone functions. If the EMU was not in a position to help one of its smaller members, then it would lose its standing in the international community. The Greek government had taken the measures which the member states of the Eurozone asked it to, now they (the Eurozone) had to take note of their own responsibilities. The French Finance Minister, Christine Lagarde, drew attention to structural problems within the EMU, premised on the German economic model, in which German growth was primarily driven not by domestic consumption but rather by exports across the Union. The fact that the largest economy of the continent was oriented towards export had contributed significantly to the imbalance of the whole Eurozone. Lagarde continued her analysis to assert that Germany had a pivotal role in redressing this imbalance; Germany should look to promote higher domestic wages and consequently domestic consumption. By making moves to reduce national competitiveness, it would facilitate relative improvement in the competitiveness of the less competitive countries of the Eurozone, such as Greece. However, such analysis received criticism in the international media; it only furthered division and made an unnecessary contribution to an already convoluted debate. Furthermore, currency speculators were the primary beneficiaries, to the detriment of the euro and the Greek economy. By the time the March summit took place, the value of Greek bonds had tumbled dramatically in just 20 days.

The summit, held on 25 March, was conducted in a positive and cordial environment, following a compromise reached between Germany and France the previous day. The statement released by the heads of state and government of the Eurozone acknowledged that 'the Greek authorities have taken ambitious and decisive measures which are expected to allow Greece to regain the confidence of the markets'. The Greek government gave an assurance that it did not need, nor had it asked for, financial support. In the context of the efforts to ensure the stability of the Eurozone, and to prevent damage from further speculation on the markets, the member states announced that they were prepared to proceed with bilateral lending for any one of its members, should this be necessary. This new mechanism would constitute a measure of last resort and would be implemented only when financing from the market was insufficient. Furthermore, they agreed, in principle, to the simultaneous financing of a member state by the IMF.

The provision of any bilateral loans must, according to the statement, be done only on the basis of unanimous agreement and under 'strict prerequisites, as well as the oversight of the European Commission and the European Central Bank'. Interest rates would not be overly favourable; there would not be any elements of a subsidy. Finally, the member states declared the 'strong coordination of their economic policies' and a will to improve the overarching 'economic governance of the European Union'.

All the signatories to the agreement made public declarations of their satisfaction.[18] The Greek Prime Minister stated: 'Greece and the euro are safe; Europe has taken a big step.' In a prior statement he paid his compliments to the resolve of the Greek public, and the efforts of the administration: 'the efforts and sacrifices of the Greek people are bearing fruit. The policy of responsibility has been vindicated. Greece has proved its strong will and the merits of its timely reaction to the crisis.' With regard to the bilateral mechanism now available, he insisted that 'we shall not need to have recourse to the mechanism – that the gun is on the table is sufficient'. The Prime Minister's metaphor of the gun on the table was directed at the markets. Media analysis agreed, in less triumphant terms, that Greece had 'got the weapon it sought'. The speculators would now be afraid to play with interest rates. Lenders would carry on lending at sustainable interest rates. 'We shall not need anything or anyone.' Greece would be in a position to stand on its own two feet.

The German Chancellor stated: 'The members of the EMU shall not allow the destabilisation of the euro.' There would be assistance only if Athens were unable to borrow funds from the market; all financing would constitute only a measure of last resort. Any notion of a subsidy whatsoever was out of the question; the interest rate on loans would be higher than that of the market. President Sarkozy put on record his pleasure at the outcome; he had ensured help for Greece and for any other member of the EMU that might face problems in the future. The standing and stature of the Eurozone would remain intact. As had been the German desire, the provision of finance for any struggling member states would remain a primarily European affair, avoiding the humiliating excessive intervention of the IMF. Sarkozy asserted 'the Eurozone is taking its fate in its hands'. This arrangement would deter speculation against Greece and would ensure that its challenges could be overcome in a structured and reasoned fashion, without fear of the markets.

The President of the ECB, Jean-Claude Trichet, stated in a post-summit press statement that he was confident that 'in all likelihood, the mechanism decided upon will not be put into effect. Greece shall regain the confidence of the markets.' He may, however, have recognised that this might not suffice to allay anxiety in the markets. In an additional statement he announced that the ECB would continue to accept bonds of the Greek state as collateral. This ensured both that Greek banks would have access to capital through the ECB and that Greek bonds would be honoured by foreign banks, which could then use them as collateral with the ECB. He thus averted a liquidity crisis in the Greek banking system.

Commentary in the international media remained sceptical, however. A piece in the *Financial Times* read:

> Another knife-edge summit in Brussels, another late-night agreement, followed by self-congratulatory plaudits from European leaders: the 'emergency funding agreement' for Greece sounded like a significant deal on Thursday night. But then you wake on Friday morning, examine the details and realise it was mostly smoke and mirrors. They had you fooled for a minute.[19]

In a leading article, the most eminent conservative German newspaper, the *Frankfurter Allgemeine Zeitung*, reiterated the German position and maintained that conditions had hardly changed.[20] It insisted, in fact, on the need for stricter oversight, so that similar problems would not re-emerge in the Union. The conclusion to be drawn was less clear in the French media. They still considered it possible that Strauss-Kahn might be called upon to provide support to Greece. The Greek press highlighted the 'grey areas of the support accord' and hoped that day where they would need clarification should never arise. They commented that the famous 'gun' was probably lacking bullets. Domestic media in Greece did maintain, however, that if Greece proceeded with immediate implementation of the measures to control the deficit, and managed to gain the necessary confidence of the markets, the worst might be over.

A few days later, Greece floated seven-year bonds on the markets. The sum sought through the bonds was a modest €5 billion; however, the markets did not respond as positively as had been hoped. The interest rate officially on offer was 5.9%. In reality, however, it exceeded 6%. The government sold the bonds below face value so as to present the misleading public image of a fall in interest rates.

This development showed that the Brussels accord had not solved Greece's problem. The country's problem was not merely one of liquidity, as the Greek government had maintained. Greece was not an economy with rates of growth able to cover its borrowing needs. The crisis was compounded by issues of credibility, but had major structural issues at the heart of its cause: the size of its debt, low competitiveness, repeated budget deficits and recession. The country, however, did not wish to acknowledge the true severity of its problems, nor the need for long-term and painful reform. Greece's public position was convenient for its partners in the EMU; it allowed them to avoid responsibility for involvement in redressing these underlying challenges. They could avoid difficult discussion concerning draconian intervention, or major reforms to the regulatory framework of the EMU. However, the markets, the banks and potential financers had realised that the root cause of the crisis was much greater than simple concerns of liquidity. This could be seen in the continuation of high interest rates, expensive CDS policies available and ongoing speculation, not to mention sustained demands for guarantees from Core European nations.

The Brussels accord did nothing to redress the Eurozone's structural imbalances. Mention of disparity was entirely absent from the common statement. References to *economic governance* remained little more than rhetoric, and no substantive effort was even discussed to rectify these shortcomings. The accord, in essence, was a weak compromise of rhetoric and public statements of support, designed to remove anxiety in the markets. However, nothing had truly changed, and once again events would drive policy, and not the other way round.

## Notes

1 D. Gros, 'The Greek fiscal adjustment programme', European Policy Centre, 21 April 2010.

2 Institute of Economic and Industrial Research, 'The Greek economy', *Quarterly Review*, March 2011, p. 8: 'There is no doubt that the Eurozone's supervisory and control system failed to identify Greece's fiscal derailment in a timely manner. This could have been achieved through checks of the fiscal data provided by the government.'

3 *Le Monde*, 11 February 2010.

4 *Le Monde*, 10 February 2010.

5 See Statement by the heads of state or government of the European Union, Brussels, 11 February 2010.

6 See Statement by the heads of state or government of the euro area, Brussels, 11 February 2010.

7 Published in *Le Monde*, 12 February 2010.

8 Lex column, *Financial Times*, 12 February 2010.

9 Economic and Financial Affairs, 6477/10 Presse 28, Brussels, 16 February 2010.

10 *Eleutherotypia*, 27 February 2011.

11 See his interview in *Le Monde*, 23–24 May 2010.

12 *Eleutherotypia*, 27 February 2011.

13 See *Kathimerini*, 20 February 2011; *Eleutherotypia*, 27 February 2011; D. Mitropoulos, 'Cries and whispers for the recourse to the IMF', *Ta Nea*, 8–9 September 2012. The government denied that the contact was related to recourse to the IMF. A few days later, the Prime Minister stated in Brussels that recourse to the IMF was out of the question: 'We are not on the edge of the cliff', he stressed.

14 According to the *IHT*, 19 March 2010, he stated to journalists in Brussels that an offer of assistance from the EU 'would be enough to tell the markets: hands off, no more speculation, let the country do what it's doing, leave it in peace to be able to move ahead'.

15  *Imerisia*, 17 March 2010.
16  In mid-March the Prime Minister visited Hungary, which had requested and received help from the IMF. The object of his visit, according to his statement, was to exchange experiences of 'the management of a difficult economic crisis' (statement, 16 March 2010).
17  *Ta Nea*, 20–21 March 2010.
18  Their statements were published in all the newspapers of 26 and 27 March 2010.
19  Wolfgang Münchau, *Financial Times*, 28 March 2010.
20  *FAZ*, 27 March 2010.

# 6

# The bitter truth

The only thing that Greece gained was a little breathing space. But the government did not realise that. They thought they had achieved a great success. Many celebrated: they believed the interest rate crisis had been resolved, Germany had been obliged to yield and the IMF would not be dealing in detail with the Greek problem. The government's policy of giving absolute priority to the positive spin of its policy, of glorifying its actions and downplaying the problems served only to obscure the real situation. The government itself was led astray by its 'success', and for one more time did not do what it had to, that is, to draw up a long-term plan to deal with the crisis. This superficial approach made the situation worse. Accordingly, the respite did not last for more than a few days.

After the Easter holidays, more and more doubts began to be expressed over whether the assurance of support for Greece was sufficient to ensure its financing. The swift rise in the payable rate of interest was indicative, should Greece wish to borrow from the markets. From 6.5% at the end of March 2010, it climbed to 7.4% on 8 April, a level that precluded any borrowing. The high cost of interest was an indication that the markets deemed loans to Greece particularly risky, owing to its high level of debt.

Contrary to the expectations cultivated by the government, financial analysts ascertained that Greek debt as a percentage of GDP would rise at a rapid rate owing to the recession and the consequent shrinking of GDP. The annual rate of interest on borrowing for Greece was already much higher than the annual rate of growth of GDP. When this happens, sovereign debt does not simply feed on the annual budget deficits. It feeds itself further by continually adding new amounts of debt, owing to the interest which cannot be paid because the weak performance of the economy cannot ensure repayment. The figures then show a continual rise in debt as a percentage of GDP, a continual deterioration in the situation. Tangible proof of this is how Greek debt developed, despite the attempts to stabilise the country in 2010. In the spring of 2010, it fluctuated around a level of 140% of GDP; a year later, despite austerity, it had reached 150%. Calculations showed that by 2020 it would fluctuate at levels above

170%![1] The Greek public was not informed of this aspect of the problem and was mystified over why debt was rising. At the time, the government tried to play down the recession, presenting it as a passing phase without particular consequences. However, in this way it only made its planning harder.

Developments were worsened by two additional factors. The first was that the Greek economy kept coming up against greater problems than had been originally forecast. The deficit for 2009, which had been calculated at the unusually high level of 13.5% of GDP, turned out to be even higher by 2%, rendering its correction even more painful. The Greek banks requested that the balance of the help that had been provided for in 2008 by the previous government, amounting to approximately €18 billion, be granted to them. The flight of capital out of the country had accelerated and it was calculated at about 5% of deposits. The result was that the economy's liquidity was negatively affected.

A second factor was the lack of clarity over the terms of the EU's intervention. What amount would the EU grant and how much would the IMF, should the bilateral lending be activated? Various rumours circulated that financing would amount to €30–40 billion. However, French and German banks alone held Greek bonds worth an equivalent of €100 billion; therefore the amount of financing had to be greater, if the aim was to secure the banks. A second question was, who would determine the terms conditions of the loan? The view prevailing in the Greek press was that the IMF would lay down its own conditions, since its managing director had stated that the IMF would set its own conditions for Greece, as it did for other countries. It was concluded that negotiations would be needed with both the IMF and the EU, something that did not happen of course. The matter of the rate of interest was also significant. Germany wanted a high rate of interest, so as to convince Greece that it must proceed with the reforms necessary for it to return to the markets. In Greece, talk was of a possible rate of interest of 4%, lower than the market rate, even though the Ecofin statement determined that it should be higher than the market rate. Finally, it was unclear how the matter would proceed. In answer to journalists' questions to the President of the ECB on 8 April, as to whether Greece would be granted the aid, Trichet answered that: 'that is up to the Greek government', which, however, according to *Le Monde* newspaper, stated 'that it shall continue to borrow in accordance with its planning'. And, indeed, the government cultivated the impression that those matters were of no interest to it.

Government leaks, statements from its officials and a continual stirring up of matters fed into and sustained the general uncertainty prevailing. Despite the decision of the Eurozone taken on 25 March, at the beginning of April it was reported that the government and the European socialist parties would be presenting a 'more effective proposal' for a new support mechanism, one without the IMF. A government official stated that he was not satisfied with the Brussels accord. 'The government accepted it because it had no other choice', but 'an even stronger defence against speculators is needed'. When reactions against these announcements were manifested, 'an official of the Ministry of Finance' denied what the 'government official' had said.[2]

On 9 April, the *International Herald Tribune* summarised the situation in the following headline: 'Looming over Greece: Specter of bankruptcy'. On 10 April, officials of the Union and representatives of the member states drew up a draft agreement on the loan to be granted to Greece. On 11 April, the ministers of finance of the Eurozone decided on the conditions for financing Greece, should it request such financing. The loan would amount to €40–45 billion: €30 billion would be granted by the countries of the Union in the form of bi-lateral loans, and €10–15 billion by the IMF. The rate of interest on three-year borrowing would fluctuate between 4.85% and 5%. The rate of interest that would be calculated by the IMF under its own rules would probably be 2.8%. The basic queries were answered by this decision, but yet again this lasted only a short while.

The next day, Greece raised €1.2 billion from the markets through the auction of treasury bills, an amount of no particular significance. The rate of interest was very high, 4.50–4.35%. The rate of interest critical for evaluating the picture of the country's economy, that for 10-year bonds, moved upwards. The Minister of Finance stated that Greece would continue to borrow from the markets smoothly and he underlined that the Greek government had not requested activation of the support mechanism; nevertheless, it remained available to Greece should it become necessary.

International analysts had a different view. They ascertained that the situation had not changed and that Greece would require financial support to avoid default. Trichet pointed out that the condition of Greek banks remained difficult and could become worse; the Prime Minister, however, called on the Greek public to be certain that the efforts they were making were 'bearing fruit', giving public opinion the impression that he was trying to find another solution, such as a loan from France, according to information published.

On 21 April the spread between the German and the Greek interest rates reached 501 basis points, and the interest rate on Greece's borrowing rose to 8.1%, from 6.5% 20 days earlier. According to the newspaper *Ta Nea*, the decision to have recourse to the support mechanism was taken on the afternoon of Thursday 22 April subsequent to the agreement reached between the Prime Minister and the Minister of Finance, and after a telephone call from the latter, Giorgos Papaconstantinou, to the US Secretary of the Treasury, Timothy Geithner. Geithner warned 'that if one more day were lost it could prove catastrophic' and that Greece 'had no reason to wait'.[3] It is difficult to understand why the telephone call to the US government was made. Why would Greece ask the USA whether it should activate the arrangements it had agreed with the Europeans? The telephone call gave rise to assumptions that there had been previous talks with the USA and a quest for 'allies' beyond the EU which had been fruitless.

On Friday 23 April, the Prime Minister proclaimed in a public announcement to the Greek people from the island of Kastelorizo that he would be requesting 'the activation of the support mechanism which we have created together with the European Union'. Among other things, he stressed that 'We have drawn up a plan, we have taken difficult measures many times, measures that have often been painful, but we have regained our credibility'. The markets were not convinced. Either because they did not believe in the will of the EU, or because some people decided to continue speculating. 'Our ultimate destination is to free Greece from supervision and custodianship.'[4] These long-winded words were uttered with the intention of covering up the fact that Greece, despite what the Prime Minister maintained, had not regained its credibility and was therefore accepting far harsher supervision than anything it had ever known from 1974 onwards.

On the same day, Papaconstantinou, in an official letter, requested from the EU, the ECB and the IMF that negotiations be held in order to put into effect the implementation of the decisions of 11 April. With this move, the government admitted that it no longer possessed the ability to deal with the sovereign debt crisis. The reason behind this development was not only the speculation of the international markets against Greece, as government officials heavily hinted. Speculation is a permanent feature of markets. It intensifies when opportunities are on offer. The uncertainty of economic developments in Greece, in conjunction with the high level of its sovereign debt and lenders' fears that they might lose their money, created favourable conditions for speculation.

The performance of the economy and the government's inability to deal with it played a decisive role. During the months and even the days before the request for financing was made on 23 April, various amounts for the assistance now deemed unavoidable were mentioned from the Greek side, ranging from €26 billion to €100 billion. The EU, the ECB and the IMF offered a greater amount in May 2010, €109 billion. But even this did not prove to be enough. Within a year, in the summer of 2011, another €100 billion or so became necessary, without it being certain that even that amount would be sufficient. Neither in April nor in May 2010, nor in July 2011, did public opinion understand what the Greek side's version was with regard to what was really necessary. Those responsible had failed to pay the necessary attention to matters of decisive importance to forecast economic developments, such as the fall in the rate of growth, the failings of the tax collection mechanism, the reduction in income and also the whole way the clientele system functioned, which increases expenses and benefits and reacts when these are squeezed. The contingency plans of the Greek government proved scrappy. The expression 'black hole', which was used ad nauseam to describe the inability to cover the budget targets, became a part of daily speech. Without a plan and precise forecasts for a longer period of years, there can be neither a proper negotiation nor efficient handling of the means at your disposal. You accept whatever turns up and you apply the principle 'wait and see'. You hope you can pull through, but you do not have a realistic strategy to seek to achieve your goals with much probability of success.

Before October 2009, the New Democracy governments were not in a position to seriously negotiate with Greece's partners in the EU. Constricted by the policy of hand-outs and the clientele system, they cared only about winning the next elections and staying in power, and not in formulating a common stand with the EU. After 2009, the PASOK government could rely on the party's previous positive engagement with the EU. But this time round, it avoided full engagement with its partners. It appeared in two minds over European cooperation. It believed it had the ability to pull through under its own steam. It deemed that recourse to the EU would put obstacles in the way of the programme it wanted to implement. It wanted to handle the various matters without the restrictions deriving from the Stability Pact and super-vision of the country. The advances made to the IMF at the end of 2009, and the talks with the US Treasury, indicate its desire to determine a path without European directives. But even later, in the first months of 2010, when help from Europe proved inevitable, it did not adjust its policy to the situation but followed a tactic of bilateral contacts, in which France played a central role, thereby downgrading Greece's relations with other countries. Differentiating between the central players of the EU is not useful. In these contacts the government did not specify what it really wanted to achieve. Its object was to gain moral support for the country, and not the planning of the necessary long-term financing. The Prime Minister repeatedly stressed that he did not want help, and his interlocutors made assurances that help had not been requested by him. Valuable time for sounding out solutions was lost in this way. By April 2010 it was no longer possible to keep avoiding the issue, neither for Greece nor for its partners. The necessary preparations for sustainable, long-term solutions had not been made.

Negotiations, when they were held, followed unusual methods for the EU. The main negotiators for Greece were the Prime Minister and the Minister of Finance. They had inadequate staff to prepare the ground with the staff of Nicolas Sarkozy or Angela Merkel – with discussions, plans, alternative proposals, research of the data. The problems, however, presented so many different aspects that a substantial discussion without extensive preparation in bilateral or multilateral meetings was not possible. So unusually frequent discussions at the highest level prevailed and decisions were rushed on the basis that 'we cannot do it differently'. Greece's presence in important organs of the EU was low calibre. Its representatives had 'political instructions'. They could not deal with their European colleagues, who had participated in negotiations for years. 'Technocrats' of the other countries determined decisions.

The governing party's communication tactics up till then had a negative effect. Domestically it was triumphal with regard to its efforts, and accusing with regard to countries that put up obstacles. The domestic audience formed the impression that everything was going well, and that the back-tracking was due either to the reluctance of certain states to help Greece or to the continual speculation against the country. The external audience watched these communication shenanigans and wondered whether Greece was working with the seriousness such problems demanded.

Greece's partners were, of course, also responsible for this development. The Union wanted to gain time. Each time the markets ratcheted up their pressure for the EU to intervene and limit the risk of a default on Greek bonds, the major countries promised an extraordinary meeting of the Ecofin, a summit, a new plan from Rompuy. There were declarations of support, but no initiatives to provide financing. For months the impression prevailed that some parties were willing but that Germany either refused or was avoiding the issue. And, indeed, the German government, either owing to the reactions of public opinion at home or because it thought it was obliged to support fiscal discipline against all those remaining indifferent to it, appeared reluctant to become actively engaged. The continual hesitations of Greece's partners over what must be done and their endless discussions, in conjunction with the procrastination and indecision of the Greek side, made the situation worse. Had a decisive intervention been made from the beginning, the extent of the disaster would have been limited. There was, however, an excuse for this inertia. The Greek crisis was an unprecedented phenomenon. The Treaties made no provision for how to deal with it. Whatever solution was given would create a precedent for the future; it should therefore be well processed and as widely acceptable as possible. Owing to the way the Union functions, it takes time. Greece should have sounded the alarm bells much sooner.

From 21 April 2010, representatives of the EU were already in Athens. Officials of the IMF and the ECB were added to them to look into the problems. The government had said, a few days earlier, that new burdens would not arise, should Greece have recourse to the support mechanism. However, it became immediately obvious that the discussions with the representatives of the Troika[5] would begin with a total evaluation of the Greek economy, from scratch. New measures in addition to those already planned were certain to be imposed, as both the international as well as the Greek press observed. Changes in labour relations, restoring public companies to health and extensive privatisations were mentioned as examples.

New measures were inevitable a few days after the Greek request, because the situation had deteriorated even more. On 27 April, Standard & Poor's downgraded Greece by three notches. Greek bonds had now been reduced to 'junk' status. Immediately after the downgrading there followed a mass sell-off of Greek bonds on the market. Prices toppled. Greece's borrowing rate of interest, which constitutes the risk index for financing, reached 9.69%. This rise affected the borrowing interest rate of other countries of the Periphery, such as Portugal. The value of the euro fell, the price of gold rose. Shares of banks and insurance companies holding Greek bonds worth billions fell on the stock markets. The international press ascertained that the crisis was extending

to Spain, perhaps even to Italy: 'The precedent of Greece, which obliges countries with deficits to support countries with greater deficits, is particularly
toxic'.[6] The President of the ECB, Trichet, and the managing director of the
IMF, Strauss-Kahn, visited Berlin on 28 April to put pressure on the German
Chancellor, but mainly on German MPs, to speed up the process of financing
Greece. Strauss-Kahn stated, on this occasion: 'Every day lost is a day that
makes the situation worse and difficulties increase for everyone'.[7] According to
the European press, panic prevailed.

The Greek crisis found the members of the Eurozone unprepared. There
were no provisions in the Treaties. The silence of the statutory texts expressed
the conviction that prevailed: the inability of one country to pay its liabilities,
resulting in a generalised economic flurry, was not allowed. It meant that this
country had contravened its commitments immeasurably, and that the EU had
ignored its gross violations. They had, therefore, to deal with a problem which
should not have existed. All of a sudden they found themselves obliged to
proceed under pressure with arrangements for something which was impossible to have happened. Their first reaction, on 11 March 2010, was a wish:
'Things will be all right. We shall not abandon Greece.' When, despite hopes,
the situation was not fixed, they remained inert again. For three whole months,
they did not manage to formulate a common stand. Consequent to this, the
markets undertook the handling of the problem. They put pressure on to
formulate the necessary framework, as much for the current crisis in Greece as
for future turbulence in the Eurozone.

### Notes

1  *Kathimerini,* 17 July 2012.
2  *Eleutherotypia,* 2–3 April 2010.
3  *Ta Nea,* 24–25 April 2010.
4  *Ta Nea,* 24–25 April 2010.
5  The Troika was a three-member group, comprising the European Commission, the
   IMF and the ECB. It was the basic negotiator of the official lenders with the Greek
   government. 'It is a vehicle for economic and financial evaluation and negotiation.'
   The discussions with the Greek authorities were held jointly and agreements on
   the conditions for assistance had to be accepted by all three members. See Jean
   Pisani-Ferry, André Sapir and Guntram Wolff, *EU–IMF Assistance to the Euro-Area
   Countries: An Early Assessment,* Bruegel, May 2013, p. 20.
6  *Le Monde,* 28 April 2010.
7  *Le Monde,* 30 April 2010.

# 7

# The first Memorandum: a medicine with dangerous side-effects

Greece was considered the source of the crisis. It was in Greece, therefore, that the necessary measures to prevent it spreading had to be implemented immediately. Intense and challenging consultations between the Greek government and representatives of the Troika (the European Commission, the ECB and the IMF) concluded on 1 May 2010 with a framework agreement. The following morning, that framework agreement was approved by the Greek Cabinet. Later that afternoon the Eurozone ministers of finance convened in Brussels and ratified the framework agreement. On 6 May, the Parliament in Athens voted on the agreement, passing the bill into law. The 'Memorandum of Understanding' was thus born. Leaders of all the Eurozone member states (the EU-17) ratified the agreement of the ministers of finance on 7 May. The programme for Greece's salvation was thus wrapped with all the necessary formalities so that it would be binding for all members of the Eurozone. Additionally, on 3 May, the ECB announced that it would continue to accept Greek bonds as collateral for granting liquidity. Greek bonds thus secured the continuation of their financing from the ECB.

In a statement from the ministers of finance on 2 May it was indicated that, in total, €110 billion would be provided over a three-year period, with the EU-17 shouldering €80 billion and the IMF €30 billion. The financing would be effected through bilateral loans between Greece and the European Commission (representing the other members of the Eurozone), on the basis of conditions agreed between Greece and the Troika. The loan would be disbursed in tranches, the first on 19 May. The coordinator of the programme on behalf of the lenders would be the European Commission.

Certain basic matters were not mentioned in the statement, but could be deduced from the accompanying documents. Repayment of each tranche was to start approximately three years after receipt and was to continue for two years in eight quarterly instalments. The interest rate on the EU-17 share of the loan would be around the 6% mark but for the IMF share 3.8%. Repayment of the first €20 billion tranche that was disbursed in May 2010 and interest thereon would thus begin in May 2013 and end in May 2015. The largest part of the loan would be repaid from 2013 to 2016. Greece would not have to resort to borrowing from international markets for the next 18 months. It would be able to issue long-term bonds again at the beginning of 2012. It should be noted that the €110 billion rescue package corresponded roughly with Greece's debts to German and French banks.

The EU-17 heads of state and government described the aims of the Memorandum as both 'ambitious and realistic … it addresses the grave fiscal imbalances, will make the economy more competitive, and will create the basis for stronger and more sustainable growth and job creation'.[1] So that there would be no doubt about Greece's obligations to implement what was decided, the statement of the EU's heads state and government recorded categorically that 'the Greek Prime Minister has reiterated the total commitment of the Greek government to the full implementation of these vital reforms'.[2] Beyond oral assurances, the agreement provided mechanisms to ensure compliance. Prior to receipt of each new tranche, the Troika would check for 'correct application of the programme'. Funds would be released only subject to its approval. Greece's continued liquidity would thus depend on adherence to the conditions attached to the bailout package.

The Memorandum reflects the dominant view in the IMF and European Commission on how to confront an economic crisis in a nation carrying an excessive sovereign debt and unable to secure funds from the international market. The remedy prescribed is the quickest possible reduction of the fiscal deficit, to stop any growth in the level of debt. At the same time it is deemed imperative that the root causes of the crisis, which usually include declining competitiveness, be dealt with.[3] The aim is to return the country to the inter-national markets as soon as possible so that it does not burden other countries. The prerequisite for the success of this prescription is debt sustainability. The Troika judged the Greek debt sustainable. Thereafter, the Memorandum was structured to achieve three central objectives:[4]

1 the reduction of the budget deficit to 3% of GDP, in line with the provision of the European Treaties, by 2014 (this reduction would be front-loaded, the brunt of the efforts to reduce the deficit being borne immediately, to send a convincing message to the markets, and to ensure that further support from Greece's partners would not be necessary);
2 the reduction of state expenditure, with permanent reforms to the func-tioning of the state, such as changes to the social security system and the curtailment of pensions;
3 the improvement in the competitiveness of Greek enterprises, by opening closed or protected professions, the liberalisation of labour law and, above all, an internal devaluation (i.e. a reduction in prices and incomes), effected through administrative measures, in order to secure lower costs.

The Memorandum sought to transform the Greek economy into one operat-ing according to the standards of the advanced nations of the EU. It sought to do so via a 'big bang' and presumed it could be achieved in three years, by the middle of 2013.

The need for extensive reforms that would, among other things, result in a reduction of the annual deficit from 15% of GDP in 2009 to less than 3% in 2014[5] was laid out in the Memorandum, and would receive ongoing review by the European Commission and the IMF. To achieve such a turn-around, a reduction in expenditure of approximately 18% of GDP over the period 2009–14 was stipulated. This exceeds by six percentage points the 12% fall, from 15% to 3%, stipulated for budget deficit by the Treaties. This additional reduction was required to offset falls in tax revenue caused by the recession, failure to achieve budgeted revenue, delays in tax collection and so on. The intention of these stipulations was to contain sovereign debt at 146% of GDP for 2014. The recession (in terms of the reduction in GDP), according to the Memorandum, would be of the order of 4% in 2010 and 2% in 2011. From 2012 onwards, the rates of growth were predicted to be positive and be increasing. The primary surplus (the balance of the budget prior to debt servicing) would grow from 1% in 2012 to 5.7% in 2014, and would continue to fluctuate around 6% over subsequent years.

The Memorandum[6] was an exceptionally detailed text, specifying the form and timetable for all the reforms. Every target was precisely specified so that implementation could be monitored. The majority of the reforms were to be implemented in the first two years of the programme, so as to increase the likelihood of recovery. Implementation would receive evaluation on a quarterly basis. The Memorandum cited the following actions, among others, as necessary for fiscal rehabilitation. Straight from the first quarter, to redress Greece's financial situation, it demanded a rise in VAT rates, with a projected yield of €800 million in a full year, and a cut in the salaries of the public sector, through the reduction of the 'extra salaries' for Easter, Christmas and holidays (known as the thirteenth and fourteenth salaries), and reductions in other allowances paid to public sector employees, with net savings to amount to €1,500 million in a full year. The Memorandum even detailed the need for the deregulation of road transport in the final quarter of 2010: 'Government adopts a law on road freight transport that removes restrictions not provided for in Directive 96/26/ EC of 29 April 1996 on admission to the occupation of road haulage, including minimum fixed prices.'

Since devaluation of the currency was not possible, the measures set out in the Memorandum were said by its authors to be able to achieve the same results by other means. When a currency is devalued, real wages decline and the prices of imported goods are reduced. The population becomes collectively poorer, but more competitive, thanks to the reduced real earnings of workers and more competitive prices. When it is not possible to devalue the currency, as in the case of Greece, comparable results must be achieved through an 'internal devaluation', accomplished by administrative measures. State intervention leads to a reduction in income, medium-term recession and a fall in prices. The authors of the Memorandum did not invent this policy; they followed prevailing economic theory.

The government did not adhere strictly to the instructions in the Memorandum. Rather, it sought to limit reactions through adjustments it deemed politically and socially necessary. It did not, for example, completely abolish the extra Christmas pay. It frequently acted with the political cost as the criterion. However, it steadfastly defended the Memorandum and the policy it incorporated. In the Cabinet meeting that took the decision to implement the Memorandum, the Prime Minister said:

> Think of where we would have been today. Without this European support mechanism, our problems would be insurmountable.... An unprecedented support package for an unprecedented effort by the Greek people.... We are talking about historical changes for the citizen. Historical changes that will definitively pull Greece out of the crisis.[7]

In the first quarterly review of the progress of the programme, both the European Commission and as the IMF ascertained that impressive progress had been made in the efforts to stabilise the economy. Their conclusion was that 'the strategy and the targets of the programme continued to be the appropriate ones'.[8]

The reaction of the majority of Greek public opinion was intensely negative, not only because IMF intervention was popularly associated with inevitable reductions in income and a rise in poverty, but also because, in the specific case of Greece, the Memorandum provided for cuts in salaries and benefits, a rise in the retirement age and cuts in pensions, and a systematic reduction in privileged arrangements and acquired rights. The newspapers spoke of a 'bloody rescue' and of a 'taxation storm to fill the coffers'. They considered the measures 'the greatest economic and social intervention ever attempted in Greece. If it turns out successfully, Greek society may come out of it economically healthier. But if not ... success is far from secure.'[9]

On 5 May 2010, one of the largest demonstrations of recent years clearly showed the intensity of the reaction but also its dead ends. Demonstrators set a bank on fire, resulting in the death of three employees. Anarchists and extreme right wingers attempted to occupy Parliament. The following months were dominated by extreme confrontations familiar in Greek political life, with its permanent excesses and personal attacks that obstruct any examination of a problem that aims to achieve a widely acceptable solution. In this intense battle, there were of course cooler heads than those demanding the complete rejection of the Memorandum, or the paying off of all debts by the individuals responsible for the current state of affairs. They recognised the need for tough intervention, but expressed doubts over whether this intervention, in the way it was shaped, was the most suitable. The domestic political situation, however, did not permit a calm dialogue over what other solutions were possible. A super-simplistic 'yes or no' approach dominated.

The government did not try to prevent the explosion of protest. It maintained an equivocal stance on the Memorandum. It did not demur when party officials publicly proclaimed that the measures did not correspond to government ideology. It let it be tacitly understood that the Memorandum reforms had been imposed, and that it would have followed another policy, had it been free to decide. The Troika representatives were described by one minister as 'middling to minor employees of international organisations', to whom ministers should not stoop to talk.

The government did not make any serious efforts to inform the public as to the true size of the problem and the degree of adjustment necessary in the Greek economy, or the extent of the forthcoming restrictions. It did not explain 'what the innocent remarks concerning competitiveness, productivity etc. actually concealed'.[10] Instead of a public awareness campaign above party expediency, it harped on the mistakes of governments 'of the last 30 years', and on its own decisive initiative to mend the situation. Instead of offering an economic and political analysis that would make comprehensible the necessity of interventions in matters of state expenditure and the social security system, it emphasised the responsibility of politicians, speculators, banks and tax evaders. Public opinion failed to realise that the country was in a situation that, without profound reform, was incompatible with staying in the EMU and that it had been on a path that was likely to have catastrophic consequences for all citizens. It did not appreciate that there was an overwhelming need for the return of economic stability, irrespective of whether it was demanded by the European Commission and the IMF.

New Democracy played an important role in this negative development. During parliamentary discussions over the Memorandum that took place in May, it took a clear rejectionist stand. It declared that 'we shall do what we can to get out of the mechanism the soonest'. Its main argument was that the measures would worsen the recession. However, its own solution remained obscure. In July the party's president, Antonis Samaras, sensing an opportunity to profit politically from the prevailing public sentiment, adopted sharper tones. In a speech at Zappeion on 7 July 2010 he opined that a necessary condition for an 'alternative solution is for us to get out of the coercive one-way street of the Memorandum'. He asserted that he would be capable of reducing the total budget deficit to zero by the end of 2011. He claimed that state-owned assets amounted to €272 billion, and that a small percentage of this wealth would be sufficient 'to reduce debt, and to get us out of the vicious circle and the commitments of the Memorandum'. 'We are literally an extremely wealthy country'. The plan he presented offered a 'path of hope.'[11] This was the standard mix of accusations, hyperbole, unrealistic plans and unsubstantiated assertions. He was drawing a line between 'the bad', those who supported the Memorandum, and 'the good', those who were subject to it but fighting against it. Samaras's plan became New Democracy's 'Zappeion I' programme, which was replaced, in May 2011, by the 'Zappeion II' programme.

The Memorandum's projections were not realistic. Its main objective – to reduce the deficit – required, as already noted, an expenditure reduction of the order of 18% of GDP by the end of 2013. Reductions on such a scale are not possible in a developed country. Experience teaches that attempts to squeeze incomes and state expenditure to such an extent will inevitably spark an intense public reaction that will frustrate the desired 'adjustments'. The prediction that Greece would return to the bond markets in 2012 was also totally unrealistic. As the second Memorandum proved, the debt was not sustainable and it needed to be restructured if Greece were to return to the markets by 2020, after a decade of severe austerity.

In 2009, Greek debt had reached 129% of GDP and was forecast to reach approximately 160% of GDP by 2014. A country with such debt needs rates of growth of GDP exceeding the rate of interest it pays on its loans by at least one percentage point, so as to have some resources to spare for reducing its debt and financing investment at the same time. In the case of Greece, the average rate of interest on its loans was approximately 5%. But its nominal growth, according to the Troika's predictions, would only just return to a positive rate by 2012. From 2015 onwards it would reach a level of the order of 4%, up to 2020. It would, therefore, be notably lower than the rate of interest.

The rate of interest Greece had to pay was lower than the rate it would have had to pay if it borrowed from the market. It was, nonetheless, punitive because it was higher than a level that would allow for the recovery of the Greek economy.[12] It was reminiscent of lenders who finance over-indebted households at rates of interest so high that they will be driven to certain bankruptcy. A whole year had to pass before it was officially recognised, in July 2011, that this rate of interest was having negative consequences, and it was reduced thereafter.

The Troika took the view that revenue would steadily exceed expenditure after 2012. Greece would thus be able to ensure the repayment of its loans. The primary surplus would in fact fluctuate, according to Greece's lenders, around 6% of GDP from 2014 onwards. With the exception of Norway, an oil producer, no other European country has ever shown such a large surplus over so many consecutive years. This target of the Memorandum was unachievable.

Tangible proof of the predictions' falsity was the estimated effect of the measures on growth. The cumulative forecast for the years 2009–12 was a decline of GDP of 7.5%. But it reached three times that figure, approximately 23%. When recession exceeds 20% over four years, the economy needs time to return to steady growth. The second Memorandum predicted that there would be a recovery in 2014, not 2012, as the first one had stated. It is probable, however, that this too will not be realised.[13]

The miscalculations were not without consequences. When rates of growth are far lower than the levels necessary to pay off interest and there are no surpluses with which to discharge the debt, borrowing rises in order to cover obligations. Despite efforts at stabilisation, debt follows a rising course. A comparison of the data on sovereign debt in the IMF report of July 2010, with the data, also from the IMF, a year later (i.e. July 2011), clearly shows this rising course of debt, contrary to the predictions set out in the Memorandum. According to the 2010 forecast, debt was to have reached 133% at the end of 2010 and 145% in 2015 of GDP. A year later, the figure for 2010 was reported to have been 143%, and was estimated at around 166% for 2011.

From the start of the programme, 'black holes' kept appearing in the tax revenues, and deviations from the forecasts were observed. The Ministry of Finance attributed this to a rise in tax evasion, the inertia of the tax collection authorities and the refusal of citizens to pay their taxes. These were not, however, the only reasons for the shortfall. The main cause was the drop in demand and the recession. When GDP shrinks by 2%, a 4% increase in taxes does not yield a 4% increase in revenue for the state, nor a corresponding reduction by 4% of the deficit. The Troika, however, did not undertake more detailed calculations. It did not entertain any extension to Greece's period of adjustment beyond 2013, because it wanted to use Greece as an example, to put pressure on other countries.

The Memorandum did not consider the probable social reactions, nor did it make proposals to gain the cooperation of citizens. It was imbued with a moral lesson the strong countries of the Eurozone wanted to give: that agreements and rules are meant to be applied, otherwise there are unpleasant consequences. Its style was highly technocratic. Such a text, however, neither moves nor convinces citizens. They feel that their interests and their difficulties are being ignored. As has been correctly observed, the EU is a political entity that considers social justice as one of its basic goals. 'As a consequence it cannot demand the reduction of the minimum wage and consider as a secondary matter the tax avoidance of the 10% of high earners which results in the loss of one quarter of tax revenue.'[14] Such a stand has consequences. The protests returned aggressive politics to the foreground. Expectations of swift and un-contested implementation of the Memorandum were spectacularly overturned.

For society to cooperate with such radical changes, it needs motivation. Under the Greek conditions, such motivation could only be produced by some evidence of growth combined with increased employment. The Memorandum indicated that growth would come about more or less automatically as a result of the restoration of healthy public finances, the lowering of the cost of labour and the opening up of markets. It did not contain special measures that would have helped, such as exemptions from the restrictions on public investment, spending cuts or compulsory Greek co-financing for the funding of public works by the EU. Nor was some kind of 'dowry' provided to finance investment that would have supported a new development pillar, such as the exploitation of wind energy. Nearly two years had to pass, marked by the victory of the socialists in the French elections in May 2012, before any serious discussions began on promoting growth. No attention was paid at that time to privatisations, which could have been a means for attracting investment – that came considerably later and mainly in the context of funding debt repayment. As a result, both public and private investment was drastically restricted, and recession and unemployment were worse than expected.

The foreseeable result of the crisis and the Memorandum was the loss of the public's confidence, the anxiety of the people over future developments and the consequential withdrawal of deposits as the insecurity crossed to the banking sector. The expansion of credit to the private sector had already reached zero in 2010 and this was followed by credit contraction thereafter. The banks did not lend and private companies could not borrow. Entrepreneurs avoided new investment and initiatives. Recession worsened to unforeseen depths. This was not the simple 'correction' intended by the Memorandum. There was no antidote to hand.

The President of the ECB, Jean-Claude Trichet, described the conception underlying the Memorandum as follows:

> When a household spends more than it earns and its debt keeps growing, it realizes very quickly that it can no longer continue to live in the same way. Common sense demands that it should correct the situation. The same holds for a country. For it, also, it is a matter of prudence and common sense to return, after a while, to a sustainable situation with regard to its expenses. Policies leading to fiscal orderliness favour growth. They enhance the confidence of households, businesses and investors. And confidence is absolutely necessary for growth.[15]

The case of Greece gave an opportunity to commentators in various publications to question this analogy. As the economist Paul Krugman has repeatedly noted, while it is important to maintain a prudent fiscal policy in the long term, a sudden and drastic reduction of expenditure in the middle of a crisis serves only to intensify the crisis and leads to recession; it is a policy that is self-cancelling. Others have observed that 'When you raise taxes and at the same time reduce the benefits and income of those at work, you kill off demand and growth'.[16] In the case of Greece it has been maintained that a reduction in spending of 1% led to a reduction in growth much greater than 1%.[17]

The success of an economic policy that follows a theoretical model of corrective interventions in countries with high fiscal deficits and reduced competitiveness depends on the extent to which it takes into account the particularities of each case. It depends also on evaluating the country correctly. It must take account of: its production possibilities, the probability of a fast recovery, the efficiency of the state in adapting its apparatus, and the social and political dynamics. Not all deficits present the same problems. The size of a deficit and its causes may require different approaches. The imposition of a uniform percentage cut in all salaries, for example, cannot be resorted to if it is going to result in the pauperisation of a section of the workforce.[18]

The Memorandum did not take into account the particularities of the Greek case. It applied an invariant recipe, with the aim of concluding the cure as soon as possible. To achieve this it fitted the necessary steps to the desired time frame and not the time frame to the economic conditions. The recession that followed from this hurried and pressured implementation was far greater than had been projected, and indeed far greater it needed to be. It resulted from an unrealistic and dogmatic design.

In the case of Greece, the rate of reduction of the deficit should have been correlated to the rate of growth (or recession), with regard to both extent and timing. Had this been done, following the first measures and the subsequent drastic fall in economic activity that they brought about, the next wave of measures would have been milder, the targets more achievable and the reactions more limited. There should have been a greater period of adjustment for the reduction of the deficit, exceptions to the cuts in public investment and provision for the implementation of community support programmes, the funds for which remained largely unused. The absence from the Memorandum of any correlation between the implementation of the measures and the outcomes they generated meant that, despite the recession and the popular insurrection, the drastic cuts continued.

The Greek crisis coincided with a broader economic predicament in the South of Europe. To avoid a worsening of the situation, there should have been a more comprehensive approach to the problem of competitiveness in the countries of the Periphery. The Memorandum was addressed to one country only and its specific problems. This self-limitation overlooked the extent of the problem and the need for parallel measures. Germany, for instance, should have been asked to reduce its domestic taxes, to increase domestic demand and thus to facilitate imports from the peripheral countries. Such a move would have been a quid pro quo for Germany having been the chief beneficiary of the Common Market, the single currency, and the trade and exchanges with the countries of the European South.

The Memorandum underestimated certain obstacles. Its implementation requires an efficient administration. However, the administrative mechanisms in Greece are suffering gravely. The extent of tax evasion was merely one indicative example of administrative weakness. Another example, which came to the fore during work with the Troika, was the lack of the data needed to design the measures and estimate their effectiveness. In 2010 a census of public employees was required to ascertain how many there were and where they worked. In the developed countries of the EU the existence of such data is taken for granted. Administrative dysfunction is not an accident. It reflects professional and guild interests, chronic compromises between government and the trade unions and, mainly, clientelistic arrangements and mentality. Under these circumstances, resource-saving changes are impossible to implement overnight. They require careful preparation, targeted action and public support. In times of wide-reaching austerity, however, public support is far from being a given.

The authors of the Memorandum conceived the reform programme on the premise that Greece is a developed country, with the state and social infrastructures of its European partners. They thought it capable, therefore, of implementing a stabilisation programme as had been done, for example, in Germany in the 2000s, or Sweden in the 1990s. The Greek problem was one of excessive public expenditure and lagging competitiveness due to high earnings. It was deemed possible to redress these failings over a three-year period with a targeted and decisive policy. Greece had the capacity, it was presumed, but it would have to demonstrate the necessary will. To bring about such a will, the lenders thought it appropriate to use, as an instrument of pressure, a high rate of interest and the repayment of the loans by 2017. They thought Greece would comply with their demands when faced, as the country was, with the risk of having to continue paying a 5% rate of interest, and under the pressure of fast repayment of loans. It was a miscalculation.

The poor state of the country was due not only to the misdemeanours of the governing class, which could be easily corrected. It was also due to a system of politics and government, clientelistic and guild-based, that rejected both the control of expenditure and a policy of economic rationality and stability that would ensure growth and solidarity. This system had evolved over decades, with the support of the political parties and aided by the intense populism that they cultivated.[19] There were some politicians who endorsed rational policies of convergence with the advanced countries of Europe but they did not remain in power long enough to bring about substantive change.

Overcoming this system would require many years of effort, changes in mentalities, radical reforms in the organisation of the state, actions to pull down the walls protecting clientelistic and guild practices. It would demand sustained and intense confrontation of established interests. It was not something that could be achieved in three years, as the authors of the Memorandum believed. Nor was it an economic matter alone: it was a deeply political one.

The shortcomings of Greek society, and those of the administration in particular, were shown clearly in efforts to implement the programme of investments financed by EU Structural Funds.

During implementation of the programmes of the Community Support Framework (the EU's regional policy funding for Greece, 2000–06) there was deliberate and misleading obfuscation by the New Democracy governments as to how much was being achieved. There was all-round ignorance about what was going on. Funding absorption varies over a project cycle: exceptionally low during the planning stage, higher during the initial implementation stage and extensive at the stage of completion. For proper oversight of progress, the data must be recorded at each stage. Ministers continually referred to the overall rate of absorption during their period of office, but this is a meaningless number without a more detailed breakdown of the data. Almost all ministers asserted that the programmes were proceeding satisfactorily and that problems were being overcome. The 'Competitiveness and Entrepreneurship' programme, for instance, showed an absorption rate of 43% for 2010. Upon further requests for clarity concerning the meaning of these figures from the

European Commission, it was reported that this percentage included payments 'which have not yet reached the enterprises', that is, payments that had not yet been made. The Minister for Development, Competitiveness and Shipping, M. Chrysochoides, made it known in May 2011 that there were 4,768 'dead projects', that is, projects for which there was no tender, legal commitment, contract in place nor, of course, payment. These projects held €5.5 billion frozen owing to bureaucratic processes, inadequate planning and clientelistic interventions by mayors, heads of public organisations or regional prefects. In the same month – May 2011 – 'live' projects, contributing to the absorption of EU funds, numbered in total 2,259, that is, barely half the number of 'dead' projects.[20] Efforts to increase efficiency were being made, though. The number of 'dead projects' was reduced, new projects were added to the planning and the legal framework was simplified, but there remained issues that overall caused delays.[21] At the heart of the problem, as more generally in the public sector, was the lack of a systematic approach and the clientelistic demands, the localisms and the amateurishness at the lower levels of the ministries.

The European Commission felt that the country was not in a position to propel the programmes. A Task Force for Greece was created and the EU appointed an official to act as a consultant/supervisor of the processes of programme implementation. The EU also reduced the compulsory national co-financing to 5% and recycled back to Greece the funds that the country had failed to absorb. The Greek government presented this recycling of funds, previously lost owing to non-absorption, as a new 'Marshall Plan'. It thus created the impression that this was a grant which it had secured through its negotiating ability and thereby attempted to cover up its failure to take advantage of the funds in the first place.

Greece was obliged to repay the loans in instalments, starting in 2013, with the majority to be repaid by 2017. This short period for the repayment of the loans was backed by the argument that the country was simply facing a temporary liquidity crisis, which could quickly be overcome via the measures set out in the Memorandum. The loan was designed as a short-term facility, for a solvent country in a position to meet its liabilities. In December 2010 the Commissioner responsible gave assurances that Greece would be able to return partially and gradually to the markets from May 2012 to May 2013. This self-deception was not sustained for long, however. Before a year was out, it was decided to reduce the interest rate, and then to extend the repayment period for the debt. Next, in July 2011 it was decided to add some new funding and, finally, in October 2011 a new loan of €130 billion was agreed, as the decisions of the previous July were now considered inadequate. This was a grand recognition that the first attempt had failed.[22] It had failed because the crisis was not one of liquidity, but was due to Greece's continual inability to meet its liabilities, as the country was insolvent. The effort made in May 2010 was not commensurate with the problem it sought to solve, and proved unrewarding. For the Greeks, ensuing developments proved that planning done on the back of an envelope had been short-sighted and had shown no real concern for citizens.

The agreements between the Eurozone and Greece provided for a strict process of scrutiny regarding the Memorandum's implementation. Disbursement of each instalment of financial assistance was subject to the approval of representatives of the Troika after they had performed a series of checks, the object of which was to ascertain the progress made in achieving the quantitative and qualitative targets of the Memorandum.[23] The Troika had the right to request new initiatives or revision of decisions taken by the Greek authorities, if it spotted deviations from deadlines or targets. The Greek authorities were obliged to consult the Troika with respect to policies that were not consistent with the Memorandum, as well as in the case of failure to achieve the agreed targets. To make checking possible, they had to provide all the information needed to ascertain the economic and fiscal situation. Before every instalment was paid, they had to compile a report on the progress of the programme.[24] The quintessence of these provisions was that the Troika had direct oversight of all matters relating to the financial assistance and it had the right to reject government initiatives. In the case of disagreement, the government was in a weak position. The Troika possessed the decisive weapon, in that it decided whether the instalment due would be disbursed. If it did not give its approval, Greece, not having any other means, had to yield. Otherwise it risked insolvency and exit from the euro.

The Memorandum restricted the country's autonomy. In accepting it, the government drastically reduced its scope for independent economic policy. It had to comply. But even without the Memorandum, any Greek government would not have had the freedom to shape policy to its will, because it could not ignore the political or economic environment. The debt, the inability to find other means, the scarcity of liquidity and the probability of national insolvency all drastically constrained its moves. Any other creditor could demand the same stringent conditions, or possibly even more severe than those stipulated by the Memorandum, in order to lend to the country. The harsh truth is that a country's autonomy and power are won or lost in proportion to its economic and social performance, towards growth and economic robustness. Greece had lost a large part of its autonomy long before it signed the Memorandum, when governments, following the downhill path of clientelistic hand-outs and of servicing the social groups that supported them, began to borrow at an increasing rate.

The loss of autonomy is not an argument adduced only by the Greek side. It constitutes also the counter-argument of the German side in making the case against the provision of finance to member states that are facing a debt crisis. In the German view, the responsible state, one which handles its economic affairs carefully, resigns power when it provides support to a country with unreasonable economic and fiscal behaviour: 'it becomes exposed to adventures it cannot control effectively'.[25] Responsible states, which accept such self-restrictions, encourage the avoidable by rewarding dangerous and irresponsible behaviour.

However, both the Greek and the German conceptions are incompatible with the broader goals of a union of states seeking closer cooperation and a common path for its members. Mutual support in such a case must be a *sine qua non*. But it has to be subject to rules. The stronger must not exploit the weaker and the weaker must not take advantage of the more developed, for example by continuously cheating on their obligations. Common rules inevitably restrict autonomy, in proportion to the challenge faced. In the case of Greece the restriction was large, whereas for Spain the restriction was much smaller.

The argument focusing on the loss of autonomy disregards also the idea that international cooperation – here, the operation of the EU but in fact every project undertaken by a community of nations to pursue common goals – leads to constraints on the nation state for the sake of the supranational whole. In the era of globalisation, every country has to accept constraints in order to secure opportunities and liberties which could not be enjoyed otherwise. In this way the modern nation state can ensure a qualitatively superior autonomy, one that it could not experience were it to follow a path of isolation for the sake of a nominal but not substantive independence.[26]

The public's negative assessment of the Memorandum questions why the Greek government accepted this agreement, and did not react by seeking another solution more in keeping with the Greek reality. The answer is simple: it did not know how to act differently. It did not have a plan of its own, it had not formulated a view on how to deal with the situation and it had neither the time nor the arguments to change the minds of its interlocutors. It had wasted all the time after the elections in dead end explorations. It did not immediately recognise the gravity of the situation and it neglected the formulation of realistic solutions of its own. By the time the dangers were recognised, in all their magnitude, there was a matter of days left to avoid default. It agreed to what was being offered in order to avoid a worse outcome.

France, Germany and the institutions of the EU were well aware of this fact. Their aim was different. They wished first of all to assist their banks and avoid the negative effects on their own banking systems of a possible Greek default. The 'unofficial assessment that they were saving their banks', as opposed to the 'official assertion that they were saving Greece', was true.[27] Through the loan package, the EU bought itself a little time to evaluate the situation in depth, to acquaint itself with the dynamic of developments and to prepare its next steps. However, it also served another purpose, of equal importance. Greece's debts to the European banks were being transformed into debts to member states of the Eurozone. That is, the banks were escaping the risk of losing their assets, and the EU was acquiring the ability to handle the problem as it deemed appropriate through various measures: delaying repayments, reducing rates of interest, and partial writing off of debt or demanding full repayment.

Notes

1 Statement of the heads of state or government of the euro area, after the summit of 7 May 2010.
2 Ibid.
3 Ch. Iordanoglou, in his article 'The Memorandum: a post-mortem', *Athens Review of Books*, December 2011, p. 28, analyses the ideology of the Memorandum.
4 See *European Economy: The Economic Adjustment Programme for Greece*, Occasional Paper 61, European Commission, May 2010; *Greece: Staff Report on Request for Stand-By Arrangement*, Country Report No. 10/110, IMF, March 2010.
5 The deficit should have fallen to 8% of GDP in 2010, to 7.6% in 2011, to 6.5% in 2012, to 4.9% in 2013 and to 2.6% in 2014. These targets turned out to be impossible and were revised in July 2011 and March 2012.
6 The text of the Memorandum was published in the daily press. See *Ta Nea*, 5 May 2012, special supplement.
7 From www.naftemporiki.gr, 2 May 2010.
8 *First Review under the Stand-By Arrangement*, Country Report No. 10/286, IMF, September 2010, p. 4; *European Economy: The Economic Adjustment Programme for Greece. First Review, Summer 2010*, Occasional Paper 68, European Commission, August 2010, p. 7.
9 Yannis Pretenteris, *To Vima*, 2 May 2010.
10 G. Lakopoulos, *Ta Nea*, 5 September 2012.
11 Speech at Zappeion, 7 July 2010. For New Democracy's position, see T. Pappas, *When the Cat Became Reconciled with the Mouse*, Polis Editions, 2012, pp. 69ff.
12 J. Pisani-Ferri, *Le réveil des démons*, Fayard, 2011, p. 7.
13 On the recession, see Chapter 21.
14 J. Pisani-Ferry, 'Economie', *Le Monde*, 21 February 2012, p. 2.
15 'Economie', *Le Monde*, 1 June 2010, p. 15.
16 A. de Tricornot, 'Economie', *Le Monde*, 11 May 2010, p. 5. See also P. Krugman, 'Austerity, Italian style', *New York Times*, 25 February 2013.
17 'Dossier', *Le Monde*, 6 September 2011.
18 See Chapter 22 on the matter of austerity and growth.
19 R. Hermann underlines this point, 'Fessel Klientelismus', *FAZ*, 24 August 2012, p. 10.
20 'Growth', *To Vima*, 25 November 2011.
21 According to *Kathimerini*, 12 September 2012, p. 20, 'almost one-third of the projects are up in the air and risk not being executed in time before financing ends..... The projection for projects which shall not be executed in time has worsened by €1 billion compared to the projection which had been made in May.'
22 See Chapters 16 and 20.
23 Since instalments were disbursed quarterly, checks were also done quarterly.
24 For the practice adopted during implementation of the adjustment programme, see Chapter 9.
25 O. Hoffe, 'Souverän ist, wer uber Verstand verfügt', *FAZ*, 10 August 2012
26 See Panayiotis Ioakimides, *Ta Nea*, 25 October 2011: 'Approximately 65% of public decisions taken that concern us as a society and as an economy are taken by the organs of the Union, and only 35% by national institutions'.
27 M. Wolf, 'Economie', *Le Monde*, 11 March 2010.

# Part II
# The Memorandum's first year
# of implementation

# 8

# The crisis spreads to the Union

As well as ratifying the decision to grant the loan to Greece, the extraordinary summit of the Eurozone held on Friday 7 May 2010 discussed developments across the whole of the Eurozone. The President of the ECB, Jean-Claude Trichet, had already expressed concern that the Greek crisis could develop into a 'systemic crisis'. American and Asian investment groups had agreed, according to Trichet, to speculate against the euro. Its value kept falling, while Spain's and Portugal's borrowing rates were rising rapidly, creating further risk of a default within the EMU. A solution had to be found during the weekend because the Asian markets would on the Monday morning (10 May) react to any hesitation on the part of the EU and set a negative tone. The leaders left Brussels on the Saturday morning without a result. They continued to differ, but had agreed that the problem should be solved by the finance ministers on the Sunday.

After many gruelling hours of negotiation and phone talks between Angela Merkel and Nicolas Sarkozy through the night from Sunday to Monday 10 May, at 2 a.m. the finance ministers of the Eurozone agreed upon the implementation of the European Financial Stability Facility (EFSF).[1] During the negotiations, Germany had initially insisted that the mechanism should ensure that loans were granted on the same bilateral basis as had been done in the case of Greece. France, however, favoured a framework of collective funding to be provided by the EU as a single entity. This view met with intense objections, not merely as it was in violation of the existing Treaties but also as the smaller countries stressed that they were not willing to provide capital but only guarantees, since they did not have at their disposal budgets comparable to those of their larger counterparts. There were also disagreements about the amount of capital that the fund would require. The amount originally discussed was €750 billion; however, reservations were expressed and the fund shrank. The final agreement on 17 June provided for the creation of a fund of €440 billion. Every member state within the Eurozone provided a guarantee relative to its own liability, through this new common framework.

Access to capital from the EFSF would be structured according to the framework agreed upon at the Eurozone summit, subsequent to a unanimous decision by the member states of the Eurozone. The interest rate on the loans granted would be determined by market conditions but would also account for expenses incurred by those parties contributing the necessary funds. The EFSF was a provisional body and would be in operation till 30 January 2013.

According to its mandate, the EFSF would provide financial support to 'a member state of the Eurozone facing economic or fiscal trouble owing to extraordinary circumstances that it cannot control.... Should the mechanism be activated, strict conditions over fiscal policy must be imposed, with the aim of ensuring the sustainability of the member state's fiscal economy and restoring its ability to draw financing from the markets.' Thus it was clear that lending would take place only under extraordinary circumstances and with stringent conditions attached.

This agreement marked a significant break with the policy and discourse that had preceded it. The Eurozone had taken the first step towards a collective effort to combat crises, despite the framework of the Treaties indicating that every member bears independent responsibility for the fulfilment of its financial liabilities. The need to avert a major crisis proved stronger than the commitment to the framework of the Treaties. The Treaties were not accordingly amended, however, as this was politically unpalatable. Nonetheless, the violations were understood to be crucial.

France felt that the establishment of the EFSF was a significant step towards achieving the long-discussed common economic governance but, even though an institution of common crisis management was indeed established, this was not the case. Dealing collectively with crises does not constitute a common fiscal policy nor a common economic policy; it does not create a coherent framework for common economic governance.

The crisis had thus led to the establishment of a framework for regulation and support, in form of the EFSF, but the underlying causes of the turbulence had not been addressed. The members of the EU continued to maintain that strict fiscal discipline, in the form of limitations upon structural deficit and levels of sovereign debt as designated by the Treaties, guaranteed stability and economic performance. A crisis, however, can arise despite adherence to discipline. As mentioned, Spain did not have a structural deficit at the start of the crisis; rather, the government had surpluses in its budget. Despite this Spain rapidly found itself drawn into the crisis, through the bursting of the speculative bubble in the Spanish construction industry.

Furthermore, the EFSF made no mention of the broader imperfections of EMU. The loss of independent monetary control entailed in EMU severely limited the policy tools available to member states when faced with a crisis. They could no longer under take quantitative easing to ensure liquidity in the economy, they could no longer devalue their currency to bolster competitiveness, and they no longer had any monetary tools to impede imports or help exports in an effort to combat economic decline. National central banks no longer had the ability to finance the commercial banks in a capacity of lender of last resort. National central banks found themselves dependent on the decisions and the fortunes of the others. Furthermore, when the GDP of the countries of the Periphery is significantly lower than that of the Core nations, there are major implications for levels of development, competitiveness and convergence over the longer term. In a country with its own currency, the central bank has the available tools to overcome the state's challenges when it encounters a major downturn in the economic cycle, and can still ensure that the state adheres to its financial obligations. This is not possible in the EMU. The regulations under which the ECB operates forbid it to lend to member states. Member states must have recourse to the markets. When, however, a state finds it is no longer able to acquire the necessary liquidity to service its debts, the market interest rates will inevitably reflect the increased risk. In the case of Greece, the international market's exponential reactions made the continued acquisition of credit unsustainable. The liquidity crisis turned into a crisis of solvency.

A mechanism providing capital to counter a crisis, such as the EFSF, is a useful solution in extreme cases. It does nothing, however, to avert the growth in divergence across the EMU to the detriment of the weaker states. In a system of monetary union, a coordinating authority is required, a directing agent managing the sustainable economic governance of the whole area. Only then is it possible to counter the trends in divergence mentioned above; only then is it possible to ensure a policy directed at growth for all and the coherent management of any common financial challenges. Following the establishment of the EFSF, a widespread opinion, reflecting on its shortcomings, was that the euro had been saved but not cured.

After the establishment of the EFSF, there was a belief that optimism would return, that the situation would gradually improve and that interest rates would decline to reflect this. No such reversal in fortunes was forthcoming. The fall in the value of the euro against the dollar continued. While it was recognised that the Eurozone's plan had bought time and countered contagion, it had not allayed doubts over the future of the euro. The fear that the austerity measures in the various member states would have detrimental consequences for the prospects of growth across the Eurozone remained pronounced.

In Greece, however, the bailout package exceeded expectations and this did create a climate of optimism. The Prime Minister asserted that 'the country had been saved'. In the Cabinet meeting held on 2 May, at which the Memorandum and its measures were discussed, he noted that 'for the first time in very many years, the government is operating with the greatest devotion to the mandate given to it by the citizens. I say this sincerely, we are a different kind of government.' The Minister of Finance claimed that the fiscal measures were more than enough. 'Greece shall return to the markets earlier than 2012.' He could see the 'light at the end of the tunnel' and predicted that the situation by the end of the year 'shall be better than expected'. 'Greece shall have returned to growth by mid-2011.' Furthermore, he foresaw 'the recession will be lower than expected ... for 2010' and rejected the 4% decline in GDP projected by the EU.[2] Events proved his predictions premature. By mid-2011 not only had Greece not returned to the markets, but it needed further support. Recession not only reached 4% in 2010, but it continued to worsen throughout 2011 and 2012.

The Greek government, however, was not the only party guilty of premature optimistic analysis. The representatives of the European Commission who drew up the first report on the progress of the country's adjustment programme in August 2010 were equally complimentary:

> Greece has managed an impressive budgetary consolidation during the first half of 2010. It has also achieved impressive progress in major structural reforms which will help to transform the economy. Some of these reforms have been undertaken earlier than the schedule set.[3]

As an example of these positive developments they drew attention to reforms to the pension system made in July. The report also contained a review of the situation and an enumeration of the many more measures that were deemed necessary. Despite the praise in the report there was recognition of the work that was yet to be undertaken.

Others, however, were very sceptical with regard to the progress made. Many realised that any solution to the sovereign debt problem in Europe, and particularly in Greece, would not be possible without a restructuring of that debt, that is to say a 'haircut' of lenders' claims. They noted that the European authorities and the member states remained averse to such calls because they feared such a measure would have alarming effects on the balance sheets of their own commercial banks, and inevitably have serious repercussions on the whole of the economy. It was increasingly believed, however, that in the end such action would be inevitable. Calls were made for the creation of a body to oversee the restructuring of the debt. In Greece no one paid any attention whatsoever to these comments; they were decried as completely unrealistic.

On 17 June the European Council convened and adopted the 'Europe 2020' Strategy, a new strategy for employment and growth, which would determine the policy of the EU over the coming years. With regard to fiscal discipline, it imposed penalties on any member state that did not adhere to the regulations. In terms of stricter fiscal supervision, it now obliged member states to submit stability programmes every six months, and much tighter economic oversight was written into the Strategy, particularly with regard to levels of sovereign debt. The European Council referred to the European Commission for further examination the matter of what punitive measures would be taken in the face of further violations. It stressed, however, that the Union would proceed with greater decisiveness from here on in dealing with problems.

The climate in the markets saw a marked improvement. The panic over the future of the euro receded significantly. Cautious optimism prevailed. Stock markets saw a return to growth, banks began to lend to each other again without fear of a default, the gulf between rates available to peripheral countries of the Union versus those available to Germany shrank, and the price of CDS policies for the Periphery fell significantly. This reversal in fortunes led many to question whether the gravity of the situation had not been over-played, the risks overestimated and the EU's capacity to react underestimated. However, most financial analysts kept repeating that the risks remained and that future difficulties had not been overcome. They considered that Greece had achieved a deferral through the loan. A restructuring of its debt remained a necessity at some juncture over the next three to five years, despite the categorical declarations to the contrary made by Greek officials. In any case, significant problems remained unresolved, such as the structural imbalances between the countries of the Core and those of the Periphery.[4]

By the second half of 2010, the Greek crisis was no longer to the fore in the international news. Attention had turned to Ireland and Portugal, to the necessity of taming the debt crisis that was spreading to more and more countries. Greece had been the first case, but was far from the last. The risk of contagion plunging the whole of the EU into turbulence was obvious, as was to become apparent very soon in Ireland.

Ireland requested help from the EFSF in November 2010 and Portugal in April 2011, after mounting pressure from the Eurozone, concerned that delaying the inevitable would only aggravate the situation.[5] In Ireland, the cause of the collapse was the crash in real estate prices. This made apparent the levels of toxic debt now held by the Irish banks that had fuelled the country's expansion in construction. Losses arose from the previous senseless and speculative expansion of the banks' activities. In order to avert the insolvency of its banking sector, the Irish government guaranteed the payment of all the banks' liabilities, with regard to both deposits as well as other activities. Ireland's sovereign debt, which had stood at 25% of GDP before the crisis, shot up to 125% and was now one of the highest in the Eurozone. In Portugal the cause of collapse was comparable to that in Greece: the low productivity and competitiveness of the country; dependency on imports and the decline in exports; the large balance of payments deficit; high state expenditure; and the exponential growth in borrowing that followed from all these. Portugal's austerity programme, which both the government and the opposition agreed to, turned out to be ineffective and compounded the recession. The negative picture across the EU was completed by developments in Spain and Italy. From as early as the start of 2010, it had been noted that they would face difficulties in meeting their growing liabilities. The rates of interest they agreed with the international banks fluctuated at levels higher than was sustainable in the long term.

Thus, despite the idiosyncratic qualities of the Greek problem, it did not constitute an isolated case. It was also indicative of the broader failings of the EMU, those of a single currency across such divergent member states. The system, as was increasingly apparent, created imbalances.

Furthermore, it was becoming obvious that the EFSF would be insufficient. It had enough funds available to deal with the problems of Greece, Ireland and Portugal, since their economic activity combined amounted to barely 6% of the EU's GDP. However, Spain made up 9% approximately and Italy about 12% of the Union's GDP. The capital required to save them would be three or four times that available in the EFSF. It had become obvious that the sovereign debt crisis was not a transient matter. Problems would re-emerge after the temporary mechanism had ceased to operate. A more permanent solution was necessary. Once this realisation became apparent, intense anxiety arose in the markets and drove a spectacular rise in the rates available to member states facing problems.[6] Additional measures to those provided by the temporary mechanism were vital to reverse anxiety in the markets.

Negotiations bore fruit at Deauville on 21 October 2010. Sarkozy and Merkel, after a private meeting, agreed that there should be a permanent financing mechanism for states in need of help. This was something of a 'retreat' on the part of the German Chancellor. What she won in exchange was that private lenders (the banks) should participate in the restructuring of a nation's debt.[7] This would have significant consequences for future decisions concerning Greek debt.

A few days later, the European Council agreed to the institution of a permanent mechanism to ensure financial stability for the entire Eurozone: the European Stability Mechanism (ESM).[8] The temporary mechanism (the EFSF) would continue to function until July 2013.[9] The final form of the ESM was decided upon at the European Council summit held on 24–25 March 2011.[10] The ESM would provide financial support to a member state of the Eurozone, provided that a 'macroeconomic adjustment programme with suitable conditions (dependent upon the severity) ... of the imbalances observed in the said state' could be agreed upon. Financial support would be made available following 'a detailed analysis of the sustainability of the member state's debt, and whether there is a risk for the Eurozone's financial stability'. The nature and the extent of the private sector's participation would be specified on the basis of this analysis. Should the 'programme of macroeconomic adjustment be able to realistically return debt to a sustainable course, the member state shall take initiatives' to ensure continued involvement of the private sector in the provision of credit. Should, however, 'the programme of macroeconomic adjustment be unable to realistically return debt to a sustainable course', the state would have to negotiate a plan with its lenders whereby they could participate in reinstating the sustainability of the debt. These regulations allowed a member state to access the Mechanism if it was facing serious problems. Aside from the statement that access to the ESM 'requires a macroeconomic adjustment programme with suitable political conditions', the nature and extent of the conditions was unclear.

The Greek government considered the creation of the ESM a positive development, as indeed it was. In the future, the Eurozone would have a mechanism to support countries facing difficulties, which Greece could apply to in the event of further crises.

With regard to the central question of fiscal discipline, on 29 October 2010 the Council decided to implement: an annual appraisal of the stability and reform programmes of each member state, in order to identify macroeconomic imbalances and implement countermeasures; the scrutiny of each national budget to ensure compliance with targets and regulations; the introduction of fiscal targets for all member states, even those not afflicted by large deficits; and the mandatory reduction of debt (as a percentage of GDP) for countries whose debt exceeded 60% of GDP.[11]

The important matter of the supervision of banks was approved by the European Parliament in September 2011. The new supervisory framework was applicable to the entire EU. The European Systemic Risk Board (ESRB) now monitors the macroeconomic environment, provides an early-warning mechanism and makes recommendations with regard to any important risks it identifies. The supervision of banks is now the responsibility of the European Banking Authority (EBA). The European Insurance and Occupational Pensions Authority (EIOPA) now monitors insurance companies and pension funds. The European Securities and Markets Authority (ESMA) is now responsible for the supervision of stock brokers and investment companies.

By the end of 2010 significant progress had been made both in terms of monitoring financial developments across the EU and with regard to the Eurozone's ability to intervene to maintain the stability of the euro and the economies of its member states. How effective these mechanisms would prove under severe pressure was yet to be seen. Nonetheless, the conviction prevailed in the Union that this new regulatory framework would face the challenge. The mechanisms were now in place that would ensure identification of risks, and either its prevention or suitable management and containment.

Commentators held a more cautious view about this. They noted that these decisions not only marked a significant u-turn in EU policy but also contravened existing Treaties. There was recognition of the need for a coherent and collective strategy to combat the risk of economic crises, and by extension the need for supervision and intervention where deemed necessary. The need for solidarity between member states was also articulated. The German Chancellor declared to the Bundestag in December 2010: 'No one in Europe shall be left on his own; no one in Europe shall be left to his own fate'.[12] The leaders of the member states appeared determined to take all the necessary measures to protect the euro. They considered the defence of the single-currency imperative.

However, there remained justifiable frustration. The decisions did not ensure that the Eurozone would function better; they did not create the long-discussed common economic governance. All these reforms dealt with risk prevention and mitigation. They were in essence a short-term response to a long-term problem. By the end of 2010 problems were emerging for which there had been no control mechanism instituted. The capital available from the EFSF and the ESM was not adequate to deal with an expansion of the crisis in Spain or Italy. Unanswered questions arose during the next two years, and they required further changes to the institutional framework. The decisions taken in 2010, while they may have prepared the ground for dealing with them, proved insufficient. They avoided the elephant in the room: how to reconcile monetary union with the absence of a common fiscal policy.

The Greek government hardly made any contributions to the debate in 2010, or to the subsequent decisions concerning the regulation of the Eurozone. Its primary concern was to attack any policy suggestions that would make Greece's position even more difficult. The suggestion of a suspension of a country's voting rights following repeated violation of the Treaties provoked an understandable Hellenic backlash. The Greek government should, however, have focused its efforts on preparing itself for the developments the country would face in 2011. Proposals on the ramifications of the programmes of austerity, the need for a coherent model for the common economic governance of the EMU and the challenges posed by divergence in the economic performance of member states stemming from structural imbalances would all have been of great value. However, the government remained satisfied. The Prime Minister presented Greece as returning to a position of standing within the EU: 'Greece can now negotiate with its partners on an equal basis'.[13]

Under conditions of scarce information and led astray by government spin, Greek public opinion formed an image of events in Europe which was very far removed from reality. Every meeting of the European Council was usually preceded by a heightening of anxiety following media reports and government statements; continual coverage of every European summit indicated that 'the coming days' would be 'critical for the future of the Eurozone'. The 'will of European leaders to effectively protect economic stability in the Eurozone' was put in doubt prior to every summit. If developments were not favourable the consequences could be dire for the country. After every summit, public opinion was relieved to see that another disaster had been averted thanks to the valiant efforts of the government. When the problems reappeared later, uncertainty and anxiety would again intensify.

From 2010, the extent of the crisis clearly indicated the need for a comprehensive strategy; the member states should have a clear picture of the Eurozone's shortcomings as well as what measures were needed to overcome them. The formulation of such a strategy proved exceptionally painful.

The inability to control economic developments in the Union follows from monetary unification (despite oversight from the ECB) while fiscal policy remains an exclusively national competence. Economic policies are highly determined by national goals. Economic management, in terms of both prevention of and reaction to crises, would be far more effective if the states exercised fiscal policy on the basis of uniform rules. The transfer of new powers to the European centre, however, met and continues to meet with intense objections.

Countries of northern Europe reject unification, arguing that every state must retain responsibility for the decisions that it makes. The UK, in particular, resists any effort to weaken its independence in the financial sector and its ability to apply special taxation regimes for business. In contrast, France and the countries of the South support efforts at unification in the field of fiscal policy. Such longstanding disagreement over the matter of fiscal integration affected the development of the crisis. The dizzy pace of debt expansion could have been avoided if, from the inception of the EMU, strict supervision and economic governance had been implemented. This would have reduced deficits and made senseless expenditure impossible, while at the same time a policy matrix could have been in place to promote the gradual convergence of the Core and the Periphery.

According to the German analysis, the countries of the Eurozone should reduce their expenditure significantly; they should subsequently produce surpluses which would allow them to pay their debts. They should avoid deficits and increases in sovereign debt. Germany has followed a restrictive policy, through the strict control of inflation and income, which improved its competitiveness and economic performance from 2000 onwards. Germany then advocated the same policy matrix for other member states; it was vital that the Eurozone adhered to strict rules with regard to borrowing and expenditure. Countries with excessive budgets had to adjust their behaviour to reflect their actual economic capacity. This meant not only movement towards frugal budgets, but also major structural reforms to increase their competitiveness. Financing by the Eurozone was necessary and correct only in a context where it was required in order for a country to proceed with economic adjustment. However, a country not in a position to or unwilling to implement the reforms required should receive no financial assistance. Germany felt that there should also be punitive measures to discipline any member state in continued violation of fiscal regulations.[14]

France, as well as other member states, held view that the strict restrictive policy advocated by Germany would be counterproductive at a time when demand needed to be bolstered to enhance economic activity. France was concerned that the EU was running the risk of limited recovery and the possibility of a new recession. Focus should be directed towards driving growth and investment. The Minister of Finance for France, and later head of the IMF, Christine Lagarde, advocated in the spring of 2010 that Germany should increase its domestic demand. This would serve to provide a greater export market for other member states and enhance recovery across the Eurozone. Countries with the robust economy of Germany should, she insisted, support weaker countries by boosting domestic demand.

It was the German view that came to dominate, without ever becoming the official position of the Union. However, in its efforts to impose a system of automatic penalties, including the suspension voting rights for repeat offenders, it was unsuccessful.

Another point of friction was the role of the ECB. According to its statute, the ECB is an independent institution. It determines policy on its own, with the overall aim of ensuring stability. The Treaties do not allow it to finance the member states to cover their liabilities. Despite these restrictions, the ECB indirectly financed states with borrowing problems, either by purchasing their bonds on the secondary market, or by accepting their bonds as collateral against loans to commercial banks. According to the French perspective, the role of the ECB should be expanded and the restrictions on its activity should be lifted. The ECB should have a role similar to that of the Bank of England, or the Federal Reserve in the USA, which can undertake quantitative easing and the direct provision of finance to the state and national commercial banks when deemed necessary. Germany did not view a change in the Treaties as advisable with regard to the ECB. Lifting restrictions could lead to inflation or to an enormous burden on member states – especially Germany – if it became necessary to cover the Central Bank's losses following issues of solvency in any given member state. There was also conflict concerning the extent of the Bank's support for private banks, if the latter found themselves in difficulties following the emergence of any toxic assets on their balance sheets or negative externalities in the market. The ECB provided credit at limited levels. However, many within the banking sector felt more generous lines of credit should be extended to them to guard against risk and exposure to such externalities.[15]

The divergence in opinion had not receded by the beginning of 2011, despite the ever-growing need for action. France maintained that funds exceeding €1 trillion should be found to finance the ESM. Germany asserted that such an amount was excessive. It maintained that the mission of the ESM could be re-examined, together with any possible changes in the role of the ECB, at a later date.

One solution which was widely discussed in Greece in the context of the crisis was the issue of eurobonds to institute mutual guarantees and to reduce exposure to fluctuations in the market. Greece would not be obliged to issue its own bonds, and could use the support of its fellow member states to reduce the levels of interest available to it. The eurobonds at its disposal would be guaranteed by all member states, and as such would offer a mechanism to allow those afflicted by crises to continue to acquire capital from the markets at sustainable levels.

This solution was not accepted, because it would ultimately result in the Core states guaranteeing the debts of other countries, without limitation. If there were to be any agreement on such a bond, there would have to be clear and stringent conditions attached to ensure this did not simply sustain poor economic policy, or permit the countries of the Periphery to rest on the economies of their more affluent neighbours. However, such conditions would undermine democracy in the recipient nations, as it would permit the Core nations to oversee and potentially veto policy, even if ratified by national parliaments. The EU would end up an autocracy directed by its wealthiest nations, so as to mitigate any perceived risks to the Core. In the discussion over eurobonds it was also highlighted that the bonds would actually incur higher rates of interest than were currently available to certain member states. If they lost the ability to issue their own bonds, these states would be obliged to pay higher interest rates than they currently received – a change they were not willing to contemplate.

It was also proposed that the members of the Eurozone proceed with the common issue of bonds for 60% of their GDP, the amount which, as laid down in the Treaties, a country is allowed to borrow.[16] To acquire credit in excess of this figure, member states would have to issue their own national bonds, for which they would be exclusively responsible. For this solution to function there would have to be much closer scrutiny in the EMU of the economic management of each member state, to ensure that economic mismanagement in one did not afflict all. The proposed solution, in any case, hardly helped countries such as Greece, with sovereign debt standing at approximately 150% of GDP. The fundamental difficulties on the markets derived from having exceeded the 60% limit. Had that limit been kept to, Greece (and others) would have been readily able to borrow at an interest rate much lower than that actually paid.

The issue of eurobonds was also proposed with regard to the need to increase the capital available for the EU's own budget. The bonds could cover the finance required for the implementation of major continental projects, which would provide benefit to numerous member states, such as investment in energy supplies. The Union would bear responsibility for the repayment of these. The eurobond could be a useful mechanism for the provision of capital, independent of the economic problems of each member state. These preliminary proposals were rejected.[17] Again, the aversion stemmed from opposition to the concentration of any further powers in Brussels.

The issue of eurobonds remained in limbo after these preliminary suggestions, till the conditions attached and the responsibilities of member states guaranteeing repayment could be clarified. At the beginning of January 2011 Greek Prime Minister George Papandreou announced his strong desire to lead a European initiative with regard to eurobonds. He assigned the implementation of this proposal to a Special Parliamentary Committee of PASOK MPs. His initiative fell on deaf ears and was quietly abandoned. It was obvious that the other countries had no desire to undertake the repayment of Greek debts.

Intense arguments continued over the matter of debt restructuring. The basic principles of its management had already been resolved. However, in the second half of 2011, Germany asserted that the crisis could not be overcome unless measures were taken to reduce the levels of sovereign debt in the ailing nations. The restructuring of debt, referred to as 'haircuts', were required to reverse the situation. This would entail a reduction in the debt owed, as well as the extension of payment periods, and would serve to reduce levels of interest available to struggling member states. Germany increasingly asserted that states willing to help a country should not assume the entire cost of saving it. The costs must also be borne the creditors, at least in part. Lenders bore responsibility because they were careless in their provision of credit. It was not right for taxpayers to be liable for the balance sheets of careless banks. Restructuring was appropriate because it would distribute responsibility to the culpable. Nonetheless, it would be advisable for it to be implemented in collaboration with the creditors, to ensure it was managed correctly and did not produce a counter-reaction from the markets. Otherwise lenders would seek punitive measures, either in court or through further speculative action in the markets. If lenders cooperated in the restructuring, they would ensure that they would be repaid at least part of their loans. If they did not, they risked losing all their capital, as a nation was driven to default.

The ECB, though, was against debt restructuring in any form in 2010 and this opinion continued to prevail. Its main argument was that such a move would provoke a flurry of negative reaction in the markets. It would also fuel insecurity in the banking sector, as a range of banks would have redundant loans on their balance sheets. It would lead to a rise in interest rates for all, owing to the higher levels of risk for banks. Finally, it would actually aggravate the difficulties experienced by the weaker states when they did return to the markets. If bond buyers were not certain that they would be able to make the returns apparently guaranteed, they would turn to other forms of investment.

Sarkozy was also sceptical with regard to restructuring of debt. The French banks had the largest share of exposure to Greek bonds. A haircut would cause major losses and would pose major risks to the credibility of the French banking sector. France was finally convinced to embrace the German analysis, after the meeting of their leaders at Deauville in October 2010. From that moment on, it was certain that there would be a restructuring of Greek debt. Financial analysis was almost uniform in observing that restructuring was absolutely necessary, otherwise Greece would be driven to default.[18]

The Greek government, however, refused any such restructuring. In November 2010, the Prime Minister asserted that the involvement of the private sector in any restructuring of Greece's debt 'could push the county into default'.[19] Indeed, the government framed the entire debate concerning the 'haircut' in negative terms. It felt that such a debate threw the ability and resolve of the government to handle the crisis into doubt. The government's efforts were being subverted. The reasons for this intense resistance were not apparent, since Greece only had to gain from a restructuring that would reduce its debt. The argument that a reduction in debt would cause a collapse in the Greek banking sector, since all the Greek banks had bought government bonds, more or less under duress, had only limited value. The restructuring, as would come to pass, could be done only in a coherent and planned fashion. External support for the recapitalisation of the banks was imperative. Collapse was not likely. However, recapitalisation could bring about a reshaping of ownership relations and an increase in power for shareholders. The business elites were therefore afraid that they might lose control of their banks.

## Notes

1 Ecofin Council, Extraordinary meeting, Brussels, 9–10 May 2010, Council conclusions, Press release 9596/10, Presse 108.
2 See *Ta Nea*, 2 May 2010.
3 *European Economy: The Economic Adjustment Programme for Greece. First Review, Summer 2010*, Occasional Paper 68, European Commission, August 2010, p. 7.
4 See, for example, R. Taylor, *IHT*, 10 August 2010.
5 See Gavin Hewitt, *The Lost Continent*, Hodder and Stoughton, 2013: for Ireland, pp. 2, 46, 112; for Portugal, pp. 125–128; for Spain, pp. 6, 37, 277; for Italy, pp. 132, 301.
6 On 15 December 2010, interest rates on 10-year bonds were 3.03% for Germany, 11.86% for Greece, 8.24% for Ireland, 6.43% for Portugal, 5.51% for Spain and 4.62% for Italy.
7 However, the risk of losing money grew for lenders, which is why they demanded higher interest rates from then on.
8 See European Council, 28–29 October 2010, EUCO 25/1/10 Rev. 1, CO Eur 18, Concl. 4; European Council, 20 April 2011, EUCO 10/1/11 Rev. 1, CO Eur 6, Concl. 3.
9 A later decision designated that it would function until the ESM began functioning in 2012.
10 European Council, 24–25 March 2011, EUCO 10/1/11 Rev. 1, CO Eur 6, Concl. 3. It was decided that the ESM would have at its disposal €700 billion. At the Eurogroup meeting held on 2 March 2012, new decisions were taken on this amount (€800 billion) and on how it would be financed. See Chapter 22.
11 EUCO 25/10, CO Eur 18, Concl. 4. The points were further set out in *Strengthening Economic Governance in the EU: Task Force Report to the European Council*, European Council, 21 October 2010. These arrangements became known as the Six Pack, because they contained six directives and regulations.
12 *FAZ*, 16 December 2010.
13 *Kathimerini*, 30 October 2010.
14 See for example articles by W. Schäuble and J. Stark in *Europe's World*, autumn 2010, p. 56 and p. 62.
15 *Financial Times*, 2 December 2010.
16 See Jacques Delpla and Jakob von Weizsäcker, *Eurobonds: The Blue Bond Concept and Its Implications*, Policy Contribution 2011/02, Bruegel, March 2011.
17 On 10 July 2012, Ecofin approved a pilot programme for the issue of eurobonds to draw €4.5 billion from the private sector, to finance the construction of 'strategic infrastructure'.
18 See for example J. Pisani-Ferry, 'Economie', *Le Monde*, 4 November 2011.
19 *Kathimerini*, 16 November 2010, p. 4.

# 9

# Implementing the Memorandum: an obstacle race

In 2010 the Greek government devoted itself to extending the repayment schedule of the first loan made under the terms of the first Memorandum. The Prime Minister put the matter 'officially on the negotiating table' at his meeting with the President of France in Paris in November of that year. This initiative was presented as a significant move. Under the circumstances prevailing at the time, it was rather self-evident that an extension would be granted. When creditors realise that they will soon be obliged to grant new loans to ensure the continued solvency of their debtor, the first thing they do is extend the repayment schedule of the existing debt. The matter was over-stressed by the Greek government in an effort to present this as a success. It would have been more advisable for it to direct its efforts toward a discussion of the effects of the recession and a revision of other conditions of the loan; such a debate could have prompted a recognition of the impossibility of reducing the annual budget deficit to 3% of GDP over a period of three years.

Cautious optimism prevailed in the country up until the end of 2010. The shared impression was that Greece had made a 'strong start' and taken important steps forward with the reform of the pensions system. The assessment that 'no one can be absolutely certain when the Greek economy will come out of the crisis'[1] was widely accepted, but the various risks inherent were considered manageable.

In mid-December 2010 discussion of the budget began in Parliament. Both at home and abroad the Finance Minister repeatedly asserted that Greece would be borrowing again from the markets 'within 2011'. The report on the draft 2011 budget stated that 'confidence is already beginning to return to the Greek economy and large structural changes that will ensure the sustainability of fiscal stability and the country's growth have already begun being implemented'.[2]

Earlier optimistic assessments were related to the municipal elections, held on 7 November. In an interview broadcast on all channels, the Prime Minister affirmed that no new measures would be taken, apart from those already set out in the Memorandum. According to the government spokesman, there was no question of taking additional measures; rather, the government was examining 'ways in which those who have been hurt by cuts may be supported'.[3] Official statements created the impression that the government had the economic crisis under control: 'we were the first to enter the storm that began through sovereign debt, but we hope that we shall also be first to get out of the crisis'; 'we have a national plan as an alternative agenda to the Memorandum'; 'in the space of a very few months we have achieved more than what has needed to be achieved over decades'; 'we have regained confidence in our country'.[4] The government made an undertaking that if the result of the municipal elections demonstrated disapproval of its policy, it would call for early general elections. This displayed its self-confidence and certainty.

Abroad, the impressions of the economic developments in Greece were largely set by the comments and analysis of the Troika. Its representatives supervised the progress of the programme set out in the Memorandum, they evaluated the implementation of the measures, they judged whether the government's efforts were sufficient or not, and they suggested additional action. They had the ultimate word on the matter, since disbursement of the loan and continuation of the country's solvency depended on their verdict. The team of representatives of the European Commission, the ECB and the IMF functioned freely and at their own discretion, so they could be certain of access to all salient data, and confident in its accuracy. Supervision was carried out according to the procedures laid out in the Memorandum. The team's visits took place towards the end of each quarter, prior to the release of further funding. The aim was to ascertain to what degree the agreed objectives had been achieved. In preparation for and to help in the conduct of this review, the Greek government presented a report on the results achieved during that quarter. On the basis of this text, the team carried out its own audits and drew up its own 'report on compliance', which indicated whether or not the country had adhered to its commitments. In parallel with this compliance report, another text updating the agreement (the Memorandum) was also created. This recorded actions which had been completed as well as any new initiatives required. Such initiatives were to be in response to new developments, so that progress could be ensured in achieving the targets of the Memorandum. These two documents, the quarterly progress report and the one indicating further action required, were examined by the Troika and the Greek authorities. They were to be finalised following negotiations with the Ministry of Finance. The quarterly instalment of the loan was disbursed by the Eurozone and the IMF on the basis of these documents, following evidence that the quarterly targets had been met and that updates of the Memorandum had been agreed and approved.

This procedure meant that the content of the Memorandum continually grew, to ensure that the original targets for the reduction of the deficit and debt were achieved. Following the November 2010 audit, the 'updating' included an obligation on the part of the Greek government to reform the costly health-care system. The 'updating' that followed the next quarterly review, in February 2011, contained detailed measures on how to achieve this and included directions on how doctors should be paid, as well as proposals on how to calculate the price of generic drugs.

For this amended version of the Memorandum to become binding for the Greek government, it had to be passed into law. Over a period of time the government would gather together the various 'updates' from the audits in a single text, and introduce it as a parliamentary bill. This process constituted the 'Medium-Term Fiscal Strategy Framework to the end of...'. This pompous title concealed the inescapable reality, that the Memorandum was a dynamic document that would incorporate endless amendments and additions.

This apparently simple procedure was in fact complicated. Disbursement of the third instalment of the loan is a prime example. The end of November 2010 marked the end of the second quarter, following the previous instalment in September. The third instalment was supposed to be disbursed in December. An assessment group from the Troika arrived at the beginning of November to prepare for negotiations with the Greek government on technical issues. In their initial meetings, the Troika representatives indicated that the deficit had not been reduced to the level specified in the Memorandum. They decided extra measures were needed, such as the closing down of public companies and the firing of personnel. Otherwise, Austria and Germany threatened to suspend the next instalment. In a meeting between representatives of the Troika and the Finance Minister held on 17 November, the new measures, amounting to approximately €4 billion in cuts, were agreed. The following day, well placed sources claimed that agreement was far from being reached. The Troika had reservations over whether the actions proposed by the Greek government would achieve the results required. On 23 November, the newspapers reported that consensus had been achieved on the Memorandum update. They also reported that the Troika was unhappy with the speed of reform, that the deficit had not been reduced to the desired level and that the target had been missed. Despite this, the next instalment would be disbursed to Greece.

Soon after, however, the text detailing the government's revised obligations was under discussion again. The Troika pressed for a number of draft bills to be submitted to Parliament, including the deregulation of 'closed professions' and the restructuring of state-controlled utilities, accompanied by a clear road map on their eventual privatisation. A key point of friction was the relationship between sectoral and company-specific agreements, affecting remuneration and employment rights. The Greek side maintained that sectoral agreements overrode company-specific ones. The Troika insisted on the opposite and the conflict soon escalated to Brussels. At the beginning of December, the Minister of Labour travelled to Brussels and proposed that sectoral agreements could be overridden by company-specific ones only where a recognised trade union operated at the company level. Although no agreement was reached, it was decided that the two sides would return to this issue in due course. On 10

December it was announced the next instalment had been given the green light. The European Commission underlined that 'the time is right [for the government] to redouble fiscal consolidation and reform efforts, and to demonstrate enhanced resolve to implement programme policies'. The instalment was released, finally, on 19 January, instead of mid-December.

This system of continual supervision, repeated negotiations, leaks about the shortcomings of the Greek reforms and assurances to the contrary by the Greek government kept fuelling the media with news, rumours and comments, which in turn provoked widespread uncertainty. Within the space of a few weeks, towards the end of 2010, the public had read that there would be cuts in allowances and increases in taxation to amount to €6.7 billion, reductions in basic pay and cuts in expenses amounting to €2.4 billion and new labour regulations, including reform in public companies. It was announced that €6 billion was needed to close the black hole for 2010, and a further €12 billion for the three-year period 2012–14. The amended first Memorandum was to have multiple further amendments.

The relentless talk of 'measures and more measures' became a permanent feature of media coverage, intensifying confusion and anxiety. The public simply could not understand why one 'black hole' after another kept appearing, why there had to be one amendment to the Memorandum after another, and why more and more new measures were required. Were these coherent programmes or simply exponential demands being made of them? The complicated and convoluted mechanism was constantly producing more and more burdens, with no guarantee that the pain would ever prove worthwhile. The logic of 'we must achieve the targets' became less convincing with each amendment. Public opinion was at a loss to understand how targets already repeatedly amended by the government and the Troika could require further reform. A return to normality no longer seemed feasible; the citizens had become convinced that they would live in a state of constant emergency, where tomorrow could never have any certainty again. It became increasingly apparent that predictions of complete despair had as much chance of materialising as the blind optimism that preceded them. In discussions over how Greece would ever manage to repay its colossal €110 billion debt, the Troika remained unclear. The matter 'was not something to be discussed now'.

In the meantime, New Democracy had reassessed its position, and sought to make a break with its former sources of support during the debate on the Memorandum in Parliament. It was now of paramount importance to renegotiate the Memorandum and seek 'the implementation of another policy mix'.[5] It was no longer a policy of austerity that was needed but a programme of investment to combat the recession. It was necessary to return to the markets in order to escape the shackles of the Memorandum and the restrictions on state expenditure. How New Democracy would achieve renegotiation, and what specific measures it had in place to counter the recession without increasing deficits and debt, appeared nowhere in its new statements. New Democracy gave no answer to public questions about why Greece's partners would permit a complete renegotiation given that, to date, they had systematically refused to do so. It confined itself to vague statements, naïve claims and descriptions of what it sought to achieve. The party did not seem the least bit concerned with the construction of a coherent and comprehensive policy that might have practical value in reversing Greece's fortunes. It sought simply to return the debate to one of partisan conflict, serving no helpful national purpose. New Democracy looked to capitalise on the pain and disillusionment of the electorate. It wished to appear, at the same time, as the advocate of change and the defender of vested interests, decrying everything citizens were losing faith in. Its message bore no relation to reality.

The conflicting messages of the government and the opposition compounded public confusion. According to the government, the political and economic problems stemmed from a clash between Greece and foreign forces, inimical to the country's stability, which wanted to undermine the government's valiant efforts. The government alone could reverse the fortunes of the country. The opposition presented the crisis as a battle between the draconian 'advocates of the Memorandum' and all those who wanted to defend the country's independence and freedom. In resorting to such platitudes, both of the main political parties sought to steer the argument away from the complex and painful economic debate, and instead to frame the validity of their own position in moral terms. What one side framed as evil, the other would frame as just, and vice versa; the open and critical discussions so crucial to the functioning of a democracy were lost as each party made repeated declarations in an effort to monopolise the truth.

Following their visit in November 2010, the representatives of the European Commission indicated that

> implementing the policy has proved more difficult.... Slower progress reflects a combination of changes, including the electoral cycle,[6] the resistance of vested interests and in a few cases – difficulties in the design and activation a number of complex reforms within a short time-span.[7]

It was stated to the government that it was time to redouble its efforts and to show greater conviction in driving the agreed reforms.

At the beginning of the New Year in 2011, urban transport workers, pharmacists, lawyers and engineers began to strike. The 'Won't Pay!' movement gathered momentum; it called upon citizens not to pay the tolls on the highways or to purchase tickets for public transport. Angry citizens began insulting politicians in public. Government confidence stemming from the positive results in the municipal elections, and the optimism the election had brought to the public, began to wane. Citizens were increasingly anxious, and social unrest grew.

The government declared it would not be intimidated by demonstrations and strikes. The Prime Minister's entourage informed the press that he was extremely annoyed by the image of compromise resulting from negotiations with certain groups. If the government was to concede or compromise with those responsible for civil dissent, he stressed, it would spark a reaction from taxpayers and pensioners, who were already being asked to give so much. In the coming months, though, the commitment to abolish regulations that favoured union interests began to weaken. It gradually receded into compromise, first with the truck drivers and the taxi drivers, then with the pharmacists.

The municipal elections held at the beginning of November marked a shift to a more flexible policy, resulting in delays to crucial reforms. In September commentators highlighted that 'even though the effects of the recession are visible, the government has not formulated a convincing plan to deal with them. It has been drifting between cuts in public investment programmes ... platitudes ... and obsolete methods of managing state subsidies.' Attention was also drawn to the growing doubts in the market 'over whether Greece will ever manage to achieve the targets of the Memorandum'.[8] The spread, that is the difference between the interest rate paid by Germany and the rate charged by the markets to Greece, was 9.73% by 6 January on 10-year bonds. It continued to follow a gradual upward trend.[9] This rise indicated that Greek bonds were losing their value and were being sold at lower and lower prices by bond holders who wished 'to get rid of them' while they could. The General Index of the Athens Stock Exchange on 5 January 2011 fell to the lowest level it had seen since November 1977 (1,373 points).[10]

Anxiety in international public opinion concerning the future of the Greek economy was heightened by discussion over the restructuring of Greek debt; the 'haircut' on Greek bonds would reduce the amount the Greek state owed its lenders, but could have wider consequences.[11] To put an end to this discussion, the Finance Minister categorically stated that 'there will not be a restructuring of Greek debt'.[12] The Prime Minister himself supported this statement a few days later, and denied any possibility of a restructuring.[13] The French Minister of Finance displayed greater caution when asked if there would be a restructuring: 'not within 2011', he responded.[14] However, restructuring was announced in 2011, subsequent to a decision taken by the Eurozone in July of that year.

During the same period, a counter-proposal to the restructuring of Greek debt was made. The EFSF would purchase Greek bonds on the market at the increasingly low prices at which they were available, and would sell them back to Greece at a later date for approximately the same value. Greece would gain from the difference between the high nominal value of the bond and the lower price at which the EFSF had bought them. It was also envisaged that this proposal would contribute to the lowering of interest rates on the country's borrowing. Noting the EMU's support for Greece through the EFSF, the banks would no longer be so anxious and would lend to Greece at sustainable interest rates. Initially, Greek officials denied that these ideas were being discussed. Following a few days of denial, the European Commission, the Minister of Finance and the Prime Minister confirmed that they were examining the matter 'in the context of an all-encompassing answer to the sovereign debt crisis'.[15] The major condition to this solution was ensuring the EFSF had sufficient capital to purchase the bonds. This obstacle, though, proved insurmountable and this option, which the Greek government had begun to believe might finally master its woes, was soon abandoned.

The fact that this potential recourse for Greece was so quickly dropped inevitably compounded anxiety and further fuelled the recession. The rate at which economic activity was shrinking was higher than forecast. According to the original calculations, the recession would peak in 2010 and from 2011 onwards would continue but at diminishing rates. By 2012 there would be a return to growth. Indicators at the beginning of 2011 were not positive. Recession in 2011 would be greater than in 2010 and the contraction in the economy would exceed 4% of GDP. Subsequently, debt as a percentage of GDP would climb to 153.8%. The prospect of debt at such a level inevitably fuelled further anxiety in the markets; it was considered to be out of control. The forecast that by 2020 debt would be reduced to 131% had no positive impact on the economic climate. The level of unemployment was the most glaring indication of the health and trajectory of the Greek economy. Data from the Statistical Service published in January 2011 indicated that as early as October 2010 it had reached 13.5%. This was the highest level of unemployment since the Statistical Service began making records.

During 2011, Greece was obliged to borrow €63.6 billion to meet its liabilities. This was a colossal sum, approximately twice its expenditure on pensions. It was obvious that the country could not resolve its problems alone. It needed support again. Since May 2010, however, when the first plan of assistance for Greece had been implemented, things had changed drastically. Not only Ireland and Portugal, but other, more economically significant countries, notably Spain and Italy, were facing problems. No longer could one simply look to address the Greek question: an all-encompassing answer to the Eurozone's sovereign debt crisis was required.

## Notes

1   Yannis Stournaras, *To Vima*, 19 September 2010.
2   Minister of Finance's speech on the budget during the budget parliamentary debates, 18–22 December 2010.
3   See *Kathimerini*, 13 October 2010.
4   Statements by government cadres in various newspapers on 16 October 2010.
5   See p. 57.
6   This was a reference to the forthcoming municipal elections, due in November 2011.
7   *European Economy: The Economic Adjustment Programme for Greece, Second Review, Autumn 2010*, Occasional Paper 72, European Commission, 2010, p. 1.
8   *Kathimerini*, 5 September 2011, p. 4.
9   Reaching 10.45% on 15 April 2011, 15.30% on 23 August, 20.9% on 16 September, 20.87% on 7 November, 30.90% on 6 December 2011, and the highest level for the

first half of 2012, on 2 March 2012, was 37.10%. The spread was indicative of the level of risk for 'the Greek patient'.

10  These were still 'days of glory' for the Greek stock market. On Tuesday 14 August 2012 the index was at 621 points.

11  See forecasts by the American Citigroup and the German press, *Kathimerini*, 20 January 2011 and 22 January 2011.

12  *Kyriakatiki Kathimerini*, 23 January 2011.

13  See *Imerisia*, 28 January 2011.

14  News on Mega TV, 7 January 2011.

15  See *Kathimerini*, 29 January 2011.

# 10

# An 'all-encompassing plan' to solve the crisis in the Eurozone?

In the Eurozone, the more economically stable nations had begun efforts to develop a holistic and 'all-encompassing plan'. At a meeting held on 17 January 2011, they examined a series of initiatives such as increasing EFSF funds, bringing forward the establishment of a permanent stability mechanism, reforming the Stability Pact and instituting common economic governance. Negotiations, however, did not produce any results. The European Council summit held at the beginning of February 2011 made calls for a fresh impetus.

The Greek government argued forcefully – at least in the public debate – for the introduction of a eurobond. It was felt that a eurobond would not only ensure a return to stability among the ailing European economies but would also guarantee access to the funds needed to service the alarming levels of sovereign debt now accrued. However, not only did the arguments fail to convince, but the demands antagonised Greece's partners in the EMU. Greek calls were made for the immediate issue of eurobonds without limitation, but at the same time the Hellenic camp rejected the institution of economic governance, with the strict fiscal policy and oversight of member state activity that it would entail. Athens wanted to be free to determine the Greek budget, but for the other nations in the EMU to guarantee Greek debt through the issue of the eurobond.

A few days before the European Council held on 4 February,[1] the Chancellor of Germany proposed a 'Competitiveness Pact' for the countries of the Eurozone, which received French support. As a German official expressed it, the object of the Pact was economic stability and hence greater solidarity; this was to be achieved by taking the necessary structural measures to enhance confidence in the euro on the international markets. The plan actually comprised six initiatives to promote this stability and, more broadly speaking, structural convergence across the Eurozone. It called for: the adjustment of the pension systems to reflect demographic developments; the unification of taxation systems; the abolition of automatic indexation of public sector salaries; the establishment of statutory limitations within each member state on the level of sovereign debt; the review and unification of regulations governing the compilation of economic and social data; and the implementation of uniform frameworks for the response to the banking crisis.

Reactions were prolific and heated. The European Commission indicated that Germany had exceeded its authority, as such an initiative was the remit of the Commission and the creation of structures in the EU parallel to the Commission was not permitted. Other member states observed that competitiveness could be promoted through various frameworks and that the German proposals were not the only available solution. Dissent also emerged as claims were made of possible double standards. Were policies to be applied to all member states, even those countries with surpluses in their balance of payments, such as Germany? Or was this new framework just to be imposed on the ailing nations of the EMU?

The European Council deferred examination of the proposals till its summit in March. The critical matter of any increase in the funds of the temporary EFSF was also deferred to March. The Council did not share the anxiety prevailing in public opinion. In its assessment, 'the overall economic situation [was] improving'. The inaction on the part of the Council was due to Germany and France not being willing to proceed with immediate measures. First, they would ascertain what they felt was the most appropriate course for the EMU, and then they would seek to drive the Eurozone in the direction they favoured. In February 2011, the 'all-encompassing plan' for the Eurozone was still under consideration. Further time was needed. It was increasingly apparent that economic governance and financial stability would dominate debate across the Union for many years.

Greece, and any other nations suffering under the crisis, would have to adjust as and how was seen fit. Reforms and initiatives were no longer likely to be undertaken with regard to a single member state, but would be undertaken with the entirety of the EMU in mind.

The Greek government appeared calm at the end of the summit. 'Greece is no longer the problem, but part of the solution', the Prime Minister asserted. He also added, reassuringly, that Greece had already undertaken 90–95% of the proposed measures![2]

## Notes

1  European Council, 4 February 2011, Conclusions, EUCO 2/1/11 Rev. 1, CO Eur 2, Concl. 1.
2  *Imerisia*, 7 February 2011.

# 11

# An 'all-encompassing plan' to solve the crisis in Greece?

The May 2010 agreement on the Memorandum initiated a short-lived period of optimism; while uncertainty remained, there was acknowledgement of Greece's efforts. This optimism came to an end with the European Council held in February 2011, which was followed by a period of insecurity, which turned into intense anxiety and anxiety into calls for further action. This culminated in the Eurozone summit held in July 2011, at which new terms were set to deal with the Greek crisis. The major source of renewed pessimism was the growing doubt over whether Greek sovereign debt was sustainable.

The Bruegel think-tank – an organisation financed by EU member states to study the problems of European unification – published a report on the debt crisis in the Eurozone in February 2011. According to this report, the Greek crisis differed from that of the other peripheral countries. The problem of Greek sovereign debt was primarily due to the 'bad management of public finances'. The behaviour of the banks played only a secondary role, contrary to events in other member states. 'The country is undoubtedly on the edge of insolvency with its debt to GDP ratio reaching 150% in 2011 and set to continue growing over the coming years.'[1] The study proposed the following for dealing with the problem: (1) reduction of the rate of interest paid on loans granted by Eurozone members to 3.5%; (2) the extension of repayment on loans granted by the EU to 30 years; (3) that the EFSF purchase bonds held by the ECB, with repayments made at the price they were purchased by the Bank; and (4) the restructuring of debt held by the private sector, through a 'haircut', by cutting the claims of private sector bondholders by 30%. Through these actions Greek sovereign debt would be reduced to 60% of GDP, the upper limit designated by the Maastricht Treaty, within 20 years.

According to the weekly German news magazine *Der Spiegel*,[2] the head of the EFSF had submitted a similar proposal, based on the arrangement the IMF had applied in the Philippines in the mid-1980s. This plan, called the 'Manila' plan, provided capital for Greece to purchase its bonds at the current market value, which fluctuated around 70% of their nominal value. In other words, it proposed a reduction of debt equating to a 30% haircut. Foreign commentators and international media increasingly indicated that 'the haircut' was unavoidable. 'But what is needed is to find an orderly way to restructure debt.'[3]

Following the continued deterioration of Greek state finances, debate concerning an imminent 'haircut' grew. International ratings agencies downgraded Greece to such an extent that the markets demanded a 15% interest rate on its two-year bonds. By that time Greek debt was 'beyond junk'.[4] The reports of the EU and the IMF presented an alarming picture. In its third quarterly review of the implementation of the Memorandum, in February 2011, the European Commission stated that 'the programme is broadly on track, and has made further progress towards its objectives'. But it noted immediately afterwards that:

> Going forward, there are major challenges. A number of important hurdles have emerged. They include a tense fiscal situation, contagion of the other peripheral economies, persistent deficiencies in tax collection, some delays and capacity problems in delivering complex and far-reaching structural reforms. Delivering on programme targets will require much stronger resolve to implement the agreed policies than in the past two quarters.[5]

In its own review of the same period, the IMF added an analysis of the sustainability of debt under various possible circumstances. For instance, a delay in implementing a 10% fiscal adjustment, an extremely likely eventuality, would result in the level of sovereign debt falling no lower than to 142% of GDP until 2020, 12% higher than the original target.[6] The conclusion derived from various analyses was that the level of debt would remain, in all cases, at a disconcertingly high level. Its sustainability was highly doubtful.

The government kept rejecting every thought of restructuring the debt. The Prime Minister had repeatedly made reassurances that a restructuring of Greek debt would harm the country's credibility and the health of the European as well as the Greek national banking system. It would be a very heavy price to pay. Such a scenario was in the interests of neither Greece nor the European economy.

The discussion over restructuring Greek debt was, in essence, a discussion about ensuring the sustainability of debt and averting bankruptcy. The sustainability of debt is never a given, in any case. That is why the international organisations examined what would happen in the case of a Greek default, while Greece remained completely silent, both domestically and internationally, on the matter. The Maastricht Treaty set a maximum level for a country's sovereign debt at 60% of GDP. At such a level, debt can be serviced in an orderly way; it is sustainable. It is widely acknowledged that in order to avert crises in the Union, the Treaty had taken a conservative stance in designating this maximum level. Research in many developed countries has indicated that debt as high as 90% of GDP is sustainable. The conditions prevailing in a particular country inevitably determine what may be sustainable. For example Japan, whose debt is primarily held by domestic banks, can handle the financing of its debt with limited concern for the sentiment of international bond markets, and can therefore safely exceed a level of 90%. The same applies to a country with high rates of growth or the production of high-value commodities, such as oil.[7]

With very low rates of growth, the majority of its debt held in foreign banks and without internationally valuable assets or commodities, Greece was not in a position to sustain levels of debt exceeding about 90% of GDP. According to international estimates, debt would fluctuate at approximately 140% of GDP in 2020, even under favourable circumstances. The conclusion was that additional and distinct intervention was required. Otherwise, Greece would inevitably end up defaulting on its debt.

To deal with these increasing concerns, Athens proposed the revision of the Memorandum on the basis of three points:

1  an extension of repayments on the €110 billion loan;
2  a reduction in the rate of interest;
3  the repurchase of Greek bonds either by the EFSF directly, or by Greece with capital from the EFSF.

The first two points were self-evident. The repayment schedule of the loan provided by the Memorandum was unacceptably short. The rate of interest was higher than had been available to Ireland, and should be reduced, at a minimum, to a rate comparable to the Gaelic package. The third request was met with staunch refusal by the European partners, which stated formal and substantive objections. Greece did not participate in the EFSF; it had borrowed through a bilateral framework and the use of the EFSF required unanimous support from the member states, support which would be hard to achieve. In addition, the EFSF was designed to deal with new crises in other member countries, such as Portugal. It was widely held that movement on the first two points alone would not radically alter Greece's fortunes. 'They have already been discounted by the markets to a great extent.'[8]

The Greek government, however, did not agree. It felt that the ability of the European support mechanisms to buy bonds directly from member states would 'send a message [indicating the] sustainability of Greek debt to the markets'. It expressed the belief that 'the recent decisions taken by the leaders of the Eurozone will facilitate Greece's return to the bond markets much earlier'! With regard to its progress on reforms, it asserted 'the government is working at unprecedented speeds, not only compared to Greek but to international practice. Within the space of a few months, reforms [normally] requiring decades have been instituted.'[9] In reference to the matter that antagonised and infuriated Greece's European partners most, that of inadequate tax collection, Athens claimed 'no country up till now has managed to carry out such radical changes to its taxation system in less than two years'.[10]

Greece's proposal concerning the repurchase of bonds within an EFSF framework was never formally examined by the Eurozone, as it was never formally submitted; it was not submitted because aversion to the proposal was widespread.[11] No other solutions were officially discussed, since there were no other substantive proposals.

The deepening recession and the fall in state revenues resulted in the Troika representatives augmenting the pressure 'for more to be done'. In mid-February 2011, at a press conference, they announced that state assets must be sold and that the proceeds should go towards redeeming the debt. They set a target of €50 billion from privatisations. This announcement provoked heated reactions. Media reports indicated that 'the government is selling off everything' and 'the Troika has the initiative in determining the country's policy'. The Greek government immediately released a strongly worded statement asserting 'the behaviour of the European Commission, IMF and ECB representatives was unacceptable. They must understand, however, what their role really is. It is obvious that the development of publicly owned real estate ... does not mean selling off public land' and 'only the Greek government has the right to take such decisions'. Despite these statements, following a Eurogroup meeting on 12 March 2011, it was confirmed that Greece agreed 'to carry out the programme of privatisations and development of real estate ... [worth approximately] €50 billion'. Initially the programme was expected to yield €8.5 billion by 2013, with a further €24 billion by 2016.

Agreement to such a programme of privatisation is indicative of the inadequate planning and negotiation on the part of the Greek government. There was no preparation, no comprehensive study nor feasibility plan to indicate that €50 billion could be accrued from the sale of public assets. No list of state assets valued at a total of €50 billion was made known. The press mentioned many examples of possible privatisations, such as the OPAP (the Greek Gambling Corporation), the Post Office Savings Bank, the State Lottery, but the total value of these companies was nothing near the target mentioned. It was clearly doubtful whether such a sum from the sale of state assets was attainable. Experience has shown that time is needed for a structured and well managed privatisation of state-run services or assets.

Preparatory action began in 2011 for the programme of privatisation, including the establishment of the Fund for the Development of State Private Property. The most optimistic analysis of that programme suggested that, at best, a few billion might be raised in 2012. Other proposals were not made public. The problem was not confined to the fall in demand for and value of Greek assets, resulting from the crisis: in many cases privatisation would prompt fierce and popular resistance, and encounter long-existing vested interests. Time would be needed, and it seemed that 'it would be impossible to square the numbers'.[12] By the end of 2012, a mere €1.6 billion had been raised. Following this realisation, a reappraisal was made of the forecasts for revenues to be generated by privatisation. These were reduced to just €2.6 billion by the end of 2013 and €8.5 billion by 2016. Accounts that simply did not add up should not have been agreed to.

Recurrence of these same shortcomings enhanced the belief, both domestically and internationally, that there was no exit from the crisis. While the
Minister of Finance continued to claim there were encouraging signs, such as
the rise in exports, the IMF noted that costs of production remained 20–30%
higher than what would make Greece internationally competitive. With regard
to the internal devaluation the Memorandum sought to achieve, commentators
observed that not only had reforms actually deepened the recession, but, far
more alarmingly, the 'objective conditions of social tension are being created',
and social tension 'impedes the consensus necessary to promote reforms'.[13] The
country was at a dead end. 'The austerity programme is paralysing the Greek
economy.'[14] 'The country's economic vitality has been paralysed for one and
a half years, while bureaucrats, political parties, syndicates and professional
groups endeavour to maintain all real or imaginary privileges granted to them
by the defunct system, which cannot provide them any more in any case.'[15]

In early 2011 hope was again focused on the EU. There were expectations
that either the Eurozone summit to be held on 11 March or the European
Council to be held on 24–25 March could produce the long overdue 'all-
encompassing plan' and end the never-ending turmoil in Greece. The Prime
Minister visited both Angela Merkel in Berlin and Nicolas Sarkozy in Paris.
He restated his 'conviction that the country's salvation will come through the
summit meetings of the Eurozone and the Union'. He even made reference
to the 'threat of a veto if decisions were not favourable for Greece'.[16] He put
all matters before both summits, including the issuing of a eurobond and the
possibility of buying back Greek debt. The results, however, were again very
disappointing. Negotiations in both summits only reaffirmed what had already
been agreed: an extension for the debt repayment and a reduction in the rate of
interest.[17] The maturity of the loans was extended from 4.5 year to 7.5 years.
The interest rate on the Eurozone loans was reduced by one percentage point,
from around 5.5% to 4.5%. These arrangements improved Greece's position,
but only marginally. They reduced the debt, amounting to €345 billion, by
approximately €10 billion. Their only tangible value lay in the time Greece had
gained to repay the debts.

The European Council held on 24–25 March, following the decisions taken
in October 2010, set out the operational framework for the implementation of
agreements reached the year before:

- It established the ESM, which 'shall be activated should it be deemed necessary to ensure stability in the Eurozone as a whole'. The ESM was an
  institution that the EU had lacked until then, one mandated to deal with
  the serious financial problems of member states. It was to be the permanent
  solution which would succeed the EFSF or other ad hoc solutions, such as
  those that had been implemented in the case of Greece.
- It acknowledged that debt restructuring was imperative for dealing with
  countries whose debt level was not sustainable.[18]

The European Council focused primarily on discussions regarding the Competitiveness Pact, which had previously been postponed from February to March. The Pact was presented in its new form as the Euro Plus Pact. The new Pact sought to promote competitiveness and employment, and to contribute to fiscal stability, as well as to the orderly functioning of the financial markets: 'Every head of state or government shall undertake specific national commitments every year. Fulfilment of these commitments shall be monitored yearly on a political level by the heads of state or government.' With regard to the promotion of competitiveness, emphasis was placed on wage restraint in order to increase productivity. In reference to the labour markets, the need for 'flexibility and security' was noted. The 'enhancement of the maintainability of fiscal accounts' was to be attempted through monitoring the sustainability of pensions, health-care expenses and social benefits. From now on, member states would be obliged to undertake commitments with regard to domestic policy and to accept that their policies would be monitored.[19]

The Council also ratified prior decisions from Ecofin concerning the establishment of the 'European Semester'. According to these decisions, all member states were to present 'multi-year stability plans which shall contain special targets for deficits, state revenue, state expenses, the strategy to achieve these targets and the schedule for implementation thereof'. States would be audited with regard to adherence to their programmes. The March summit therefore finalised an overarching operating framework for member states, which would seek to ensure the coordination of their economic policies and the oversight of all developments so as to prevent further economic mismanagement.[20]

With regard to developments at the summit, it was widely understood that they constituted a significant step. But commentators stressed that, even though these developments did deal with many of the major problems, serious questions remained fundamentally unanswered.[21]

The principal defect of the Eurozone was not examined: the gulf in competitiveness between the Core and the Periphery. It did not touch on the creation of surpluses in the countries of the Core and corresponding deficits in the countries of the Periphery. This phenomenon is far more salient in any holistic discussion of the causes of crises than the violation of fiscal discipline, which lay at the heart of the decisions taken at the summit. The operation of the new permanent stability mechanism, the ESM, was also pointed out. It was underlined that its funds should be sufficient to deal with liquidity crises in more countries. It was also noted that this matter had been known for some time and should have been addressed long before.

The summit's decision on the need for restructuring when a debt is not sustainable was clear. It was deemed unacceptable that taxpayers should bear the burden of reckless activity by the banks. Banks should accept the cost of their risk taking. After all, they had enjoyed long periods of incredible profits, owing to the high interest rates they charged. How restructuring should be undertaken, however, remained unclear.

Failure to recognise the need for the meticulous auditing of all banks, to clarify which were solvent and which were not, was criticised. The recapitalisation of banks should proceed on the basis of such audits so as to avert another crisis. Granting loans to countries of the Periphery to service their debts to the reckless banks undermined efforts to hold the banking sector to account.

Greece did improve the terms of its debt, with regard to both interest rates and payment schedule, but Greece saw no movement at the summit in the form of an 'all-encompassing plan' required to avert future problems and restore confidence in the Greek economy. Hopes for an 'all-encompassing plan' were, unfortunately, unrealistic. Such plans do not materialise out of the blue at a single summit. They can be realised with meticulous planning and relentless negotiation with major European powers. Visits to the Chancellor of Germany or the President of France, aiming to convince them of the Greek position, could not bear fruit if the negotiation team was not convincing in terms of the validity of its arguments and the preparation it had put into them. From the end of 2009 up until March 2011, Greece was guided by little more than good intentions, a friendly disposition towards continental partners and bellicose terms of debate when the government spoke to its domestic audience. There was no plan. The government followed an ad hoc policy. It was always reacting to changing events, but never able to direct them. Such behaviour might mitigate or defer problems in the short term. However, medium- to long-term planning is integral to any competent economic management.

## Notes

1  Z. Darvas, J. Pisani-Ferry and A. Sapir, *A Comprehensive Approach to the Euro-Area Debt Crisis*, Policy Brief 2011/02, Bruegel, 2011.
2  Issue 4, 2011.
3  Interview in *To Vima*, 13 March 2011, p. A21. See also *Le Monde*, 24 March 2011, p. 18.
4  See 'Greek downgrading', *Financial Times*, 8 March 2011.
5  *European Economy: The European Adjustment Programme for Greece, Third Review, Winter 2011*, Occasional Paper 77, European Commission, February 2011, p. 1.
6  Country Report No. 11/68, IMF, March 2011, p. 55.
7  On the sustainability of debt, see C. M. Reinhart and K. Rogoff, *This Time Is Different: Eight Centuries of Financial Folly*, Princeton University Press, 2009. See also: Th. Herndon, M. Aschand and Robert Pollin, *Does High Public Depth Consistently Stifle Economic Growth?*, Working Paper Series 322, Political Economy Research Institute, University of Massachusetts, April 2013. The latter maintain that high levels of public debt 'do not inevitably entail sharp declines in GDP growth'. Gavyn Davies added, 'If the economy is working well below capacity, a rise in the budget deficit may raise aggregate demand and thus boost GDP growth'. G. Davies, 'How much of Reinhart/Rogoff has survived?', http://blogs.ft.com/gavyndavies/2013/04/19/how-much-of-reinhartrogoff-has-survived/, 13 April

2013. A reply by C. Reinhart and K. Rogoff to such criticisms was published in the *IHT*, 27/28 April 2013.

8  Statements by an EU cadre, *Kathimerini*, 27 February 2011, p. 6.

9  Statements by G. Papaconstantinou, *Kathimerini*, 16 March 2011, p. 22.

10  G. Papaconstantinou, *Imerisia*, 19 March 2011, p. 5.

11  According to *Ta Nea* newspaper, 11 March 2011, the President of France warned that any insistence in promoting an unfounded request to buy back Greek debt could provoke negative reactions, with the result that even the extension might be lost.

12  Y. Pretenteris, *Ta Nea*, 14 March 2011. See *European Economy: The Second Economic Adjustment Programme for Greece, First Review, December 2012*, Occasional Paper 123, European Commission, December 2012, pp. 4, 33.

13  Y. Pretenteris, *Ta Nea*, 10 March 2011.

14  *Kathimerini*, 19 March 2011, citing *The Economist*.

15  Ph. Gerogeles, *Athens Voice*, 10–16 March 2011.

16  *To Vima*, 20 March 2011, p. A4.

17  The ability of the ESM to buy bonds on the primary market was presented as a gain for Greece by government sources (*To Vima*, 20 March 2011). However, this referred to the future activity of the ESM, and not to the repayment of the existing Greek loan.

18  See 'Activation of financing assistance, monitoring of programme', in Appendix 2 of the European Council's conclusions to the summit meeting of 24–25 March 2011.

19  Greece's obligation annually to reduce its debt over 60% of GDP by one-twentieth derives, among other things, from these provisions. Violation of this obligation would entail fines as a penalty.

20  According to M. Hallerberg, B. Marjinotto and G. Wolff, *On the Effectiveness and the Legitimacy of EU Economic Policies*, Policy Brief 2012/04, Bruegel, November 2012, p. 1: 'The introduction of the European Semester economic policy surveillance system has not resolved problems. Policy guidance deriving from the Semester is not focused enough on areas of significant spillovers and on problem countries, and national compliance is often procedural rather than actual.'

21  See M. Wolf, *Financial Times*, 30 March 2011, p. 11; W. Munchau, *Financial Times*, 28 March 2011, p. 11; 'Not so grand deal', *Financial Times*, 26 March 2011, p. 11.

# 12

# A year of the Memorandum: seeking a new solution

After the March Eurozone summit, a short-lived sense of optimism returned to the EU. But Portugal's request, on 11 April 2011, for financial assistance from the EU and the IMF indicated that nothing had changed. The crisis was far from resolved.

Mirroring such sentiment, the English journal *The Economist* was particularly despondent in its analysis. It deemed that the summit had been 'something between a fudge and a failure':

> The Brussels gathering did little to help Greece, Ireland and Portugal.... Their situation is getting worse – and Europe's lenders bear much of the blame.... Greece should stop pretending that it can bear its current debt burden and push for restructuring.[1]

Restructuring became the major point of discussion in the following months. The headlines in Greece were dominated by the subject: 'The possibility of restructuring Greek debt has become a bone of contention in the Eurozone', 'Restructuring yes or no?' Restructuring was presented to the Greek public as akin to disaster; it had to be avoided at all costs.

In the EU the arguments in favour and against remained substantively unchanged. Economists, academics and commentators in major newspapers insisted that the only possible recourse for Greece was through restructuring. To pay the banks back in full would burden the taxpayers of all nations called upon to help, for generations; the banks' losses would be 'socialised'. This was increasingly unacceptable; the responsibility for the reckless extension of credit should be laid at the feet of those agents of capital who had so willingly granted such unsustainable loans. To expect the costs of such behaviour to be shouldered by the taxpayer would inevitably lead to social unrest, a rise in poverty and increases in austerity. Creditors' participation in restructuring of debt was therefore a logical conclusion. In order to avoid mutually damaging developments, a consensual arrangement, involving the private sector and the indebted nation, had to be sought.[2]

The reduction in the interest rate and an extension of the repayment schedule did not alter the debt to GDP ratio, and a debt of the order of 150% of GDP is a colossal burden. 'Greece has taken steps, but even if she managed to achieve a swift recovery, there is no doubt that she should seek a restructuring.'[3]

The IMF, the ECB and the European Commission remained steadfastly opposed to any restructuring. The Troika felt that such a course of action would undermine efforts to ensure Greece made all the necessary reforms to make the economy competitive once again.[4] The President of the European Council, Herman Van Rompuy, insisted that 'the risks entailed in any kind of restructuring of Greek debt are far greater than any possible benefits'.[5] The Greek government equally maintained its position that 'there is absolutely no possibility that Greek debt will be restructured'.[6] Instead, Athens made calls for a much greater period of grace, limiting current liabilities to the payment of interest, while the full repayment of bonds held by the private sector would be made over many years. The discussions that took place concerning such proposals, according to Greek accounts, were not met with any interest in Brussels.

The German news magazine *Der Spiegel* noted, nearly a year after the decision to grant Greece the bailout package, that 'things went a lot worse than the countries of the Eurozone had expected'.[7] The German Minister of Finance, along with many of his European counterparts, felt that the Memorandum's forecast that Greece would be able to borrow from the markets again in 2012 was utopian. It was evident that other solutions were necessary, but what these would be remained uncertain.

The news of a further bailout package for Athens met with intense reaction from the Bundestag. A member of the governing coalition put on record the growing dissatisfaction. He stressed that if the German government subscribed to the flawed logic that it must definitely help, then there was a danger that it would be unable to resist perpetual calls for more and more financing for Greece.

The date 23 April 2011 marked the anniversary of the Prime Minister's announcement 'We shall officially ask our partners for the support mechanism to be activated'. In the months following the Memorandum, the government had appeared determined to drive through the economic reforms. A year later, it was increasingly apparent, both at home and abroad, that reform fatigue had taken its toll. Efforts appeared absent of conviction, courage or structure. The annual statement of the Bank of Greece for 2011 indicated 'a strong re-evaluation of the efforts [was necessary].... The deficits, mainly of the broader public sector, had not been brought under control and the reforms that were legislated for, remained on paper [only].'[8] Media reports were indicating that the European Commission felt that the target of returning Greece to the markets in 2012 was now impossible; it was in discussions concerning an alternative plan. A year had passed, but anxiety, uncertainty and the fear of what the future held had only grown. Hope of a swift return to normality had evaporated.

Confusion over what should be done peaked with the convening of a 'secret summit' in Luxembourg, on 6 May 2011. Greece and the most affluent members of the Eurogroup were in attendance. Despite the intention to keep this meeting secret, the media got wind of it. They immediately questioned the need for secrecy. The meeting was convened by the President of the Eurogroup, the Prime Minister of Luxembourg Jean-Claude Juncker, who had favoured a covert summit in an effort to limit speculation in the financial markets. One report in the Greek media indicated that it was the Greek Prime Minister who asked him to convene the Eurogroup, fearing mounting 'pressure ... to leave the euro'. Concern was also growing in Athens with regard to 'any restructuring of Greek debt ... [and its possible] disastrous consequences'.[9]

At the beginning of the meeting of the Eurozone's finance ministers, pressure was brought to bear on Greece 'to speed up the reforms and strengthen the austerity measures'. The German minister raised the matter of restructuring Greek debt and the necessity of the participation of private bondholders in this. The reaction of the President of the ECB was intense. He requested that it be put on record in the minutes that he objected in the strongest terms to the participation of the private sector in any adjustment of Greek debt, and departed from the meeting.[10] The meeting examined other proposals following this acrimonious departure. These included the voluntary extension of Greek bonds maturing in 2012, to make a little more capital available to Greece to address mounting social concerns. Further proposals were made regarding a more extensive transfer of maturity dates over the coming years. Yet again, no major decisions were taken.[11]

Intense criticism mounted once again. For instance, Wolfgang Munchau in the *Financial Times* commented that the Eurozone had proved once again that it was 'politically incapable of handling a crisis, [one] that is now contagious'. He said the crisis was going from bad to worse because of a fundamental inability to agree collective action.

> This is not a debt crisis. This is a political crisis.... The leaders of the Eurozone will soon face the choice between an unimaginable step forward to political union, or an equally unimaginable step back.[12]

The major questions and painful decisions, such as any restructuring of Greek debt, were just being perpetually postponed; one can only posit a lack of political courage or the naïve belief that an imminent reversal in circumstances would remove their necessity. The more one defers the resolution of such a problem, however, the greater the cost will finally be.[13]

Precisely what the Greek side sought remained unclear. The target had not altered – a return to stability and to the markets upon sustainable terms – but a coherent plan as to how this would ever be achieved appeared as distant as ever. The government continued to postpone any decisions, believing 2012 would present Greece with more favourable circumstances. In France, a socialist victory in the upcoming elections looked highly probable. In Germany, Greek analysis forecast a collapse of Angela Merkel's coalition, with a replacement government comprised of the Social Democrats and the Greens. These new governments would likely be far less stringent in their demands for austerity, and far more sensitive to the growing social consequences for Greece. Such optimistic predictions from Athens were misguided to say the least. The new governments would certainly be no more willing to support Greece unconditionally. Again, the debate returned to Greece's need to construct a genuine alternative to the Memorandum, if it wished to see movement on the part of the Franco-German axis, regardless of what administrations were in place following elections.

In an interview I gave on 17 April 2011,[14] I made it clear that Greece must proceed with the restructuring of debt as soon as was possible, in agreement with our partners. I did originally indicate that restructuring would be imposed on the country in 2013, if we requested help from the ESM and the debt was deemed unsustainable, as it in fact was. Comprehensive preparation was vital, to ensure the negotiations were not only fruitful but also that any agreement that followed reflected the best efforts of the Greek government to defend the interests of its electorate. The crux of the issue of restructuring also had a significant temporal dimension. Through the use of the EFSF and the ESM, sovereign debt was in part being transferred from a private to a public liability. That is to say, debt previously held by private bondholders was increasingly held by member states of the Eurozone. A 'haircut' on a private bond would inevitably have significant positive consequences for the sustainability of Greek debt. However, debt held by fellow member states could not be restructured, according to international practice. By postponing the restructuring, therefore, Greece was exchanging debt that could be cut with debt that could not be cut.

The day after this interview, the Prime Minister's 'displeasure' was leaked from his office. The government felt that this public intervention on the part of a previous Prime Minister had come 'at the most inopportune moment', and the Minister of Finance stated during a visit to Washington that 'the public debate on restructuring is not helpful for the country'.[15] The government maintained its dogmatic insistence that the debt was sustainable and imminent developments would be favourable. Y. Pretenteris wrote a commentary in which, among other things, he said:

> Everybody knows that there will be a restructuring of Greek debt, ... the whole of the international press knows it, ... the European Union knows it.... And yet what the whole world knows, we wish to keep secret.[16]

All that happened over a few short months showed how tragically misguided the government had been. When, in July, the Eurozone proceeded with the restructuring, Greece was yet again fundamentally unprepared.

Debt restructuring should have been supported by Greece from its very inception in the debate on the crisis. If this had been the case, it could have been undertaken much earlier.[17] The belief that a change in circumstances would favour Greece was criminally naïve; the onus was on Athens to instigate developments that would reverse Greece's fortunes. The government did exactly the opposite: statements and repeated reassurances from the Prime Minister made it quite apparent that he did not seek restructuring.[18]

The representatives of the Troika arrived in Greece at the beginning of May 2011 to undertake their quarterly review of progress made, prior to release of the fifth Memorandum instalment in June. Reports in the international media suggested the adjustment programme had lost all its momentum, negating any progress that had been made.[19] Laws that had been enacted were not being enforced. Efforts to combat tax evasion were disappointing. The privatisation programme had been delayed. The promise that by 2015 the sale of public assets would generate close to €50 billion was proving entirely unrealistic. Greece was nowhere near being able to return to the markets in 2012; the rate of interest available to the country had reached 17%. The deficit for 2011 would be approximately 10% of GDP, not the 8% as forecast. Sovereign debt would reach a record level of 153% of GDP. Media coverage increasingly spoke of a vicious circle of recession and continually rising debt. The cost of CDS policies to guarantee Greek bonds had reached such a level that default appeared increasingly imminent. The Troika's findings were no different.

Statements were more diplomatic in the reports of the European Commission and the IMF. The Commission stated:

> The implementation of reforms presented substantially lower rates of progress.... The recession is deeper and more extensive.... The fiscal targets for the first quarter of 2011 were achieved, but the country's underlying problems have not been solved. Delays in implementing structural reforms reflect limited managerial skills and a lack of political coordination.[20]

The conclusion of the reports was, according to Reuters, that the financial strategy needed serious revision; Greece was not expected to return to the markets and needed further capital injections. Most alarming, however, was that Greece had not made sufficient progress in terms of the Memorandum targets to qualify for the next instalment of funding.

The IMF requested 'serious guarantees from Greece and the Eurozone' in order to disburse the next instalment because, according to its rules, an instalment can be disbursed only when a country is able to service its debt liabilities over the course of the next 12 months.[21]

To overcome the deadlock, a discussion of funding under revised conditions began. This loan, amounting to €30–35 billion, would be available only under strict terms, including rapid privatisation. The package would also be combined with a change in the repayment terms for private bonds, to ensure the availability of some €60–70 billion.[22] The Troika also indicated the need for major layoffs in the broader public sector, in conjunction with the closure of a range of public organisations, as well as the strict supervision of activity in the ministries and the ability to intervene in decision-making.

These demands met with fierce resistance in the public sector, especially among the labour unions. From 2010, the number of strikes exceeded every precedent. In May 2011, two general strikes, in addition to one in honour of 1 May, were held to protest against the government's measures. Citizens proceeded to occupy Syntagma Square in Athens, the White Tower Square in Thessaloniki and squares in many other cities, following the model of the *Indignados* protestors in Madrid.[23] The first demonstration march, on 25 May, assembled 30,000 people and drew much public attention because it gave the impression of being a spontaneous, non-partisan event. Cases of citizens refusing to pay the new increased tolls on the highways or their dues to the public utilities companies grew in frequency. The 'Won't Pay!' movement received widespread support across Greek society as indignation spread over the range of new charges. Continual marches in the centre of Athens, clashes between dissenting groups and the police, repeated strikes affecting public transport, and protests outside Parliament all disrupted life in the centre of Athens and gave the impression of permanent turmoil and relentless conflict with the government.

Research undertaken looking at the social costs of austerity indicated that over 50% of the population had difficulty in covering their monthly outgoings, seven out of ten households felt that their financial position had deteriorated and would deteriorate further; the overriding majority of public opinion was very alarmed over what the future might hold. Figures confirmed the significant fall in the income of working people. The reduction in remuneration in the public sector was, by the end of 2011, 22.2% on average, while for people working in the private sector it had fallen by 12.6%. The government's levels of support had deteriorated staggeringly. At the beginning of 2011 only 20% of voters stated that they would vote for the governing party again in a future election, and by the end of the year that had fallen to 14%.

The growth in dissent across Greek society fuelled anxiety inside the European Commission and the key member states of the Eurozone. It became increasingly apparent that Greece required a cross-party consensus and support for the programme of austerity. Referring to bi-partisan support for the adjustment measures in Portugal, one Commissioner stated that 'this stand constitutes an example for Greek politicians'.[24]

In Greece, pressure for such agreement between the government and the parties of the opposition had grown. The Prime Minister's initiative for a Council of Political Leaders to be convened under the President of the Republic at the end of May came to nothing, however. No meetings ever took place. Partisan conflict continued to dominate, the government still lacked anything in the way of a coherent plan for action and the opposition simply looked to exploit the record levels of dissent and dissatisfaction. Such political positioning and the inability to put bellicose political loyalties aside, even temporarily, enhanced the impression across the EU that Greece did not have the will to overcome its problems. Lack of faith in Greece continued to grow.

At the beginning of May, New Democracy produced its own 'proposal to counter the crisis', 'Zappeion II', overturning its previous statements on the status of Greece.[25] The central premise of the proposal was to 'change the conditions of the Memorandum in order to restart the Greek economy'. This 'restart' would be driven by: a reduction in tax rates; 'removing any guilty feelings about engaging in business'; broader reform of the taxation system; the registration of all unregistered domiciles and commercial buildings; an obligation on the banks to provide liquidity to the market; the payment of all outstanding public debt to the private sector; and support for those with low pensions. New Democracy claimed all this would be possible, while at the same time the deficit would disappear and surpluses would be created within a four-year window, with which the sovereign debt could then be serviced. This was not realistic. It failed to mention that the €110 billion loan was not sufficient to repay outstanding debts and that at least €200 billion more was needed. It failed to mention that the members of the Eurozone were far from likely to agree to a further bailout package on Hellenic terms. It grossly underestimated the ability of the Greek public administration to raise a supposed €50 billion from the sale of state assets, or to combat tax evasion. It exaggerated the likely reward of any public investment. It promised to reduce the deficit to zero, while maintaining at the same time that it would reduce levels of taxation. It is indicative of the extent of the fantastic claims contained in the proposal that it guaranteed 'the codification of all taxation stipulations in a few statutes', something not seen in any developed country in the world. The most important failing of Zappeion II was, however, that it entirely disregarded the views of the members of the Eurozone. Their desire not to let Greece default did not mean they would have terms dictated to them, especially given that they had no faith in Greek planning, administration or even conviction. The Greek side could convince them only with action, either through structural reforms or decisive improvements in taxation. Till then, promises and grand theories, not believed or shared by Greece's partners, would not be enough to get them to part with their money.

By mid-2011, the majority of public opinion rejected the Memorandum and government policy. It felt that efforts at reform and austerity had been riddled with incompetence and mismanagement. Data justified doubts over whether the reforms would lead to an exit from the crisis. The Memorandum's first aim was to ensure Greece's capacity to borrow from the markets in 2012. In mid-2011 it had become obvious that this goal was impossible. A new bailout package was therefore required. The second major aim of the austerity programme was the reduction of the budget deficit to around 8% of GDP in 2011. However, the deficit would reach approximately 10%. The temporary recession that the authors of the Memorandum had promised had developed into an unprecedented fall in economic activity. It followed that it was not possible for fiscal adjustment to be realised as had originally been planned. The continued recession rendered impossible the rest of the Memorandum's goals, regarding growth and the acquisition of primary surpluses, in the space of time provided. The programme of austerity simply gave rise to new problems. Social tolerance of the measures was at breaking point, conflicts in society intensified, politics lost its standing and efforts to modernise were met with increasingly violent responses. The situation deteriorated hand in hand with the government's ability to act.

From the beginning, the government had wished to avoid dissent and major protests. It focused efforts on public relations activities rather than the substantive challenges of the crisis. Repeated measures were followed by repeated assurances that they were to be the last. Indicative of this focus on public relations over substantive concerns was the government's response to the Troika's announcement that public assets worth €50 billion were to be sold. After categorically denying that assets were to be sold, the Greek administration later spoke of the 'development' of assets and compliance with the decisions of the Eurozone. The government blamed speculators and ratings agencies, even though market reactions were in no small part due to its inability to implement reform. An announcement by PASOK, the ruling party, in May 2011, placed blame for Greece's woes on 'public chatterers, be they the opposition parties, the media or supposedly independent analysts and anxious academics, who choose to play the role of Cassandra' and 'prophesy the restructuring of our debt on a daily basis'.[26]

Debt was restructured just three months after this announcement. Inevitably it followed that efforts at public relations and the continued rejection of calls for a restructuring of Greek debt left the government completely absent of credibility when it was obliged to undertake this u-turn. Abroad as well, the government's inability to adhere to its commitments gradually turned support into doubt and finally into a lack of faith in Greece.

The referendum which led to the resignation of the government in November 2011[27] was a prime example of such public relations activities. After a 'proposal' from the Federation of Greek Industries that a referendum on Greece's new bailout package should be held in May 2011, aides of the Prime Minister conveyed that he was 'positive' with regard to the idea. A few days later, the Prime Minister indicated that 'for major matters we must always examine the possibility of holding a referendum'. At the beginning of June the media spoke of 'the Papandreou obsession with a referendum'.

Speculation on the complexities and the fallout of a referendum circulated in the media. Some reports spoke of constitutional concerns, others of the ramifications for the relationship with the EU. In fact, an adviser to the Prime Minister had been assigned the task of coming up with various possible referendum questions, questions that would ensure a strong majority in favour of the government. The goal was for there to be a resounding 'Yes' to certify the government's popularity and to expose its critics. To legalise the whole operation, a special law was passed in October concerning referenda, with the grandiose title 'Expansion of direct, participatory democracy through holding referenda'![28]

The loss of confidence in the government had decidedly negative effects on the economy. In 2011, capital was being withdrawn from the country, no investments were being made, transactions were being postponed, credit granted to Greek importers shrank and the banks could not borrow; the economy was suffocating owing to the lack of liquidity. In this unfavourable environment, the political administration's lack of expertise and inability to undertake necessary reforms exacerbated doubts, inertia and the crisis. It was impossible to deal with even secondary matters, such as the opening of pharmacies on Saturdays, without conflict, owing to the reactions of the unions. The government deferred examination of any matter that risked major dissent or internal strife. Taxi licences preoccupied the government and public opinion more than economic policy.

Statements, continual meetings, negotiations with vested interests, discussions with the Troika, trips abroad and the promotion of an image of constant mobility was no substitute for decisive action.

## Notes

1  *The Economist*, 2 April 2011, p. 14.
2  See M. Wolf, 'Economie', *Le Monde*, 24 May 2011, p. 2.
3  *FAZ*, 20 April 2011, p. 9; see also, N. Economides, Economics section, *Kathimerini*, 23–24 April 2011 p. 6.
4  'Economie', *Le Monde*, 10 May 2011, p. 14.
5  See 'Restructuring a horror scenario', *Kathimerini*, 25 May 2011.
6  G. Papaconstantinou, *Kathimerini*, 5 April 2011, p. 23.
7  Issue 15, 2011, p. 66.
8  *Ekthesi gia to etos 2011*, Trapeza tis Ellados, April 2012.
9  See *Kathimerini*, 7 May 2011, p. 4.
10 See *Kathimerini*, 30 December 2011, p. 16, which refers to a *Wall Street Journal* report.
11 *Financial Times*, 9 May 2011, p. 1; *Kathimerini*, 8 May 2011, p. 11.
12 Wolfgang Munchau, *Financial Times*, 8 May 2011, p. 11.
13 See Norris, 'Delaying default only extends pain', *IHT*, 8 May 2011.
14 *To Vima*, 17 April 2011, p. A12.
15 See *Ta Nea*, 18 April 2011, p. 9.
16 See *Ta Nea*, 19 April 2011.
17 According to the IMF (see p. 293), debt restructuring should have been attempted at the outset. Buiter and Rahbari maintain that 'the ideal moment for such a restructuring was May 2010'. W. Buiter and E. Rahbari, 'Greece and the fiscal crisis in the EMU', in *From the International Crisis to the Crisis in the Eurozone and Greece*, Livani Editions, 2011, p. 440.
18 Prime Minister's interview on CNN, 3 November 2010: 'The government's political agenda does not include debt restructuring'. Prime Minister's interview in *Le*

*Figaro*, 16 November 2010: 'The restructuring scenario is not even being discussed. It would be disastrous for Greek citizens.' Prime Minister's interview in *Die Presse*, 29 January 2011: 'Debt restructuring does not constitute a choice for Greece'. Prime Minister's speech to the parliamentary PASOK group, 15 April 2011: 'Many say that debt restructuring will solve the problem. Is that the problem? The country needs restructuring, not the debt.'

19  See *Financial Times*, 4 May 2011, p. 25, 9 May 2011, 10 May 2011, p. 1, 30 May 2011.

20  *European Economy: The European Adjustment Programme for Greece, Fourth Review, Spring 2011*, Occasional Paper 82, European Commission, July 2011; see also *Greece: Fourth Review*, Country Report No. 11/175, IMF, 2011.

21  See *Kathimerini*, 27 May 2011, p. 23; 'Economie', *Le Monde*, 28 May 2011, p. 15.

22  *Financial Times*, 30 May 2011, p. 3.

23  On the *Indignados* (the 'Indignant'), see T. Pappas, *When the Cat Became Reconciled with the Mouse*, Polis Editions, 2012, p. 120.

24  'Economie', *Le Monde*, 18 May 2011, p. 15.

25  'Zappion II', Speech by President of New Democracy, Antonis Samaras, Proposal for an exit from the crisis, 12 May 2011.

26  PASOK, press and media sector, 28 April 2011.

27  See Chapter 17.

28  Law 4023/2011.

# Part III
# Debt restructuring and power games

# 13

# Debt restructuring: the decisions of 21 July 2011

Owing to the IMF's reservations over the sustainability of Greek debt, disbursement of the fifth instalment of the €110 billion loan, along with any further support, remained pending at the beginning of June 2011. It had not been determined how additional assistance would be provided; nor had it been clarified whether private sector bondholders would participate in this. Views continued to differ intensely. What was widely recognised, however, was that a solution was urgently needed. The prolonged indecision, on a European level, had compounded investor insecurity and this was reflected in the markets. According to reports in the international media, if the inertia was to continue, or if any miscalculation was made, the ramifications would not be confined to Greece or even Europe, but would be felt by the USA and the global economy as well.[1]

The German Minister of Finance, Wolfgang Schäuble, addressed a letter to his colleagues at the beginning of June 2011. In it he clarified Germany's position. He stressed that 'any additional support for Greece has to involve a fair burden-sharing between taxpayers and investors, and has to help foster Greek debt sustainability'.[2] Bondholders, he wrote, must make a material contribution to the effort. He indicated that the most appropriate way to achieve this would be through the exchange of the old bonds for new ones maturing seven years later. Finally, he noted that the matter must be solved by the end of July; otherwise, Greece would be at risk of a disorderly default. The President of the ECB, Jean-Claude Trichet, reacted immediately. He said that if Greece's private sector creditors were to be party to any solution whatsoever, this would be tantamount to a default, and would cause a great flurry of activity in the already unstable financial sector. In his opinion the private sector could participate in other ways, through privatisation or investment.[3] France agreed with Trichet's analysis and reasserted objections to any restructuring of Greek debt.

Germany's proposal was known as the 'Vienna scenario'. It had been implemented in 2009 when the financial crisis had spread to Eastern Europe. The European Commission, the IMF and the ECB had convinced the Eurozone banks not to request immediate payment of the liabilities. Rather, the debts held were to be serviced over a significantly expanded temporal framework. This was all undertaken on a voluntary basis. The Commissioner responsible, Olli Rehn, proposed a comparable solution for Greece. The ECB withdrew its absolute rejection of this proposal when the representatives of the international banking sector (the International Swaps and Derivatives Association, ISDA) indicated that any voluntary extension of the payment schedule would not constitute a 'credit event'.[4] Crucial in this debate were the indications from the financial sector that CDS policies would not be eligible for indemnity, because repayment of debt had only been deferred. Nevertheless, the ECB felt that if such a solution were approved, there was still risk of a range of negative reactions across the markets.

Objections had not been confined to the ECB. Representatives of the banking sector in particular observed that Rehn's proposed solution would not resolve the Greek crisis conclusively; it would serve only to buy a little time for Greece. The matter would inevitably raise its head once again; under a worst-case scenario this might afford Greece a year, while at best it could provide four. At that juncture, the same questions would remain: who would provide Greece with capital, and under what terms? Commentary in the international press concurred with such an analysis: 'the European Union delays surgery with painkillers'.[5] 'Any solution must be a long-term one and get to the root of the evil.'[6]

According to the *New York Times*, Greece had developed its own proposals for the major reconstruction of the terms and holders of its sovereign debt.[7] The newspaper reported that the Prime Minister had envisaged 'a radical plan' whereby Greece would transfer €133 billion or 40% of its sovereign debt to the ECB, which would then issue eurobonds to raise sufficient capital to service the debt. Astoundingly, a member of the British Labour Party was charged with the task of presenting this proposal to the Commission. The proposal did not go any further; according to the *New York Times*, the plan was nothing more than a 'fantasy'.

Official discussions concerning the Greek problem were held by the Eurogroup and Ecofin on 19 June, in Luxembourg. At least four months had passed since February, when it had been recognised that Greek sovereign debt was not sustainable and that a novel solution was needed to reverse Greece's deteriorating fortunes.[8] Once again, reports in the international media spoke of excessive delays and widespread inertia in the Eurozone.[9]

There were of course serious difficulties in reconciling the views of the creditor nations with those of the peripheral member states afflicted by sovereign debt crises. Citizens of the latter were exasperated. They were afraid that they would be indefinitely paying the cost for the indiscretions of previous generations and the failures of their political elites. They turned against their governments, increasingly believing those in power were no longer defending their interests, but rather servicing the needs of the creditor nations. Resentment was growing towards the EMU, which was viewed as an agent demanding unrelenting commitment and progressively removing the rights of the sovereign member states and their populations. In the elections held in Finland in April 2011, the Eurosceptic party Real Finland won approximately 20% of the vote. Eurosceptic parties also saw significant gains in elections in the Netherlands and Austria. Protest and anger grew as the electorate in creditor nations became increasingly unhappy to service the debts of 'profligate countries' that had squandered European funds.

In the Periphery the Eurosceptic opposition saw even more pronounced growth, but here it was driven by the relentless austerity measures and the continual fall in people's standards of living that followed. The austerity programmes were viewed as draconian and without tangible value or an end in sight. All they did was to fuel the inescapable circle of recession, unemployment and poverty. Public fury rose against the creditor nations. The delays in support and the inadequate sums provided were sustaining this vicious circle. In Madrid and Athens indignant citizens occupied the city centres. In Portugal and Ireland strikes were held and clashes with the police occurred. In Brussels, the centre of EU decision-making, the impression was growing that the adjustment programme for Greece was only serving to delay the inevitable default.[10] The climate of anxiety and distrust was compounded by the inadequate efforts of the Eurogroup and the behaviour of its President, Jean-Claude Juncker. The failure of the 'secret' meeting in Luxembourg was indicative of these shortcomings.

Once again, speculation mounted throughout Europe as to what the upcoming meetings of the Eurogroup and Ecofin, scheduled for 19 June, would produce. The day before, the President of the Eurogroup publicly indicated that a solution was essential; otherwise, a Greek default risked dragging down Portugal and Ireland, and, even more alarmingly, Italy and Spain, due to the high level of sovereign debt now exposing these nations.[11] The IMF was represented at the meetings because of that institution's involvement. Its representative made it clear that the IMF required specific commitments from Greece before it could permit the release of the pending instalment. The country's ability to service its debt and its compliance to a programme of reform had to be guaranteed for the following year. The Belgian minister proposed that the instalment should be released incrementally in order to avoid the worst, namely Greek bankruptcy. But the other finance ministers of the Eurogroup did not support this proposal. In their common statement, released on 20 June, they indicated that important and necessary reforms were already in place in Greece. However, the sustainability of its debt depended decisively on the speed and success of the programme of privatisation and the sale of public assets amounting to €50 billion, as well as the programme of structural reform designed to promote growth in the medium term. New obligations had to be placed on the Greek government arising from failure to adhere to the existing reform programmes and the key laws concerning privatisation and the new fiscal measures had to be ratified by the Greek Parliament prior to the release of the next instalment of funding, due in mid-July. The Eurogroup recognised that it would be impossible for Greece to access the markets. It was therefore agreed that it was necessary to ensure the provision of further funding, from both member states as well as private sources. The private sector was again to proceed with the voluntary relaxing of payment schedules and the reduction of the monthly liabilities in order to avoid the risk of a disorderly default. However, once again, the major decisions regarding a revised financial strategy were postponed, until the beginning of July. Finally, the ministers of the Eurogroup called on all the Greek political parties to cooperate in their efforts at reform. Their announcement concluded with the remark that 'national unity constitutes the prerequisite for success'.[12] It was a clear indication to the opposition parties that their political positioning had negative implications for any effort at exiting the crisis.

According to the international media, the Greek Minister of Finance made clear his intention at the beginning of the meeting to table the challenges Greece had been encountering in honouring existing commitments, most notably in the efforts at privatisation. His statements indicating he wished to discuss existing agreements met with fierce reactions. As a result, the ministers of the Group requested guarantees that prior commitments would be honoured, and indicated categorically in their announcement the need for legislative ratification of the measures.[13] The Greek contingent was all but ignored when the text was drawn up, because it was now viewed with distrust and scepticism. Greece, therefore, had to proceed as quickly as possible in updating the Memorandum and legislating in all relevant areas, following a review of the Troika's recommendations.[14]

In mid-June the ratings agency Standard & Poor's downgraded Greece to the lowest level available for nation states, as it now viewed default as no longer a question of probability, but rather of time.[15] The interest rate on Greek borrowing reached a new record high, approximately 17% for 10-year bonds. The Greek stock exchange continued to fall. The general index slid to levels not seen since February 1997.

The Troika representatives, who arrived in Greece after the June meeting of the Eurogroup, realised that the country's adjustment programme for the period up to 2015 would have to be revised. Additional funds amounting to €5.6 billion were needed, of which €600 million would have to be secured by the end of 2011, in order to achieve the targets of the budget. This deficit arose because the government in Athens had modified the measures that had been agreed during the Troika's previous visit.

The public were in no position to follow exactly what was happening. The 'facts' seemed to be in constant flux, and there was no end to the alarming news. In May they read that 'the fifth instalment is up in the air', because of a shortfall in revenue amounting to €1.9 billion. Three days later, they were informed that the shortfall was actually €7 billion. This figure was later decreased to €5 billion. At the beginning of June, it was announced that revenue over the first five months had shrunk by 4.6%. The fifth instalment, due in June, was finally disbursed in July. Not long after, new discussions began, based on the revised data, concerning the release the sixth instalment, due in September 2011. These funds would actually be made available much later than originally scheduled, in December. Conflicting reports emerged in the media. Was this change in schedule a response to the shortcomings of the Greek government, or was it perhaps an effort to renege on the financial commitments made in the Memorandum? Critical comments came from various investment groups highlighting the administrative hurdles that had to be surmounted to access EU Structural Funds in Greece. The analysis repeatedly drew attention to the inertia and complex bureaucracy in the Greek administration, stifling any chance of growth: 'the system obstructs economic growth'.[16]

Indicative of the shortcomings in the efforts to reduce expenditure in the public sector was the handling of the abolition of the corps of agricultural guards – originally instituted to prevent crop theft but unnecessary in modern Greece. The staff were not made redundant, as detailed in the programme of austerity; rather, they were seconded to other parts of the public administration and continued receiving their salaries. This decision could not be justified on grounds of social concerns. It was taken only in order to avoid the political fallout. The 'employees' of the agricultural guard had been hired in 2004 by the New Democracy government, without applying the official procedures. Hiring was, astonishingly, based on lists that had been drawn up by the previous New Democracy government, back in 1993. This list was the product of the long-established system of political patronage.[17]

Throughout all efforts at implementing and engaging with the demands of the Memorandum, the government exhibited a lack of systematic preparation and planning. The June negotiations with the Troika were very much an incremental, stop–start affair. Marathon formal and informal Cabinet meetings were held one after the other, with limited progress. Agreement could not be reached on the amendments necessary to the Memorandum prior to further European meetings at the end of June. Negotiations were delayed until the beginning of July. These delays resulted in the Finance Ministry struggling desperately to cover the state's capital needs and obligations, 'in a fight for survival, under extremely difficult circumstances'.[18]

The irrevocably damaged confidence the international community had in Greece's financial management was dealt a further blow by political developments. On 15 June, the Prime Minister, George Papandreou, tried, impulsively and without the necessary preparation, to establish a government of 'national unity', feeling that 'national consensus' was an imperative. He believed that such a government was vital to manage growing domestic strife and the increasingly invasive demands of the reform programme. Antonis Samaras, leader of the New Democracy opposition, initially responded positively to the suggestion, upon the condition that Papandreou tendered his resignation and the premiership be assumed by a mutually acceptable figure. In the discussions between the two that followed, no agreement was reached over the duration of the new government, its aims or mandate. No decisions were taken regarding a time scale for any elections. According to sources inside New Democracy, during these discussions the Prime Minister indicated he was willing to step down. When this news disseminated through leaks to the media, it fuelled surprise and turmoil in the ranks of PASOK. However, in a statement made later that same evening, Papandreou announced that his efforts were in vain and no new administration would be formed. This was due to the behaviour of the opposition, who had not handled the matter in a politically and nationally responsible way. Once again, political positioning and actions driven with one eye on public relations had been given precedent over any effort at the consensus now, more than ever, vital to Greece's national interests.

There followed a Cabinet reshuffle. The most significant change was the promotion of Evangelos Venizelos to Deputy Prime Minister and Minister of Finance. On the part of Papandreou, this was an effort at conciliation with the faction of the party that had been against his election as leader in 2007. He hoped that in this way he would be able to improve both his own public standing and that of the government. Government policy with regard to the economy remained unchanged after the reshuffle, even though the new minister was more pronounced in his defence of government policy and the valiant efforts of the party. He indicated that he would implement the economic policy steadfastly but creatively. However, the Eurogroup meeting of 19 June had severely curtailed any scope for flexibility or opportunity for economic creativity. The ministers of the Eurogroup were insistent that Venizelos honour existing obligations.

Neither the Cabinet reshuffle nor the brief effort at a government of national unity did much to reverse the tangible contempt with which much of Greek public opinion now held the administration. The reshuffle did not revitalise the government as had been hoped. In any case, hopes for a reinvigorated administration or reversal of Hellenic fortunes were quickly dashed by the constrictions of the Memorandum and the mountain of sovereign debt. Papandreou subsequently announced that he was considering the idea of a national referendum in the autumn on constitutional matters. Following the failure of his above efforts to reassert his mandate and improve his party's public standing, this was his next scheme to regain some notion of credibility and public support. This was a step that, a few short months later, would prove self-destructive.

From May onwards, the image of Greece in the international media was of a nation riddled with strikes, demonstrations, protests and widespread strife. This was most evident in Athens at the end of June, when Parliament was debating the 'Medium-Term Fiscal Strategy Framework 2012–15'. The objective of the widespread protest was to force a change in government policy: a reversal of the Memorandum; the rejection of the Medium-Term Framework; or the resignation of the government and fresh elections. In the centre of

Athens, in Syntagma Square, from 28 to 30 June, clashes raged between the police and demonstrators, but also between demonstrators of different political persuasions, while the presence of the 'hooded ones' became the norm, with intimations of violence. The police response was swift and intense. The use of tear gas by the security forces was met with violence. Molotov cocktails, broken marble, crow bars, slabs from the streets and building facades were used as weapons by the demonstrators. Images of burnt-out and ransacked business premises flashed across media outlets the world over. The aim of the demonstrators was to interrupt debate in Parliament and to pressure the government into rejecting any further demands for austerity by the Troika. Demonstrators formed a ring around the Parliament building; MPs were 'spirited away' through side exits leading to the National Gardens, when they wished to leave at the end of discussions. Those who used the normal exits were vilified and humiliated.

The number of people participating in these demonstrations was initially very impressive; however, it progressively diminished as the clashes raised the stakes involved. The crowd of *Indignados* was eventually limited to groups whose aims were clearly undemocratic: anarchists and fascists. The demonstrations and clashes revealed not only the extent of social disharmony but also the existence of a section of society so disillusioned it sought chaos and the complete destruction of the status quo; this extremist fringe recognised the historic opportunity to undermine democracy. It cultivated the rhetoric of despair and the rejection of every policy, in an attempt to promote violence and revolution as both appropriate and necessary. The economic crisis served as a catalyst that brought to the surface all underlying challenges in terms of social cohesion and the existing social conflict so prevalent in Greece; it indicated just how far behind the nation was in forming a modern society.

On 24 June 2011, the European Council confirmed that an agreement had been reached between the Troika and the Greek government regarding measures to be taken in order to secure financing for the years 2011–13.[19] On 29 June, the Greek Parliament voted in favour of the Medium-Term Framework, that is the revised Memorandum, and on 30 June it ratified the relevant legislation. All the conditions set on 20 June by the Eurogroup for release of the fifth instalment had now been met. In the EU these developments were hailed with relief. Such sentiment was mirrored in Greece; the country had avoided a default. Events, however, quickly undermined any premature notions of security or stability; rapidly the climate of political and social hostility returned.

In its meeting on 23–24 June, a few days before the vote in Parliament and the turmoil in Athens, the European Council reiterated the Eurogroup's requests of 20 June. The tone was less than cordial. The Council said that all the parties involved were under an obligation to support the 'basic policies' of the Memorandum. The Council approved the Commission's plan to alter the regulatory framework for the release of Structural Funds, to redirect funds from investment to structural reform and the management of liabilities. It agreed to the establishment of a technical assistance programme for Greece, and gave limited further discussion to the idea of economic governance and oversight of member states' economic policy.

It was a routine meeting and the scope of any progress was limited. In Greece its prescriptions were framed in terms of a small temporal allowance: 'they are keeping us on life support, while at the same time they are asking us to implement an adjustment programme that is exceptionally difficult to carry out, in terms of both time and the measures required; nothing is over and nothing has been conclusively decided'.[20] Outside the EMU it was felt that the countries of the Eurozone were recycling the same policies, vainly hoping for different results. International opinion increasingly favoured more radical measures, such as debt restructuring; it was felt this continued desire not to engage with any notion of an 'end game' was motivated by the desire not to truly acknowledge the exposure of the European banking sector to the Greek crisis. It was easier to continue to prop up Greece than to risk the fallout of a disorderly default on balance sheets held in banks the continent over.

By the end of June, preliminary discussions began with the private sector. The President of France announced that agreement had been reached between the French government and those French banks with Greek liabilities on their balance sheets over how they would participate in the new financing plan. The banks would reinvest the capital due by 2014 in new long-term Greek bonds, further extending the payment schedule. Nicolas Sarkozy made calls for a comparable plan from Germany. The French proposal was central to discussions at the next Eurogroup meeting, in Brussels, on 2 July.

From the statement issued,[21] it appeared that ministers were cautious about future steps. They took into consideration the willingness of banks to participate in an arrangement 'for a substantial reduction in Greece's year-by-year financing needs while avoiding selective default'. But, yet again, the substantive decisions concerning the nature of the private sector's involvement, as well as the figures involved, were deferred to a later date. These would be determined over 'the next few weeks'. Just over a week later, on 11 July, at another meeting of the Eurogroup, no significant progress was made regarding these major issues. Representatives of the banking sector, from the International Institute of Finance (IIF), were also in attendance. The primary consideration for all concerned was that the involvement of the private sector in any restructuring of Greek debt should not constitute a 'credit event' – that is, an event which would force the payout of the CDS policies underwriting Greek liabilities. The figure under discussion was approximately €85–90 billion. The statement issued indicated that a task force had been assigned to enhance the effectiveness of the political handling of the Greek crisis. In particular, the main concern of the task force would be the elaboration of a long-term plan for Greece's macroeconomic consolidation, steps to reduce interest rates on Greek debt, as well as other measures to improve the sustainability of Greek sovereign debt. The finance ministers also noted, in rather vague terms however, that they would improve the Eurozone's capacity to prevent the crisis dragging on for longer than necessary. These proposals included further extensions on repayment schedules, a reduction of rates of interest and assistance in the provision of guarantees.

This was the latest in a line of postponements. The repetition of such proposals and the failure to produce any meaningful let alone definitive solution is indicative of the indecision of the EU. The international media levelled at the leaders of the European Union accusations of 'irresponsibility and mean mindedness': 'For many months they have been squabbling over the formulation of a second plan of assistance for Greece, after the deficiency of the first one'. 'Every one of their meetings concludes with the announcement of a new critical summit' but never do the meetings produce what is required. [22]

These perpetual deferrals fuelled the growth of far more alarming debates regarding the future of both Greece and the overall structure of the EMU. In mid-July the Fitch ratings agency downgraded Greece's credit rating as far as the scale permitted, in response to the continued debate concerning private sector involvement in the restructuring of Greek debt,[23] while another ratings agency indicated any such involvement would constitute a default and a 'credit event'. Discussions again returned in earnest to the prospect a Greek default and whether it was inevitable, if not imminent. The Greek Minister of Finance spoke of a 'selective' default of the country, 'which is not a default' but 'an evaluation of government bonds by the rating agencies'.[24] The use of the term 'selective' default further fuelled anxiety and perplexed Greek public opinion, unsure of what this would entail. Abroad, it was increasingly noted that Greece was no longer in a position to fulfil its obligations.[25] The proposals and actions of the EMU were consistently failing to remedy the situation, let alone provide any notion of closure. Not only was debt restructuring clearly necessary but, to make the sovereign debt once again sustainable, creditors needed a cut of up to 80%. Without any major restructuring of the terms of Greek debt, it would exceed a staggering 400% by 2050. The IMF expressed its growing concern over 'the unstable condition' of Greek debt, and stated that continued assistance was vital to avert the risk of contagion to other countries.[26]

The fundamental question was whether the solution that had been proposed by the French was sufficient and appropriate. Doubts were expressed. Germany, the Netherlands and Finland wanted the private sector to be involved in the reduction of Greek debt, through a cut in their claims of up to 50%. Economists maintained that the deferment of repayment proposed by France would not rectify the situation. 'A write-down of debt is necessary.'[27] This suggestion encountered intense objections from within the ECB and the banking sector, which were both very conscious of the turmoil this could trigger in the markets. The fear was of a rise in the rate of interest for all countries. Further, a write-down would in essence be a default, and would prevent the Greek banking sector from having any further access to the markets. The European Commission and France proposed that the EFSF should be used to finance

Greece and other ailing member states, as a conciliatory solution. The capital from the Facility should be used to repurchase their bonds from the market, available on the market far below their nominal value. Such a proposal could ensure a major reduction in overall liabilities, without risking the major fallout of a credit event or an orderly default. However, such proposals failed to consider that once Greece, or the EFSF, appeared on the market and made any effort to purchase the bonds, they would rapidly return to their nominal value.

The German government fundamentally disagreed with the proposals; such action would place a huge cost on national taxpayers and did nothing to involve the private sector. Similar criticisms were made of proposals regarding the issue of eurobonds by the EU to pay off Greek debt. German public opinion increasingly held that any efforts to help Greece were futile. German discourse spoke of a temporary 'Grexit' from the EMU, which would allow Greece to recover its competiveness, through the return of control over monetary policy such a move would ensure. The theory was that, after two years, say, once the situation had normalised, Greece could return.[28]

Various nations raised proposals regarding state assets as guarantees against debt. This would allow member states both control over and responsibility for their own sovereign debt, but would, more importantly, permit a return to the markets on sustainable terms, as all loans would be guaranteed by tangible assets. The markets would lend again and the disastrous consequences of compulsory cuts would be avoided. The IMF and Italy indicated that the onus was on the German Chancellor to make clear how private bondholders might be involved in any agreement concerning Greek sovereign debt, as the continuing uncertainty would subvert the Eurozone.

The President of the European Council proposed that a summit be convened on Friday 15 July so that this problem could be discussed at the highest level. Germany made clear its objections that national preferences were too divergent to be bridged in such a short time frame. The markets, the media and public opinion would expect a conclusive proposal. However, as every preceding summit had shown, this was highly unlikely. A further failure to produce any closure on the debate would only fuel further anxiety and insecurity.[29]

The continued deferrals of any final solution to the Greek problem had already had negative consequences for other members of the EMU. The rate of interest on Italian borrowing reached its highest level in 10 years. In the first week of July, Portugal's credit rating was downgraded and the same fate met Ireland on 14 July. The euro was continually losing its value against the dollar. The value of bank shares was falling on all the stock markets. In Europe, newspaper reports spoke of a 'storm … raging with no end in sight'. Most analysis did not view the euro as the root cause of the crisis, but rather the indecision and inertia of the European political class. The relentless cycle of negative developments was a result of politicians failing to deal with the problems.

In this cacophony of pejorative assessment and conflicting proposals, Greece was continuing its calls for a decision to be taken. At start of the Eurogroup meeting on 11 July, the Prime Minister addressed a letter to the President of the Eurogroup, Jean-Claude Juncker. In it he stressed the need to take a decision and that that decision needed to be made soon, because, if Europe continued to be riddled with such inertia, it risked fuelling renewed and possibly global turmoil in the markets: 'The ball is with Europe and not with Athens, as the situation in Italy and Spain proves'.[30] However, Greece did little to help; it did not make its own position clear, or offer any substantive proposals. The French policy preference to continue to roll over the debt was described as 'unrealistic'. Debt restructuring was feared, for concern over the ramifications it would have for the markets. The Greek Minister of Finance expressed support for the proposal of purchasing bonds below their nominal value, through the use of the EFSF.[31] However, official Greek statements indicated flexibility or, more likely, an absence of a coherent strategy. Other solutions would be acceptable provided they ensured sustainability of debt – through a reduction in debt of up to 50% and a reduction in the rate of interest – and guaranteed the protection of citizens' deposits in Greek banks. If these terms were accepted, the 'Greek government could discuss the matter of a selective default'.[32] Despite the continuing turmoil, the Greek administration appeared extremely optimistic. The Minister of Finance promised a return to the markets within 2014. However, the call for a 'haircut' of up to 50% marked a full u-turn for an administration that not so long previously had categorically ruled out such a move and had conveyed to the public that this would be a disaster; that administration would therefore now find it very difficult to convince the public that some kind of restructuring was inevitable, and might even prove a salvation. Had the Greek government at any point thought to found a think-tank devoted to the crisis, 'it would now be ready to evaluate the cost–benefit balance between the various proposals (French and German)'.[33]

A summit of the European Council convened in Brussels on 21 July 2011. Heated negotiations on an acceptable solution preceded it. The most critical meeting took place in Berlin the previous evening. Discussions were initially held between Chancellor Merkel and President Sarkozy. Subsequently, the President of the ECB, Trichet, the Pesident of the European Council, Rompuy, and the German Minister of Finance, Schäuble, were called in to join the discussions.[34] There were no Greek representatives. According to journalists, Greece's marginalisation stemmed from the emerging realisation that the Greek minister 'did not actively participate in dealing with the crisis'.[35] The summit closed with nothing more than a statement of principle: private creditors should contribute to the solution of the Greek problem. The EFSF was to be enhanced, to bolster its ability to limit contagion. The former statement was reflective of German preferences, while the latter reflected those of the French administration. The specifics of how these aims were to be realised would be picked up on the return to Brussels the following day.

The key points hammered out in 10 hours of negotiations in Brussels on 21 July in Brussels were as follows:[36]

- The formulation of a new support programme with the joint involvement of the IMF and the private sector (on a voluntary basis). Funds amounting €109 billion (€60 billion under the new agreement and €49 billion from the balance of existing loans) would be made available to Greece. The EFSF would provide the capital for the new loan. Financing would be accompanied by a stringent adjustment programme for the Greek economy. The Troika would supervise its implementation.
- The payment schedule would again be revised; the new loans from the EFSF would be paid over the next 30 years, with a period of grace of 10 years. The interest rate would be approximately 3.5%.
- A strategy for economic growth and investment in Greece would be developed. Funds from the EU would be used to provide a stimulus to the Greek economy. In addition, the EU would support Greece with technical assistance.
- The private sector would contribute through a reduction in the rate of interest and an extension of the repayment schedule, measures amounting to approximately €37 billion.
- The EFSF's capacity to intervene in the secondary markets for bonds would be enhanced, in order to curtail contagion.
- The provision of guarantees, where deemed necessary, to any ailing member states, would be financed by the EFSF.

The framing of the terms with regard to the involvement of the private sector stressed, in no uncertain terms, that it constituted an extraordinary initiative of a unique nature. That is, it would not be permitted to set any precedent.

The proposals were accompanied by other texts, clarifying how they would be implemented. These texts, along with statements made by the leaders of the EU, indicated that the contribution of the private sector would be effected through the choice of one of four alternatives for the exchange of government bonds. Private bondholders with bonds maturing before 2020 would lose 21% of the value of their bonds. Greek sovereign debt would be reduced by approximately 25%. Finally, Greece would be given access to €15 billion from the Union's Structural Funds. Greece's mandatory contribution to the financing of Structural Funds projects would be 5%, rather than the conventional 25%.[37]

Immediately following the summit, the President of the ECB, Trichet, announced that the Bank would guarantee the liquidity of the Greek banking system to the value of €35 billion. This ensured that the Greek banking sector would survive any losses entailed in the restructuring of national debt. It was the latest in a long line of various measures, throughout the crisis, designed to support the Greek banks. However, the EMU requested that the Greek banking sector primarily manage its recapitalisation through capital increases, mergers or sale of assets. The Greek banks could also have recourse to the Hellenic Financial Stability Fund, which had been established in Greece by the Troika and which made available funds for financing banks.[38]

The summit of 21 July brought about a significant change in EU policy. Many things that had been deemed highly inadvisable were now acknowledged to be imperative. For the first time, the Eurozone recognised the responsibility of the private sector in the crisis and, as such, the role it must play in any effort to fund recovery. Greek debt was deemed unsustainable, something the Eurozone had refused to acknowledge up until then, as such an acknowledgement implicitly recognised the mistakes in the first Memorandum. Finally, the member states broadened the EFSF's capacity for action, acknowledging that the crisis was not only a Greek problem. These decisions signalled the beginning of a new period, in which the bodies of the EU would play a more pronounced role in the management of the crisis. It must be noted that the EFSF did not become a 'European IMF', and the Commission did not (and still does not) oversee a regime of complete and coherent economic governance, to the displeasure of the then French President, Sarkozy. However, concrete steps were taken in the direction of closer consultation and common action.

During negotiations at the summit, officials from the French six-month EU presidency distributed a draft proposal which referred to 'a European Marshall Plan'. This grandiose reference did not appear in the final text. Such language stemmed from the Greek government's claims that support from the Structural Funds constituted a Marshall Plan.[39] This reference did not recognise that while the Marshall Plan was a grant, the funds from the structural programmes were not. These were funds Greece was entitled to but had not managed to absorb in earlier efforts and had risked losing them entirely. European financing, in the form of Structural Funds, was the result of Greek participation in the EMU, and not a result of global conflict, as the Marshall Plan had been.[40] The availability of Structural Funds was a step to counter criticisms that Greece was not receiving any support in its efforts to return to growth. A reduction in the Greek contribution to EU programmes was a further significant concession. However, Greece's inability to absorb EU funds was only partially due to the fact that the government was unable to provide its share of funding (on the basis of the co-financing principle). The inadequacies of the Greek public administration and of private stakeholders were the primary reason the funds had remained unused.[41]

The critical question posed at the end of the summit was whether these proposals made Greek debt sustainable. On this matter, widespread analysis was less than positive. It was widely held that any conclusive effort to make the debt sustainable would have to entail a reduction of no less than 50%. Scepticism remained regarding the capacity of the EFSF to stem the tide of the spreading crisis reaching Italy and Spain. The funds of the EFSF were deemed insufficient to deal with any adverse development in these countries. According to a commentator in the *Financial Times*, 'the second loan package to Greece will be fine as long as we realise that there needs to be a third'.[42]

There was also criticism of the involvement of private bondholders. The relevant stipulations and specifics of associated texts were considered complex and unclear, 'to a degree justifying anxiety'.[43] Banks, insurance companies and other entities that held bonds were far from eager to participate in the voluntary programme. Following repeated delays, only half the number of participants forecast had volunteered. The private sector remained reluctant. This may have stemmed from dissatisfaction with the terms of the restructuring. However, it is far more likely this reluctance was a result of the recognition that the summit agreement had not made Greek debt sustainable. While the cuts requested from the private sector were approximately 20%, the fall in the value of Greek bonds was twice that. To the markets it was apparent that such a cut did not ensure sustainability of the debt. At the same time, it gave rise to the argument that the proposal actually returned to the banks a large part of the money they had lost through the fall in the value of Greek bonds. The market value of the bonds had been reduced by 40–60%, but the Greek taxpayer would now have to pay 80% of their value.

The Greek government was satisfied. It had avoided defaulting and had succeeded in securing sufficient capital so that the sword of Damocles was no longer hanging over its head. The administration felt that 'debt sustainability, the country's borrowing requirements and an impetus for growth had all been ensured'.[44] It downplayed the significance of debt restructuring, of which it had once been so vocally critical. This necessary intervention would not have taken so long if Greece had actively promoted such measures earlier.[45]

Germany was in two minds over the results of the summit. Undoubtedly, Chancellor Merkel had ensured German preferences were at the core of the agreement. She had blocked any calls for a relaxing of conditions imposed upon Greece. It was widely accepted that any support was conditional upon wide-reaching measures to reduce expenditure, as well as major reforms to modernise both national economies and the European single market. However, the agreement was not received well by German public opinion. German citizens felt that they were again being forced to pay for the mistakes of others. The President of the German central bank articulated nationally held fears that these agreements marked a step 'towards collective risk [sharing], should other countries follow absurd fiscal policies'.[46]

In France, the agreement was viewed favourably; the French had achieved their main object. The EFSF was now a European monetary fund – on the model of the IMF – which would buy bonds of states in crisis on the secondary markets; it could recapitalise banks and it would proactively finance countries such as Spain and Italy. Under such conditions, they believed, the economic governance of Europe would become much more effective.[47]

However, many commentators indicated that while the summit might have assuaged anxiety and insecurity, it had done so only in the short term. The agreement had bought time, nothing more. The questions regarding complete fiscal union were no closer to being answered, despite the evident shortcomings of a monetary union without common fiscal rules.

## Notes

1  *The Economist*, 18 June 2011, p. 30.
2  *IHT*, 9 June 2011, p. 1.
3  'EZB verweigert sich Zahlungsaufschub', *FAZ*, 10 June 2011.
4  See *Imerisia*, 9 June 2011, p. 4.
5  *IHT*, 14 June 2011, p. 24.
6  *Le Monde*, 17 June 2011, p. 1.
7  'Greece's fading dream of easing pain', *New York Times*, 9 June 2011, p. 13. See also the related Y. Pretenteris, *To Vima*, 12 June 2011, p. A61; Y. Varoufakis, 'Crisis bulletin', Protagon news and comment website (www.protagon.gr), 10 June 2011.
8  See Chapter 11.
9  See for example *Der Spiegel*, issue 25, 2011, p. 38; *The Economist*, 18 June 2011, p. 29; 'Der zahlungsunfähige Musterschüler', *FAZ* online, www.faz.net, 10 June 2011.
10  'The adjustment programme of May 2010 is not sufficient to save Greece', *Le Monde*, 17 June 2011, p. 1.
11  *Le Monde*, 21 May 2011, p. 15.
12  Statement of the Eurogroup, 20 June 2011.
13  See *Le Monde*, 22 June 2011, p. 14; *IHT*, 23 June 2011; 'Political veteran takes on Greek challenge', *Ta Nea*, 6 October 2011, p. 10.
14  See *Ta Nea*, 21 June 2011, p. 8; Y. Pretenteris, *To Vima*, 26 June 2011, p. A46.
15  *IHT*, 14 June 2011, p. 18.
16  *IHT*, 20 June 2011, p. 1.
17  See P. Mandravellis, 'Stuck on agricultural guards', *Kathimerini*, 29 June 2011.
18  *Kathimerini*, 12 June 2011.
19  See Council of European Union, 11406/2/11, Rev. 2, 12352/11.
20  P. Panyiotou, *Ethnos tis Kyriakis*, 26 June 2011, p. 62.
21  Statement by the Eurogroup, 2 July 2011.
22  *Le Monde*, 13 July 2011, p. 1. See also *Ta Nea*, 6 October 2011, p. 10.
23  *Ta Nea*, 14 July 2011, p. 9.
24  *Kathimerini*, 13 July 2011, p. 3.
25  'Lex Greece', *Financial Times*, 14 July 2011.
26  *Financial Times*, 14 July 2011, p. 1.
27  'Greece needs debt to be written down', *Kathimerini*, 8 July 2011.
28  See interview with H. W. Sinn, *Le Monde*, 16 July 2011, p. 11.
29  See various views expressed in: *Le Monde*, 15 July 2011, p. 9; *Financial Times*, 12 July 2011, p. 1 and p. 3; *Financial Times*, 13 July 2011, p. 1 and p. 3; *Financial Times*, 15 July 2011, p. 1; *IHT*, 13 July 2011, p. 1.
30  *To Vima* online, www.tovima.gr, 11 July 2012.
31  See *To Vima*, 10 July 2011, p. A44.
32  *Ta Nea*, 14 July 2011, p. 9.
33  G. Karelias, *Eleutherotypia*, 16 July 2011, p. 11.
34  A lengthy description of the meeting appears in *Le Monde*, 26 July 2011, p. 3.
35  *Ta Nea*, 6 October 2011, p. 11.
36  Council of the European Union, Statement by the heads of state or government of the Euro area and EU institutions, Brussels, 21 July 2011.
37  This was a confirmation of a decision taken on 23–24 June 2011.

38  The Hellenic Financial Stability Fund (Tamio Chrimapistotikis Statherotitas) was quite separate from the European Financial Stability Facility. It was a legal entity under Greek law. It was established by law 3864 of 2010. Its capital derived from the money granted to Greece as a loan by the EFSF. The Greek state is its shareholder. Its purpose is to enhance the capital sufficiency of banks, provided this is, in its judgement, necessary. Beyond the Fund, there is the local support mechanism of the Bank of Greece, ELA (Emergency Liquidity Assistance), which can be used to intervene exceptionally to support a bank.

39  See *Le Monde*, 23 July 2011, p. 12.

40  See *Ta Nea*, 22 July 2011, p. 10; *Financial Times,* 23 July 2011, p. 8, 24 July 2011, p. 9; *IHT*, 22 July 2011, p. 1. 'The National Strategic Reference Framework (NSRF) funds, provision of technical assistance for absorption thereof, and also for the improvement of Public administration ... are very good but do not constitute a Marshall Plan'. *Kathimerini*, 26 July 2011, p. 3.

41  See p. 62.

42  W. Munchau, 'The eurozone crisis is on hold, not over', electronic edition of *Financial Times,* 24 July 2011.

43  *Financial Times,* 22 July 2011, p. 14.

44  *Kathimerini*, 22 July 2011, p. 4.

45  'If you can see that you will be forced to take a measure, it is always better to do so sooner rather than later. The more you delay, the more the cost of any move you finally make, rises.' F. Bergsten, *Kathimerini*, 8 April 2011, p. 10.

46  *Der Spiegel*, issue 30, 2011, p. 21.

47  *Le Monde*, 23 July 2011, p. 10.

# 14

# A dead end

August 2011 was anticipated to pass quietly. EU leaders had taken decisive steps; they believed that they had used the 'atomic weapon', as they called it, to combat anxiety and uncertainty. Time was no longer of the essence, collapse had been averted; their decisions simply had to be ratified by domestic parliaments for negotiations with creditors over Greek debt restructuring to take place. However, the complacency was short-lived. The tide started to turn just a fortnight after the European Council summit of 21 July.

On 2 August stock prices tumbled the world over. Rates of interest on Italian and Spanish bonds began to rise. Investors turned en masse to the security of German bonds. The activity was compounded by fears of a crisis in the USA and its effects on the Eurozone. This was not a phase. It continued and became a determining factor in future developments. In order to stop the crisis spreading, the ECB decided to buy Irish and Portuguese bonds by way of support for the two countries; however, it was soon obliged to extend its action to Italian and Spanish bonds. The crisis had an entirely predictable consequence: the loss of confidence led to major drop in intra-bank lending. Major deposits were made in the ECB instead, despite the limited returns available. The Eurozone found itself in a rapidly deteriorating international economic climate.

The French President, Nicolas Sarkozy, and the German Chancellor, Angela Merkel, met in mid-August. The meeting was intended to demonstrate collective resolve to protect the common currency by taking the measures deemed necessary. The results were, yet again, disappointing. Among other things, the two leaders decided that 'the golden rules' of the Eurozone relating to the balancing of budgets and the restrictions on levels of sovereign debt should be incorporated into the constitutions of the member states of the Eurozone. However, they rejected the introduction of eurobonds. They both indicated there were no simple solutions. Progress, they asserted, would be incremental. Their negotiations, once more, did not rise to the occasion. The meeting did little to allay anxiety; nor did it do anything to broach the issue of reducing sovereign debt in the long run, as there were no discussions concerning the promotion of a return to growth.[1]

The international climate was increasingly strangling Greece. The country's rate of interest had reached 18% on 10-year bonds by August 2011. Banks were afflicted by increasing liquidity concerns, leading to talk of recourse to extraordinary measures, such as support from the EFSF. The recession went in the face of many forecasts, exceeding expectations and further undermining confidence.

Despite all this, the Greek government continued to appear optimistic. It believed that the Greek problem was a small dimension of much deeper European and international concerns. Greece could 'function as the starting point for transcending the crisis'.[2] Hellenic analysis viewed developments after the European Council summit favourably; it had created the conditions 'for the exchange of Greek bonds'. The Prime Minister made telephone calls to European officials and, 'according to informed sources, the dead line for completion of the procedure concerning the private sector involvement had been set for 26 September'.[3]

The exchange of bonds did not take place in September, or later. The short-comings of the 'historic decisions' made in July and continued procrastination were not the appropriate means to reverse the fortunes of Greece and the EU.

The July decision provided that guarantees could be given to any of the member states financing Greece through the EFSF.[4] On the basis of this clause, the Finnish government requested that Greece provide certain guarantees to ensure that the Finnish Parliament could approve the lending of €1 billion to the EFSF to finance Greece. To avoid any delays in the process, the Greek government came to an agreement with the Finnish government in mid-August to deposit an amount in a Finnish bank which, together with interest on the deposit, would reach €1 billion on the date the Finnish contribution was repayable. In this way Finland in essence cancelled its contribution to the new support package by taking back as a guarantee the amount it would be granting.[5]

When this agreement became public knowledge, other countries also requested comparable arrangements to limit their own exposure. If agreements of this nature were concluded with all creditor nations, Greece would in fact not get the loan granted to it. Greece turned to the Eurozone to find a solution. This move led to endless negotiations; the Eurogroup decided that any conclusive decision concerning such guarantees would be deferred to the next summit, to be held in mid-September. According to the *Financial Times*, these discussions, as well as the agreement between Greece and Finland, 'were bringing the Greek economy a step closer to default'.[6]

A second factor impeding progress, stemming from the July summit, was the aversion of many banks and insurance funds to participate in the bond exchange programme. That programme required participation that would represent 90% of bonds that were to mature over the next 15 years. This would entail a 'haircut' of 21% or a reduction of debt by approximately €26 billion. Information on the scale of participation in the private sector was contradictory. The Minister of Finance gave a reassurance that both the Greek as well as foreign banks would be participating. At the end of August, reports in the media indicated that, to the contrary, the participation of the private sector had only just reached 70% of the total amount of bonds. Even the Greek banks were reluctant to participate, owing to the losses they would incur in a period of increased instability and reduced revenues.

The third factor which had a profoundly negative effect on the implementation of the agreement of 21 July was the confrontation between the government and the representatives of the Troika during negotiations over the quarterly review and subsequent funding in September. The negotiations were anticipated to be painful, since the targets that had been set in the previous quarter had not been met. New Democracy continued in its assertions that the Memorandum should be renegotiated, with growing approval from public opinion. The parties of the traditional left of Greek politics were also increasingly vocal in their criticism of the government and in their rejection of the Memorandum. Much dissent was emerging, with people angry because the government was offering no objections to the demands of the Troika. The Prime Minister's American advisers also expressed their objections to conciliatory tactics. The new Minister of Finance was under pressure to take a more assertive stance than that of his predecessor.

In their talks with the Greek administration, the representatives of the Troika indicated that the deficit would be 8–8.5% of GDP, rather than the 7.6% forecast. They felt that further measures were required, amounting to at least €1.7 billion. The Greek administration countered that the shortfall was due to the recession, which would only be compounded by additional measures. The Troika rejected such claims, asserting that the recession was responsible for only a 0.5% percentage of the overshot target for the deficit. The balance of the overshot deficit was due to the delays in the structural changes agreed at the last quarter. Talks were interrupted at midnight on 1 September. Evangelos Venizelos, the Minister of Finance, is said to have asserted to the Troika that he could not continue with talks, and that he would seek political negotiation at the Eurozone level in order to avoid taking new measures. In an extraordinary press conference shortly after, he attempted to downplay the matter, saying that this was not a rift but an agreed interruption in the talks, with the aim of giving the Greek side the necessary time to present its proposals. The representatives of the Troika stated that the talks had been interrupted to enable 'the Greek authorities to complete their work of a technical nature, among other things, with regard to the 2012 budget and the structural reforms'.[7] Indicative of the mounting tension and fundamental disagreement, talks did not resume within the 10 days initially planned. It was not until 29 September that the parties were back around the negotiating table.

It appears that the Greek administration was actually seeking political talks, with the aim of securing a bailout amounting to €109 billion to be disbursed by the end of 2013, not mid-2014 as previously agreed. At the same time, it was seeking a further extension in the deadline for the reduction of the deficit to 3%, beyond 2013. These requests were reasonable, but the way in which they were sought was less than tactful, considering that extensive negotiations had just been concluded and there had been no public discussion or planning regarding further support. The demands were met with instant refusal by the Union. The efforts on the part of the Greek government to present a more assertive stance in the face of the Troika's demands did little more than defer the next instalment of Memorandum funding. This left Greece in a far more precarious position, with no real gain to show for the demands.

For Brussels, the talks had been interrupted because the Greek side had not kept its promises in three areas: the establishment of a single payroll for the public sector; the designation of which companies would be included in the programme of privatisation; and the continued failure to address the shortcomings in taxation.[8] The President of the Eurogroup publicly stated that things in Greece were not proceeding at the proper pace and that results were not being achieved. Greece, it appeared, was heading full throttle towards default. 'The taboo has been broken, Greece's exit from the Eurozone is being discussed in low voices by the European lenders', *Le Monde* observed.[9] The Dutch Minister of Finance stated: 'if a country does not wish to comply with the requests of the Eurozone, then all it has to do is abandon it'.[10] The severity of the situation was widely acknowledged, and it was recognised that there was no way out, other than compliance with the Troika's demands: 'There is no room for manoeuvre'.[11] Greece and the Eurozone were back to square one, back to May 2010, when the first bailout had been agreed.[12]

On 14 December the Greek Prime Minister had a teleconference with Sarkozy and Merkel. According to Greek accounts, the result was satisfactory: it had been confirmed that 'the future of Greece is in the euro'. Yet French and German accounts said discussions had concentrated on Greek compliance with existing obligations and avoiding a 'disorderly default'. According to the international media, there was no scope for manoeuvre left to Greece. Greece's partners inevitably doubted the Greek government, 'which does not keep its promises and does not achieve its targets.... There is no room left for mistakes and delays.'[13]

The deterioration of the situation fuelled mistrust. On 12 September the rate of interest on 10-year Greek bonds reached a record high 23.544%.[14] The rise in interest rates on short-term bonds was also explosive. International markets now viewed the possibility of a Greek default as a near certainty, or, more precisely, a 98% probability.[15]

The IMF, the European Commission and the ECB urgently noted the need for further measures to be taken and for absolute compliance with regard to their existing demands. The Troika indicated in no uncertain terms that it needed to see movement in terms of changes in the labour market, structural reforms, the deregulation of markets, and the audit and recapitalisation of banks. The Greek government had already announced a 'hurricane of measures' on 6 September in an effort to counter the distrust so widespread among its European partners. It announced that it would swiftly proceed with job losses in the public sector (by placing employees near retirement age onto a 'reserve list' on reduced pay), the adoption of common rules across the public sector payroll, the 'opening' up of 'closed' professions and a programme of privatisation worth €5 billion, all within 2011. It was an impressive list, which was publicly announced and widely referred to. In light of the scale of the proposed reforms, journalists predicted intense reactions, not least from those directly affected. However, cynicism remained. What mattered was not the 'hurricane' of reforms announced, but the tangible results: 'They announced things … without knowing how exactly these would be done … seeking to achieve them with opportunistic, slip-shod prescriptions, written off the cuff, and in many cases contradictory and paradoxical.'[16]

As for the results, a few short months later, by the beginning of 2012, the programme had, as before, proved to be little more than rhetoric. The reserve status for public sector employees turned out, in the words of the government itself, to be a 'fiasco'. The opening of closed professions was still under discussion, and no significant movement was made in terms of privatisation. The resistance of the unions and the privileged position of vested interests remained as prevalent as ever. Once again, the government was guilty of over-promising and under-delivering. What had appeared to be a comprehensive programme of adjustment was in reality little more than yet another public relations exercise. Charges of 'incomplete actions, delays and tricks' were again levelled at the Greek administration.[17]

On 16 September Ecofin convened in Warsaw. It was the first chance since 21 July to discuss the Greek problem with reference to the wider context, and to seek Hellenic compliance with the decisions of the Eurogroup. The Greek side was naïvely optimistic, feeling it had taken substantive steps in carrying out its commitments, as it was moving towards a single payroll and a reserve status for public employees. The principal aim for Athens was the disbursement of the pending instalment. The instalment, however, was not released. Disbursement was made dependent on the Troika's progress report on the Greek programme. The return of the Troika was agreed for mid-October, over a month after it had abandoned Greece for '10 days'. The climate was less than amicable. Ecofin reminded the Greek delegation of its pending obligations, stressing that if they were not fulfilled, the country would be abandoned to its fate. Discussions over the implementation of the decisions made on 21 July were postponed until a more holistic picture of developments could be ascertained. At the Cabinet meeting held after the delegation had returned to Greece, the Prime Minister and the Minister of Finance 'described the ruinous position the country had found itself in, in the darkest of colours, and that it was now in a particularly hostile environment'.[18]

At the Eurogroup meeting held on 16 September, discussions focused primarily on the size of the EFSF, and whether the Facility should be increased to such an extent it would be able to intervene in every case and loan the amounts necessary for both the indebted countries and banks no longer able to access the markets. The US Secretary of the Treasury called upon his European counterparts to increase the Facility to deal with the crisis. The European reaction was icy. Certain ministers felt that the USA, with greater deficits than the Eurozone, was in no position to lecture.

After the Ecofin meeting in Warsaw, Greece sought to normalise its relations with the nucleus of the Eurozone, so that the agreement of 21 July could go ahead and the instalment still pending could be disbursed. In repeated discussions with the Troika, the Minister of Finance tried to come to an agreement over the measures to be implemented. The aim of the talks was further reform, including the readjustment of property tax and a drastic cut in tax exemptions. According to leaked information, the Troika insisted on substantive interventions to reduce the deficit. Its preferred solution was a policy mix on deficit reduction, which would rely two-thirds on spending cuts and one-third on tax increases, so that the impact of the programme on incomes would be moderated. However, cuts in pensions and tax rises remained the main tools of reducing the deficit, as these were considered a 'safer' and quicker way of balancing the books, in contrast to the reduction of government expenditure.

The Troika finally returned to Greece on 29 September, approximately one month after it had left. The interruption in talks had been an episode which cost Greece dearly. It put the country in an acutely disadvantageous negotiating position.

Germany and France were seeking to isolate the Greek crisis, so as to limit wider exposure or further contagion. This meant Greece would receive assistance, at least for as long as was necessary to undertake the recapitalisation of banks at a European level, so that a default would not shake the entire European banking sector. Time was also needed to ensure the necessary preparations for an orderly default by Greece, and for negotiations with creditors. Germany felt that all these concerns could be addressed by the time the permanent European Stability Mechanism (ESM) came into operation, in 2013. It was therefore certain that Greece would be given assistance but only to buy time for wider contingency planning to be done; it was questionable whether any support still existed at the European level to solve the Greek crisis. Any permanent arrangements would have to be included in the ESM's programme of intervention, which would evaluate the situation together with that of the other over-indebted nations of the Eurozone.

This logic led to growing doubt over the value of the agreement of 21 July. Even if the full target of a 90% participation of the private sector in the bond exchange were to be achieved, the agreement would lead to only minimal debt relief. What was needed was not a 'haircut' of 21%, but of 50% or even more, so that the debt could become sustainable, at least until the ESM came into operation. To compound criticism of the agreement, it became clear that capital speculation was actually using its terms to profit. Hedge funds were increasingly trying to speculate with Greek bonds. They bought them at a price lower than their nominal value, usually around 50% or 60% lower. They would then, in case of a haircut, seek to exchange them for new bonds, whose value would be 80% approximately of their nominal value. They would thus realise a significant profit. Germany felt that such speculation should not be rewarded.

In the beginning of October, the European Commission started discussions with representatives of the banking sector about the possibility of a much larger haircut, but always on a voluntary basis. These negotiations had led to concurrence of views on various matters, but left the fundamental question unanswered: what would the exact scale of the cut in the creditors' claims be? Objections to a 'deep haircut' were expressed by two sides. Inevitably, there were widespread objections from the banks, in particular the Greek ones. They felt the proposed level of 50% was excessive, despite the fact the bonds were not worth more than 50–60% of their nominal value on the market. The ECB also felt that the debt restructuring would set an ominous precedent, which might encourage other nations to seek a comparable solution to their sovereign debt concerns.

The Greek government did not appear to hold a clear position. It neither defended the existing agreement of 21 July, nor advocated a deeper haircut. Either it did not want to antagonise the Greek banks, or else it was waiting for information on the wider ramifications of any such proposal, for instance on how the recapitalisation of the banks would be financed. On the Prime Minister's return from Brussels, on 14 October, the newspaper *Ta Nea* wrote: 'The good news he brought back in his suitcase … was that ultimately Germany's intention to impose a haircut of Greek debt of 50% to 60% does not appear to have been adopted'. Thirty per cent was 'the highest rate that the Greek banking system and the social security funds can bear'. This position was the closest the government could get to realising the apparent necessity of a 'haircut', in contradiction to its prior assertions that restructuring was in no way desirable.

## Notes

1  See *IHT*, 17 August 2011; *Le Monde*, 18 August 2011.
2  See the statements of Evangelos Venizelos, Finance Minister, in *Kathimerini*, 7 August 2011, p. 5.
3  *Ta Nea*, 9 August 2011, p. 9.
4  Point 9 of the Eurogroup statement.
5  *Kathimerini*, 17 August 2011, p. 17.
6  On this, see *Kathimerini*, 31 August 2011, p. 3, and also 19 August 2011, pp. 3, 4, 20 August 2011, p. 3; and *Ta Nea*, 27–28 August 2011, p. 11; *Imerisia*, 26 August 2011, p. 4.
7  In a comment in *Ta Nea*, Y. Pretenteris wrote: 'It is obvious that the recession blew the economic programme sky high, but it is equally obvious that the recession is only partly to blame for what has not been done or has come to a halt.… The

recession is not to blame for public organisations being neither closed down nor merged.... The recession is not to blame for tax avoidance reigning supreme.... This is what the Troika sees and invokes. What is worse, though, is that it uses government dithering as an excuse to cover its own crowning responsibility for its failed policy.'

8  *Le Monde*, 4–5 September 2011.
9  *Le Monde*, 10 September 2011, p. 38.
10  In an interview he gave in 2012, the then President of the Eurogroup, Jean-Claude Juncker, said that he opposed 'those who were trying to push Greece out of the Eurozone', as well as the implementation of plans 'which left Greece with no option other than to leave the Eurozone'. *Kathimerini,* 18 March 2012, p. 10.
11  W. Schäuble, German Minister of Finances, *Kathimerini,* 11 September 2011, p. 12.
12  Leading article, *Le Monde*, 4–5 September 2011.
13  *Le Monde*, 16 September 2011, p. 19; *IHT*, 14 September 2011, p. 1.
14  Source, Bloomberg.
15  *Imerisia*, 13 September 2011, p. 5.
16  P. Panayiotou, *Ethnos*, 10 September 2011, p. 2.
17  Y. Pretenteris, *Ta Nea*, 8 September 2011.
18  *Ta Nea*, 19 September 2011, p. 9. According to the Greek Minister of Finance, Schäuble proposed that Greece should exit the Eurozone, which he rejected. See *Ta Nea*, 9–10 March 2013. This has not been corroborated by the German side.

# 15

# More hitches

Anxiety and uncertainty mounted. The Troika report on the sustainability of Greek sovereign debt published in October 2011, conducted as part of the fifth quarterly review on the progress of reforms, did not bode well.[1] The report indicated that substantive change in the Greek economy was driven more by the recession than by the structural reforms of the Memorandum. The reforms were not stimulating the internal devaluation they were designed to achieve: 'The situation in Greece has taken a turn for the worse'. The report indicated that the recession was expected only to deepen in 2011, and that trend to continue into 2012, with growth forecast to return by 2013. As to when Greece might be able to return to the markets, no clear indication could be given. Conditions that would precede a return to the markets, upon sustainable terms, were unlikely to be seen until 2021. The debt to GDP ratio was expected to peak in 2013, at a staggering 186% of GDP. The country's borrowing needs till the year 2020 were calculated at €252 billion over and above that already granted, and after the debt had received a 21% haircut.

The report's conclusion was that Greece needed extensive, long-term and generous international support. The provisions agreed during the July summit would not suffice. The claims of creditors would have to be cut by at least 60% if debt were to become sustainable. A further reduction in the rate of interest would be required, along with additional support from the EFSF, 'in accordance with the promise made by the leaders of the Eurozone to help Greece throughout the whole time it will need to acquire the capacity to borrow from the markets again'.

The analysis from the Troika indicated indirectly that all preceding efforts to address the crisis had failed. Extensive debt restructuring would be needed if any conclusive progress were to be made. At the same time, however, it was no less relentless in its demands for the reduction of the deficit, so that a primary surplus might be achieved as early as 2013. No reference was made, and no analysis undertaken, with regard to the social costs of continued austerity. The severe fiscal targets placed huge pressure on the Greek government to rapidly force through cuts in social security, regardless of the social consequences.

Such a singular emphasis on the fiscal concerns augmented social reaction and criticism of the programme. Many European economists noted that the imposition of further measures on Greece was counterproductive; it did little other than to compound the recession. The country's ability to endure much more austerity was being tested to breaking point: 'the medicine being administered may prove useless, if not criminal'.[2] Consumption had deteriorated to a huge degree in a very short space of time. Incomes had shrunk dramatically, up to 40% in some cases. Unemployment was growing month by month; it would not be long before the number of unemployed would exceed 1,000,000, a record figure for Greece. The result was a continual fall in tax receipts, with a corresponding rise in social security expenditure to support the loss of income or employment. The crisis was not being resolved by the reform programme and austerity continued without an end in sight; the country was being driven further into the depths of recession by the policies. Public dissent in Greece was fuelled not only by disillusionment with the Memorandum, but also by the government's handling of the situation. The shortcomings of the administration, in terms of management of the state and the reduction of expenditure, left few options for the reduction of the deficit. These failings were paid for by the taxpayer, with ever-increasing demands being placed on ever-decreasing incomes. Public sentiment was increasingly furious at wave after wave of tax hikes, with no end in sight. The measures taken in the autumn of 2011 are indicative of this trend.[3]

To ensure that receipts were issued for the procurement of goods and services (ensuring the payment of VAT), the government established a system whereby tax rebates would be tied to the receipts submitted by the taxpayer. The system was not calculated correctly and resulted in the loss of tax receipts amounting to €1.4 billion. In order to balance this mistake, a reduction in the tax-free bracket was discussed. At the same time, MPs' concern for those at the lower end of the income scale led to the establishment of a social solidarity contribution on higher incomes. This measure did not, however, make up for the shortfall, so the contribution was extended to a four-year period, rather than the annual scheme originally conceived. Despite this extension, the tax receipts were still insufficient. The tax-free bracket was reduced, even though the solidarity contribution had originally been established to avoid this. The recession increased the fall in receipts. In an effort to bolster revenue, a new tax was imposed on real estate, dubbed the *Harachi*, after the harsh land tax imposed on Christians in the Ottoman Empire. This was supposed to be limited to just one year, but it was quickly extended to two. Initially, this *Harachi* was collected through the electricity bill, so if any household failed to pay the tax, the electricity would be cut off. However, the Supreme Court for Administrative Affairs ruled that tying the provision of electricity to the payment of tax was unconstitutional. For weeks, confusion continued as the Ministry of Finance did not respond to the ruling. At the same time, there were other taxes on real estate which remained uncollected (ETAK – Uniform

Duties on Real Estate – for 2009 and 2010). Finally, the original measure taken to guarantee the collection of VAT receipts was withdrawn, and replaced by a new system which removed any exemption in tax liabilities and increased administrative complexity.

This brief example does much to highlight the cause of growing public exasperation and protest. Throughout the autumn of 2011, demonstrations, strikes, occupations of public buildings and workplaces, and clashes between the police and demonstrators became virtually daily occurrences. Public and private sector employees, in education, law, health care, municipal services, haulage and transport, all sought to fight reforms affecting their industries. Many felt their 'fundamental rights' were being withdrawn with the pro-grammes of reform. This resistance inevitably impeded structural reforms. The protest of every social group was widely accepted and legitimised by the emerging public narrative, disillusioned and critical as it was of every new austerity measure.

Public opinion was framed by the chaotic dynamic so evident across the country, the paralysed state apparatus and a governing party that had lost both its cohesion and its credibility. The attempt to deregulate the taxi market indicates just how deep the division between government and electorate had become. After fierce clashes with taxi owners, the government finally put forward a proposal for the regulation of the industry. After the summer Cabinet reshuffle, the plan was rejected. An alternative proposal was submitted, resulting in renewed clashes at the peak of the tourist season. Subsequently, the second plan was suspended. On 1 September 2011, the Prime Minister again gave 'the green light' to the responsible minister to 'proceed immediately on the front with the taxi owners in order to answer the Troika's criticisms on delays'.[4] However, no further action was actually taken till after the formation of a new government, in November. The new government then retreated, agreeing with the representatives of the sector to a limited deregulation of the market in order to put an end to the matter.

The above examples go a little way towards showing the systemic and repeated failings of the government. Inadequate planning and a complete failure in terms of diligent preparation were characteristic of every piecemeal attempt at reform. Each attempt would be driven by the singular focus on one of the Troika's stipulations, but was neither considered in context, nor assessed for feasibility or fallout. Explanation and public information were never satisfactory; nor did any official statements appear to carry conviction or confidence. Often fearing the public backlash, no government official would even attempt to defend or justify any reforms, framing them as prescriptions of the Troika, over which they had no room for manoeuvre. In this context it is no wonder that the programme of reform never received the public support it needed. Media criticism of the government's handling of the crisis, even from outlets that supported the administration, was widespread. Reports highlighted the lack of coordination between ministers, their unwillingness to defend the government position and the complete absence of constructive or coherent discussions regarding the political management of the situation.[5] The principal obstacle to any substantive progress in combating the crisis was the failure of the Greek government to conceive a credible counter-proposal to the Memorandum, one that would not be tainted by any association with the Memorandum but would make clear the necessity of certain targets, designed to provide a significant stimulus to the Greek economy and return the country to growth. Not only might such a plan be able to reverse some of the damage from years of obligatory austerity but, if well constructed, it could also return a little leverage to the Greek government in its negotiations with the Troika. Greece, however, did not make any contributions to the European discussion on growth, despite the utmost relevance of the matter to Greek interests. Hellenic requests focused on little more than the introduction of eurobonds: nothing more than further borrowing to pay off sovereign debt.

In mid-October discussion of another attempt at a cross-party consensus between PASOK and New Democracy emerged in the media. A meeting between the two leaders, George Papandreou and Antonis Samaras, took place a little before an upcoming European summit. However, rather than promoting reconciliation, the talks aggravated the rift between the two. The Prime Minister proposed to Samaras that they go to Brussels together, a first step in a broader convergence; however, Samaras was offended by the absence of a formal role for himself. The leader of the opposition refused, because the government had not made him aware of the pending negotiations and national objectives had not been drawn up. These talks were political gamesmanship, designed to create the impression of consensus. They were a failure in all respects.

For the members of the Eurozone, the Greek problem was now a secondary concern to the more pressing matter of securing funds for the EFSF and determining how it would function. It had been agreed at the previous summit that the Facility would have €440 billion at its disposal. Many felt, though, that this was insufficient to ensure it could act as bulwark against the contagion of the crisis. Support for Ireland and Portugal had already reduced the capital reserves of the Facility. Should Italy require comparable support, the Facility would prove wholly insufficient. Through various measures to augment its capacity, the Facility was to be increased to €1 trillion. The proposals included member states granting guarantees, borrowing from the ECB and the acquisition of capital on the markets. The debate over the expansion of the EFSF took place against the background of the long-established concerns over access to liquidity, a lack of faith in the markets and issues of both credibility and exposure in the banking sector.

The President of France, Nicolas Sarkozy, and the Chancellor of Germany, Angela Merkel, met on 9 October in Berlin to develop a mutually acceptable solution to these concerns. No substantive progress was made. In a common statement they indicated they would continue discussions aimed at achieving an all-encompassing and sustainable strategy for the recapitalisation of European banks and the fiscal union of the Eurozone. As to the Greek problem, both sides agreed to wait for the Troika's report on the sustainability of the debt before taking any further actions. The European summit scheduled for the middle of the month was postponed until 23 October.

The meeting between Merkel and Sarkozy, and those that would follow, marked a significant shift in the style of discussion of the major European challenges. Negotiations between member states, often conducted away from the limelight, and usually with the involvement of one or more EU institutions, were replaced by public deliberations between the leaders of the two most powerful countries of the Union. EU institutions and other member states were increasingly called upon to express their opinion, or voice their concerns, only after the major deliberations had taken place.

German and French views differed considerably. France felt that the EFSF should take the form of a bank and be financed directly by the ECB. This would bypass the prohibition of the ECB financing member states. Both Germany and the ECB disagreed. France then proposed that the ECB should provide guarantees for the EFSF so that it could acquire capital directly from the markets, so that the €1 trillion figure could be secured. Germany disagreed, viewing the matter of the recapitalisation of banks as a sovereign affair, for which each member state must bear its own responsibility. In contrast, France wanted recapitalisation to be effected through European institutions, very aware that the exposure of the French banking sector to Greek debt could pose a significant risk to France's international credit rating. Furthermore, the two countries fundamentally disagreed over the scale of any haircut of Greek debt. Germany favoured a figure as high as 50%, while, due to the exposure mentioned above, France was anxious it should not exceed 21%.

That the Eurozone had not managed to construct a mutually acceptable solution did little to inspire public confidence. Indecision and inertia from the European political elite had allowed the crisis to spread. It now posed a major risk to both Spain and Italy, not to mention the increasingly global ramifications of such a sustained downturn in the world's largest single market. A former President of the European Commission, Jacques Delors, observed that 'the euro is on the brink of the abyss'.[6] Throughout October, the institutions of the Eurozone as well as those of the EU strove to reach the 'all-encompassing strategy' which they had failed to determine in the March and July summits.

## Notes

1 See the Troika report on Greek debt, *European Economy: The Economic Adjustment Programme for Greece. Fifth Review, October 2011*, Occasional Paper 87, European Commission, October 2011.
2 *Le Monde*, 6 October 2011, p. 18.
3 See Y. Pretenteris, *To Vima*, 16 October 2011, p. A61.

4   *Kathimerini*, 1 September 2011, p. 1.
5   See for example: *To Vima*, 9 October 2011, p. A8; *Ta Nea*, 15–16 October 2011, p. 20. The headlines are typical: 'Few are trying to pull the cart out of the mud', 'Co-ordination has disappeared … into the rubbish bin', 'The appearance of government paralysis a headache for the government'.
6   *Le Monde*, 19 October 2011, p. 18.

# 16

# The new solution

Despite six hours of negotiations, negligible progress was made at the Euro-group meeting on 3 October 2011. The only tangible progress was with regard to guarantees on Finnish loans made to Greece. The ministers agreed that Finland had a right to demand guarantees. 'Collateral' would consist of AAA-rated bonds, which would be gradually deposited in a special account. Greece's request for the release of the pending instalment (due in September) was rejected. It would be reviewed after the Troika had submitted its quarterly report on the progress with the Memorandum reforms. Finally, it was agreed that the EFSF funds would be augmented through 'leveraging'.[1]

On 4 October the Council of General Affairs (bringing together the EU's foreign ministers) approved the compromise reached with the European Parliament regarding the reform of the framework for economic governance. These reforms strengthened the rules of fiscal discipline, and were designed to ensure the continued reduction of the deficit and debt of member states. The Council also approved the supervision of the economic policy of all countries, in order to avert and limit macroeconomic imbalances.[2] This was a step that Germany had proposed in February, to monitor economic developments across the Union in a more coordinated and efficient way.

Rumour and speculation grew that France and Germany were preparing a 'Plan B', which might entail Greece exiting the Eurozone. Intense negotiations were taking place, to which Greece had not been invited. Greek requests for involvement in the talks were rejected. The Greeks were informed that the discussion pertained to the whole Eurozone, rather than any specific country. The Prime Minister visited the President of the European Council, Herman Van Rompuy, to voice his anger at this exclusion. This meeting, presented as an important one, did not result in any reversal of Greece's exclusion.

On 20 October, Nicolas Sarkozy visited Angela Merkel in Frankfurt, in a last effort to resolve their differences before the summit on 23 October. Yet again they did not manage to reach a consensus. The EU summit would go ahead, as Sarkozy wanted, but no major decision would be taken, at the insistence of Merkel.

They would seek conclusive agreements in a second summit of the Eurozone member states, to be held on 26 October. A French negotiator commented on developments: 'We are on the brink of the abyss'. President Barack Obama spoke with both leaders, highlighting increasing risks to the American economy that such ongoing indecision posed.

The summits were held in an extremely tense climate. In France it was widely observed that Europe needed fresh impetus. The principal concern was to guarantee the safety of the euro, once deemed the 'key to success' for Europe. The currency was no longer the flagship of integration it had been. Nevertheless, its health was the 'prerequisite for the orderly functioning of the EMU'. But how Europe functioned in terms of coherence and solidarity was also very important. All this had to be re-examined 'if we want to stop the fire and rebuild the house at the same time'.[3]

In a speech she gave to the Bundestag, Chancellor Merkel spoke of the 'greatest crisis in Europe since World War II ... if the euro fails, the European Union will also fail'.[4]

The discussions at the EU summit on 23 October covered little more than the Union's economic policy. Priority was given to the single market and the creation of jobs, a reduction in administrative costs, fiscal policy, structural reforms, energy, research and innovation. The measures to strengthen economic governance were recapitulated once again. These were the Europe 2020 strategy, the European Semester, the Euro Plus Pact and the 'package of six legal acts'. All were designed 'to achieve new and better coordination and a higher degree of supervision'. These aims and frameworks were merely the ratification of policies that had already been agreed.[5]

More fundamental concerns were addressed at the Eurozone summit on 26 October. The meeting began at 6 p.m. and ended a little before 4 a.m. It was interrupted at 0.44 a.m., after which negotiations continued between Merkel, Sarkozy, the head of the IMF, Christine Lagarde, and the President of the Council, Van Rompuy, in the privacy of his office. They were mainly deliberating on how a restructuring of Greek debt through a 50% cut might be operationalised. The Greek representatives were present for parts of the discussion. Reports in the German media indicated that, despite the importance of these talks to the Greek side, there appeared to be little enthusiasm for them on the part of the Greek government, which was subsequently 'removed' from the discussions.[6] Lagarde played a pivotal role in all progress made at the summit. At a parallel meeting at a lower level, the technical advisers of the Greek delegation were excluded. A member of the delegation commented that 'They are sick of us in Europe. They are tired of dealing with Greece.'

The release of the sixth instalment to Greece was finally approved. The European Commission was assigned to set up a panel of experts to help the Greek implement the necessary reforms.

Private sector involvement was considered vital to ensure Greek sovereign debt could become sustainable. Greece and members of the private sector were called upon to agree to a voluntary exchange of bonds. This would entail a reduction in the nominal value of the bonds held by private investors by 50%. The agreement was designed to cover virtually all existing Greek bonds, unlike the one reached on 21 July, which limited itself to bonds maturing before 2020. Member states would contribute €30 billion to limit, to a degree, the losses to the bondholders. The bond exchange was scheduled to take place during the early months of 2012.

The member states agreed to provide Greece with an additional €100 billion, to ease liquidity concerns until 2014. This figure was calculated with sufficient capital for the recapitalisation of the Greek banking sector. The conditions of the loan and the obligations to be placed on Greece were to be agreed by the end of 2011. The new bailout package would inevitably entail a new adjustment programme, with revised macroeconomic and fiscal targets, and would specify the necessary structural measures and privatisation. This second Memorandum would replace the first and would be, after its acceptance by the Greek Parliament, the determining factor for relations between Greece and the Eurozone. This support for Greece was a 'solution of an extraordinary and unique nature', and would not set a precedent for other ailing EMU member states to follow. The new adjustment programme would be combined with increased oversight and greater direct involvement in financial management. European Commission personnel already present in Greece would be bolstered for this purpose.

According to the agreement, the objective of the EFSF was to provide support to member states encountering difficulties in accessing capital on sustainable terms and to help stabilise the international bond markets. The EFSF required access to the highest possible credit rating to ensure its ability to do so. Two choices were approved for leveraging EFSF funds: either it could issue CDS to private investors buying bonds on the primary market, or it could combine ways of financing third parties through private and state financing institutions issuing securities to be sold on the market.

The member states calculated that through such a mechanism the EFSF would be able to raise approximately €1 trillion. The IMF, which had already indicated its intention to support any efforts to counter the growing Eurozone crisis, would also be available to provide further capital if required.

It was deemed necessary to recapitalise the banking sector to satisfy the regulatory framework regarding the capital ratio.[7] This target would have to be met by 30 June 2012, once the level of exposure to the restructuring of the debt had been ascertained. The decision underlined the states' intention to bolster coordination of their economic and fiscal policy, as well as to strengthen centralised supervision of management and compliance in this sphere. The need to improve 'the governance of the Eurozone' and to promote economic convergence[8] was stressed in no uncertain terms.

However, the European Council's arrangements were not sufficient to satisfy the targets set for Greece. The target had been a reduction in Greek debt to

120% of GDP by 2020, a figure considered sustainable. The 50% cut did not guarantee such a result. As a consequence, the targets for reductions in expenditure and increases in revenue still remained very high. The restructuring of the debt was not the only measure to reverse Greece's fortunes; much was still expected of internal efforts. A member of the Greek Ministry of Finance made this quite apparent: 'this will be a decade of discipline and control'. It was widely noted, however, that 'in the early hours of Thursday, Greece bought time'.[9] Given the gravity of the situation, and the difficulty of the challenges, the results had been satisfactory. It provided sufficient respite for Greece, so it might have the opportunity to improve its economic performance and negotiate from an improved position at a later date.[10]

Despite the above-mentioned achievements of the summit, it was not received well in all quarters. Within the banking sector, many felt that the size of the cut in liabilities was excessive. Initially, discussions had indicated that the imposition of an involuntary haircut upon the holders of Greek bonds would constitute a 'credit event' for the markets, and there was fear of the inevitable fallout. Chancellor Merkel indicated that the 50% cut was the only and last offer by the Eurozone and the Greek administration was far from happy with such an ultimatum. Within a space of an hour, however, differences were overcome. The banks were persuaded to support the proposal and agreement was reached. However, significant technical details, such as the rate of interest on the new bonds from the bond exchange, their duration, the possibility of a period of grace or the requirement for guarantees of the sort previously demanded by Finland and Slovakia had not been covered in the agreement. These matters were, yet again, to be clarified at a later date.

The details of how the EFSF would function also remained unclear. The French President wanted 'a big bazooka', with sufficient capital at its disposal to deter speculation against member states. However, there remained widespread cynicism that the EFSF would prove adequate to serve its purpose. According to the French, it would have the ability to raise in excess of €1 trillion. Other countries doubted this. The French proposal to turn the EFSF into a bank with unlimited access to capital from the ECB was widely rejected.

The agreement reached at the summit was more detailed on its terms regarding the recapitalisation of the banks. According to an announcement by the European Banking Authority (EBA), €106.5 billion was needed to strengthen 21 European banks. The banks were now obliged to secure this figure under the supervision of the EBA. They could also secure guarantees from the EFSF to borrow from the markets. After the decision, most of the heads of the banks indicated that they would secure private funds to undertake this recapitalisation. Some of them expressed their displeasure at imposed restrictions on their capacity to grant loans, as a result of this obligatory recapitalisation, citing the negative fallout this would have upon liquidity in European economies.

Developments in Italy preoccupied the leadership of the EU. The Italian Prime Minister, Silvio Berlusconi, submitted a letter detailing measures to be taken to counter the alarming developments in the third largest economy of the Eurozone. However, the measures were not considered satisfactory. Chancellor Merkel and President Sarkozy, in a 'discussion between friends', reminded the Italian Prime Minister that he would have to honour his commitments. States at risk of punitive rates from the markets, they stressed, could not delay balancing their budgets.

Euphoria prevailed after the summit. Merkel announced that a step had been taken towards greater stability, towards a stable Union. However, no one should have expected that all the problems would be solved in one moment. The German Minister of Finance highlighted the strategic character of the agreement: 'We are building a new institutional structure for the Eurozone, which will ensure more Europe and more stability. We have a long way to go in solving all the problems. But the probabilities of success are, after the last decisions, greater.'[11] According to the French government, Sarkozy had led Europe on the road to responsibility. US President Obama hailed the agreement.

The markets also reacted positively. Prices rose on stock exchanges, the euro reached its highest level for 2011, while rates of interest available to the EMU's ailing nations fell. The international media were positive in their analysis of the agreement, drawing attention to the convergence in the policy preferences of the member states of the Eurozone.

The Greek Prime Minister, George Papandreou, described the results as extremely significant, and stressed that the Brussels decisions had vindicated the sacrifices that had been made in Greece over the last two years. In line with established partisan division, the opposition rejected the decisions in their entirety. They spoke of a decade of austerity and failed to mention that before the restructuring of the debt the period of austerity had been anticipated to last twice as long. Yet again, the criticism was based on unsupported claims and unrealistic premises and the focus was on public relations activities and political gamesmanship. Public opinion remained divided in Greece. For months, both the government and the opposition had framed the notion of debt restructuring in absolute terms: it had been an evil to avoid at all costs. It is not hard to understand how public opinion remained sceptical in face of claims of great success. At the extremities of the political spectrum, the agreement was seen to be a direct assault on national sovereignty. It was felt that 'national sovereignty has been torn to shreds' and it was an insult that 'Greece has been placed under supervisory control'. Neither PASOK nor New Democracy drew attention to the fact that membership of the EMU had already transferred wide-ranging sovereign competencies to the European institutions a long time before.

The summits of both the EU and the EMU, on 23 and 26 October respectively, demonstrated the shift in impetus now directing political action. Efforts to combat the Eurozone crisis were being directed entirely by Germany and France. The European Commission played an extremely limited part. This downgrading of the role of the Commission did not conform to EU norms and procedures for policy direction. Such a trend was not well received by the smaller nations of the EU, which felt the Commission provided a bulwark against domination by the key nations of the Union. As was becoming increasingly apparent, however, Europe was now being directed by those making the largest contributions to countering the crisis.

At the European summits, there was clearly divergence emerging between those inside the EMU and the other members of the EU. The latter were not entitled to participate actively in EMU summits, despite the clear ramifications any deliberations would have for the broader EU. A two-tier Union was thus being formed, with the Eurozone constituting its central nucleus. The Polish Prime Minister, who was presiding over the EU for the second half of 2011, did not attend the Eurozone summit, but observed that this fragmentation lacked logic and that the unity of the Union must be fortified.

While the summit and the subsequent agreement clearly marked significant and substantive progress, it did not provide the 'all-encompassing solution' many sought. It quickly became apparent that the agreement raised a range of new problems. The scale of Greek debt was underestimated. Consequently, the restructuring should have provided a greater cut, to ensure the country could return to the markets on sustainable terms. The reduction in debt through the private sector involvement, even if debt were to reach a level of 120% of GDP by 2020, which was doubtful, did not ensure sustainable debt. The agreement did not make substantive efforts to stimulate growth in Greece. Most economic analysts concluded that a further agreement would be inevitable; it was merely a matter of time.

Discussion over the EFSF continued, as doubt grew over its ability to meet its mandate. Uncertainty remained as to whether it would be able to counter a major crisis in Spain or Italy. The EFSF did not have the mechanisms at its disposal to provide unlimited capital as it saw fit, such as those possessed by the Bank of England or the US Federal Reserve. The questions regarding exposure to a liquidity crisis remained, should neither the markets nor fellow member states be willing to provide support; the EFSF was not 'the lender of last resort'.

The summit made clear that the leading states of the Eurozone did not wish to commit to any long-term common economic planning. There was no coherent effort to address the root cause of turmoil in the EMU, namely divergence in levels of economic development and the structural imbalances this drove. A substantive effort to provide closure to the crisis would have provided a long-term mechanism for support of the Periphery, addressed the need for a common fiscal policy and provided a coordinated approach to concerns about competitiveness and growth. Instead, the leaders limited themselves to the pursuit of permanent and stable fiscal discipline. For the stability of the Eurozone to be achieved, the perennial questions of coherence and competence needed to be addressed. The partial political unification of the Eurozone was needed.[12]

## Notes

1 'Eurozone postpones Greek loan, agrees on collateral', *EurActiv*, 6 February 2012. Leveraging is the ability to ensure funds beyond those whose repayment is guaranteed by the paid-in capital, which, in the case of the EFSF, was anything beyond €440 billion.
2 Council of the European Union, 14998, Presse 344.
3 'Le sursaut ou le chaos', *Le Monde*, 26 October 2011, p. 1.
4 *FAZ*, 27 October 2011, p. 1.
5 European Council, 23 October 2011, Conclusions, EUCO 52/1/11 Rev. 1, CO Eur 17, Concl. 5.
6 *FAZ*, 28 October 2011, p. 3.
7 That is, their capital must cover at least 9% of its liabilities.
8 The decision also determined the structure of the Eurozone's organs: (1) the Euro Working Group was to be responsible for the preparatory work, and its operations were of a defining nature; (2) the ministers of finance would also attend the Eurogroup and would have their own president; (3) the European summit would be presided over by a permanent president, elected by the leaders. It would convene at least twice a year.
9 V. Zeras, *Kathimerini*, 29–30 October 2012, p. 4.
10 L. Feld, one of the five members of the Economic Council of Experts that was advising the German government, said in an interview he gave to *Kathimerini*, 13 November 2011, p. 10: 'I believe there will be a renegotiation of Greek debt next year'.
11 *Der Spiegel*, issue 44, 2011, p. 30.
12 A. Greenspan, *Financial Times*, 7 October 2011, p. 9.

# 17

# Political games with unpredictable consequences

Immediately upon his return from Brussels on 31 October, the Prime Minister announced his decision to the PASOK parliamentary group to hold a referendum over the agreement of 26 October. He did not specify with any precision what the terms of the referendum would be, but he said that all Greeks should decide on whether to accept the decisions of the summit. In the Cabinet meeting held the next day, he indicated what was at stake with this vote: 'yes or no to the deal, yes or no to Europe, yes or no to the euro'.[1]

This decision took public opinion by surprise. It was, however, a move that had been conceived some time prior to the announcement. The Minister of the Interior had repeatedly referred to the value of a referendum and had already ensured the passage of relevant legislation. He had already announced that 'the question to be formulated shall be about the fundamental interests of the Greek people, in view of the current economic and fiscal situation'.[2] A university professor and adviser to the Prime Minister had already undertaken public discussions concerning the formulation of possible questions for a referendum. The intention was obvious. The Prime Minister wanted to use a referendum to recapture his waning support and renew his mandate, or at least isolate himself from the political costs of further reform. Through approval of the country's membership of the EMU he sought approval of his own power, by extension. He wanted a misleadingly simple question to ask for support for the European path, or outright rejection, hoping the former would provide him with renewed political legitimacy and impetus. Anxiety quickly grew in his close political circle. What would happen should such support not be forthcoming? Would the Prime Minister tender his resignation, or would he continue to exercise his power despite the fallout such a vote would inevitably provoke?

In assessing their preferences with regard to a referendum, the electorate's voting is determined by government approval ratings and the socioeconomic context in which the vote is to take place. These conditions are far more causally significant to the voting behaviour of the electorate than the terms of the question. The rejection of the European Constitution by the French and Dutch electorates in 2005 were due in no small part to domestic climate and context. In both these cases, voters wanted to express their dissatisfaction with their prime ministers and governments.

In light of these realities, a referendum in Greece's current climate was a huge risk. A decisive rejection of the Memorandum could have led the country to bankruptcy and exit from the EMU and the EU. It could also raise comparable debates in the creditor nations of the EMU regarding the democratic endorsement of support for the Periphery. If Greece was to have the opportunity to vote on whether it accepted the support, were other nations not entitled to vote on whether they wished to provide it? Any comparable referenda in Core nations would be likely to return negative results. This could lead to the withdrawal of all support from Greece.[3] The Dutch Labour Party, for example, announced that it would vote against the agreement of 26 October when it came before the Dutch Parliament for approval if Greece proceeded with holding a referendum.

The Prime Minister's announcement provoked intense reactions both at home and abroad. Sources inside the Greek government claimed that Greece's partners had been previously informed about the proposal and no problems would arise. But the reactions of Germany and France proved this was not the case. Representatives of Merkel and Sarkozy made it clear in no uncertain terms that the agreement of 26 October in Brussels was a final and non-negotiable offer for Greece. Neither France nor Germany had been previously informed of the Greek Prime Minister's intentions. Both nations indicated they wished to proceed with the agreement as soon as possible.[4]

To ensure this was done a meeting was scheduled for Wednesday 2 November in Cannes, with Sarkozy, Merkel, the head of the European Council, the European Commission, the IMF and the Prime Minister Papandreou.[5] It was quickly made public that, despite the decisions taken at the summit, no further funding would be released, in light of the Greek government's discussion of a referendum. That is, the next instalment, initially scheduled for release in September, would still not be released.

Domestic criticism was intense and internal division within PASOK grew. The Prime Minister was asked 'why he was setting a question, one prong of which would lead to an exit from the euro and Europe, a closed question not raised by anyone today'.[6] New Democracy announced it would not engage in 'such adventurism'. The press described the decision as incomprehensible: 'How is it possible that the Prime Minister wants to ask the citizens about a supranational decision which he has already accepted as a solution…?'[7] Commentators highlighted that the Prime Minister had 'managed to inflict a very strong blow, that could even be the knock-out one, to any credibility Greece may have had left'.[8] However, the Prime Minister stood firm on his decision. He attacked the media for rabidly reacting against the referendum and claimed their stand served vested interests, in particular those of the banks, which were against the agreement of 26 October. He had now, in public at least, completely forgotten that he himself had previously been hostile to any debt restructuring.

In Cannes, the Greek delegation met a hostile reception. President Sarkozy and Chancellor Merkel expressed their surprise and anger as to why they had not been informed on 26 October of the Prime Minister's intentions. They demanded that the question of the referendum be one and only one: yes or no to Greece remaining in the Eurozone. Both underlined that the matter of a referendum must be settled by 4 December, and not in January, as the Greek government had indicated. The next instalment of the bailout would be released only if and when all preconditions of the Memorandum were satisfied, and upon the return of a positive vote in the referendum. Germany and France indicated they were not prepared to discuss again what had already been agreed. The Greeks would have to decide whether they would continue the adventure with the EU or not, since they had invoked Union solidarity. They also stated that a broader political consensus was necessary in Greece, like that in Portugal and Spain.

On the flight back, Papandreou continued to think that it was possible to hold a referendum. Evangelos Venizelos, the Finance Minister, disagreed. After their arrival at 4.45 a.m. he made his disagreement public in a written statement: 'Greece's position within the euro constitutes a historic conquest for the country that cannot be placed in doubt. This vested benefit the Greek people have acquired may not depend on the outcome of a referendum.' After this public statement, it looked increasingly unlikely the Prime Minister had sufficient political support, at home or abroad, to hold a referendum. At midday, on Thursday 3 November, Antonis Samaras, leader of the opposition, made clear that he would vote in favour of the loan agreement and requested the formation of an interim government. That afternoon, in his speech to his parliamentary group, Papandreou hailed the fact that New Democracy would vote in favour of the loan agreement. He expressed objections to the proposal for an immediate interim government, but indicated it was a matter that had to be discussed, along with the question of whether elections should be held. He concluded: 'In any case, I at least am glad, even if we do not hold a referendum, which in any case was not an end in itself'.[9] This was an acknowledgement that his original plan had to be abandoned. The same evening in Parliament, he repeated that he was not insistent on holding a referendum, and that he was willing to discuss the formation of an interim government with New Democracy, even if that meant losing the premiership. The response was positive, both at home and abroad, but comments on how the matter had been handled were widely critical. Commentaries pointed out that great damage had been done to Greece's already lamentable international standing and credibility. The Prime Minister rejected this analysis 'as if it were nothing.... As if all the things that had happened over three days were figments of our imagination, that they had only happened ... in the minds of Sarkozy, Merkel and all the other Europeans.'[10]

The story of the referendum thus came to an end and the curtain went up on the next show: the formation of a coalition government. That same evening, in a vote of confidence, the government won the necessary majority. PASOK would thus take the principal role in the formation of a new government.

The new administration needed to be formed in as expedient a fashion as was possible, so the country could regain the capacity to deliberate with its partners in a climate of mutual trust. However, this did not happen. It took five days to select the new Prime Minister. During this period both parties provoked public anxiety and exasperation and compounded the deteriorating image Greece had abroad. The headlines and reports in the newspapers were widely critical: horse trading on the *Titanic*; the country is sinking and the politicians are engaged only in their party interests, their entirely personal ambitions and traditional cleavages. Foreign correspondents in Athens commented that one day an agreement was concluded, the next day it was cancelled and on the third day nobody knew where the country, in a state of paralysis, was headed.[11] Papandreou was putting forward for Prime Minister individuals totally unsuitable for the job, on the basis of his personal preferences. Samaras sought to manipulate the situation to his own political gain, advocating snap elections that would inevitably favour the opposition. Political positioning and partisan conflict continued in spite of the realisation there was not the slightest room for their usual little games. Citizens drew the conclusion that despite the patriotic veneer under which it was hiding its pursuits, the political system was incapable of rising to the occasion.[12]

On 10 November 2011 Lucas Papademos, formerly Governor of the Bank of Greece when the country entered the EMU, and Vice President of the ECB for many years, was selected to be the new Prime Minister. He was the most qualified person to handle the country's economic challenges. Three parties would participate in the government, PASOK, New Democracy and the right-wing group Popular Orthodox Rally (LAOS). Partisan opportunism yet again prevailed in the formation of the new government. Ultimately, 50 ministers and junior ministers participated in the government, a counterproductive number and totally incompatible with the mantra of a reduction in public expenditure.

The parties decided that their mandate would principally be the implementation of the summit agreement of 26 October. As such, the administration was to be known as a 'special-purpose government'. As to elections, a specific date was not agreed upon; initially, New Democracy had wanted them to be held on 19 February 2012. However, agreement was reached that elections must be deferred until the aims of the government had been achieved. Critics argued that only with elections could political stability be ensured. However, those arguing for a focus on the economic concerns asserted that stability could be ensured through a longer-term Papademos administration.

In his policy statement, the new Prime Minister detailed the actions required to 'implement the decisions taken on 26 October and the application of the economic policy associated with these decisions', and stressed the need to improve competitiveness through structural reforms. With its predecessor having failed to implement the decisions of 21 July, the vote of confidence in the new government renewed the effort to control debt and stabilise the Greek economy.

The PASOK government under Papandreou had failed massively in its attempt to control the economic crisis in the country and to set the economy on course for recovery. The EU contributed significantly to these shortcomings, through indecision and miscalculation. However, the government must take the brunt of the blame. It repeatedly proved that it was not up to the task. When PASOK took office, the adverse economic climate was widely recognised. The leadership of PASOK remained in a state of denial for far too long. At no point did it construct a comprehensive strategy to manage or combat the crisis. It made no effort to combine the necessary stabilising measures with the structural changes to improve competitiveness; nor did it seek to promote investments through the European Structural Funds. Its focus may have been on the demands of Memorandum, but it did not do this with competence or conviction. In negotiations it did not present any substantive analysis worthy of debate. Its responses were continually reactionary; it never directed events or developments. It focused on utopian demands, such as the unlimited issue of eurobonds.

This behaviour was rooted in the norms and practices cultivated in PASOK under Papandreou. The party focused on public relations activities, in an effort to maintain popular support and retain power. The assurances during the 2009 election campaign that 'the money is there' was an indicative example of such spin. All the Prime Minister's actions were presented as important, successful and pioneering, regardless of how true such claims ever were.

The government repeatedly claimed that changes that had not been made in the preceding three decades were finally being made. It portrayed its reforms as the most ground-breaking Greece had seen in that time frame. The Prime Minister claimed that the government had changed the Greek mentality through its efforts. Such extreme hyperbole was self-defeating. The Emir of Qatar was depicted as Greece's saviour, and was anticipated to invest billions, but disappeared when he became sceptical of such repeated exaggerations. Citizens were kept in the dark, and when analysis was presented it was often contradictory. Regurgitated grandiose claims left the public disillusioned and disheartened.

The Greek government lacked organisation in its deliberations with the EU. Staff across the Troika, assigned to help Greece in the efforts to reverse the country's fortunes, became very disillusioned with their Greek counterparts. Frustration was widespread at the perennial lack of preparation, open division within delegations and the entire absence of any long-term vision or coherence demonstrated by Greek representatives, time and time again.[13] Representatives of other government ministries confirmed that the Ministry of Finance refused to provide an official stance or policy preference prior to meetings with the Troika; nor did it take advice or request data from other salient ministries. It was more preoccupied with its internal division. In its discussions with the

Troika, the Ministry of Finance contributed little more than ad hoc policy formulations. The entire ministry was seemingly devoid of any notions of unity or coordination.

The civil servants working throughout the Greek ministries, despite their best intentions and ability, lacked the experience and expertise to deal with a crisis of this magnitude and complexity. Their counterparts in the European Commission, Germany, France and other countries had been through countless negotiations, and had experience of both the EU structures and the staff and representatives across the Union and its member states. Greece fundamentally lacked intellectual or political capital at this level.[14] The permanent Greek delegation in Brussels, despite its experience and expertise, was rarely involved in any discussions with the Ministry of Finance.

The power structure under the Greek premiership was centralised to an unprecedented degree but the Prime Minister lacked the expertise to oversee such a top-down administration. Despite this, he did not assemble a Cabinet with sufficient ability or experience in financial matters. Initially, he did not even consider close cooperation with the EU necessary. He believed that with the support of the USA he would be able to address the crisis in isolation from his continental counterparts. Greece sought advice from US advisers, but they either were ignorant of the intricacies of European politics or were unsure how to translate their advice into operable policies to counter the Hellenic crisis.[15] Papandreou collected views and advice on an unstructured and ad hoc basis. There was no continuity in policy or preference. His advisers, unprecedented in number, made up various factional groups and provided conflicting and counterproductive advice. This was detrimental to Papandreou's relations with the other members of the EMU. The Prime Minister preferred direct personal deliberation with his European counterparts to structured and ongoing talks between officials. However, as was proven time and time again, the coming to-gether of heads of state, while it might provide newspaper headlines and photo opportunities, could make little progress without the painstaking groundwork and preparation that Greece simply did not undertake.[16]

The activities of the various ministries lacked centralised coordination and supervision. The Cabinet was a thoroughly disorganised entity. Papandreou's close advisers, regardless of whether they held a Cabinet position, or possessed sufficient experience or expertise, held the Prime Minister's ear. Decisions were taken in a small circle, rarely though the same circle, and predominately behind closed doors. Dissenting voices were ostracised and long-existing democratic institutional procedures were paid only lip service. Every policy decision or government reform was viewed as a public relations activity, constructed to function as an advertisement for the government; little attention was paid to the course or benefit of any political action after it was taken. Policies were selected on the basis of their political costs, not their tangible value.[17]

Despite the obvious importance of the working relationship between the Bank of Greece and the ECB, in light of the crisis, no effort was made to foster or develop such a relationship. The Greek government, for example, did not involve the Bank of Greece in its crisis management efforts and, as a result, its concerns were not uploaded in the monthly meetings of Eurozone's central bankers.[18]

The government did, though, succeed in reducing the deficit. It reformed the social security system, it took measures to significantly reduce health expenditure and it tried to implement necessary structural reforms. At the same time, however, it tried to minimise the political cost, to appease popular dissent and seek compromise. This inevitably led to delays and the government's involvement in endless confrontations and inefficiency. The abolition or merger of public organisations was one of the first measures to be announced, but after two years of reform results were disappointing. Elements of the privatisation programme did not go ahead. Public opinion quickly lost confidence or faith in reform programmes, as a result of systemic mismanagement. The continual announcement of intentions, the revision of announcements and contradictory statements fuelled anxiety, anger and confusion.

Typical of this confusion was the effort to introduce an electronic tax card, so citizens could register purchases without having to collect numerous paper receipts. The tax card was announced as a major policy, designed to simplify the life of the electorate, but this was before any logistical planning had been undertaken. When the card was finally introduced, it did not fulfil the grandiose claims previously made and it had virtually no impact. Most retail businesses refused to acquire the special terminals for the tax card to work, and most citizens realised that they were encumbered with processes and waiting time when they used it. Taxpayers feared that the amount of their purchases as registered through the tax card could be used against them as proof of income higher than what they had declared. Thus the tax card fell into disuse.

Criticism of the government was dealt with by assigning responsibility for any failures or shortcomings to previous administrations. Such practice simply served to fuel the public perception that politicians were just self-interested and not in a position to respond to the needs of the country. Rejection of politics and politicians was intense and widespread. This impression was compounded by the significant deterioration in the quality of public administration. This deterioration resulted in staff who were both disillusioned and angry. This was not helped by long-term vacancies in key positions and a fundamental lack of centralised oversight or vision.

As a party, PASOK no longer acted as an agent capable of promoting growth or modernisation. The party elite promoted by Papandreou belonged to the old guard of the party, which fiercely opposed modernisation. It was indifferent to the grass roots of PASOK. Members offered the president of the party the support he asked for in exchange for the power which he ceded to them. An inevitable consequence of the decadence of the party was Papandreou's political demise. The fall of the government and the collapse of the party were two dimensions of the same phenomenon: a failure of leadership.

## Notes

1 *Kathimerini*, 9 November 2001.
2 *Kathimerini*, 4 October 2011, p. 1.
3 V. P. Ioakimides, 'The wrong way to take political decisions', *Ta Nea*, 2 November 2011, p. 14.
4 *FAZ*, 2 November 2011, p. 2; 'EU leaders battle to save Greek deal', *Financial Times*, 1 November 2011.
5 The meeting took place on the sidelines of a G20 conference.
6 A. Loverdos, *Kathimerini,* 2 November 2011, p. 3.
7 G. Lakopoulos, *Ta Nea*, 2 November 2011, p. 6.
8 A. Stangos, *Kathimerini*, 2 November 2011, p. 5.
9 *Kathimerini*, 4 November 2001; also www.imerisia.gr, 3 November 2011.
10 Y. Pretenteris, *Ta Nea*, 4 November 2011.
11 Kerin Hope, *Financial Times*, ft.com, 7, 9 and 10 November 2011; *IHT*, 8 November 2011; *Le Monde*, 8 November 2011.
12 S. Polymilis, *To Vima*, 6 November 2011, p. A9.
13 D. Kroustalli wrote the following (*To Vima*, 6 May 2012, p. A14) with regard to negotiations with the Troika in Athens: 'The members of the Troika expected that the Greek government would present a plan with proposals and solutions for the matters arising, on which they would formulate their caveats or would give their approval. Most of the ministers expected the Troika to draw up the plans: "No one assumes responsibility for the reforms" they protested to the Prime Minister.'
14 Yannis Stournaras was the first Minister of Finance since the beginning of the crisis in 2007 to have had first-hand experience of EU negotiations prior to his ministerial appointment in July 2012. This experience had equipped him with better skills to represent the country effectively.
15 See for example Professor Richard Parker's article, 'A personal journey to the heart of Greece's darkness', *Financial Times*, 15 February 2012.
16 See also Chapter 6 on the government's way of negotiating.
17 The Minister of Finance at the time, George Papaconstantinou, described the prevailing conditions in an interview he gave to *Le Monde*, 20 July 2012, p. 11. See also on this T. Pappas, *When the Cat Became Reconciled with the Mouse*, Polis Editions, 2012, pp. 50ff.
18 An example of the lack of understanding between the ECB and the Bank of Greece was the decision to refer the Greek banks to the Emergency Liquidity Assistance (ELA) for their financing requirements in July 2012: the ELA had rather limited capital, which was anyway meant to be used only in emergencies – its purpose was not the recapitalisation of banks.

# Part IV
# Coalition government, private sector involvement and the second Memorandum

# 18

# A flicker of hope

Public opinion welcomed with relief the new coalition government. Opinion polls indicated the new Prime Minister's popularity rating was high. In a vote of confidence on 15 November 2011 the government received 255 votes of support from the 300 Members of Parliament. The climate improved significantly. Demonstrations on the streets of Athens were not as frequent, and violent confrontations with the police subsided. There was hope that, despite the temporary nature of the government, it would be able to improve the situation decisively. The EMU summit's decisions of 26 October had created a framework for the management of the debt. The government could now move quickly to redress Greece's woes. However, anxiety had not been removed entirely. Antagonism between the parties supporting the government was still intense and their willingness to cooperate very limited. They were far more interested in positioning themselves for the elections that would follow.

The European Council detailed the plan for action: negotiations with the Troika and agreement on the content of the new Memorandum; ratification of this second Memorandum by the Greek Parliament and its approval by the Eurogroup; a decision on the recapitalisation of Greek banks; negotiations with lenders and completion of the arrangements for private sector involvement (PSI); and finally parliamentary endorsement of the new Memorandum in other Eurozone nations, as required. Subsequent to the agreement on, and endorsement of, the second Memorandum, further parliamentary and administrative action would have follow in Greece, to foster the required fiscal measures and structural changes mandated in the text. Given the Greek track record on legislation and executive leadership, this would be no small feat. Optimistic analysis anticipated that this could be done by February; however, many remained understandably sceptical that such predictions would prove correct.

The programme required intensive work and left little scope for inertia or delay. Developments in the Eurozone and continued anxiety in the markets continued to pose a risk to the programme of reform and the time frame laid out for its implementation. The delays and shortcomings that had plagued efforts to implement the summit agreement of 21 July presented a clear indication of the difficulties ahead.

By mid-November the government was still working to create suitable conditions for the programme of reform. The sixth instalment of the first loan, approximately €8 billion, initially scheduled for release in September, had been approved by the Troika for release in October. However, the referendum debacle had prevented the release of the instalment. The funds were required by mid-December if Greece was to be able to meet pending liabilities; otherwise, a disorderly default would follow.

A necessary precondition for the release of the instalment and the continued engagement of the EU was the unequivocal acceptance by the leaders of both the government and the main opposition political parties, George Papandreou and Antonis Samaras, of all existing commitments made by Greece. Samaras was less than tactful in this matter and framed such commitments in terms of an assault on 'national dignity'. Multiple heated meetings took place, with lines of conflict being drawn up inside New Democracy. Samaras announced that 'he will not vote in favour of new measures' and he did 'not intend to sign the letter expected by the Eurozone'.[1] There followed meetings between representatives of New Democracy and Commissioner Olli Rehn. Finally, the much-debated text was signed on 21 November.[2] This whole discussion demonstrated how little Greek politicians cared for the substance of the matter; every political interaction was seen as a zero-sum game and an opportunity to score partisan political points. Such narrow-minded political gamesmanship understandably infuriated Greece's European partners.

The budget for 2012, imperative to the success of the reform programme, was voted through by all three coalition parties (New Democracy, PASOK and LAOS). The new budget provided for cuts and increased tax receipts amounting to at least another €11 billion, due to the failure to sufficiently reduce the deficit the previous year. Nevertheless, the government remained optimistic that in 2012 it would be in a position to show significant improvement. However, in January 2012 expenditure had risen above the target fixed by the budget. IKA, Greece's main social security fund, had used 50% of its annual allowance by January.

Two texts detailed the condition of Greece. The first was a report of the Commission's Task Force for Greece, whose mandate was 'to identify and coordinate all the technical assistance Greece needs to implement the EU/IMF the adjustment programme'.[3] It was a detailed record of the challenges encountered in efforts at administrative reform, as well the broader shortcomings of the public sector. It described the great delays in absorbing the funds granted to Greece by the EU for regional development projects. It noted the need for swifter take-up of available funds and improvement in the efficiency of their use. However, its proposals focused on major infrastructural projects and administrative reform. They were of a general nature and did not offer any scheme of action to redress the tumbling Greek administration.[4]

The Task Force had agreed with the Greek government to create, as a top priority, a stable inter-ministerial coordination structure. The Greek government, according to the report, had promised to establish within a few weeks a high-level steering group to supervise and monitor the reforms of the administration. Such a group was never formed. Numerous Greek governments had made efforts to improve coordination between ministries, but without success. The Task Force did not need to reiterate the problem, but rather to make operable proposals as to how to redress it. The report was indicative of the scant understanding among the EU Core nations of the idiosyncrasies of the Greek problem. It followed the mantra that highlighting the problems alone was sufficient and then, once aware of the shortcomings, the government in Athens would quickly be able to redress them. While there was limited recognition of the 'lack of know-how' in Greece, the challenge of political and social change was never given the attention or focus it required.[5]

The other report came from the IMF and was published in December 2011.[6] It was the fifth report from the Fund regarding the progress made by Greece in the efforts at reform. According to this report:

> the economic situation in Greece has taken a turn for the worse, with the economy increasingly adjusting through recession and related wage reduction, rather than through structural reform-driven increases in productivity.... The authorities have taken steps to bring the fiscal program back on track, taking meaningful measures to cut public wages, employment and pensions, and to broaden the tax base.... The new financing strategy can place the program on a sustainable foundation assuming that the PSI [private sector involvement] strategy delivers the targeted gains via near universal participation of creditors.... Still, risks to the program remain large, both from external sources (the worsening outlook for the Euro area), and internal sources (a relapse into weak implementation).[7]

In its analysis of the sustainability of debt, the IMF re-evaluated its former assumptions and concluded that, from now on, predictions should be more conservative. The recession was expected to last longer and be deeper, while growth was predicted not to return before 2013 and then at a rate of only 1.25%. Primary surpluses would fluctuate around the level of 4.5% of GDP, from 2014, and not 6% as had originally been predicted. The return to the markets for capital was not anticipated until 2021, provided Greece had achieved 'three years of growth, three years of primary surpluses and once debt drops below 150% of GDP'. The authors of the report noted that this was a rather arbitrary conclusion, but was presented 'for illustrative purposes' to give an indication of the scale of official support that could be needed to fill any funding gap until market access was restored in 2021.[8]

The report was a reminder of the difficult conditions the country found itself in. It indicated that the agreement of 26 October had done no more than create the opportunity to deal with the crisis. For this to be more than a wasted opportunity, sustained and coherent efforts were required. There was but a flicker of hope.

The government faced two serious obstacles in its efforts. The first was the question of confidence and credibility: Greece commanded very little of either. The second was the question of public fatigue. Greece had been subjected to continued demands for austerity for years now and public opinion was not merely tired of such demands but deeply sceptical they would ever reverse Hellenic fortunes. Disillusionment with reform was widespread and any faith that further austerity would do anything other than deepen the recession was all but gone. Diligent and sustained efforts by the new government did improve Greece's European standing and by the end of February 2012 the government had succeeded in greatly improving international confidence in the country. Domestically, however, the new austerity measures had significantly harmed its public image. The Prime Minister's popularity dropped and by the end of February public opinion was negative in its perception of him, despite progress made in implementing the agreement of 26 October. It was increasingly clear that political efforts were needed to defend and argue for the merits of the European path in the increasingly Eurosceptic Greece. Given its 'technocratic' character, the Papademos government found it increasingly difficult to see out its full term. In Italy, the need for an interim technocratic government, led by Mario Monti, was widely accepted, but not so in Greece.

## Notes

1  *Kathimerini*, 15 November 2011, p. 1.
2  Samaras said that New Democracy intended to bring the matter of the adjustment programme to the fore, 'together with alternative sustainable policies strictly within the framework described in the programme'.
3  Task Force for Greece, *First Quarterly Report*, European Commission, 2011, pp. 2, 7, 15.
4  According to the Greek newspaper *Naftemporiki*, 19 April 2013, p. 3, the Commission indicated in a report published in April 2013 that no other Eurozone nation was as unsuccessful in absorbing EU funds as Greece. The Task Force's advice obviously had not changed the situation.
5  There was, though, an indirect reference to this in the Task Force report: 'The country's fiscal problem is directly related to the sluggish public sector'.
6  *Greece: Fifth Review Under the Stand-By Arrangement*, Country Report No. 11/351, IMF, December 2011.
7  Ibid., p. 1, and see also 'Debt sustainability analysis', p. 64.
8  Ibid., p. 65.

# 19

# Conflicts at the highest European level

Following the October 2011 summit, anxiety over instability in Greece continued to have ramifications across the EU. Italy was looking increasingly exposed to contagion from the crisis, and at risk of a similar exponential rise in borrowing costs. Even though Italy's debt to GDP ratio was 120%, Rome had continued to access the markets at a rate of interest hovering around the 4% mark. However, 2011 saw a rise of two percentage points in this interest rate.[1] Under these terms, its debt was no longer sustainable. Despite urgings from the Union, the Italian government did not take the necessary measures to stabilise its economy. Media speculation mounted concerning the possible need for a restructuring of Italian debt and the possibility that Rome might go the way Athens did. The loss of confidence led to a government crisis and the formation of a new technocratic government in Italy in mid-November. Mario Monti, a former European Commissioner with many years' experience, took the premiership of the new government. He immediately announced drastic measures to reduce Italy's deficit. Analysis widely held that it would take years to return to normal conditions and that the required reforms would inevitably have major social and political costs.

At the same time, international ratings agencies were becoming increasingly anxious over the performance of the French economy. A growing number of discussions were taking place regarding the continuation of France's AAA status. The downgrading of this status would clearly indicate that the crisis had now struck at the heart of the EU and was no longer confined to the peripheral countries. There were growing indications that the crisis was indeed spreading: industrial output had fallen dramatically and the rate of growth had dropped to a level of virtually zero across most of the Union.

Alarm bells went off in the Eurozone. Banks started selling off their sovereign bonds, they avoided subscribing to newly issued bonds by Italy and Spain, and they did not renew their loans to smaller banks. A crisis in liquidity looked increasingly likely. The *International Herald Tribune* noted that 'two years of gross mismanagement of the Eurozone debt crisis have all too predictably produced a wider crisis in market confidence that now threatens the entire 17-nation Eurozone'.[2] In its forecasts of the European economy's performance, the OECD even examined the possibility of default by one of the Core nations of the Union, and underlined that the political repercussions would be dramatic and could lead to a collapse of confidence in the entire European project, as well as deep recession.[3]

Conflicting opinions were voiced across the Union. The Anglo-Saxon analysis levelled much of the criticism at German policy: Berlin ought to have provided much greater assistance to those members of the EMU in a crisis and directed the ECB to take a more central role in the provision of liquidity through the purchase of sovereign bonds. The real danger for Germany lay in the prospective collapse of the Eurozone and not in the risk associated with a mildly inflationary policy.[4] Indeed, German policy became the object of intense criticism. Countries finding themselves in a debt crisis indicated that the imperative above all else was growth, and German domestic policy was not conducive to Europe-wide growth. Without the support of the German import market, many nations risked a crisis of liquidity and even the possibility of a default. To combat the perennial gap between the countries with high competitiveness and those of the Periphery, the former were required to enhance their domestic demand, even if this would drive an increase in inflation. This would fuel an increase in imports from the Periphery. The ECB should aim to frame its policy to promote growth rather than limiting its mandate to liquidity control to ensure price stability. The policy of continued austerity might lead to the possibility of the EMU needing to provide indefinite support to a member state in permanent recession or, even more dramatically, it could undermine the euro itself.[5]

It was now common knowledge that Germany played the decisive role in European developments. The demands of the German electorate therefore had clear and tangible ramifications for the direction of European policy. The German government favoured 'fiscal union'. This term indicated the need for greater coordination of fiscal policies and direct supervision of the fiscal policies and budgets of member states. According to Germany, there should be common limits for deficits and debt; member states failing to adhere to these should be referred to the European Court and risk punitive measures to ensure compliance. Germany rejected the establishment of eurobonds to deal with the crisis, along with broader increases in the support available to the Periphery or a more active model for the ECB in terms of the purchase of sovereign bonds for ailing nations. Berlin was equally opposed to the conversion of the ECB to a central bank with powers comparable to those of the Federal Reserve in the USA or the Bank of England. In the Chancellor's view, there were no 'quick fixes' to exit the crisis: many months if not years of work were needed.

While France did not subscribe to the German analysis, its primary concern was any threat to France's prized AAA credit status. Moves towards the mutualisation of risk or a greater role for the ECB would likely have detrimental ramifications for that status. The markets would inevitably demand a higher rate of interest on French bonds. In recognition of this risk, Sarkozy and the Italian Prime Minister, Monti, in several discussions supported Merkel, and indicated that Germany, France and Italy wished to be the motors of a more united, more stable Europe, with regulatory mechanisms that eliminated cheating. Member states must strive to limit their debt and to converge in the way they stuck to their budgets. They decided to proceed with reform of the Treaty framework, and to institutionalise punitive measures for any member states of the Eurozone violating the limits on deficit and debt.[6]

The agreement was limited to the concerns of debt and deficit; it did not engage with the broader systemic challenges afflicting the Eurozone. No discussion was given to the possibility of converting the ECB to a lender of last resort for the member states. Nor was a relaxation of its regulations examined so that banks could be financed generously. Even the level of capital that should be at the disposal of the EFSF was not debated. The €440 billion originally accepted was no longer adequate, due to the growing crisis in Italy. Additional sources for capital as agreed at the summit in October turned out to be insufficient. Calculations indicated that these sources would provide only half the capital now needed.

Finally, despite German aversion, the discussion in the Eurozone did return to eurobonds. The European Commission published a discussion paper on possible ways of introducing 'stability bonds'.[7] The paper indicated that their introduction would require fiscal discipline, economic competitiveness on a national level and more intense control of national budgets by the EU, in conjunction with provision of guarantees to ensure credit worthiness. The Commission rejected the immediate issue of eurobonds without prior completion of the fiscal stability measures.

The existing difficulties also affected discussions of the agreed haircut for Greek debt. As the days passed and despite negotiations regarding the implementation of the existing agreement of 26 October, anxiety once again grew as to whether this agreement had provided the long-evasive closure that the crisis needed. The limits on capital available to the EFSF fuelled this concern. The EFSF would not be in a position to replace the old Greek bonds with its own bonds of lower value and thus help with the reduction of the Greek debt. The Greek state had to change its proposal. It offered the banks an exchange of the old bonds with a combination of new Greek bonds and bonds from the EFSF. This offer was rejected by the representatives of the banks. The failure of these negotiations once again raised the risk of a Greek default.[8]

At the summit of the EMU heads of state and government held in Brussels on 9 December, it was decided that the member states should establish a new fiscal pact (later adopted as the Fiscal Compact). Its central aim was the establishment, 'in parallel with the single currency', of 'a strong economic pillar.... It will rest on enhanced governance.'[9] The Compact would therefore be a regulatory framework which would deter member states from non-compliance and would enhance fiscal discipline. According to this framework, budgets would be balanced or in surplus; that is, 'as a rule their annual structural deficit would not exceed 0.5% of nominal GDP'.[10] This principle would be legislated into the constitution (or equivalent) of every member state. Exceeding the highest deficit limit set by the Treaty of Maastricht, which is 3% of GDP, would incur punitive measures. These penalties could be suspended only by a special majority of member states. Sovereign debt exceeding 60% of GDP would have to be reduced by 5% per annum. Arrangements for the evaluation of draft budgets and the correction of excessive deficits would be cemented in a binding manner for all member states. All countries would be obliged to comply with the Commission's suggestions. The Compact was not limited to control and oversight. It also sought to actively shape a common economic policy, through regular summits. It stated that 'all major economic policy reforms ... will be discussed and coordinated at the level of the Euro area with a view to benchmarking best practices'.[11]

As to immediate action, it was decided to speed up the establishment of the ESM, which would begin operating from July 2012. The sufficiency of the capital available to the EFSF and the ESM, amounting to €500 billion, would be re-examined in March 2012. The voting rules in the context of the ESM were to be amended, so it would have the ability to act decisively in response to an emergency. The member states would provide €200 billion to the IMF, giving the Fund sufficient means to deal with crises.

Finally, in order to allay the anxiety aroused by the restructuring of Greek debt, reassurances were given that the Greek 'haircut' would not set a precedent. Such a restructuring of debt would not be repeated.

The President of the European Council announced, at the end of the negotiations, that it was possible that the Compact would be subscribed to by all the members of the EU, aside from the UK, which had already made its disdain for the agreement apparent.

The terms 'economic policy' and 'economic governance' in the text were used to legitimise and underwrite stricter fiscal discipline. Key European protagonists hailed this as a significant step forwards in achieving improved coherence and stability in the operation of the Eurozone. 'This is an extremely good result for the members of the Eurozone', the President of the ECB, Mario Draghi, pronounced. Angela Merkel described the summit as 'a breakthrough to a union of stability. The fiscal union will be developed step by step'.[12] Public opinion was more reserved. Following monetary union, the need for a common fiscal policy was now acknowledged. The Compact was a step in this direction. No country would any longer be in a position to ignore or contravene common policy. An important transfer of power had been effected, significantly reducing national sovereignty. This new framework upgraded the role of the European Commission, which undertook new responsibilities regarding oversight and compliance.

The announcement of these measures to limit the crisis and enhance the Eurozone's capacity to intervene was not without criticism. The measures were described as unclear, a result of compromise and competing preferences. As had been the case in previous decisions taken by the Council, compromise and complexity would cultivate uncertainty. 'There is nothing substantially new', a report in the French media commented.[13]

It was widely noted that the UK's failure to participate in the agreement, as well as the wider continuing divergence between members and non-members of the Eurozone, was creating a two-tier Europe. The French said that the British had never believed in the euro and that it was therefore pointless to expect their participation. The UK raised a caveat against the use of EU institutions, such as the European Court or even the European Commission, in the execution of the Fiscal Compact. These were contemporary manifestations of the perennial lines of conflict that had accompanied European integration for many years.

The markets reacted positively to the Compact. The initial enthusiasm receded, however, when the American ratings agencies warned that the crisis would continue throughout 2012 and very possibly for several years more. A little optimism returned when, in mid-December 2011, the ECB made €489 billion available in three-year loans to over 500 banks. It sought to achieve three targets: to avert the collapse of any bank which would have unforeseeable consequences for the system; to increase liquidity, in order to avert recession; and finally, to facilitate lending to states. This intervention greatly improved the climate and confidence in the markets.

The Greek press spoke of a 'Pax Germanica', of fiscal discipline within the Eurozone and of a policy of eternal austerity; 'the German Chancellor imposed her plan for the Eurozone'.[14] Another commentator noted that the Compact 'fails to address the underlying problems, and it has hardwired austerity into the framework of the Eurozone'.[15] According to the critics, a broader review of the problem was necessary.[16] Fiscal discipline was not, and is not, the only problem that needed to be fixed. Over the period 1999–2007, the deficits of just 12 countries of the Union did not exceed the limit of 3% of GDP. While nations including Italy, Germany, France and Austria did not always comply with the regulations concerning deficits and debt, Spain and Ireland did adhere to the 60% of GDP cap on sovereign debt. However, both Dublin and Madrid were quickly engulfed by the crisis. Ireland's debt shot up from 25% to 108% of GDP, and Spain's from 40% to 70%.[17] These data indicate that caps on deficit and debt are not sufficient to prevent crises. It was the gulf in competiveness that drove the countries of the Periphery into recession.[18] The current-account deficit, an indicator of a lack of competitiveness, was particularly high in countries like Greece, Portugal and Spain. In these nations, regardless of whether they adhered to policies regarding fiscal discipline or not, imports inevitably exceeded exports. The Fiscal Compact did not broach this matter at all.

During the EMU summit on 9 December, there were public statements made indicating that the establishment of a regime of control for fiscal policy across the Union posed major political challenges, to which excessive centralisation might not be the only solution. In light of popular dissent, there needed to be a mechanism for public participation in EU policy. Inevitably, economic and political unification entails the transfer of competencies from national to European level, as well as a reduction in the ability of a member state to undermine collective action. At the same time, however, it is imperative to have safety valves to ensure democratic scrutiny. Furthermore, the inter-governmental framework, under which 27 distinct member states had to reach consensus for all major decisions, had proven incapable of making expedient decisions when faced with crises. It was evident that to counter such inertia a new framework was required.

A report by the Spinelli Group,[19] following the summit of 9 December, indicated that coherent and legitimate economic governance could be overseen only by the European Commission, accountable to the European Parliament. The Vice President of the Commission should be responsible for the economic governance of the EMU. The Vice President's staff should consist of all Commissioners with portfolios for economic, social and environmental matters. The Spinelli Group also proposed a range of changes in the operations of the European Parliament, as well as the revision of the Treaties in order to increase its areas of competence and achieve the active participation of citizens in European policy.

## Notes

1  The interest on 10-year Italian sovereign bonds on 10 January 2011 was 4.85%; on 24 November 2011 it was 7.11%.
2  *IHT*, 18 November 2011, p. 8.
3  See M. Wolf, 'What the IMF should tell Europe', *Financial Times*, 29 November 2011.
4  *IHT*, 18 November 2011, p. 8.
5  M. Wolf, 'Does the Eurozone advance or risk ruin?', *Financial Times*, 22 November 2011.
6  See *Le Monde,* 6 December 2011, p. 8, 7 December 2011, p. 4; also *Le Monde*, 24 November 2007, pp. 6–7, 25 November 2007, p. 4.
7  'Green paper on the feasibility of introducing stability bond', COM (2011) 818 final, European Commission, 23 November 2011.
8  See *Kathimerini*, 4 December 2011, p. 4.
9  See European Council, Statement by the euro area heads of state or government, European Council, 9 December 2011. Also 'Remarks of Herman Van Rompuy', 9 December 2011, Euro 157/11.
10  Annual structural deficit is the deficit which is not circumstantial and which does not include interest or extraordinary expenses.
11  On the Fiscal Compact see also p. 175.
12  *IHT*, 10 November 2011, p. 4.
13  *Le Monde*, 10 December 2011, p. 3.
14  *Ta Nea*, 11 December 2011, p. 1.
15  S. Tilford in S. Castle, *IHT*, 10–11 December 2011, p. 4.

16 See M. Wolf, 'Germany has to make a fateful choice', *Financial Times*, 12 December 2011; M. Wolf, 'A disastrous failure at the summit', *Financial Times*, 13 December 2011; S. King, 'Why the Eurozone deal will fail', *Financial Times*, 12 December 2011.

17 J. Pisani-Ferry, 'Economie', *Le Monde*, 13 December 2011, p. 1. See also M. Wolf, 'L'échec de Merkozi', *Le Monde*, 13 December 2011, p. 2.

18 See pp. 7ff.

19 A group promoting European unification. See Spinelli Group, 'Against the temptation of a Franco-German "coup de chefs d'etat"', 9 December 2011, at www.spinelligroup.eu.

# 20

# The new agreement with the Eurozone (the second Memorandum) and private sector involvement

Anxiety swiftly returned to Greece after the summit of 9 December 2011. The government's primary concern was to satisfy the preconditions required for the release of the €130 billion loan. Two agreements needed to be drawn up. The first concerned the conditions of the loan. It would clarify the still unclear arrangements for the new fiscal measures and the structural changes needed to achieve the agreed targets. In sum, this constituted the new Memorandum. The second agreement would be drawn up with the private sector, after the conditions for private sector involvement (PSI) had been clarified. No release of funds would occur until both these agreements had been concluded.

While this project was clear in its aims, it proved particularly difficult in its execution, for two reasons. First, Greece's partners fundamentally doubted the Greek administration's credibility. On numerous occasions Troika representatives had indicated that failure to implement the programme was primarily due to delays on the Greek part and failure to adhere to its obligations. While the Troika recognised criticism of the first Memorandum and acknowledged that mistakes had been made, it indicated that the excessive emphasis on concerns of taxation was a result of initiatives of the Greek side and not a result of the Troika's demands.[1] The ECB, the Commission and the IMF made it clear that the new regulatory framework, the fiscal measures and the structural changes should be agreed in January 2012 and implemented in the first quarter. It would not be possible to sign the agreements if this was not done. They rejected the proposition that the measures should be enacted by a new government after elections. The Troika stated it would not be willing to release the €90 billion due in March while the reform of the regulatory framework remained pending.

The second challenge stemmed from the partisan behaviour of the parties of the government coalition, principally that of New Democracy. New Democracy was far more concerned with how any reform might affect its position in the upcoming elections than satisfying the terms required for the release of further support. The party behaved as if Greece had overcome the crisis and once again politicians could draw partisan lines and speak in favour of their clientele. Its leader repeatedly drew 'red lines' in order to prevent cuts in the size of pensions or new burdens to taxpayers. However, after his objections were widely advertised he agreed to proceed with the changes in the context of the new programme.

The ongoing party positioning and partisan conflict fuelled intense discussions over whether and when elections would be held. Any reasoned analysis clearly indicated that the government needed to fulfil its mandate before any fresh elections could be undertaken. That is to say, the interim administration needed to complete the outstanding agreements with the Troika and the private sector, as well as satisfying the terms for the release of further support. The time needed to complete this whole process could not be determined with any precision and so discussion of, or preparation for, elections was wholly premature. As would soon become apparent, a range of matters were still outstanding and would take longer than anticipated to resolve. Holding elections prior to the resolution of these concerns would very probably lead to default and had, therefore, to be avoided at all costs. The view that the Papademos government should have remained in power for the full parliamentary term was also unrealistic, however, since the Prime Minister had not posited such a situation and had in fact agreed to the opposite. In any event, a frenzy of media reporting continued to cultivate uncertainty on the future of the government. The elections were finally set for 6 May 2012.

The representatives of the Troika left at the end of December and announced that they would return in mid-January. By then the government should have reached decisions regarding how to cover the 2011 deficit and how best to satisfy the conditions attached to the release of further funds. The Troika was determined to counter the internationally held image of a Greece marred with reform fatigue and inertia. In the meantime, the IMF and the EU, in negotiations with the private sector, had started calculations regarding the sustainability of the total Greek debt. Data showed that the target of a reduction of Greek debt to 120% of GDP by 2020 was increasingly unlikely. A re-examination of PSI looked both likely and necessary. Commentators observed that 'The IMF has got harsher because reality has got harsher and they are responding to it'.[2]

January was to be the critical month for the new government, whose agenda had to focus on three fronts. The first related to outstanding commitments undertaken by the Greek government which needed to be resolved by the end of February, prior to the release of further funds and the signing of the PSI agreement. Among the most pressing of these were cuts in auxiliary pensions and the minimum wage, as well as the abolition of the 'extension clause' of collective agreements.[3] A second front consisted of 'additional measures', adapting the programme's initial provisions to the new conditions. It was estimated that these additional measures amounted to €2.2 billion. These were considered necessary in order to ensure that deficit projections for 2012 would remain on track. Such measures included further cuts in defence and health spending. The third front concerned the reforms for the years 2013–15. There was a need to minimise the risk of further delays in the implementation of the programme. These reforms included the adoption of a new tax system and the axing of 150,000 public sector jobs. Negotiations over these matters proved exceptionally difficult.

New Democracy, LAOS and also a section of PASOK did not want to acknowledge how critical the situation was, or risk tainting themselves with the political cost of more painful reform. Pressure was intense and patience or a willingness to seek a compromise was virtually non-existent on the part of the Troika. Its representatives believed that 'the country has neither the ability nor the will to carry out the broad economic changes ... it had promised in exchange for aid'.[4] 'The deficit in credibility was as high as the fiscal deficit.'[5] The Troika wanted immediate action: the implementation of the various laws that had been passed but remained unenforced and the completion of the decrees and ministerial decisions that had not yet been issued. At the beginning of January they sent a letter to the government indicating various matters had to be settled so that negotiations could begin on 16 January. They cited continual dysfunction in the labour market and combating tax evasion. Neither was a minor or easy issue to resolve. At the same time, they made public their displeasure with the positions taken by certain members of the Greek government, who, despite their tacit support of the reform programme, continued to frame the debate in terms of 'measures imposed by the Troika'. The release of the further funding could not take place while these salient concerns remained outstanding, and so Greece still remained at risk of a disorderly default.

There remained a fundamental lack of faith in the Greek government. The discourse and conflict within the administration gave the impression of a coalition of divergent parties which viewed this interim government as a necessary evil rather than a vehicle for the pursuit of a common goal. On 19 January the Prime Minister convened a meeting of the heads of the three parties, to present them with a policy 'road map'. However, a further meeting had to be scheduled to hammer out a compromise. Divergent views emerged from parties within the government as to the future course of the administration. New Democracy made evident its desire to hold elections as soon as possible, while PASOK believed an extension of this government's life was absolutely necessary. Such conflict affected efforts to debate and legislate for the required reforms. The Members of Parliament of the government coalition voted according to their personal sentiment and interests, in what was becoming an increasingly 'mutinous' environment.[6] Government officials tried in vain to reassure public opinion by insisting that 'the project of maintaining communications channels between the three parties, so as to avert crises, is already underway'.[7] But the Troika was already in Athens trying, in vain, to ascertain the position of the government on a number of issues that had been placed on the table.

The new government's primary mandate was the reduction of expenditure in line with the demands of Greece's creditors. A coherent plan and policy matrix had been absent in Greece since the start of the crisis in 2009; it did not look like this would change under the direction of the two main political parties, each of which was adamant that it did not subscribe to the analysis of the other. At an EU summit held on 30 January 2012, the Prime Minister limited himself to the presentation of a framework he had hammered out with the leaders of the three coalition parties regarding matters of employment, growth and the Fiscal Compact. He also underlined that the results of the country's efforts were far more significant than they appeared. These assertions had been heard before, however, and would do little to alter the way the other EU nations viewed Greece. At the end of the summit, the members of the Eurozone issued a statement in which they urged Greece to conclude negotiations on the new programme 'in the coming days.... Restoration of credibility requires that all political parties irrevocably commit to the new programme.'[8] Eurozone leaders also delegated to their ministers of finance the task of undertaking all the necessary actions regarding the second Memorandum in an expedient fashion, so that the PSI arrangements could be implemented in mid-February. Their orders for all were, simply put, 'get on with it'.

A German proposal for a 'commissioner' for Greece, with the capacity to intervene in budgetary matters, was rejected by the Prime Minister.[9] This proposal had already aroused widespread and fierce criticism in Greece, as well as in France, where President Nicolas Sarkozy said that it 'would be unreasonable, not be democratic, nor would it be effective'.[10] Chancellor Angela Merkel had also distanced herself from the proposal at the beginning of the summit, indicating that 'we are discussing a matter which we should not be discussing', even though many members of the German government supported it.[11]

The primary concern for the EU Council was the acceptance of the Fiscal Compact, which had been agreed at the beginning of December. The related intergovernmental Treaty for the Compact was accepted with minor amendments. The European Commission did not acquire, as had been in the initial proposals, the right to bring *any* member state of the EMU that failed to comply with the deficit limit before the European Court: it acquired such a right only for those nations that were party to the Compact. It was decided that any nation continually failing to adhere to the controls on debt and deficit would have to submit a detailed programme of structural changes to the EU in order to ensure 'a permanent correction of its excessive deficits'. The Compact was accepted by all members of the EU, with the exception of the UK and the Czech Republic. The non-members of the Eurozone that signed the Compact requested and were granted attendance at at least one Eurozone summit per annum. The Compact was to be signed at the next summit, to be held in March 2012.

The substantive value of the negotiations at the January summit did not stem from the text of the Compact, but rather the statement of political unity. Virtually all the countries of the EU, even if they were not part of the Eurozone, accepted that the stability of their fiscal policies constituted a priority. The member states recognised that limited coordination and fiscal indiscipline had made the markets arbiters of their credit worthiness and debt sustainability. The markets determined their credibility and their rates of interest on borrowing. The Fiscal Compact sought to mitigate the risk of these externalities, instituting objective criteria on the basis of which each member state had to be judged. However, it was doubtful whether it would achieve this. The Hellenic example clearly indicates that fiscal control depends not only on adherence to financial regulations, but is equally affected by issues pertaining to the structural framework of the economy and its relative competitiveness.[12]

The declaration made at the end of the summit related to growth and employment. Those responsible in the EU wished to conceal their inertia in dealing with the crisis and instead to convey a positive message regarding the substance and conviction of their efforts. The announcements included the reiteration of a series of existing measures and an indication of future plans 'to boost employment, complete the single market and enhance financing to small and medium-sized businesses'. The text was littered with phrases referring to 'enhanced efforts', 'full development', 'renewal of efforts', 'swift implementa- tion of', 'greater activation of' and so on.[13] This indicated that the EU had not yet developed a coherent and comprehensive plan to bolster growth across the single market, or the Eurozone. It was a text that simply expressed preferences and aspirations.

Over the last 10 days of January into mid-February, the government and the Troika representatives tried to find a commonly acceptable solution regarding the necessary measures to be taken in order to avert a Greek default. On 20 March, Greece had to redeem bonds totalling €14.5 billion; time was a currency in short supply.

Negotiations between the government and the Troika were as slow as ever. The Greek newspapers described them as a 'marathon'. The original demands of the Troika were replaced during deliberations, owing to compromises or newly arising challenges. The perpetual meetings of government ministers and civil servants, the daily visits by the Troika to Greek ministries and con- tradictory statements from those involved, all under mounting international pressure, did little other than to create the impression of chaos. Public support in Greece deteriorated as a result of a range of factors: the relentless and unbearable pressure from international partners; the virtually complete retreat of the Greek administration, despite the 'heroic statements' by some of the members of the governing coalition; the domination of German preferences for continued stringent and draconian interventions; and the unrelenting wave of austerity programmes driving Greece ever further into recession.

The critical final round of negotiations began on Sunday 5 February, with a five-hour meeting between the Prime Minister and the leaders of the parties of the government coalition. The list of the Troika's demands was extensive. It included: the reform of the system of auxiliary pensions; the reduction of the minimum wage; the reduction of the thirteenth and fourteenth salary; the abolition of the extension of the sectoral contracts for six months after their expiration; the abolition of special payrolls of the public sector; and a drastic reduction in medical and defence expenditure.[14] At the same time, the Troika reserved the right to adjust its demands if it felt the circumstances merited such. For example, it initially demanded a reduction in expenditure of €3.3 billion, which it later reduced to €2.8 billion. In the course of negotiations it indicated that it sought personal guarantees and reassurances regarding Hellenic commitments from all three party leaders. The Troika was clearly concerned about the prospect of fresh elections and the possibility that a new administration would renege on existing obligations. During the meeting, the political leaders agreed to the following: (1) to take measures in 2012 to reduce public expenditure by 1.5% of GDP; (2) to ensure the sustainability of the auxiliary pension funds; (3) to reduce non-payroll costs, with the aim of enhancing employment and competitiveness; and (4) the recapitalisation of the banks. Through their own statements, two of the party leaders – Samaras of New Democracy and Karatzaferis of LAOS – made public that they had disagreed with the government's line. One of them indicated that 'he was fighting' to avert measures that would lead to recession, while the other stated that he would not allow a revolution to occur by plunging Greece into misery.[15] The participants agreed to meet again as soon as possible.

Across the coalition, there was some agreement on a rejection of the pre-scriptions of the Troika. The members did not agree on the reduction of the minimum wage by 25–30%, or to the abolition of the thirteenth and fourteenth salary. They also had common objections to the size and speed of the fiscal adjustments.[16] But extensive internal disagreements were also apparent, which did not permit the formulation of a common Greek position during negoti-ations. The only too familiar postponements of the next planned meeting with the Troika occurred once again. These perpetual postponements also affected the planned meetings of the Eurogroup, which needed to assess the reform programme as prescribed by the Troika and determine the subsequent steps and the terms of the final agreement.

The statements made by Merkel and Sarkozy[17] were indicative of inter-national pressure on Greece. The former stated that time was getting short and it was particularly important for the Eurozone that an agreement be reached. Sarkozy stated, 'together we say to our Greek friends that decisions must be taken now.... The situation in Greece must be settled once and for all.' Both of them, expressing their doubts over the country's credibility, proposed that the financial assistance to Greece should be deposited in a special account which would be used to service Greece's debts, as a means of minimising uncertainty over whether such payments would be honoured in the future.

The next meeting of the party leaders, held on 8 February, lasted ap-proximately seven hours. Both during and after the meeting, the Prime Minister telephoned Commissioner Rehn, the President of the Eurogroup Jean-ClaudeJuncker, Merkel and others, in order to evaluate how far various compromise proposals could be accepted. According to media reports, these requests for further compromise were met with anger. Agreement was finally reached, with the clear exception of cuts in pensions. The coalition leaders assigned the negotiation of this matter to the Troika and the Prime Minister. The result of their deliberations was a compromise which provided for a reduction in auxiliary pensions over the next two years. At the same time, however, the agreed cuts in expenditure were less than the target figure. Cuts amounting to €325 million had still to be made. The compromise was approved by the leaders. The Prime Minister's office subsequently announced that a general agreement over the content of the programme had been reached.

All the decisions were presented at the Eurogroup in Brussels on Thursday 9 February. The Greek party tried to table a request for a milder adjustment, by deferring the reduction of the deficit to less than 8% of GDP by a year. The request met the staunch opposition of members of the Eurogroup, who were frustrated by the continual delays and revised positions. Certain ministers in Brussels believed that 'Greece cannot implement any other programme to restore its economy to health ... and they are looking for an excuse to push it towards exiting the euro'.[18] They referred to the 'theatricals' of the political leaders, as evidence of the Greek side's lack of commitment or conviction.

The Eurogroup made its final decision on the further release of funds dependent on three preconditions:

1  a reduction in expenditure amounting to €325 million (the cuts in the defence budget proposed by the Greek government were considered a 'one off', rather than a sustainable cost-cutting measure and, as such, were rejected by the Troika);
2  the written commitment of the leaders of PASOK and New Democracy that they would implement the policies of the new Memorandum;
3  ratification of the Memorandum in the Greek Parliament.

Provided these preconditions were satisfied, there would be a new meeting of the Eurogroup on 15 February, for final approval to be given.

Turmoil and strife spread across Greece in response. The labour unions in both the private sector and the public sector, as well as many of the professional associations, went on strike and called for national mobilisation. There were continual demonstrations in the centre of Athens, clashes with the police and a broader breakdown of civil order. By Sunday 12 February, the day on which Parliament was to vote, organised groups committed arson, destroyed property and began looting. The police focused on the protection of Parliament and neglected disturbances elsewhere. This reaffirmed the internationally held perception of Greece, not only as a weak state, but also as a nation in economic collapse. The chaos in the capital signified the extent of the social breakdown.

The LAOS party withdrew from the government coalition and its ministers resigned. Governmental advisers to the PASOK party also resigned, while a number of its MPs indicated that they were against the new Memorandum.

The Prime Minister stressed to MPs in the speech he gave to Parliament that their actions

> will affect whether the country shall remain in the euro or whether it shall be led into a disorderly default, whether we can secure our place in the euro or whether, on the contrary, we shall lead the country into prolonged misery and a fateful downhill path towards marginalisation.... What is at stake is the country's choice to travel along with the others towards European unification, as an integral member of the nucleus of a united Europe and the common currency.

In the vote to approve the new Memorandum held on the Sunday, 199 MPs voted in favour of the government proposal, while 22 PASOK and 21 New Democracy MPs broke from the party line. Those who failed to adhere to the party whip were expelled from their parliamentary groups. Overall, 74 MPs voted 'no', while five abstained. It was a relative success for the government. Relative, because when it had requested a vote of confidence, three months earlier, to reaffirm its mandate to push ahead with the reform programme, it had secured 255 votes.

After the Memorandum had been voted in, the other two preconditions remained to be satisfied. The Greek government's proposal for a reduction of expenses by €325 million from the defence sector, public works and health-care programmes were rejected again by the Euro Working Group.[19] The letters from the party leaders regarding their ongoing commitment to the Memorandum were not forthcoming. Samaras's letter had not arrived in Brussels by Tuesday. In response to this, the President of the Eurogroup postponed the Wednesday meeting till Monday 20 February, with a teleconference replacing the scheduled meeting on the evening of Wednesday 15 February. The postponement of the Eurogroup meeting brought about further delays, most notably with regard to PSI. Once again, delays compounded anxiety and frustration at Greece across the Union. In the teleconference certain Eurozone ministers requested that all financial decisions be postponed until elections in Greece had been held.[20] Their proposal meant that the funds Greece needed would not be released, for an indefinite period. This proposal actually served to speed up developments in Greece. The outstanding conditions on €325 million were agreed and the ministers of the Eurogroup accepted the political commitments from the Greek party leaders.

New difficulties arose from the Troika's report on the sustainability of debt,[21] drawn up to inform the Eurozone's ministers of finance. This 'confidential' report painted a dark picture of the condition of the Greek economy. It stated that both the macroeconomic as well as the fiscal prospects for the country had deteriorated, as a result of the sustained delays in the structural changes. It considered that the country's return to the markets in 2014 was uncertain, even after the new programme. Under the most optimistic of scenarios, debt would still amount to 129% of GDP by 2020, exceeding the 120% required by the end of the decade. Simply put, debt would still not be on sustainable terms. Over the period of 2015–20, Greece would most likely need additional financial support amounting to approximately €50 billion. Without this, the restoration of competitiveness through 'internal devaluation' would simply fuel further recession and would in all probability lead to an increase in debt as a percentage of GDP. The report also noted that the Greek economy would in all likelihood be exposed to negative externalities, rendering slim its prospects for recovery. Finally, it recommended further cuts in the claims of the private sector, along with those from creditor nations, as the decision of 26 October 2011 was not sufficient to place Greece on a sustainable financial footing.

Aside from the alarming findings of the report, there was emerging concern regarding the recapitalisation of the Greek banking sector. The recapitalisation of banks had originally been calculated to require €30 billion, a figure that had been used when calculating the previous €130 billion package. Revised figures indicated the figure was significantly higher, approximately €40 billion. Germany, the Netherlands and Finland were not willing to meet the shortfall.

The Troika's report had aroused great anxiety among Dutch, Finnish and German officials. The German Minister of Finance, Wolfgang Schäuble, hardened his positioned significantly. In public statements he expressed his impatience at the ongoing uncertainty. He was no longer willing to support 'pouring money into a bottomless pit…. [Nor would he condone] relying on empty Greek guaranties'.[22] At the same time, in France it was observed that 'every time progress is achieved, the German Minister of Finance sets new conditions'. However, it was widely recognised that 'Greece's future is now in the hands of the German officials'.[23] The German position was that there must be further austerity and a more stringent adherence to the regulatory framework in order to achieve the original target, the reduction of debt to 120% of GDP by 2020. The necessity of this target was widely recognised, but there was conflict as to how it might best be achieved: through a retroactive reduction in the rate of interest on loans to Greece by the member states; through an increase in the scale of the haircut; or through the inclusion of the bonds held by the central banks of the member states in the restructuring process? The deliberations made clear there was no desire on the part of the creditor nations to provide additional financial assistance to Greece. Possible solutions should be examined only in the context of existing negotiations regarding PSI.

Schäuble's position drew intense criticism in Greece. Inside the government there was talk 'of a group of member states holding an inimical position towards Greece'.[24] In a visit to the Ministry of National Defence on 15 February, the President of the Greek Republic 'appeared exasperated' and publicly questioned: 'Who is this Mr Schäuble who thinks he can deride Greece? Who are the Dutch? Who are the Finns?'[25] These comments were not well received and sparked further negative reactions. However, some considered them an indication that the general implementation of austerity policies across the EU was causing more strain than certain economies could bear any longer. In Belgium, in fact, in protest at Commissioner Rehn's dogmatic insistence on adherence to the 3% cap for the deficit, a minister had exclaimed: 'Who knows Olli Rehn? Who knows this man's face?'[26] Such division and conflict were clear proof that a balance between the pursuit of the 'political union' required to promote economic convergence and the national policies to reduce social conflict had not been found yet.

In the run-up to the Eurogroup meeting to be held on 20 February, and to find a commonly acceptable solution, the Greek Prime Minister was in continual contact with the leaders of the other EMU member states. Following these ongoing conversations, the Italian Prime Minister, Monti, took the initiative and convened a teleconference for 17 February, which would include both his Greek and his German counterparts. Both the sustainability of Greek debt as well as possible initiatives for the ever-elusive conclusive solution were discussed. The immediate result was Papademos' 'extraordinary' trip to Brussels and his participation in the Eurogroup meeting, after 'friendly encouragement' by Chancellor Merkel.[27]

As the Eurogroup is an institution that is confined to the finance ministers, the extension of an invitation to a prime minister was a notable gesture. The invitation meant that the Prime Minister would take the place of the Greek Finance Minister, Evangelos Venizelos, at the table. The Minister of Finance had no experience in economics; he had not adjusted to the European environment; and had done a fine job of souring relations even with those sympathetic to Greece. The Prime Minister took the leading role in the Greek negotiating party, removed unnecessary frictions and found the successful conclusion to talks that had proved so evasive.

Discussions over PSI proceeded at the same time as negotiations over the new Memorandum. They had begun towards the end of 2011, and by mid-January 2012 they had reached breaking point. The government and the Institute for International Finance (IIF), which represented the bulk of the lenders, still had fundamental disagreements, which resulted in a breakdown of negotiations on 13 January. In accordance with the decision of 26 October, the claims of the bondholders were cut by 50% of the nominal value of bonds. The lenders felt that the net current value of bonds should not be reduced below 60%. There was also disagreement over the rate of interest on the replacement bonds. The lenders felt that the rate of interest must be 5%, especially for bonds maturing after 2020. The Greek government insisted on a rate of interest of 4%. According to the lenders, this entailed a haircut of the bonds' net current value of 70–80%. To ensure sufficient participation in the restructuring, the government had stated that it would legislate that participation in the restructuring would be mandatory even for bondholders who disagreed.[28] Legislation, however, was possible only if two-thirds of the lenders accepted the restructuring agreement. The lenders reacted negatively and many speculative funds did not participate in the negotiations, so as to invalidate them. Indeed, they bought up Greek bonds on the market, to raise their participation percentage and to raise pressure for an alternative solution. Figures indicated that approximately 15% of bonds were in the hands of such funds.

After the break in negotiations, the lenders returned with counter-proposals for a compromise on the rate of interest which was closer to the position of the Greek government. However, the IMF and Germany reacted. Their calculations indicated that the amount of support agreed (€130 billion) was no longer sufficient to cover the country's needs, should the lenders' proposal be accepted. They insisted on the need for a much lower interest rate, of approximately 2%, as well as on a larger 'haircut', amounting to 53% of the nominal value of the bonds (as opposed to 50%). These demands provoked retractions and a breakdown in the schedule of negotiations. There was now a growing risk that agreement might not be reached by 20 March, when Greece had to redeem bonds to the value of €14.5 billion. It seemed extremely likely that Greece would default on payment. The Eurozone exercised intense pressure on the lenders in an effort to make them back down.[29] It succeeded in changing the position of the IIF, by convincing the Institute that an unsuccessful restructuring of debt would cause far greater losses for lenders.

The €130 billion was to be allocated as follows: (1) €30 billion approximately in cash or EFSF bonds, which Greece would have to buy in order to pay the bondholders a bonus for their compromise; (2) €30 billion for the purchase of bonds by the EFSF in order to effect the exchange of old Greek bonds for new bonds, both Greek and EFSF ones; (3) €35–40 billion for the necessary recapitalisation of the banks owing to the losses they had incurred from the crisis and the restructuring of the debt;[30] (4) €5 billion for interest earned on bonds prior to the restructuring; (5) the balance of approximately €25 billion, along with the outstanding €34 billion (not yet been disbursed to Greece from the first €110 billion loan), which would ensure future payment of interest and service any emergency needs of the Greek state as well as repayment of debts to lenders not included in the bond exchange, such as the ECB and the member states of the Eurozone. However, the Troika was now indicating these figures were no longer sufficient; an even larger cut in debt was necessary.

Negotiations in the Eurogroup on 20 February 2012 were tense. They lasted over 13 hours. They were interrupted a number of times so the Greek delegation and the Eurozone ministers could discuss a larger haircut with the representatives of the private sector. The main challenge, and the cause of the most extensive discussions, was the effort to achieve a reduction of Greek debt to 120% of GDP by 2020. The Troika felt this was imperative if the debt was to be considered sustainable.

The statement from the Eurogroup on 21 February 2012 noted that the Greek side had satisfied the preconditions that had been set.[31] This meant that the new loan and the second Memorandum came into force. The Eurogroup stated that the main goals of the new programme were to ensure the sustainability of the debt and a restoration of Greek competitiveness. The prerequisite for achieving these was that Greece would be successful in attaining 'the ambitious but realistic targets of economic stabilisation'.[32] This was to be done through the programme of privatisation and structural changes, permitting Greece to present a primary surplus from 2012 onwards. The Eurozone nations felt that, in order to assist Greece in this effort, the European Commission would have to significantly enhance the Hellenic Task Force. That Task Force itself would have to provide the expertise, and the Troika's supervisory force on the ground would work towards the full implementation of the programme with the co-operation of the Greek government. In brief, the first section of the statement reiterated known targets, again designating 2014 as the year in which the deficit should not be higher than 3% of GDP.

In its second section, the statement recommended the establishment of a special account at the Bank of Greece, where Greece would deposit sufficient funds to service its debt in every following quarter.[33] At the same time, Greece was obliged to legislate for a constitutional precedence to service the country's debt above all other financial needs and commitments.

The statement proceeded to indicate that the haircut of the nominal value of bonds would be 53.5%. This final cut was greater than the original provision (50%), in order to contribute to the larger reduction in debt, in line with the recommendations of the Troika. The overall cut as a result of this restructuring would now be approximately €107 billion (rather than the €100 billion which would have arisen from a 50% haircut). The precise size of the cut would depend on the extent of participation in the bond exchange. The aim was for a participation rate of 90%. The statement indicated that Greece must now offer an open invitation to holders of Greek bonds for their exchange; however, the details of the exchange were not specified. In accordance with previous negotiations, approximately 31.5% of their original value was to be exchanged on bonds maturing in 11–30 years (to be issued by the Greek state), while those maturing in two years would receive 15% of their original value (in the form of new bonds to be issued by the EFSF). As for the interest rate, it would be 2% on Greek bonds up until February 2015, rising to 3% for the next five years up to 2020, and again up to 3.65% in 2021, and 4.3% by 2022 till February 2042. The rate of interest would rise by 1% maximum above these terms, should growth exceed the targets. These arrangements transferred the bulk of interest payments to the years after 2020.

The ECB and various national central banks (e.g. of Cyprus and Luxembourg) that had acquired Greek bonds for investment purposes would have to make their profits on these bonds available for the repayment of Greece's obligations to them up to 2020 so as to enhance the sustainability of Greek debt.

All the member states agreed to the reduction in interest rate on the first support package, limiting the profit margin to 1.5%. The estimated benefit for the Greek budget amounted to €3 billion annually. With these contributions from both the private and the public sector, it was calculated that Greek sovereign debt could be reduced to sustainable levels; by 2020 it would reach 117% of GDP. The Eurozone confirmed that 'the member states are prepared to provide up to 2014, in the form of an EFSF loan, an amount of €130 billion, with the expectation that the IMF will also make a significant contribution'. The precise amount and the way in which it was to be used would be decided at the beginning of March, when the results of the PSI arrangements would be known and outstanding reforms had been effected. The €130 billion was not given in an act of altruism, as the terms it was framed in often indicated: it was not 'help', but very much a loan with stringent conditions attached. Together with the balance of the previous loan (€34.5 billion), the sum that was to be made available to Greece was €164.5 billion. This would be needed to service:[34]

1  the implementation of the PSI arrangements;
2  the recapitalisation of the banks;
3  the payment of bonds that were maturing;
4  the payment of interest;
5  the various needs of the government.

By May 2012, Greece had received a total of €147.5 billion from the capital provided by the first and second adjustment programmes.[35]

The Eurogroup statement concluded with reassurances that the Eurozone 'would support Greece both throughout the duration of the new programme as well as afterwards, till it acquires the capacity to return to the markets, provided it complies fully with the requirements and the targets of the adjustment programme'.[36]

All the members of the Eurozone spoke positively regarding the results of the negotiations. The President of the Eurogroup remarked that Greece had won the time it needed to effect structural changes. Schäuble deemed that the preconditions now existed for the country to control its debt, for the Greek economy to become more competitive and for a return to growth. A European head of state was indicative of sentiment across continental political elites when he stressed that the preconditions had now been put in place, such that the success of the effort depended on the Greeks themselves, on their devotion to implementing all that had been agreed. Papademos spoke of a historic day and stressed that the agreement constituted 'a great step towards ensuring the future of the Greek economy but also the future of the country'.[37]

The reactions of media commentators and related experts were far more guarded. Within the financial sector there were those who did not agree with debt restructuring in principle, citing exposure to future risks and the threat of setting an ominous precedent. Investors – they pointed out – had been given a double lesson: that sovereign states can change the terms of state bonds whenever they want; and that private bondholders may be expected to bear the cost for the imprudence of a nation state. Such a change in the principles of a sovereign bond has lasting and serious consequences. Under such circumstances, critics within the financial sector felt it was extremely doubtful whether Greece would be able to return to the markets. A third bailout package was, in their view, likelier than ever.[38]

However, most of them noted that the agreement had averted a disorderly default by Greece, and anything was preferable to that. It did not, however, solve the underlying causes of the crisis; it did nothing to redress the weakness of the Greek economy or imbalances in competitiveness and development that still continued to threaten the EMU. Greece suffered from structural under-development. The agreement did not guarantee that this would be overcome. Greece did not possess any notable industry. Its industrial output contributed only 13.5% to GDP, whereas in Italy industrial output accounted for 19%.[39] Under the current circumstances, the country could reverse its disadvantageous position only by increasing exports. But required improvements in terms of competitiveness and the necessary investment in the sector would inevitably take time and money. The bailout package did not pay the necessary attention to economic growth. The austerity programme it contained rather fuelled social and political insecurity, which deters investment. Furthermore, it was far from certain that the measures prescribed would ensure a reduction of debt to 117% of GDP by 2020. The continuation of the recession and the delay in a return to growth could overturn projections. But even if the forecasts proved to be correct, debt on such a scale could not prove sustainable; its reduction to a much lower level should have been ensured. However, that did not happen, and it was consequently highly likely that a further intervention would be needed.[40]

Certain commentators linked the inadequacy of the solution to the wider European challenges: 'The heavy price Greece is paying shows that the Euro-zone is still looking for a functional mixture of adjustability, discipline and solidarity'.[41] Today, the sustaining link between the countries of the Eurozone is the enormous cost its break-up would entail for all the participants. This is not enough. What is needed above all is a common political aim and vision, one which allows the Eurozone to overcome economic differences and political tensions between its members.

Euphoria prevailed in Greece. After the obscurities, uncertainties and short-comings of the previous solutions, the impression was cultivated that a final agreement had been reached, which could lead to the end of the crisis. The Prime Minister expressed his optimism that 'if the programme is effectively implemented, the problems will be overcome in 2013 and growth will begin gradually'.[42] Public opinion felt that the risk of default had been averted, but remained deeply divided over the value of the reforms stipulated in the Memorandum. A new line of cleavage emerged – between 'pro-Memorandum' and 'anti-Memorandum' camps – on the Greek political landscape. This fuelled further intense criticism of the political elites responsible for Greece's current position. As early as February, one of the principal preconditions for Hellenic 'salvation' – unanimity in the pursuit of the necessary goals – did not exist.

In 2010, New Democracy had not voted for the first Memorandum. It had taken a critical position towards the 'policy of the Memorandum' and promised a complete renegotiation if it came to power. The Greek Communist Party (KKE) and SYRIZA steadfastly and intensely condemned the policy the

EU was imposing. The conflict between the opposition and the government regressed to traditional partisan politics; the opposition systematically and absolutely rejected the government's analysis but offered little in the way of viable policy alternatives. Opposition to the Memorandum was gradually transformed into opposition to the government on broader terms. The mobilisation of the unions, the growth of popular protests and demonstrations, anger at reductions in income and increases in taxation, along with disillusionment resulting from years of recession, unemployment and misery all contributed to an ever-growing section of Greek society rejecting the Memoranda.

New Democracy's complete about-turn, under the pressure of events as well as from members of the Eurozone, and its participation with LAOS in the Papademos coalition in November 2011, significantly bolstered parliamentary support for the Memorandum. However, this did not stem the anti-Memorandum tide. The parliamentary vote on the second Memorandum in February 2012 acted as a catalyst. In order to deal with the growing disunity and strife in their ranks, the government parties invoked the whip and threatened those who would not vote in favour of the Memorandum with expulsion. Forty-three MPs from PASOK and New Democracy refused to follow to the whip and were expelled. The loosely framed anti-Memorandum coalition gained strength from this expulsion, with corresponding losses for the pro-Memorandum PASOK and New Democracy.

The nearer the elections came, the more lines of cleavage framed in terms of support or rejection of the Memorandum came to dominate the very axis of Greek politics. The debate was increasingly expressed in black and white terms. It prohibited any reasoned discussion regarding Greece's challenges; no compromise or consensus was sought. Either implementation of the Memorandum was presented as a one-way street not to be discussed or questioned, or Greece's refusal to pay its debt was presented as the just response to the European loan sharks. While the former camp failed to engage with the challenges of reform and the need for cooperation, the latter was in denial over the inevitable horrors of a disorderly default, including certain exit from the EMU and a breakdown of relations with Europe.

When publicly questioned, both PASOK's and New Democracy's leaders declared that they were under obligation to follow the Memorandum. However, with their actions they indicated that they did so only under duress. Such tactics to avoid incurring populist wrath did little to alleviate the gravity of the situation. They did not provide the Greek public with the open public debate it required on the merits of the Memorandum. They did nothing to better the relations between Greek politicians and their European partners, and served only to further undermine the already crumbling credibility Greece had on the international stage.

## Notes

1  See *Kathimerini*, 14 December 2011, p. 12.
2  Ted Truman, 'IMF takes tougher stance', *Financial Times*, 26 January 2012, p. 2.
3  This clause allows a collective agreement to remain in force for a certain period of time after its expiry.
4  *IHT*, 17 January 2012, p. 1.
5  'Geo-politique', *Le Monde*, 15–16 January 2012, p. 4.
6  *Ta Nea*, 25 January 2012, p. 11.
7  *Kathimerini*, 26 January 2012, p. 3.
8  Communication by euro area member states, Brussels, 30 January 2012.
9  The proposal had been made by the President of the Parliamentary Group of Christian Democrats and Christian Socialists, Volker Kauder. See *FAZ*, 27 January 2012, p. 1.
10  'Victory for Merkel over fiscal treaty', *Financial Times*, ft.com, 30 January 2012.
11  'Merkel will keinen Sparkomissar in Griechenland', *FAZ*, 31 January 2012, p. 1.
12  On the Fiscal Compact, see Yves Bertoncini, '"Fiscal Compact", sovereignty and austerity', *Notre Europe Tribune*, 26 July 2012.
13  Declaration of members of European Commission, European Council, 30 January 2012.
14  *Kathimerini*, 5 February 2012, p. 5.
15  *Ta Nea*, 6 February 2012, p. 9.
16  *Kathimerini*, 5 February 2012, p. 4.
17  *FAZ*, 7 February 2012, p. 1.
18  *Kathimerini*, 12 February 2012, p. 4; *To Vima*, 13 February 2012, p. A12.
19  A permanent task force preparing the meetings of the Eurogroup.
20  *IHT*, 16 February 2012, p. 16.
21  'Greece: preliminary debt sustainability analysis', 15 February 2012.
22  'Does Germany want Greece out of the euro?', *Financial Times*, ft.com, 15 February 2012.
23  *Le Monde*, 18 January 2012, p. 1.
24  *Ta Nea*, 16 February 2012, p. 9.
25  *Kathimerini*, 16 February 2012, p. 4.
26  'Greek indignation threatens to spread', *Financial Times*, ft.com, 19 February 2012.
27  *Ta Nea*, 20 February 2012, p. 8.
28  The technical term used for this arrangement is 'collective action clauses' (CACs).
29  *IHT*, 3 March 2012, p. 9.
30  Later increased to €50 billion.
31  Eurogroup statement, 21 February 2012, at www.consilium.europa.eu.
32  Ibid.
33  This decision had met at first with fierce resistance from the Greek administration. The establishment of such an account would end the practice of transferring capital, earmarked for pending liabilities, to shortfalls in other sectors of state expenditure, such as salaries and pensions.
34  According to data from the European Commission, *European Economy: The Second Adjustment Programme for Greece', March 2012*, Occasional Paper 94, European Commission, March 2012, table 19, p. 46.

35  In total, €75.5 billion from the first and €72 billion from the second. Owing to the elections, no other instalment was disbursed till the end of June 2012.
36  The Council of European Union Ministers of Finances (Ecofin) convened in Brussels on 21 February. Matters pertaining exclusively to Greece were not discussed. The subject of the meeting was the progress in policies that had been decided on matters of fiscal discipline, competitiveness, growth, as well as 'basic principles of the Community budget for 2013'. It was evident that, despite the Greek problem, the Union continued to steadily implement the policy formulated to realise the – as it perceived it – economic governance of the European area. See Council of European Union, 2012 European Semester – macroeconomic and fiscal guidance – Euro Plus Pact – the way forward. Conclusion of member states participating in the Euro Plus Pact – Economic aspects of the road map to a resource efficient Europe, Council conclusion on the budget guidelines for 2013.
37  *Kathimerini*, 22 February 2012, p. 4.
38  'Noch ein Kreditpacket', *FAZ*, 22 December 2012, p. 1.
39  Eurostat 2010.
40  In answer to a question by the *Financial Times*, Papademos said that the full implementation of the programme would preclude the possibility of further intervention being necessary. 'FT interview transcript: Lucas Papademos', *Financial Times*, 18 March 2012.
41  M. Wolf, 'Much too much … about Greece', *Financial Times,* 14 February 2012.
42  *Kathimerini*, 22 February 2012, p. 4.

# 21

# An evaluation of the Memoranda

The second Memorandum[1] was a resounding confirmation that the first Memorandum had failed. Before the designated period of implementation was even over, its targets had proved to be impossible to achieve, and its reforms and measures had compounded the recession and all its fallout. The diagnosis had been incorrect and consequently so was the prescription. It was simplistic in both its analysis and its remedy. Greece was not sufficiently developed as a country to return to a balanced management of its economy through a stringent policy of austerity: 'The Europeans delayed in drawing up their programme, its concept was wrong, and the distribution of burdens it provided was unjust. The Europeans bear the responsibility for developments in Greece.'[2]

The Troika, of course, did not subscribe to the above analysis. Matthias Mors, the representative of the European Commission, stated in an interview he gave in October 2011:

> in general no mistakes were made in the original plan.... It is true that we underrated the depth of recession. To a certain extent, there were developments that surpassed Greece and no one could have foreseen these.... It is also true that we took many measures all at once.... We are aware that this is very tough. But ... we are at a very critical moment, where Greece must convince the international community ... that it has the will and the ability to achieve the targets which it has committed itself to.[3]

The first Memorandum had been constructed on the premise that Greek debt was sustainable.[4] This premise, as events showed, was misguided. The authors of the Memorandum placed an exclusive emphasis on fiscal discipline. As already discussed,[5] the cause of the crisis in Greece and in the other peripheral countries was not just fiscal mismanagement: much causal weight must also be ascribed to the fundamental imbalances in competitiveness across the Eurozone. The structural reforms prescribed by the Memorandum were necessary, but they were not sufficient in their own right. The Eurozone, and not just Greece, should have addressed these fundamental challenges. A small country, like Greece, could not deal with it on its own.

In order to promote convergence in terms of competitiveness the focus must be on growth. However, growth is not even mentioned in the Memorandum. At numerous summits the need to enhance growth in the Eurozone was remarked on. These remarks were, however, little more than declarations of intent. They referred mainly to the programmes of the Structural Funds available through the EU. Greece had failed to utilise all of its allocation from these Funds, owing either to poor administrative organisation and lack of related expertise or to insufficient national funds to access to European programmes. But beyond structural programmes, there should also be collective action and support to encourage investment in the less developed member states. The countries of the North should offer support to their Southern neighbours in terms of promoting research and development, quality manufacturing, the full utilisation of their natural resources and, by extension, their export sector. The focus on a reduction in expenditure across all sectors of Greek society in order to reduce the deficit inevitably had a negative effect on growth. This emphasis on austerity brought with it a loss of confidence, which led to a loss of investment. Capital allocated specifically for public investment programmes should have been excluded from the austerity programmes.

The former head of the IMF, Dominique Strauss-Kahn, in a talk he gave on European problems, indicated the multi-tiered nature of the crisis: 'It appears today as a debt crisis. More than that, it is a growth crisis. Behind the growth crisis is a leadership crisis.'[6]

Fiscal discipline is a natural product of the conservative attitude of the peoples of the developed countries of Europe. On average, the populations are older and over many years the majority of these populations have acquired a satisfactory standard of living; their concern is, therefore, directed to towards a stable financial model that safeguards their savings. They are less willing to support other countries, to agree to investments in a distant future and to support political changes on a European level. Globalisation, however, is accelerating change and existing trends the world over. The challenges it poses to the developed nations of Europe require dynamic responses, or the continent risks being left behind. While fiscal discipline is necessary, its application must at times be flexible, in recognition of the changing landscape and externalities.

Prevalent among the conservative ideologies of the developed North were punitive notions of how to treat fiscal indiscretion, a belief that 'punishment and making an example of' are imperative. This ideological framework determined the stand of the countries of the North during the first phase of the crisis. Such beliefs clouded their judgement and their ability to predict future developments. Continual pressure through public statements and pejorative comments regarding the need to 'make an example of' particular countries led to a greater and greater lack of faith in Greece, as well as to an intensification of the crisis. By the time the crisis has been overcome, the countries of the Eurozone shall have incurred far greater costs than they would have had they acted earlier and with different intentions.

In its efforts to restore normality, the EU chose what it thought to be the most effective approach, the 'shock' tactic, that is, the immediate restoration of the deficit limit of 3% of GDP. Greece is a prime example of how misguided such 'shock' tactics can be. When suitable conditions do not exist and the state machinery is incapable of implementing the necessary reforms, such tactics will act as little more than a catalyst to economic and social regression. Unprepared to restrict expenditure and committed by various promises it had made to the public sector and the broader electorate, the government made clear its preference for fiscal measures which would show immediate results. It repeatedly taxed income, and reduced pensions and salaries, instead of taking on major vested interests, including the defence industry and the unions. Experience indicates that an increase in taxation rarely generates the increase in revenue forecast. The net addition to the public budget is invariably much lower, because such measures compound recession, restrict the ability to pay tax and augment social protest. Recession and unemployment in Greece greatly exceeded projections. Poverty and misery spread to large sections of the population. It was not by chance that every review by the Troika concluded that the country was falling short of its targets; each new measure prescribed in response to the shortfall served only to worsen the symptoms that were making the targets so difficult to achieve. The new measures were a replica of the previous measures conceived to increase revenue, primarily through the same targets of taxation, income and pension provision. Time and time again, this was not sufficient. A plan to exit a crisis of these proportions is not merely a mathematical problem calculated on the basis of reliable data, but entails broader economic and social planning, which inherently includes additional variables. Factors such as the capability of the state machinery, the level of related expertise and administration as well as public comprehension and support must all be considered.

The theory that if adjustment is structured over a longer period of time it will inherently incur greater costs for the creditors is a false one. When the adjustment is forced into an extremely narrow temporal framework, it has catastrophic consequences for income. This inevitably affects tax receipts, which undermines any effort to balance the national budget. The expedient nature of the adjustment simply serves to drive the country deeper into recession, in a vicious circle. The end game of such rapid adjustment is that the overall cost to the creditors is far greater than it would have been if a programme of progressive adjustment had been adopted.[7] The most effective course to redress a crisis such as that in Greece must evidently have structural adjustment and reform at its core, addressing waste and mismanagement in the public sector, but a ruthless assault on living standards and salaries will not end a recession.

In Greece, the very rapid reduction in income mobilised massive popular dissent against the Memorandum. Wave after wave of cuts in the ongoing efforts to pull billions out of the Greek budget, followed by inevitably repeated visits of the Troika, advising that the efforts had not been sufficient, fuelled widespread fury. The unions in the public sector were capable of mobilising massive support to achieve deferrals or cancellations of policies that affected their members. The government lacked the political will or strength to take on such populist pressure, and turned its efforts on ill advised short-term measures. The result was greater and greater pressure to find funds, in conjunction with ever-mounting populist resistance.

The predictions of the second Memorandum allow a comparative analysis with the value, theory and prescriptions of the first. Table 21.1 highlights some basic macroeconomic figures from the reports of the IMF of May 2010 (Report A) and March 2012 (Report B) to support my analysis.[8] The reports of both the IMF and the EU do not designate a precise rate of interest on their loans, since interest rates fluctuate. Table 21.2 shows the reference rate of interest and the marginal rate of interest for every category of loan.

The forecasts of the second Memorandum have unfortunately been shown to have been misguided. According to Eurostat, unemployment had reached 27% in November 2012, nearly eight points above the forecast (19.4%), and the number of unemployed exceeded 1,300,000.[9]

The most spectacular failure of the first Memorandum was the forecast for recession. At the end of the four-year period 2009–12, recession was expected to reach approximately –23% of GDP, whereas the original calculations indicated it would not exceed –7.5% of GDP. It actually reached three times greater than forecast. This gulf between forecast and reality was the result of the incorrect evaluation of the effects of the reforms and the policy of austerity, as well as of the overly optimistic belief that structural measures and privatisation would rapidly drive progress and a return to growth. The recession was fuelled by the constant rise in taxation, the continual cuts in income, the suspension of construction activity, the lack of investment, the fall in tourism and the collapse in demand. In the summer of 2012 a taxpayer with real estate property had to pay: greater tax on income than in 2011, owing to the reduction of the tax-free bracket and changes in tax rates; a tax on real estate wealth for 2010 (and probably for 2011); an extra levy on real estate wealth for 2012 (also known as the *Harachi*); a solidarity levy over and above income tax. And all of this was while salaries were being cut by approximately 20%. If this was not a sufficient burden in its own right, this taxpayer was already paying more for petrol, electricity, transport and highway tolls, as well as for all consumer goods owing to the increase in VAT to 23%. It is therefore no surprise that when faced with this myriad of greatly increased expenses, the taxpayer would already have reduced consumption drastically. The same behaviour on the part of millions of citizens simultaneously restricted economic activity to a degree that many businesses – those not already insolvent – became moribund. The Troika indicated that it did not agree with the continual increase in taxation: this was the choice of the Greek government. However, the Memorandum gave the Troika the authority to evaluate the consequences of these policies, to

**Table 21.1** Comparison of some basic macroeconomic figures for the first and second Memoranda

| | Review of loans |
|---|---|
| Report A | Total financing €110 billion, in instalments. The EU to pay €80 billion and the IMF €30 billion |
| | The instalments are of different amounts. They shall be paid by the EU from May 2010 to the second quarter of 2013, and by the IMF from May 2010 to the first quarter of 2013 |
| | By 14 December 2011, the EU had paid €52.9 billion and the IMF €20.1 billion, a total of €73 billion |
| Report B | Total financing €172.7 billion, in instalments. The EU to pay €144.7 billion, the IMF €28 billion. The €144.7 billion includes the balance owed by the EU from the first loan, amounting to €27.1 billion. The IMF did not agree to pay the €10 billion from the first package which it had not disbursed |
| | The instalments are in different amounts. They shall be paid by the EU from the first quarter of 2012 to the fourth quarter of 2014; and by the IMF from March 2012 to 29 February 2016 |

| | 2009 | 2010 | 2011 | 2012 | 2013 | 2014 |
|---|---|---|---|---|---|---|
| *General government deficit as a percentage of GDP* | | | | | | |
| Report A | −13.6 | −8.1 | −7.6 | −6.5 | −4.9 | −2.6 |
| Report B | −15.8 | −10.8 | −9.3 | −7.3 | −4.6 | −2.1 |
| *Rise in GDP (% annual change)* | | | | | | |
| Report A | −2.0 | −4.0 | −2.6 | 1.1 | 2.1 | 2.1 |
| Report B | −3.3 | −3.5 | −6.9 | −4.8 | 0.0 | 2.5 |
| *Sovereign debt as a percentage of GDP* | | | | | | |
| Report A | 115.1 | 133.2 | 145.2 | 148.7 | 149.2 | 146.1 |
| Report B | 129.1 | 144.7 | 165.3 | 163.2 | 167.3 | 160.7 |
| *Sovereign debt in €billion* | | | | | | |
| Report A | 273.4 | 307.5 | 324.7 | 339.7 | 350.4 | 353.8 |
| Report B | 299.0 | 329.0 | 355.8 | 332.4 | 339.4 | 334.1 |
| *Unemployment as a percentage of the labour force* | | | | | | |
| Report A | 9.4 | 11.8 | 14.6 | 14.8 | 14.3 | 14.1 |
| Report B | 9.4 | 12.5 | 17.3 | 19.4 | 19.4 | 18.2 |

Report A = Country Report No. 10/110, IMF, May 2010.
Report B = Country Report No. 12/57, IMF, March 2012.

*Note:* Unshaded figures present actual results. Shaded figures are forecasts at the time the reports were drawn up.

**Table 21.2** The reference rate of interest and the marginal rate of interest for every category of loan to Greece from the European Union (EU) and the International Monetary Fund (IMF)

| Report | EU | IMF | Private sector |
|---|---|---|---|
| *Rate of interest* | | | |
| A | 3-month Euribor + 3% for the first 3 years | SDR rate + 2% for the first 3 years | |
| | 3-month Euribor + 4% for the next 2 years | SDR rate + 3% for the next 2 years | |
| | Lump sum charge of 0.5% on disbursement of each instalment[a] | Lump sum charge of 0.5% on disbursement of each instalment[b] | |
| | The decision of June 2011 reduced the rate of interest by 100 b.p. (1%) | | |
| B | EFSF loans: EFSF financing cost (interest rate on bonds the EFSF will issue as will be set by the market) + fee to cover operating costs | SDR rate + 2% for the first 3 years | New PSI bonds: 2% to 2015, 3% from 2016–20, 3.65% in 2021 and 4.3% from 2022 onwards |
| | EU loans already given through first Memorandum: | SDR rate + 3% for the next 2 years | |
| | 3-month Euribor + 1.5%; the new rate of interest will be retroactive[c] | Lump sum charge of 0.5% on disbursement of each instalment | |
| *Repayment schedule* | | | |
| A | A total of 5 years from disbursement of every instalment, with a 3-year period of grace for repayment of capital | A total of 5 years from disbursement of every instalment; 3-year period of grace for repayment of capital | |
| | With the decision of June 2011, a total of 10 years from disbursement of each instalment, with a 4.5-year period of grace | Repayment in 8 quarterly instalments over the next 2 years | |

| B | EFSF loans: A total of 30 years from disbursement of each instalment, with a 10-year period of grace for repayment of capital | A total of 10 years: 4-year period of grace for repayment of capital | New PSI bonds: A total of 30 years with a 10-year period of grace for repayment of capital |
| | | Repayment in 12 half-yearly instalments over the next 6 years | |

**Debt restructuring**

A    No. Greek sovereign debt was deemed sustainable

B    Yes. Greek sovereign debt was not deemed sustainable, and the restructuring was done to render it sustainable again

**Date specified for a return to the markets**

A    2012

B    2021 for a complete return. Partial return is forecast for 2016, according to the IMF

---

[a] With this arrangement the total interest rate fluctuated round 6%.

[b] Total interest rate fluctuated round 3.8%.

[c] The total interest rate fluctuated round 2–4.3% on the new bonds replacing the old ones, and around 3.5% on the EFSF loan. The highest profit margin for loans granted by member states with the first Memorandum was set at 1.5%.

Euribor, inter-bank lending rate; SDR, special drawing rights; b.p., basis points.

suspend certain measures and to insist on structural reforms and privatisations. It made no such moves. For the Troika, the primary concern was the timely achievement of the deficit targets, in order to avoid new loans. It was interested above all in immediate fiscal results. Increased taxation and cuts in income served its purposes.

Another typical example of the gulf between the Memorandum's targets and actual results was the development of the rate of interest on 10-year bonds. The Greek government requested financial support from the EU in April 2010 in response to the hike in rates available on the market. On 23 April 2010, the day the initial application for support was formally announced by the Greek Prime Minister from the island of Kastelorizo, the market rate for 10-year bonds stood at 8.66%. With the Memorandum, a lower rate of interest of less than 5% and a return to the markets in 2012 were to be ensured. Just one year later, on 22 April 2011, the rate of interest had reached 14.9%. Two years later it had risen to 21.38%. By 17 June 2012, the day the elections were held, it had spiralled to a staggering 26.43%. The full return to the markets was, therefore, postponed from 2012 to 2021, as stipulated in the second Memorandum.

The level of the current account deficit was equally indicative of the gulf between the aims of the measures and the results they produced. The Memorandum aimed at reducing this deficit by improving competitiveness. The 'internal devaluation' (through a reduction in salaries) was designed to achieve this. The deficit, however, remained high. In 2009 it was 14.3% of GDP. In 2010 it fell to 12.1% and in 2011 to 10.3%, or approximately €22 billion. This did mark a fall, but not in line with the targets of the Memorandum.[10] This high deficit indicated that competitiveness had not significantly improved; the economy continued to spend more than what it produced and it was necessary to borrow to cover the difference.

To compound these inherent flaws in the theory and calculations of the Memorandum, there were recurrent delays in implementation, on the part of the Greek administration, for fear of the political costs of the painful reforms. Much excess in the public sector, because of redundant or underperforming bodies, was not effectively cut. The more or less superfluous organisations were merged with other public sector bodies and so very few personnel were actually dismissed. Any savings achieved were so small as to be negligible. This was despite the fact that a Deputy Prime Minister was assigned the task of expediting the process, which was also monitored by the Prime Minister and the Cabinet. Though the results were meagre, each such move was announced with a triumphant public statement of valiant efforts. The closure of the 'labour reserve',[11] which would have been a significant measure to reduce public expenditure but without entailing excessive reactions, turned into a fiasco, as the minister responsible admitted himself. It only led to an acceleration of retirement among employees who were close to retirement age anyhow. The new unified payroll should have been legislated for and brought into effect in the middle of 2011. However, it was delayed for months, and implemented only under duress, in response to the threat of the sixth instalment being withheld at the end of 2011.

The new social security legislation had already been passed in 2010. It marked a significant success, and created expectations for expedient action to ensue. However, rather unsurprisingly, delays followed. The matter of auxiliary pensions, for example, was still outstanding when the second Memorandum was voted into effect. The deregulation of markets developed like a television soap, with conflicts, reversals, denials and clashes between ministers, with little substantive progress ever truly made. Privatisation programmes did need time. However, the continual deferrals in their implementation[12] indicate that the progress of the programme rarely adhered to the proposals.

With regard to the crucial matter of tax collection and evasion, by mid-2012 little progress had been made. Certain spectacular actions were made to imply progress, such as the arrest of well known business people who regularly avoided their taxes, or the incarceration of persons who, despite not declaring any income, had significant bank deposits. Major discussions over a new taxation system stalled. Public opinion widely subscribed to the belief that if tax evasion was effectively combated, then the exponential tax rises would no longer be necessary. Paradoxically, however, it was in no small part the excessive taxation that accompanied the Memorandum which caused tax evasion to become endemic.

Had the structural reforms of the Memorandum been effectively implemented, this would no doubt have enhanced Athens' credibility and fostered a more positive climate. It is doubtful, however, whether the reforms would have drastically limited the recession or whether they would have brought about a swifter return to growth, as forecast. Changes of such magnitude need time to bear fruit. They cannot be implemented in a 'social vacuum'. Society needs time to adjust and adapt to a changing environment and adopt the appropriate norms and values to accommodate such changes. The optimism of the authors of the Memorandum was such that they felt they would be able to orchestrate the rationalisation, modernisation and improvement in the competitiveness of the Greek economy through top-down legislative reform and almost overnight. They failed to realise that beyond mere legislation, political will and social mobilisation are required for such a project to succeed. If these preconditions do not exist, the prospects for success are highly limited.[13]

The Memorandum sought through structural reform of the labour market to move Greece towards an export-driven economy. In Greek society, demand for jobs is strongly determined either by the job security and higher pay offered by the public sector, or by administratively established earnings in certain professions. For example, lawyers' associations and their parliamentary lobby promoted legislation that was neither necessary nor justified but that bolstered lawyers' earnings. Greece has therefore, proportionally to its population, a far higher percentage of lawyers than other European states. However, the abolition of all unnecessary regulations, correctly stipulated in the reforms of the Memorandum, would not improve the state of the Greek economy if there were not sufficient alternative employment to be taken. The challenge of employment in Greece is inherently aggravated by the small size of the manufacturing sector, comparatively low levels of entrepreneurial expertise and educational attainment, as well as the gulf in competitiveness with the other major economies of the continent.

In April 2012, Greek public opinion hailed the 'potato movement' as a way to 'liberate' the market from intermediaries. The potato producers of Nevrokopi and other parts of the country decided to sell their produce directly to the large urban centres, bypassing the intermediary traders, and thus offering their products at much lower prices. Enthusiasm prevailed for this movement and producers of other products were urged to do the same. In Greece after 1981, the Ministry of Agriculture had sought to create in the main districts of the country markets based on the Danish and Dutch models. Producers would directly sell their goods to traders and interested parties through auctions. Cooperatives would undertake the management of these markets. However, this initiative was cancelled in 1985. Neither the farmers nor the cooperatives agreed with the initiative, while consumers remained indifferent. The market status quo, up till then, was for them less complex and more profitable, as well as being removed from direct oversight by the tax authorities and for that reason preferable for all the participants. The 'potato movement' that so impressed the media was nothing but a spontaneous version of the solution which had been rejected in Greece some 25 years previously. Established practices that restrict competition preserve high prices and maintain inefficient and multi-tiered trading structures to the detriment of the consumer; these proved (and are still proving) stronger and more entrenched than any moves towards bottom-up liberalisation. For the successful removal of such vested interests, there must be steady political will and a systematic effort to counter regressive practices.

Prices in Greece remain high as a result of high costs in materials, goods and labour that must be incurred in the production of any given product. Indicative of this challenge is the shipbuilding and repair industry. Greek shipyards suffer because their costs are notably higher than their Far Eastern or even Eastern European counterparts. The Greek state maintained this inefficient industry through the provision of state contracts. As such, the state borrowed to pay the overpriced labour costs to keep the industry alive, rather than seek to establish competitive rates. However, the EU forbade such protectionist practices. The shipyards closed. The unemployed workers demanded solutions and the yard owners were still expecting state subsidies.

The authors of the Memorandum believed that the pressure for a drastic reduction of the deficit in an exceptionally short time would force Greek society to reform such dated and costly practices. However, in the face of a crisis, entrenched industries, such as shipbuilding or agriculture, will inevitably put up a dogmatic and fierce resistance to any move to undermine the status quo. While it would always be easier to reform in times of prosperity, the retort in better times is: 'Since things are going well, why should we change them?' Such a philosophy, the populist mentality, the fear of electoral losses, along with the partisan support for opposition to any effort at reform resulted in policies that for too long avoided the painful challenges of modernisation.

A large section of Greek society considered the cause of all the country's troubles to stem from the Troika's intervention and the Memorandum. They avoided answering critical questions objectively, and viewed the status quo and times gone by through rose-tinted glasses. Such a prism leads to a failure to engage with some of the major critical questions:

### Did the state of the Greek economy imply that recourse to the EU was inevitable in early 2010?

External financial support was absolutely necessary. It could only come from the Eurozone, the IMF and the ECB. Some time previously, the EU had clarified that it would involve the IMF, should the economy of a member state need supervision. The IMF was not, as many maintain, the strictest of the lenders. The European Commission was often far more draconian. The presence of the ECB was also necessary, due to its role in supervising the banking sector and as a regulator of the monetary system. Greece had excessive budget deficits and very high sovereign debt; by 2010 it no longer retained any independent credit-worthiness. Without financial support, a disorderly default was inevitable. The Troika's support saved Greece from immediate and complete collapse and made future support and recovery a possibility.

The argument that Greece could have avoided the Memorandum, had it acted in an expedient fashion in October 2010, borrowing the necessary funds when interest rates were low, has been put forward. As events have proved, the country needed support far in excess of the €110 billion originally deemed sufficient. With rapid and covert action in October, it could have possibly ensured €10–20 billion, but not the funds necessary or sufficient to avoid external intervention.

Greece could have gone a long way to mitigate the most severe effects of the recession and the length of the crisis, had the government taken the proverbial bull by the horns, recognised the severity of the situation and directed all its efforts at a coherent and comprehensive plan to modernise the nation and drastically reduce expenditure.

### Did the European Commission, the IMF and the ECB know that the Memorandum did not 'add up'?

They probably did. The prescriptions of the Memorandum ignore standard rules for the evaluation of a nation's capacity to exit a crisis, such as the self-evident fact that the interest rate on borrowing must not be steadily higher than the projected rates of growth.

According to its statutes, the IMF can lend a country if its debt is sustainable. The Greek debt was not. The PSI arrangements and the restructuring of the debt in 2011–12 were the undisputable proof that in May 2010 the lenders had not cared about sustainability. There was a concrete reason. The Eurozone wanted to leave the creditor banks unscathed.[14] Its member states decided to take upon themselves the risk of the solvency of the debtor. They lent Greece the necessary sums to pay off the banks. The €110 billion rescue package corresponded approximately to what Greece owed to German and French banks.

Moreover, in May 2010, the Eurozone was not interested in conclusively solving the Greek problem. It wanted to ward off the threat of a Greek default, to force the country to implement a strict fiscal policy and to supervise its economic performance from then on. Its aim was to gain time and then to formulate a broader strategy for managing the crises of all the peripheral countries of the EU. Once this was done, it would then seek to re-examine the Greek problem, under circumstances that would permit a more permanent solution. This analysis is supported by the moves to establish in May 2010 the temporary stability mechanism (the EFSF) and in March 2011 the permanent stability mechanism (the ESM) after approval of the Greek loan. In discussions regarding the ESM, it was indicated that the Greek case, though a satisfactory solution was agreed, would be re-examined in the context of debt sustainability and the dangers it entailed for the financial stability of the Eurozone.[15] This indicates that in May 2010 the objectives were clearly short term, focused on the immediate control of the Greek challenge. This it achieved. But because the crisis both in Greece and in the Eurozone was affected by unforeseen developments, it fell short of ensuring any closure with regard to the Greek question. It would become rapidly apparent that the provisions concerning the EFSF and the ESM were overtaken by events and new agreements had to be negotiated.

## Was acceptance of the Memorandum mandatory?
## Could Greece have been given the money without political conditions or upon more favourable terms?

The Memorandum underpinned a loan of €110 billion to Greece. Financial support to a sovereign state or a private entity, on the brink of bankruptcy, is never going to be granted without stringent conditions to minimise the creditor's risk of losing its capital. Loans granted by international organisations, or by states to other states, have always been accompanied by reform programmes designed to drive modernisation and return the nation to a sustainable footing. Even the Marshall Plan, often cited by Athens,[16] which was a grant rather than a loan, had detailed conditions attached, to ensure the funds were not squandered.[17] The conditions of the Memorandum were conventional IMF terms, but these were not realistic for Greece. The Greek case, as mentioned above, was considered a typical case of financial indiscretion on the part of a developed country, which can, with the correct prescriptions, expedite a return to a balanced budget and a sound economic footing. The creditors were superficial and misguided in their analysis; they cared little for the social ramifications of a severe austerity programme, and rather wished to make an example to deter other member states from such indiscretions. These conditions should have been adjusted in the case of Greece. The loan, however, was not a conventional loan acquired on the international bond market, but rather blurred the lines between economic and political action and conditionality. It created a new 'political–economic relationship' in the context of the Eurozone. As such, the specific challenges and idiosyncrasies of the Hellenic crisis should have been recognised, as should the range of political, economic and social concerns; instead, purely fiscal targets underwrote the Memorandum.[18]

Athens' major shortcoming was the fundamental lack of preparation that undermined, if not negated entirely, any strength it might have had in negotiations. In discussions regarding the second Memorandum, New Democracy did not present a more coherent or prepared platform from which to conduct negotiations than PASOK had done in negotiating the first. The focus of the Greek political parties remained primarily directed towards the domestic audience rather than seeking to genuinely impress or alter the mind-set of its international creditors.

## Was there another solution?

The claims that the Chinese and Russians were prepared to offer Greece money are completely unfounded. On the contrary, they urged Greece to seek support from the IMF. Proposals indicating the country would have been able to receive unconditional financial support if it were to cede as collateral its non-existent oil resources or public land were fundamentally naïve.

It was also claimed 'that the Greek government should have raised the matter of debt restructuring with its European partners before entering the assistance programme'.[19] It is certainly true that an engagement with the re-structuring debate at the first signs of the crisis would have been of great benefit to Greece. If a haircut had been made much earlier, the entire adjust-ment programme would have proven far less painful. But it is very misguided to assume that the debate regarding restructuring would have been given even a cursory examination by European institutions or financial authorities in early 2010. As already discussed, restructuring has major consequences in terms of precedent and fallout; it is nothing short of a last resort should all else prove insufficient. The true severity of Greece's situation became apparent only in late 2010, when it became evident that the adjustment programme was not capable of restoring the country to a sustainable financial footing. Neither the ECB nor the member states whose banks had provided Greece with credit would have accepted action that would lead to widespread write-offs of debt and rewarded financial mismanagement. There is no way such an initiative could have been tabled in May 2010. On the contrary, the high levels of interest applied to Greek borrowing clearly indicated the preference for punitive terms.

## Would leaving the EMU and returning to the drachma have been a solution? Could Greece have avoided 'internal devaluation' in this way?

Departure from the EMU and a return to the drachma would in all prob-ability have led to bankruptcy; the new currency would have seen major and recurrent devaluations, with far more grave consequences than the 'internal devaluation', for income, purchasing power and living standards. At the same time, a plethora of controls and prohibitions would have been necessary in order to support the drachma. Greece would have ended up in an administra-tion of the economy comparable to the draconian regime that immediately followed World War II. The current crisis would have looked like a minor economic accident when compared with the depression that a return to the drachma would have ushered in. Membership of the EMU extends way beyond narrow economic considerations. It affects the status of Greece within the international community, the opportunities and freedoms available to its citizens, living standards, cultural norms and values, educational institutions and development. This is evident when one draws a simple comparison with Greece's neighbours in the Balkans and the Middle East.[20]

### Would a radically different policy have been possible?

Critics of the Memorandum maintain that if a Keynesian model had been adopted, rather than one of stringent austerity, economic activity would be sufficiently stimulated to drive Greece out of recession and crisis. Such critics omit to indicate where they think the necessary capital could be drawn from. As has been shown, the markets made capital available only at rates that could not be sustained, even in the medium term. Monetary union meant that Greece no longer had the ability to undertake quantitative easing as implemented in the US or the UK. Fellow member states inside the EMU would not provide the sums required for a Keynesian model, nor would they condone endlessly pouring capital into an exponentially growing sovereign debt. Those who chose to ignore the realities of the situation, favouring instead naïve idealism, did nothing to assist a reasoned, if painful, debate recognising the gravity of the situation in which Greece found itself. Athens had neither the political capital nor the international credibility to acquire support on the scale required for a radically different 'solution'. Had the 'anti-Memorandum forces' taken the reins of power in Greece, there would not suddenly have been a pot of gold available which overnight could reverse Hellenic fortunes. Furthermore, any refusal to pay debts would in no way ensure employment, production or capital. Such claims were nothing but a fallacy.

Greece was a unique case; its deficits and its debt were excessive compared with its productive capacity and ability to produce wealth. Not one of those criticising the economic model of strict fiscal discipline, whether they be Keynesian, social democrat or liberal, ever claimed that it would be possible to stabilise the economy without reducing the deficits and debt, enacting structural changes and broader reform of the modus operandi of the state. They unanimously agreed that the preconditions for 'more money' were a restoration of economic stability and economic reform, along with the modernisation of social practices, the state and the political structure. Differing views inevitably existed over how best to promote adjustment and ensure the Greek economy was once again placed on a stable footing, but little credible opinion would contest the premise that an over-indebted nation needs to be 'put in order'. Paul Krugman, one of the most vociferous critics of austerity, accepted the unique nature of the Greek case. Owing to its 'unprecedented profligacy', Greece had little choice but to follow a stringent 'programme of cutting down its deficits'.[21]

This 'order' can be the object of heated discussion: how best to achieve it, and what other targets – economic, social and political – must be served simultaneously. The Memorandum reflected majority opinion across the Eurozone. Other solutions would also have needed to be the object of serious and sustained deliberation. The starting point of any such discussions would have been the undoubted need for 'change' and not simply how to reverse the current situation.

## Were there positive results from implementing the Memoranda?

Thanks to the Memoranda, Greek society once again became conscious of the need to modernise the country. They drew into sharp focus just how under-developed Greece was compared with its European partners. The reform of the social security system, the deregulation of markets, the unified payroll or the reform of the tax system have been recognised nationally for the pressing matters that they are, even if reform has met fierce resistance. Some reform has seen satisfactory progress, but far too many programmes have stalled in the face of entrenched resistance. However, Greek society has gone some way towards recognising the imperative for change. There is also recognition of the economic challenge, whereas, prior to 2010, neither PASOK nor New Democracy wanted to admit its extent, nor its causes. There was widespread denial, indicated through claims such as 'there is money'. The economic imperatives were paid little more than lip service through vague discourse regarding the need for 'stricter control of public expenses'.

The implementation of the Memoranda contributed to a reduction of the overall deficit by over eight percentage points: from 15.8% of GDP in 2009, to 10.8% in 2010 and 7.3% at the end of 2012.[22] This is a significant fall. The restructuring of the debt cut approximately €105 billion off Greek liabilities and facilitated debt repayment. The decisions taken by the Eurogroup in November 2012 were calculated to contribute to an additional reduction in debt of €40 billion.

Greece's problem was, in no small part, due to its limited competitiveness resulting from high labour costs and low productivity. The unit labour cost in Greece had increased by over 20 points between 2001 and 2009.[23] A 'positive' result of the measures, provided we ignore obvious and painful social costs, was that the unit labour cost returned to 1995 levels, thereby creating the preconditions for competitiveness, future recovery and employment.[24]

The crisis and the subsequent programme of austerity significantly increased poverty in the country. In 2012, 19.5% of the population were deprived of basic needs, compared with 15.2% in 2011 and 11.6% in 2010. However, the increase in the unequal distribution of income was limited due to the fact that the income of nearly the whole population was compressed. Poverty reached 23.1% of the population at the end of 2012 against 20.1% in 2010. The composition of those in poverty changed. A significant section of the middle classes joined the poor. The fall in income of the upper fifth of the earnings spectrum was approximately 5%, while for the lower fifth it was 3%.[25]

The negative fallout of the Memoranda has already been given extensive discussion. In a comment on whether the Memoranda had succeeded, F. Georgeles wrote: 'It's like the joke: the operation was successful, the patient died'.[26] This vivid description should, however, be amended as follows: 'The operation succeeded only marginally; the patient continues to be in grave danger; he is in intensive care; a continuation of efforts is needed with a modified cure so he will not die'.[27]

### Was (and is) a renegotiation of the Memorandum possible?

The first Memorandum, reformed by second Memorandum, saw a significant improvement to the terms of the loan. However, the conditions related to a reduction of the deficits and the gradual achievement of surpluses remained exceedingly oppressive. They needed to be relaxed to allow the Greek people to breathe. This required cooperation and consensus, not unilateral statements from one side or the other.

The achievement of a deficit of 9.3% in 2011, as opposed to the 7.6% of GDP specified in the targets, was a result of falls in revenue and failure to sufficiently reduce expenditure. Athens attributed this failure to the recession alone. Recession bore the most responsibility, but not all of it. One must also give sufficient consideration to the effects of delays in tax reforms, the deferral of the privatisation programmes and the mergers of state organisations, and the failure to implement measures designed to limit expenditure and modernise the Greek economy. In Greece these factors were downplayed, if not ignored outright. Such denial was detrimental to Greek credibility and the prospect of any renegotiation of the Memorandum. Across Europe it was widely felt that any effort to renegotiate was little more that gamesmanship, aimed at avoiding the difficult reforms Greece was faced with. It would burden other members of the EMU with further costs. There was no appetite to pour any further funds into Greece. The opposition to support for Athens had risen drastically in domestic politics across the Eurozone; populist dissent and parliamentary opposition to such financial support saw an exponential rise.

Renegotiation might have been possible, but Greece's partners first had to be convinced of the seriousness of its intentions.[28] Such negotiations could occur only in a climate of mutual respect and cooperation, which Greece had to strive to rebuild. A comprehensive vision and well founded proposals needed to be addressed by those steering Greek efforts.

### Did the Memoranda secure the conditions for a steady course towards modernisation?

Confronting the crisis made a large proportion of the Greek population aware of the problems that the country had to address. But the ideology, convictions and practices needed for future convergence with the developed countries of the EU were not created. It is still not certain that the social causes of the crisis will be tackled effectively once the Memoranda are no longer in force.

The Commission and the IMF paid increasingly close attention to the structural reform programme which Greece had to implement. 'To ensure that the recession gradually bottoms out and gives way to a steady recovery in 2004 it is essential that structural reforms gain much stronger support and momentum', argued the IMF.[29] 'A failure to implement structural reforms would hold back investment and the economic recovery', concluded the European Commission.[30]

The Troika has indicated, imposed and monitored many structural changes, not only in sectors where its intervention was a matter of course, such as revenue administration, tax policy and the banking sector, but also in other matters, such as public administration,[31] the health-care system, the education system and the judicial system. The Troika is still involved in almost every significant matter in Greece, with the exception of foreign policy and defence. For Greeks it is a power centre, equivalent to the Greek government and in some matters outranking it. Unlike an adviser, it does not express opinions; rather, it decides what must happen, when and how. It urges the Greek government to follow its recommendations and conducts systematic checks on whether they have been implemented. Indeed, it threatens to cut off funding if they are not implemented. This mode of operation has brought it face to face with Greek public opinion. A climate of dictates, pressures and penalties cannot bring the people on board.

The reports of the IMF and the Commission have repeatedly emphasised that successive Greek governments 'have not assumed ownership' of the stabilisation programme. According to the *Oxford Dictionary*, 'ownership' means 'to acknowledge authorship'.[32] In fact, Greek governments have frequently stated that the measures they are implementing are demands of the Troika and are being accepted by Greece in order to ensure that it receives financing. The Troika also declares that it proposed and approved the Memorandum measures and that if they are not implemented it will not authorise payment of the loan. The Greek public has not the slightest doubt that the Troika is the 'author' and 'owner' of the bailout programme. That is why a continuation of the presence of the Troika after the payment of the last instalment in the year 2014 will provoke strong reactions. Domestically, this will be seen as the continuation of a 'subjugation policy'. The Eurozone could indeed continue the close monitoring of the Greek economy through other means, which are now at its disposal following the entry into force of the Fiscal Compact.

The overwhelming majority of the Greek population believes that the adjustment programme was badly designed and implemented. The example that everyone cites is the course of the recession. As mentioned above, the recession for all of the period 2009–13 was expected to be more than −27.2% in terms of GDP, although according to the forecasts of the Troika it would not exceed −7.5% of GDP. The Troika did not intervene to prevent this. It was also very slow to take action, such as restructuring the debt, to correct its mistakes.

The Troika's policy was not based on an adequate study of Greek conditions, and not only of economic issues. A typical example is the reform of the judicial system. In Greece, a judicial ruling takes years. Hundreds of thousands of cases await court hearings. The Troika correctly deemed that 'a much wider use of the e-application' was needed.[33] But the delays are not only due to the imperfect e-application but to procedural rules that benefit lawyers by increasing their billable hours. Moreover, judges are not bound to strict working conditions that would oblige them to hear cases more promptly. Decisive action to speed up the administration of justice would have to involve not only e-application but also the lawyers' and judges' lobbies.

Many of the new reforms were decided on without account being taken of the ability of the state mechanism to implement them. The result was that they were subsequently revoked and replaced by new, equally inadequate rules, so that the average person did not know what the law required. A typical example was that of tax reforms concerning the number and kind of expense receipts a taxpayer had to present to the authorities in order to get a tax rebate. In mid-2013, after repeated amendments, not even officials of the Ministry of Finance could specify the rules that would apply to incomes for the 2013 tax year. Yet another modification was needed. Under pressure to achieve results, the state administration acted arbitrarily, or ignored the objections of the public, or simply worked to rule. Rage and despair were rampant among the public. The state lost its authority. Everyday life became a nightmare. When the Memorandum expires, political parties will distance themselves from the reform policy. The matter of modernising Greek society will remain, however. Addressing the shortcomings of Greek society requires a new programme – a comprehensible, credible, feasible programme. It also presupposes an ideological, political and economic struggle to get people to understand the aims of the policy. It will need citizens who are ready to fight for the new ideas. It will need leaders prepared to rouse public opinion against the clientele system and vested interests.

After so many years of crisis, politicians will be more reluctant than ever to introduce unpopular measures. Essential measures will be rejected on the grounds that they are 'Memorandum-style'. Few politicians will be ready to actively promote social change, to explain that modernisation comes at a price and that it takes courage to combat shortcomings. Extreme nationalism, populism and demagoguery will all have a significant political presence.

### Notes

1   The second Memorandum appears in *European Economy: The Second Adjustment Programme for Greece, March 2012*, Occasional Paper 94, European Commission, March 2012, pp. 93ff.; and Country Report No. 12/57, IMF, March 2012, p. 102.

2   J. Pisani-Ferry, 'Economie', *Le Monde*, 21 February 2012, p. 2.

3   *Kathimerini*, 13 October 2011, p. 3.

4  See Chapter 7, for the central goals of the first Memorandum and the assumptions on which it was based.

5  See p. 7.

6  'Strauss-Kahn sees "growth crisis" in Europe', *Financial Times*, 19 December 2011.

7  See J. Pisani-Ferry, 'Eurozone countries must not be forced to meet deficit targets', *Financial Times,* 27 February 2012.

8  Country Report No. 10/110, IMF, May 2010; Country Report No. 12/57, IMF, March 2012. The European Commission's data are similar, but with minor differences. See *European Economy: The Economic Adjustment Programme for Greece*, Occasional Paper 61, May 2010, and *European Economy*, Occasional Paper 94, European Commission, March 2012.

9  *Naftemboriki*, 2 March 2013, p. 7.

10  Source, *European Economy*, Occasional Paper 94, March 2012, p. 16. In 2002 and 2003 it was 6.5%, whereas in 2004 it was 5.8% of GDP.

11  On the basis of the labour reserve arrangement, public sector employees ceased working but were not fired and continued to be paid a significant percentage of their salary. They could later be called back into service.

12  See *Kathimerini*, 2 May 2012. In June 2012 the newly elected government announced that it would push ahead with the draft of a law to settle 77 pending matters that had been obstructing the privatisation programme for over a year. See *Kathimerini*, 22 July 2012, p. 7.

13  D. Malliaropoulos and T. Anastasatos, *Eurobank Research: Economy and Markets*, vol. 8, issue 1, January 2013, p. 10: 'Several analysts point to the delays of the Greek government in implementing structural reforms as the main cause of the inability ... to fend off the deep recession. Undoubtedly, this was harmful for long-term prospects. However, it is well known from international experience that price competitiveness gains and, even more, structural reform require a period of 2–3 years at a minimum to yield their full benefit to potential GDP growth.'

14  M. Wolf, 'The toxic legacy of the Greek crisis', *Financial Times*, 19 June 2003.

15  See p. 74.

16  See p. 125.

17  See Christos Chadjiiosif, 'Marshall Plan and economic programming the French and the Greek way', in Thanasis Sphikas (ed.), *The Marshall Plan: Reconstruction and Division of Europe*, Patakis, 2011, pp. 183ff, pp. 101ff. Also, in the chapter by G. Stathakis, 'The Truman Doctrine and the Marshall Plan in Greece', in the same volume, pp. 295ff, a report of the American embassy is referred to (p. 304) which points out that 'AMAG (the American Economic Mission) has been turned into an invisible Greek government in practice.... It arrived determined to establish a paternalistic economy under state control, run by American advisers and technical personnel, considering Greek businessmen, industrialists and government employees corrupt and devilishly clever suppressors of the poor, almost without exception.'

18  On the matter of austerity and growth, see: M. Wolf, 'Economie', *Le Monde*, 18 October 2011, p. 2; 'Few options as Eurozone seeks path of stability', *IHT*, 9 September 2011, p. 1; M. Wolf, *Financial Times*, 19 October 2011; 'Europe and its crisis', *IHT*, 17–18 September 2011, p. 6. See also Chapter 22.

19  According to the columnist D. Mitropoulos, this view was promoted by two senior ministers of the Papandreou government who were apparently encouraged to do so by Strauss-Kahn. See *Ta Nea*, 8–9 September 2012, p. 21. See also P. Roumeliotis,

*The Unknown Goings on Behind the Scenes at the IMF*, A. A. Livanis Editions, 2012. Roumeliotis says that Strauss-Kahn insisted on the need for Greece to proceed immediately with the restructuring of its sovereign debt (p. 73) but finally abandoned this position owing to the effects it would have on the Eurozone banks, 'as well as because of possible contamination of other Eurozone countries' (p. 111).

20  The matter of a return to the drachma is examined in detail in Chapter 24.

21  See P. Tsimas, *The Diary of the Crisis*, Metechmio, 2011, p. 282.

22  Country Report No. 13/20, IMF, January 2013.

23  The nominal unit labour cost was in Greece in 2001 83.8 and in 2009 it was 113.2; in Germany in 2001 it was 99.8 and in 2009 it was 105.0. See Nominal unit labour cost index at epp.eurostat.ec.europe.eu. Thus Greece, which had been more competitive than Germany in 2001, was in 2009 far behind Germany.

24  See George Pagoulatos, 'Refuting stereotypes', *Kathimerini*, 2 September 2012, p. 10.

25  The Gini coefficient, a measure of inequality, was 33.1 in 2009, 32.9 in 2010, 33.6 in 2011 and 34.3 in 2012. See P. Tsakloglou and T. Mitrakos, 'Inequality and poverty in Greece: myth, realities and the crisis', in O. Anastasakis and D. Singh (eds), *Reforming Greece: Sisyphean Task or Herculean Challenge?*, South East European Studies at Oxford (SEESOX), European Studies Centre, St Antony's College, University of Oxford, 2012, pp. 90–9. See also Report by Governor of the Bank of Greece, April 2012, p. 89; Manos Matsaganis, *The Greek Crisis: Social Impact and Policy Prescriptions*, Friedrich Ebert Stiftung, 2013; Hellenic Statistical Authority, Press releases, 29 November 2013, 9 December 2012.

26  *Athens Voice*, 3–9 May 2011, p. 5.

27  See also G. Voulgari, *Ta Nea*, 30 December 2011, p. 9. The brief assertion 'The Memorandum has failed' sets aside the following questions: In what? In everything? Why? What else had been proposed? How far have the major problems that imposed it changed? How many different cures are there? The omission of such questions is related to political conclusions and possible cures ascribed to these.

28  On the subsequent renegotiation, see p. 269.

29  Country Report No. 13/241, IMF, July 2013, p. 25.

30  *European Economy: The Second Economic Adjustment Programme for Greece, July 2013*, Occasional Paper 159, European Commission, July 2013, p. 8.

31  'Making the public administration more efficient and effective', ibid., p. 32.

32  *Concise Oxford Dictionary of Current English* (4th edition).

33  *European Economy*, Occasional Paper 159, July 2013, p. 41.

# 22

# Austerity and growth: implementing the second Memorandum

From the end of February 2012, both the European and the Greek focus was on satisfying the conditions specified on 21 February in the second Memorandum, to enable the release of the €130 billion and to avert a disorderly default. The first challenge was to complete discussions with the private sector regarding the 'haircut'.

On 24 February 2012, the Greek government invited all bondholders wishing to participate in the bond exchange to declare their intent by the evening of 8 March. The holders of bonds to a total of €171.3 billion declared their intention to do so. This allowed Greece to activate the collective action clauses (CACs) which render the exchange of bonds mandatory. The programme now included approximately 96% of available bonds, or €197 billion (out of a total value of €206 billion). It was the largest bond exchange ever made and a significant success. The restructuring would reduce the country's debt by approximately €105 billion. In addition to the debt written off, interest rates would be reduced and repayment dates on bonds would be extended.

The arrangement harmed not only banks, both foreign and domestic, but also investment houses, social security funds and small investors who had put their savings in bonds. The government promised that it would go some way to compensate the funds for their losses, as well as the small bondholders. This promise, however, was given hastily and without due consideration. The Euro-group reacted with a statement on 9 March, clarifying Greece's responsibilities. In order to avoid the legal challenges that might arise from non-compliance with the principle of equality of treatment, the Eurogroup had indicated that 'no holder of Greek bonds shall be compensated directly or indirectly'.[1]

The exchange of old bonds for new ones began on Monday 14 March. The programme of restructuring resulted in a marked improvement in the economic and political climate in Greece. However, not all were convinced; scepticism remained on the international bond markets as to whether this move had rendered Greek debt sustainable. The impression was that while it improved the health of Athens' finances, Greece had not yet brought its deficits under control in a sustainable way; nor had it succeeded in achieving a primary surplus to reduce its borrowing needs. Equally, progress in structural reform had been slow and painful; it had been nowhere near comprehensive enough to help drive the return to growth so desperately needed. These doubts were reflected in an immediate fall in the nominal value of the new bonds by approximately 20%; in due course they were to fall by as much as 80%.

After satisfying the basic preconditions for the release of its part of the loan, the IMF indicated what its own contributions would be. Despite objections expressed at the meeting of its board of directors, its contribution was set at €28 billion, to be disbursed in 17 instalments (of approximately €1.65 billion each) over the next four years.[2] The loan from the Eurozone and the IMF was to total €172.7 billion.

On 13 March the Eurogroup finalised the terms for the release of its first instalment, of €39.4 billion. Approximately €30 billion of this was the agreed bonus in EFSF bonds, to be paid to bondholders who had participated in the PSI arrangements. Payment of the rest of the instalments of the loan would be made quarterly, and the amount of each was to be determined according to need. As had been the case with the first Memorandum, each release would be dependent on satisfaction of conditions attached. The Troika would again monitor progress with regard to the reform programme.[3]

Greece's partners expressed in various statements their satisfaction with the developments. The French President spoke of 'a solution to the Greek problem'. The German Minister of Finance said that Greece 'had been given the chance to deal with the crisis'. The head of the IMF stressed that 'the real danger of a serious crisis has been avoided'. At the same time, however, they indicated that 'the new adjustment programme must be implemented to the letter and in a timely manner'.[4]

The demands of the reform programme were not significantly relaxed when compared with the first Memorandum. In the space of two months up to the general election, among the demands placed on Greece were:

1  the recapitalisation of the banks;
2  the elaboration of the Medium-Term Fiscal Strategy Framework, which would specify all measures to be taken by 2016 in order to achieve the Memorandum targets on deficit reduction (with a view to achieving a primary surplus) and structural reform (of major importance in this regard was the Troika's insistence that, in order to avoid deviations from the targets set, the Greek government adopt fiscal measures worth €10 billion by 2014);
3  the implementation of all outstanding actions specified in the programme;
4  and finally, the government had to push forward reforms regarding the deregulation of markets and the improvement of the business climate in Greece.[5]

The primary concern of the EMU was still over mechanisms to control and regulate the fiscal performance of all member states. On 2 March the heads of state and government conclusively signed the text of the Fiscal Compact, upon the terms agreed back in December 2011. The text bore the title 'Treaty for the Stability, Coordination and Governance of the EMU'. The object of the Treaty was to ensure stability throughout the Eurozone. It would come into force as soon as it had been ratified by a minimum of 12 states. It was hoped that the ratification could be completed within 2012.

Discussion regarding the scale of funds that should be made available to the EFSF and the ESM continued. At a meeting of the Eurogroup a few days after the summit, it was decided that the funds of the EFSF and the ESM combined should total approximately €800 billion. This amount included the sums that had already been granted, or were pending release, to Greece, Ireland and Portugal. New funds, as yet unallocated, would amount to approximately €500 billion. This would be made available by the countries of the Eurozone in mid-2013. In their joint statement the ministers asserted that 'finally an effective firewall has been created'.[6]

The markets were in two minds as to the adequacy of this 'firewall'. Many nations and economic analysts indicated that the capital available to the EFSF and ESM should reach €1 trillion, to ward off the risk of market speculation and guard against any negative developments in any of the major European economies still at risk (Spain and Italy). It also remained unclear whether there would be any further contributions to this 'firewall' by the IMF. The German Minister of Finance rejected such concerns about the inadequacy of the provisions, stressing that 'there is enough capital in the budgets of the European Union to support over-indebted member states'.[7]

The meetings of the Eurogroup, Ecofin and the European Council marked the culmination Franco-German efforts to establish a new operating framework for the Eurozone and, in part, the EU as a whole. The EU acquired significant new powers and the ability to drive collective action, which would have been inconceivable only a few years before. These moves ran counter to the decline of the 'Community method' over the previous few years and the domination of intergovernmental decision-making in its place. Virtually all of the member states accepted common supervision of fiscal policy as necessary to combat economic instability. This new framework consisted of:

1 the new Treaty for the Stability, Coordination and Governance of the EMU of 2 March (the Fiscal Compact);
2 the establishment of the (permanent) ESM;
3 the financial support programmes for Greece, Ireland and Portugal, which, even though exceptional, set a precedent for intervention in member states;
4 various less substantive but nonetheless significant arrangements, such as the European Semester, the 'Six Pack' legislation and the Euro Plus Pact;[8]
5 the intervention of the ECB to bolster the liquidity of the European banking sector.

In mid-March the reports from the European Commission and the IMF regarding the situation in Greece were published.[9] Both indicated that the PSI scheme had marked a watershed and that the crisis had been tamed. However, such assessments were once again premature. The crisis was not over and the risk of regression still loomed large. The report of the European Commission, however, noted that the adjustment programme was coming up against the same challenges as before – political instability, social protests, administrative shortcomings and a recession that was far greater than originally estimated. The causes of the recession, the report indicated, were the fall in demand, 'the loss of an export drive', unemployment, political and social turmoil, and the major shortfall in credit available to businesses and households.[10] The report did not offer any analysis regarding the severity of the reforms demanded by the Troika, or their causal relationship with the degree and the duration of the recession. Neither was there any discussion of the inaccuracy of the Memorandum's predictions.

According to the IMF report, Greece had to restore its competitiveness through a 'timely reduction in nominal pay and non-payroll expenses'.[11] These measures were considered essential and inevitable, as other changes, such as improvements in productivity, would take time. The authors of the report noted that, according to a 'realistic but moderately optimistic scenario', sovereign debt would fall to 117% of GDP by 2020. However, domestic challenges and broader negative externalities, such as the painfully slow pace of structural reform or delays in economic recovery, might quickly derail the timetable and delay Greece's return to the markets. Any deviation from the schedule would inevitably require further recourse to the EU for yet more financial support. The report's conclusion stated that 'the success of the second programme (Memorandum) broadly depends on Greece itself…. Success requires the government to be decisive, enhance political cooperation, as well as acceptance of the effort by the whole of Greek society'.[12]

The authors drew attention to the danger the country was still in. Greece had little to no leeway, in terms of targets and time frames. Should there be failure or further delay, the likely results would be deeper recession and a rise in sovereign debt. Any negative developments would make additional assistance from the Troika necessary; should this not be forthcoming, Greece would inevitably default and this would be followed by a disorderly exit from the Eurozone.[13]

The report noted that any substantive improvement in competitiveness, as a result of a rise in productivity, would require a decade at least. Therefore, a strategy for the 'swift, total and effective implementation of reforms' was essential. Greece, however, 'did not have the ability to follow such a strategy'. As such, the immediate priority must be the continued internal devaluation and, in particular, the reduction in payroll costs.[14] Yet the same report indicated that the preconditions for a successful outcome of internal devaluation did not exist.[15] No substantive analysis was offered on how to enhance growth.[16]

The findings of both reports met with criticism in Greece. The anti-Memorandum forces cited these findings as evidence of an 'imminent disaster'.

Greek political elites who backed the Memorandum downplayed the significance of these reports, to limit anxiety. In statements to Parliament, the Prime
Minister attempted to present a more balanced picture of the findings. He
asserted that the first signs of recovery would appear towards the end of 2013.
However, until then, the country would have to endure even more hardship, in
both social and economic terms. For this recovery to be realised towards the
end of 2013, the adjustment programme had to be followed religiously and
Greece had to avoid any further turbulence in the economy.

The prescriptions of the EU and the reports gave rise to a new round of
discussions regarding the value of such a sustained policy of austerity and just
how appropriate efforts at an internal devaluation were for Greece. Anger rose
across the country at indications that, for Greece to regain its competitiveness,
levels of pay, along with living standards, must fall in line with those of its
Balkan neighbours, such as Bulgaria and Romania, in which the minimum
wage in 2011 was approximately €200 a month, around a quarter of that in
Greece. Reports across the Greek media voiced national anger in response to
such suggestions: 'The average Greek does not want the country to become
Bulgaria or Romania'.

The architects of the Troika's policy accepted that a policy of austerity would inevitably entail recession. But it was preferable, they asserted, to
expedite a restrictive policy to ensure a return of confidence to the markets.
Austerity would entail significant social, economic and political costs, but the
sacrifices would be justified by the eventual positive results.[17] They underlined
that if you cut expenses and increase taxes, the rate of growth will fall in the
short term. But at the same time, confidence in the country will grow. And as
soon as you regain confidence, growth will follow. Poul M. Thomsen, Deputy
Director of the IMF's European Department, asserted that the Troika 'had
achieved the appropriate balance between restoring fiscal health and reforms'.[18]
Nonetheless, in his assessment, the recession in Greece *had* been compounded
by the fact the fiscal adjustment had relied excessively on increased taxation.
Greater emphasis should have been placed on a reduction of expenditure.[19] In
a meeting of the Economic and Monetary Affairs Committee of the European
Parliament (ECON) held on 27 March 2012, the policy of austerity in Greece
was examined. The Commissioner responsible, Olli Rehn, the representative
of the ECB, Jorg Asmussen, and Poul Thomsen of the IMF underlined that
'internal devaluation in Greece is a one-way street for the improvement in
competitiveness ... through a fall in pay in the private sector and the implementation of structural reforms'.[20]

The assessment that there was no alternative to internal devaluation oversimplified the complexities of the crisis. Excessive salaries may indeed have had
detrimental consequences for competitiveness. However, this does not mean
that pay must be at the level of the lowest-paid and least-developed of all the
EU member states. Competitiveness can also be bolstered by progressive improvements in productivity, quality control, higher levels of education, research

and innovation, as well as the modernisation of business practices. Pay in other countries of the EU is significantly higher than in Greece, but the unit labour cost for product output is lower, due to higher productivity. Business costs in more developed countries are not subject to the same expenses that businesses incur in Greece. Regulations and state-imposed expenses have detrimental consequences for Greek competitiveness. In other member states, for example, businesses are not obliged to publish their balance sheets in the daily newspapers, in order to support the press. Neither are they subject to the same level of bureaucratic encumbrances or costs to attain necessary licences and permits.

An excessive deficit has to be reduced. But there are various ways to cut state expenditure. Reductions in salaries and pensions and increases in taxation are not the only solutions. For example, Greece had the highest military budget across the entire EU, proportionate to population. Defence spending as a proportion of GDP was over one percentage point higher than the European average.[21] This needed to be drastically reduced, but it was not. Even as late as April 2012, the Minister of Defence presented the acquisition of 400 tanks from the USA (at no cost) as a major achievement but made no mention of the expensive repairs required to restore these vehicles to fighting condition.[22]

The recession in Greece was compounded by the demands of the Troika. Between 2009 and 2012, GDP shrank overall by 23%, three times what was originally forecast. GDP was expected to decline by a further −4.2% in 2013. By the autumn of 2012, unemployment exceeded 27%, an unprecedented figure. Under such circumstances, the dogmatic insistence on austerity, with its inevitable social and economic costs, was futile and would never have achieved the desired aims. The policy fuelled populist resistance and rejection at every turn. The ensuing collapse provoked social tension, and made only too apparent the major deficiencies in the apparatus of the state and fundamentally deterred any investment whatsoever.[23]

The return to growth in Greece was pushed back from 2012, to the end of 2014.[24] When it does return, it will likely be very weak and entirely unstable. According to the stipulations of the Troika, Greece must adhere to a restrictive policy until at least 2020, so that sovereign debt can be reduced to 117% of GDP. How sustainable this level may be is entirely questionable. Such a policy will do nothing to counter rampant unemployment; nor will it help to promote the investment the country so desperately needs. A country on the margins of the Eurozone and the EU will not see a return to growth under a policy of austerity. Rather, in the case of a nation such as Greece, austerity fuels social unrest, poverty, stagnation and political instability, all of which are deterrents to growth. The adjustment policy for Greece ought to have been far more sensitive to Greek idiosyncrasies, in terms of both targets and time scales. Calls for a more relaxed framework are growing in number. There are many who believe that annual stringent austerity programmes should be replaced with more flexible, multi-year programmes, with targets that are less ambitious, more realistic.[25] Annual re-examinations and realistic adjustments of targets would go some way towards convincing the Greek public that the targets are attainable. Investment in infrastructure and continuing development programmes would limit the recession and maintain hope of recovery. The actions of the Troika, with its quarterly audits, eternal revisions of targets and exponential demands for cuts demoralised the nation. 'Austerity' is not a dogma, to be applied in every case of recession without regard to the context. What was valid and appropriate for Germany in 2000 cannot be considered suitable for a nation as distinct as Greece, which lacks comparable productive capacity, expertise and public administration.[26]

In Italian elections held in February 2013, political parties critical of the EU-directed policy of austerity won over 50% of the vote. Subsequently, Italy's economic woes were compounded by the inability to form a stable government. Widespread anxiety once again returned to the Eurozone. The victory of the Eurosceptics resulted from rises in unemployment and deteriorating incomes and living standards, all consequences of stringent austerity and a lack of flexibility.[27] Many commentators cited this as evidence that austerity serves only to compound the crisis when it is imposed without consideration of the specific context and challenges of any given country.[28] Austerity is traditionally a necessary instrument to force adjustment of relative costs and to achieve labour market reforms, but it is not without risk and must not be done without due consideration. 'If the domestic private and external sectors are retrenching, the public sector cannot expect to succeed in doing so, however hard it tries, unless it is willing to drive the economy into a far bigger slump.'[29]

Following the results of the Italian elections, it was noted that the European debt crisis should have been dealt with in a different way.[30] The cause of the turmoil across Europe was not the high level of deficits, but rather lenders' fears regarding the security of sovereign bonds from states that had over-extended themselves financially. Doubts over whether these bonds could be redeemed fuelled the rise in interest rates. This rise in interest rates undermined the capacity of heavily indebted nations to acquire sustainable credit on the bond markets, which in turn led to the imposition of a policy of austerity by the EU. If, however, the ECB had either guaranteed repayment of the bonds or had kept interest rates low by buying bonds on the secondary market, stabilis-ation could have proceeded at a milder rate and the recession would never have reached the depths it did. However, this argument fails to acknowledge that intervention by the ECB was not permitted by the Treaties, nor were the member states ready in April 2010 to bypass the Treaties, as happened later.[31] The member states did not ignore other possible solutions in 2010, but rejected them categorically, for fear of the consequences, as well as the precedent that would be set if political action was permitted that would be in direct contra-vention of the Treaty framework.

The austerity policy advocated by the Troika was actually questioned by the economists of the IMF itself,[32] who suggested that economic activity in developed countries is drastically restricted by reductions in expenditure and increases in taxation. They noted, in more technical language, that a rule that says a reduction in expenditure of 1% leads to a reduction in GDP (recession) of 0.5% is not correct in many cases. The 'multiplier' is not 0.5% but in certain cases much higher. In the construction of the Memorandum, however, the policy was developed with the usual multiplier of 0.5%.[33]

The remarks of the IMF experts were presented as a contribution to the theory behind the stabilisation policy.[34] In reality they prepared the way for a change in the assessment of the Greek case. A report of the IMF acknowledged in May 2013 that the actual decline in GDP was much greater than anticipated because the fiscal multipliers that had been used were too low.

Twelve nations of the EU addressed a letter to all member states before the summit of 1–2 March 2012 which finalised the Fiscal Compact. In it they stated that the economic policy imposed by the Franco-German axis needed to be re-considered, and they emphasised that the current crisis was one of an absence of growth.[35] The measures they proposed were within a neoliberal framework, maintaining the emphasis on the deregulation of markets. However, these proposals stressed the need for flexibility in the application of reform pro-grammes. It was not always possible for a member state to dogmatically pursue targets, because circumstances and externalities can change, and reform must be sufficiently flexible to accommodate such changes. While these member states recognised the need to articulate and follow a common course, they called for freedom for any given state to manage economic challenges. During the depths of a recession, a member state must have the ability to combat a continued contraction in the economy, even if this entails the temporary adoption of a policy that contravenes collectively adopted targets for levels of debt and deficit. Otherwise, the risk of sustained and deep recession is great.

Many have cited the indiscretions of Germany and France when in 2003 both their deficits exceeded the 3% cap, as well as their indifference towards the Treaties when they did not accept the 'penalties' prescribed. Both countries succeeded in the next years in redressing their economies. It was proof that a dogmatic approach involving punitive measures and the imposition of austerity at all costs is not the sole answer in times of financial difficulty.

The flexible application of rules must be combined with measures to promote convergence in terms of competitiveness, over a realistic and operable time frame. The EU needs to provide greater support to the peripheral nations to bolster development, assist with modernisation and direct investment towards export industries to take full advantage of the single market. To permit member states of the Periphery to benefit from the single market, the Core needs to be willing to accept slightly higher rates of inflation.

The former German Foreign Minister F. W. Steinmeier made clear his thoughts on the problem: 'Germany cannot continue to live as if it were an island of the blessed, surrounded by countries of the European Union sunk in recession, lacking growth. Under these circumstances, the problems the others are facing will very soon become our problems too.'[36]

The French presidential elections held in May 2012 returned the issue of growth to the forums of European debate. François Hollande, the Socialist candidate who ultimately beat the incumbent, Nicolas Sarkozy, made clear his intentions prior to the elections to renegotiate the Fiscal Compact and to redirect the European focus towards the imperative of growth. Other European voices joined his calls, for the need not only to direct efforts towards ensuring fiscal responsibility, but also actively to promote a return to growth. The President of the European Council, Herman Van Rompuy, indicated that although there could be no renegotiation of the Fiscal Compact, it would be of great value to develop 'an initiative for growth', to which Germany could also subscribe. Angela Merkel indicated that she was in favour of examining measures to stimulate growth, provided that these would not incur a rise in debt.[37]

German policy preferences did not favour major infrastructure works such as highways, but favoured investment in research and development, as well as support for small to medium-sized enterprises to stimulate economic activity. The German government indicated the management of capital for investment should be assigned to special development banks. However, Berlin still remained fundamentally sceptical: 'We do not believe that additional significant amounts can be expended to enhance growth. We have established a permanent strong stability mechanism to avert new crises; all other matters must be solved by every state on its own.'[38]

In Greece, these discussions regarding growth were presented as a vindication of criticism levelled at Germany and the indication of a shift in the emphasis of European policy. In Spain, rumours circulated that the Union would shortly be announcing a €200 billion fund directed at stimulating European growth.[39] These rumours were rapidly seized on by the Greek press. However, denial from the EU was instant.

In a text drawn up in February 2012 by the permanent representatives of the member states and addressed to the Council, the various initiatives and existing targets for the promotion of growth were detailed.[40] These included: the abolition of regulations restricting flexible employment; the reform of social security systems; and initiatives to increase productivity through improved education and training. This list indicated that the scope and scale of measures to promote growth, according to the permanent representatives of member states, was rather limited. The principal means for the promotion of growth, namely investment, was not even mentioned. This reflected the still dominant belief that investment remained the reserve of the private sector.

However, not all subscribed to this belief. In November 2011, the Notre Europe think-tank had presented a 'package for growth'.[41] According to this proposal, the European budget should contribute towards funding investment in infrastructure, especially transport, energy and communications. It should also support research programmes. Structural Funds should be put to good use, dealing with the effects of recession in countries facing difficulties, in a flexible and timely manner. In addition to these proposals, it recommended the European Investment Bank should proceed with the issue of bonds exclusively for financing investment in infrastructure and the environment. It proposed the expansion of the Bank's annual capital capacity from €80 billion to €200 billion, underwritten by guarantees from member states.

Comparable assessments were published in various European papers. The *Financial Times* [42] stated that Europe definitely needed an 'agenda for growth', in order to avoid the chaos that prevailed in 2011. It needed a programme for investment. The Commission should 'exhaust every possibility for the enhancement of expenditure on infrastructure, on a pan European basis'. Furthermore, Germany and other countries of the Core should increase their domestic consumption, in order to facilitate exports from the Periphery: 'Europe has been discussing growth a great deal and for a long time, without acting accordingly. It is about time she took action, before it is too late.'[43]

At the time of writing, the outcome of this still continuing debate, between the advocates of stringent fiscal control and those calling for a new growth strategy, was still unclear. Those pleading for growth seem to lack the ambition needed to reverse what is already in force.[44] The Fiscal Compact remains the framework that regulates fiscal policy; any initiatives for growth have to comply with the Compact. Supporters of François Hollande made it clear that France did not intend to request a change in the Fiscal Compact, but would rather seek the addition of a 'growth' clause, or a 'detailed decision' from the European Council regarding growth.[45]

This discussion offered Greece the opportunity to a request an addition to the articles of the Memorandum, regarding the need to promote growth. Greece could have proposed broader interventions, in infrastructure, transport, the tourism sector or the production of energy, all of which would have been suitable for investment from the EU directly or from the European Investment Bank.[46]

Lack of investment remains the principal shortcoming in the effort to deal with the effects of the crisis in Greece today. Owing to the turmoil, investors are afraid of losing their money. They are either avoiding Greece altogether or are waiting for the return of more stable conditions for investment. Short-term speculative investments do little to finance anything in the way of recovery or a return to growth.

For growth to return, there needs to be absolute clarity regarding Greece's future in the Eurozone; only then will it be possible for businesses to plan, and weigh the costs and benefits of their activities. Impediments such as the taxation regime, the complexity of licensing procedures and the maze of bureaucracy all need to be addressed if investment and business are to return to Greece. Till then, the government must pay particular attention to public investment and do its utmost to secure regional development funding from the EU.

As noted in the second quarterly report by the Commission Task Force (March 2012), various funds available to Greece remained untapped. For example, of the €14.5 billion from the capital granted by the European Structural Funds to Greece, approximately €4 billion was allocated for investment by small to medium-sized Greek enterprises – the sort of investment that Greece is crying out for. During the same period, the President of the European Council indicated to the Prime Minister that there were funds amounting to approximately €12 billion that were available to Greece, but remained unused. Athens was fully aware of this, but the Greek administration was not in a position to act.[47] To expedite the absorption of the funds, the Task Force of the Commission directed its efforts towards the oversight of 180 priority projects, so that their completion could be made possible by 2015. It began to monitor implementation of the projects electronically, so as to make possible the continual assessment of their progress. The electronic oversight of projects had begun under a previous administration (1996–2004), with some marked success. However, the subsequent New Democracy administration deemed such a procedure unnecessary. This is yet another example of partisan politics foiling the possibilities for the country.[48]

The Task Force did note in its March 2012 report that, for efforts directed at growth to produce results, 'time may be needed'. Due consideration also needed to be given to the suitability of proposed projects, to how much they could contribute to a Greek recovery and whether adequate infrastructure and expertise existed to ensure the effective delivery.

Indicative of the mismanagement of investment were the efforts to support small and medium-sized enterprise. In 2011, the national Fund for Entrepreneurship and Growth (ETEAN) was set up, which replaced the Fund to Guarantee Small and Very Small Enterprises (TEMPME). The new fund was designed to offer 'the development model our country needs, promoting new means of financing and facilitating access to enterprises to make them competitive'.[49] To carry out its mission, it was going to make use of EU funds amounting to €800 million and to pour into the Greek economy €2.5 billion over a two-year period. On 6 April 2012, significantly earlier than the two-year period stated, newspaper reports indicated that the ETEAN was in a critical condition financially and would be unable to attain its targets. This was a result of the need to honour loans it had granted. Astoundingly, approximately half its capital had not been invested in growth projects but in national sovereign bonds, which had seen significant losses during the restructuring of Greek debt.[50]

The development of public assets, privatisation and the attraction of foreign capital could all contribute significantly to a return to growth. The public aversion to profit-directed ventures leads to stagnation and sustains recession. The raison d'être of the state is to defend the public interest, not to indulge in business activities. Its criteria for operation must be distinct from those of the private sector. It is no position to oversee private business, to respond to the demands of international competition or to manage investment in research and development in a global market.[51]

The state must, however, strive to create the conditions conducive to growth. Social strife and the idiosyncrasies of Greek society made this no small feat. The norms and values of Greek society are such that prospects for modernisation and progressive reform are limited. Despite its association with the societies of Western Europe, the country remains inflexible and authoritarian. There are many examples of this: the inadequacy of the state administration; aversion to reform; an excessively complex legal system; the continued prevalence of systems of patronage; and the all-consuming nature of partisan division in the political structure. The educational system does not cultivate freedom of thought, innovation or critical enquiry. A swift return to growth is dependent not only on investment, but also on fostering an environment conducive to creativity and independent learning.

The partisan nature of Greek society and politics has inhibited development, as it undermines the prospects for long-term strategic planning. Greek society has not addressed up to now the question of the country's model for growth in a coordinated and systematic way. It has not thought about which sectors can offer growth to Greece and has not shaped a model that capitalises on strengths that Greece does possess. Tourism expands now in a disorderly way, remaining indifferent to the preservation of the natural environment and the quality of its services. It does not further the reputation of Greece and so fails to capitalise on repeat business. Agricultural production without sufficient quality control or standards will never make major gains in terms of market share. The same challenges afflict industrial production because of a deficiency of skilled labour. If measures are not taken to redress these shortcomings, the prospects for a return to growth are fundamentally undermined.

Throughout the crisis, Greek governments overemphasised the significance of each minor degree of progress. For public relations purposes they presented as major successes any reduction in the rate of interest or an extension to the repayment of the loan. In terms of a more complete assessment of the challenges, the only noteworthy Hellenic contribution was the focus on eurobonds. However, Athens made no detailed or considered contribution to this debate. Its initiative for the eurobonds was a resounding failure. Greece has to develop a holistic perspective in which the challenges and the time frames required to address them are recognised, and proposals are accordingly developed. Recent experience has indicated that proposals and measures premised on the most optimistic analysis are not often suitable or beneficial. It is of little help to construct a model that neither anticipates nor can accommodate further economic turbulence. Hopes of a fast return to normality are naïve. The next 15 years must be a period in which Greece has progressively to rebuild a stable economy, one over which Greece has to slowly recapture its former international status and credibility.

A plan premised on a complete and realistic analysis of the challenges Greece faces is vital if the next generation of Greeks are to have any hope for the future. Without such a plan Greece will not find a way out of the crisis, other than the relentless austerity prescribed by the Troika.[52] There has never been an open debate regarding the need for such a plan; it did not occur when the country found itself facing bankruptcy at the end of 2009, nor after the first Memorandum in 2010, when gravity of the situation became apparent, nor later, when the need for further help and a restructuring of Greek debt became evident. All decisive proposals, such as the haircut, have been initiated not by Athens but by Greece's partners and creditors, despite the misgivings of the Greeks.

## Notes

1　*Kathimerini*, 13 February 2012, p. 5.
2　And not in three years, like the EU's financing of Greece. See Country Report No. 12/57, IMF, March 2012, p. 84, table 20.
3　At the end of March 2012, the new special account for debt repayment was 'inaugurated' at the Bank of Greece and €4.9 billion was deposited in this account to repay Greek bonds held by the ECB maturing on 20 March.
4　*Kathimerini*, 10 March 2012, p. 4.
5　See V. Zeras, *Kathimerini*, 11 March 2012, p. 4.
6　Eurogroup statement, 30 March 2012.
7　*IHT*, 31 March 2012, p. 9; *Kathimerini*, 31 March 2012, p. 16.
8　The 'Six Pack' legislation was approved by the European Council on 4 October 2011 (p. 143). It has been in force since 13 December 2011. The Euro Plus Pact was approved at the European Council of 24–25 March 2011 (see p. 96) (see Background of the Euro Plus Pact, and information prepared for the European Council, 9 December 2011). The 'European Semester' constitutes a procedure for controlling and advising member states with regard to their economic policies and their reform programmes. It was first applied in 2013. It was decided on by Ecofin on 15 February 2011 and approved, finally, at the European Council of 24–25 March 2011. See: Council conclusions on European Semester: macroeconomic and fiscal guidance, 15 February 2011; Consilium, *The European Semester in 2012*, 11650/12, Presse 280, Country specific recommendations on economic and fiscal policies, Council of the European Union, 22 December 2012. For the relation of the Fiscal Compact to the 'Six Pack' see *Six-Pack? Two Pack? Fiscal Compact? A Short Guide to the New Fiscal Governance*, Directorate-General for Economic and Financial Affairs, 14 March 2011. Two regulations (the 'Two Pack') also concerning economic supervision are in process. A review of how the various regulations will function together can be found in Benedicta Marzinotto and André Sapir, *Fiscal Rules: Timing is Everything*, Policy Brief 2012/03, Bruegel, September 2012.
9　*European Economy: The Second Adjustment Programme for Greece, March* 2012, Occasional Paper 94, European Commission, March 2012; Country Report No. 12/57, IMF, March 2012.
10　*European Economy*, Occasional Paper 94, March 2012.
11　Country Report No. 12/57, IMF.
12　Ibid.
13　Ibid., Introduction.

14  Ibid., p. 13.

15  Ibid., p. 49.

16  At the end of March 2012, a report from the Bank of Greece, *Monetary Policy 2011–2012*, was published. In the covering letter to Parliament, the Governor noted the existing risks and stated that 'the most critical parameter, which shall determine the programme's success, is its diligent implementation'. Subject to this precondition, 'the programme is possible and may succeed'.

17  See interview with the head economist at the ECB, M. Praet, in *Le Monde*, 18–19 March 2012, p. 12.

18  Interview in *Kathimerini*, 1 February 2012, p. 3.

19  *IHT*, 26 March 2012, p. 1. According to P. Bofinger, ibid., p. 106, increases in taxes should be at the centre of an austerity programme and not cuts in expenses, so as not to exacerbate recession. This view may be valid for developed countries, but not for Greece, where the clientele policy led to an excess of non-productive expenses with the object of serving clients. For example, there is a technological institute at Argostoli in Cephalonia and another not far off at Lixouri, to preserve local balance. Both have very few students.

20  *Nautemporiki*, 28 March 2011, p. 3. In Germany it was maintained that 'the German path to cure the crisis' had proved the right one, both for Germany at the beginning of the decade, when the Federal Republic of Germany was considered the 'sick man' of the Eurozone, as well as for Ireland and Estonia today, as far as we can see. See *Der Spiegel*, issue 18, 2012, p. 73.

21  According to data from NATO, average defence expenditure over the period 2005–09 was 4.3% of GDP for Greece, and 2.8% for the European countries of NATO. See *Defence Expenditures of NATO Countries 1990–2010*, NATO, 10 March 2011.

22  See *Kathimerini*, 8 April 2012.

23  The head of the IMF, Christine Lagarde, stated in an interview she gave at the annual meeting of the Fund in Tokyo in October 2012, that instead of a front-loaded mass reduction in incomes, sometimes 'it is preferable to give a little more time'. See *Kathimerini*, 10 December 2012, p. 19. On the basis of this reasoning she suggested that the time frame in which the adjustment programme of Greece was to attain the targets of the Memorandum should be extended. The IMF's Troika representative, Poul Thomsen, had not expressed such a view before. On the contrary, he was particularly harsh.

24  The first Memorandum, in May 2010, had forecast a rate of growth of GDP of 1.1% in 2012, 2.1% in 2013 and 2.1% in 2014. In December 2012 the macro-economic scenario of the Commission referred to: –7.1% in 2011, –6% in 2012, –4.8% in 2013, 0.6% in 2014, 2.9% in 2015 and 3.7% in 2016.

25  See also 'Austerité en Europe: trop fort et trop vite', *Le Monde*, 21 April 2012, p. 12. Blanchard and Leigh maintain that economic activity in developed countries is negatively affected by drastic cuts in spending and extensive increases in taxation, which is why the rates of growth forecast by the adjustment programmes are not usually attained. See Olivier Blanchard and Daniel Leigh, *Growth Forecast Errors and Fiscal Multipliers*, Working Paper WP/13/1, IMF, 2013, p. 1.

26  P. Krugman, 'How the case for austerity has crumbled', *New York Review of Books*, 6 June 2013, p. 67. Krugman criticises the policy applied by the Troika. His answer to the question, 'how did austerity actually work?' is 'that the results were disastrous'.

'The countries forced into severe austerity experienced very severe downturns and the downturns were more or less proportional to the degree of austerity' (p. 72).

27  See for example: *Le Monde*, 2 March 2013, p. 7; *IHT*, 2/3 March 2013, p. 1; Jacques de Saint Victor, *Le Monde*, 5 March 2013, p. 17.

28  See P. Krugman, 'Austerity all'Italiana', *IHT*, 26 February 2013; M. Wolf, 'The sad record of fiscal austerity', *Financial Times*, ft.com, 26 February 2013.

29  Wolf, 'The sad record of fiscal austerity'.

30  Paul De Grauwe, 'Lessons from the Eurocrisis for East Asian monetary relations', *World Economy*, vol. 35, issue 4, April 2012, pp. 405–418, at p. 405.

31  The bypassing of the Treaties occurred in September 2012, when the ECB declared that it would proceed with buying bonds on the secondary market. See pp. 260–1.

32  See: Blanchard and Leigh, *Growth Forecast Errors and Fiscal Multipliers*, p. 13; IMF, *World Economic Outlook: Coping with High Debt and Sluggish Growth*, October 2012, p. 41.

33  The statements of the IMF economists provoked extensive discussions in Greece on the need to reform the stabilisation programme on the basis of correct multipliers. Blanchard responded 'that the programme has been modified and adjusted to the new estimates, e.g. through the extension of the time schedule for fiscal adjustment'. See *Kathimerini*, 10 February 2013. This discussion ignores reality. When the stabilisation programme was being elaborated, the economic-political expediency of the main states of the EU played the defining role, and not the multiplier. The protagonists wanted a strict but temporary solution so they could control their expenses till they could negotiate and shape a new broader European solution.

34  Though theoretical, these contributions led to a skirmish between the EU and the IMF. See *Le Monde*, 22 May 2013, p. 6. The European Commission leaked to the press that the failures of the Greek programme were due to the dogmatic views of the IMF. The IMF answered that the Commission was obsessed with a stringent austerity policy. Brussels replied that the IMF was particularly inflexible. It did not want the measures to be presented in a 'palatable' way so that they could more easily accepted and reactions avoided.

35  See *Le Monde*, 1 March 2012, p. 3.

36  *Ta Nea*, 2 April 2012.

37  See also 'Inclusion and participation' in Chapter 32.

38  *Der Spiegel*, issue 18, 2012, p. 73.

39  *Nautemporiki*, 30 April 2012, p. 4.

40  See Council conclusions 6113/12, Council of the European Union, 10 February 2012. With regard to the Union's activities for promoting growth in Greece, see 'Growth for Greece', Communication for the Commission, 18 April 2012.

41  'Austerity but also growth', *Notre Europe*, 19 November 2011.

42  'A growth agenda for the Eurozone', *Financial Times*, 9 April 2012.

43  Ibid.

44  See under 'Inclusion and participation' in Chapter 32.

45  *Le Monde*, 26 April 2012, p. 8; 'Economics', *Kathimerini*, 29 April 2012, p. 7. See also p. 336.

46  See P. Ioakimides, *Ta Nea*, 2 April 2012.

47  See p. 62.

48  See *Ta Nea*, 5 December 2011, p. 42; E. Georgis, 'A race for NSRF (Structural Funds)', *Kathimerini*, 18 December 2011.

49  See information on the ETEAN website, at www.etean.gr.
50  See *Kathimerini*, 6 April 2012, p. 10.
51  See also p. 306.
52  See also p. 316.

# 23

# The crisis peaks

By the beginning of April 2012, both in Greece and across the EU there was a belief that the worst was over, following the decisions made in February and agreement on the restructuring of Greek debt. Two events would rapidly derail any notions of security that had taken a temporary footing: the Greek parliamentary elections on 6 May and the French presidential elections on the same day. The major challenge was the election of a French President who had already indicated his wish to re-examine the Fiscal Compact.

Across the EU, it was recognised that the need for Greek elections was legitimate, following cross-party calls for a fresh mandate. However, many members of the Eurozone believed that they were an unnecessary risk that posed a genuine threat to any resolution of the Greek crisis. There was widespread and justified concern that the elections could detrimentally affect the economy.

At the beginning of May, prior to a fresh wave of measures aimed at reducing the deficit, it emerged that discussions had already begun regarding the need for yet another bailout. The 'new package of €14.5 billion' would be negotiated in the summer and would be for the two-year period 2013–14. This was in recognition of the fact that the economic situation was deteriorating. According to forecasts, the recession would exceed 5%, instead of the 4.5% the Bank of Greece had anticipated.[1] The country found itself in greater and greater isolation. Greek businesses could trade with their European counterparts only on the basis of cash up front; however, they could not acquire the credit required to do so from the Greek banking sector. The effect on unemployment was tremendous; levels now reached 22%. The state of the country was detailed in a letter from the Prime Minister, Lucas Papademos, to the President, Karolos Papoulias, on 11 May:

> The diminished international position of Greece and growing doubts over the country's ability to remain in the euro expressed by the media, financial analysts and international banks in conjunction with some unforeseen event adversely affecting the economic climate and citizens' confidence could fuel a sudden run on bank deposits. Such a development would have a catalytic effect on the banks' liquidity and consequently on economic activity.[2]

In other words, the Prime Minister was warning that the economy was in danger of collapsing from one moment to the next; all it would take would be one minor event to bring the entire house down. The consequence would be the country's exit from the Eurozone.

Before the elections, the government had principally been focused on satisfying the criteria for securing further financial support. Necessary regulations and reforms were driven through Parliament under accelerated procedures. Attached to legislation driven by the Memorandum were unrelated bills. The sheer volume of legislation going through Parliament meant MPs no longer had the capacity to sufficiently scrutinise the bills. Disorder prevailed. Two competing ministries tried to introduce conflicting legislation regarding the regulation of construction. The Ministry of Transport, instead of attempting to deregulate the fuel haulage industry, tried to close it through technical regulations regarding trucks.[3] When the focus needed to be on a reduction of expenditure and the cutting back of bureaucracy, costs and administration actually grew. The media spoke of 'an orgy of string-pulling', of 'pressure by unions to settle their matters' and of broader 'disruption of the government and Parliament'. With over 150 amendments, at times completely incomprehensible as they simply referred to paragraphs or articles of other laws they were rescinding or amending, vested interests ensured their preferences were accounted for, problems of a personal nature were settled and hand-outs to specific groups were arranged. This propagated the public perception that, in a time of great crisis, MPs were concerned with trivial and personal matters. Upon the realisation that 'string-pulling' legislation was flooding proceedings, the Prime Minister and the party leaders tried to impose some order, indicating that only legislation directly related to the Memorandum should be passed. However, this episode demonstrates only too clearly that, even years into the crisis, MPs fundamentally failed to appreciate the severity of the situation. Instead of serious debate and a focus on the pressing matters at hand, regression to the politics of patronage had taken precedent.

The election campaign drew an end to major activities on the part of the Papademos administration in relation to the crisis, with the notable exception of the recapitalisation of the banks. The parties were no longer willing to push ahead with implementation of the adjustment programme. They were paralysed by the fear of a populist backlash any further reform might incur.

In the course of his brief term in office, Papademos succeeded in pulling Greece back from the precipice the country found itself at following the announcement of a referendum. He managed to enact the principal decisions taken at the Eurogroup summit of 21 February, and he oversaw the resulting restructuring of debt and the negotiation of the second Memorandum as well as pushing forward the adjustment programme. These were no small feats and marked a significant success. Dialogue with the EU opened once more and the Eurozone continued to support the country, while the continual pejorative assessments of Greece dwindled a little. Papademos brought what the previous administration had lacked: technical ability, experience of European procedures, acquaintance with important political personalities of Europe and heads of banks, as well as the ability to deal with financial problems.

Papademos's political options remained severely constrained, despite the progress that had been achieved. The parties displayed no desire to plan for the future, nor to undertake any long-term initiatives. They insisted that his government was a 'special purpose' one,[4] with a mandate to govern the country only until the holding of fresh elections. New Democracy wanted to hold the reins of power on its own, at all costs, and was certain of victory in the elections. The Prime Minister, who had been chosen for his 'technocratic' abilities, could not adequately defend the need for continued cooperation and consensus. Inertia prevailed in the two-month build-up to the elections. Many measures were postponed, extreme antagonism and partisan division dominated within the country, and once again Europe lost faith in the political elites of Greece.[5] Questions again emerged regarding Greece's ability to manage its way out of the crisis and whether Greece could remain inside the EMU.

Outstanding reforms and financial challenges did not attract public scrutiny. The following were the most pressing of these:

1 *The recapitalisation of banks, along with the terms and procedures for its implementation.* It was obvious that time would be needed, but also that delays would have major detrimental consequences for the prospects of any Greek recovery.

2 *The programme for implementing the obligations of the Memorandum up to 2016.* Public expenditure needed a complete re-evaluation prior to elections, so that there could be a coherent appraisal of how to cover deviations from the targets of the 2012 budget, as well as a programme of adjustment for the period 2013–14. The ongoing public debate over the inability of social security funds to pay pensions, pressure to reduce pay, and the mounting risks of cuts across the board indicated that policy was still being developed in a piecemeal fashion.

3 *Privatisation, structural changes, reform of the tax system and the modernisation of business practices.* These all required immediate attention, so confidence might have a chance of returning to Greece. However, it was clear that the election campaign, with its partisan division, mutual recriminations and personal attacks, was leading Greece into a dead end.

The EU and the IMF issued stark warnings once again about how critical the situation remained. They reminded Greek public opinion that the obligations of the Memorandum had to be fulfilled if Greece wanted to escape bankruptcy and an obligatory exit from the Eurozone and the EU. The German Minister of Finance stated that the Greeks 'are living above their abilities and must implement cuts in expenses and reforms in the labour market'.[6]

It was not only the situation in Greece that was causing anxiety. The forecasts that indicated the reform in Spain and Italy would ensure stability in these major European economies had yet to be proved accurate. In mid-April, the Italian government announced that the recession was worse than expected and as a result the budget would not be balanced in 2013, but two years later, in violation of what had been agreed with the European Commission.

By May, Spain saw its fourth largest bank, Bankia, request state assistance, amounting to approximately €23 billion, to avoid bankruptcy. Economic analysts calculated that some €150–200 billion would be needed to recapitalise the Spanish banks, so that they could comply with international solvency rules. Assistance of such a magnitude would require the imposition of tax increases and spending cuts, which would only compound the already grave recession. 'Bank bailouts on this scale may well bring the Spanish state to its knees.... Spain's austerity–recession feedback loop is similar to the process that fed economic contraction in Greece.'[7] Anxiety over future developments in Spain spread across the EU. The rate of interest available to Spain on the international bond markets exceeded 6.5%, rendering Spanish debt unsustainable. The *New York Times* reported:

> In a season of nightmare projections for Europe, this one could be the scariest: Greece leaves the euro currency union at the same time Spain's banking system is collapsing.... if a Spanish banking collapse were factored in, Europe's long-dreaded 'Lehman moment' might finally arrive.[8]

The political crisis that broke out in the Netherlands in April 2012 was something of a surprise. It stemmed from the deficit of 4.7% (of GDP) in 2011 and disagreement regarding how to deal with it. The Netherlands was a country that had staunchly supported austerity and the deficit cap. Therefore, the expectcation was that its government would not have hesitated to impose restrictive measures. However, the emerging realisation that the European austerity policy 'is dragging one economy (after another) back into recession and the effect is not limited to the Periphery' provoked a crisis of confidence in the governing coalition.[9]

Finally, Cyprus also presented new challenges.[10] Its banks had bought Greek bonds and incurred significant losses from the restructuring of Greek debt. The European Commission stated that it would closely monitor developments in the Cypriot banking system, owing to the fears that external aid would be required. The Cypriot government raised the matter of external support at the end of June.

An unexpected fall in economic activity throughout the whole of the Eurozone in April contributed to growing anxiety regarding the prospects for the European economy.[11] According to forecasts, in the best-case scenario growth would be zero. The consequences were already evident in terms of a rise in unemployment (now at its highest level since the introduction of the euro), the volatility of the financial markets, the fall in investment stemming from the loss of confidence and the fall in the value of the euro. At the same time, social unrest and political strife were spreading across the continent. The victory of the Socialist Party in the French presidential elections, the political crisis in the Netherlands and the demonstrations across Spain, Italy, Greece and the Czech Republic all indicated a growing public anger at the policy of austerity.

Anxiety over the effects of the crisis was increasingly felt in the international community. The problems of Europe were now taking centre stage at forums such as the IMF and the World Bank. There was frustration at the inertia and indecision that undermined European responses to the crisis and anger at the consequences this had for global growth.[12] In the USA and in China as well, fear of contagion from the European crisis was mounting. In the USA this stemmed from the interconnected nature of EU–US trade and banking, while for China the loss of a major export market appeared imminent. The US repeatedly urged the EU to relax the austerity policy it was implementing.

There were also disagreements within the EU, but of a different type. The Bundesbank, for example, considered that the banking liquidity facility provided by the ECB was inflationary and, as such, should be phased out. Nonetheless, the German government did appear to be more amenable than previously to discussions about amending its absolute preference for a policy of austerity. However, it was not willing to be flexible with regard to targets for deficits and debts. It still fundamentally believed in 'internal devaluation' as an appropriate means to seek a drastic improvement in terms of competitiveness, combined with structural changes to drive a reduction in expenditure and a more balanced single market. Along with a comprehensive programme of privatisation, this would serve to attract capital and investment, and to stimulate a return to growth. Conservative circles within Germany were still very sensitive to the risks posed by an uncontrolled rise in debt of the peripheral countries. Discourse on the right, in Germany, began to consider the departure of ailing countries from the Eurozone, leaving the single-currency area to those economies sufficiently strong to ensure its stability and survival.[13] German policy-makers remained highly suspicious of any discussion of eurobonds, increases in the capital available to the ESM, or any broader proposals regarding the relaxing of fiscal control or an increase in liquidity.[14]

German preferences still held great sway in the institutions of the EU and across many member states. Conservative governments held office in many significant member states. Criticism was most vocal among the left-wing and social democratic parties of the continent, along with a notable section of the media, which drew attention to the contraction that endless austerity was driving. They argued that fiscal restrictions and the drastic cuts in public expenditure did not improve the situation in a shrinking economy:[15] 'Austerity brings about greater austerity.'[16] The example of Greece according to them indicated that continual cuts merely served to compound the recession and aggravate the crisis. A policy directed towards growth was needed, a series of measures at a European level which would help to reverse the recession. Centre-left commentators also warned against a Eurozone where the 'weak would exit' and the 'strong would stick together', an idea that was popular in conservative circles. Such a development would, however, cause serious problems for the export-driven German economy. German exports to the Eurozone constituted 42% of its total exports, while exports to China made up only 5%. The collapse of the South would inevitably have serious consequences for the German economy. In 2012, German exports were, as a result of the crisis, only marginally higher than they had been four years previously,[17] indicating how stifling the crisis had been for them.

The election of François Hollande as President of France changed the political landscape somewhat. After his election he immediately met with Angela Merkel in Berlin, to promote his views. At the informal European Council held on 23 May, an initial review of the situation was carried out. In her statements Merkel appeared conciliatory. She said: 'On the one hand we have the pillar of a healthy fiscal policy, and on the other there will be a second pole referring to growth'. Hollande posited the matter of eurobonds. He received a categorical refusal from Germany to accept such an arrangement 'for the time being'.[18] Major negotiations would begin at the European summit at the end of June. The European Commission, in conjunction with the President of the Council and the ECB, undertook to present a proposal for the necessary changes in the governance of the EU.

The question of the banking sector in the Periphery was of major concern. The banks of the peripheral countries had provided much capital to the states to deal with the consequences of the crisis. As evidenced by the restructuring of Greek debt, this close relationship transferred a proportion of the debt crisis from sovereign states to the banking sector. From as early as 2011, the banks not only found themselves unable to finance investment in the economy, but now struggled to fulfil their obligations to meet compliance targets. According to an IMF report,[19] 58 significant European banks would, by the end of 2013, have to reduce their total assets by approximately €2 trillion, so as to ensure they were not overexposed or in violation of solvency regulations. This amount was not considered excessive, compared with the total capital of European banks. The majority of these banks, however, were in the peripheral states. Consequently, any hope of the banks playing their role in providing the credit required to drive a recovery was fundamentally undermined.

Finally, in May, four of the largest Greek banks were granted €18 billion from the €50 billion that had been allocated in the second Memorandum. This injection allowed those banks to borrow from the ECB again – borrowing which had been suspended owing to liquidity shortfalls. This allowed a partial normalisation of the Greek banking sector. The Greek banks had significant debts to the ECB and to Emergency Liquidity Assistance (ELA),[20] calculated at €17.5 billion. They thus remained exposed to any developments either domestic or concerning Greece's relationship with the Eurozone.

Any European discussion concerning Greece inevitably had reverberations in Greece. Due to the elections, the mass media announced that policy changes were imminent: eurobonds were anticipated; it looked certain that Hollande had secured the reversal in German policy he sought; Merkel, despite her pejorative statements on Greece, was about to cede to the need for eurobonds, in the facing of growing European and global pressure. However, such assessment was premature and naïve; it did nothing to aid the search for tangible solutions for Greece.

## Notes

1 'Greek economy to shrink 5%', *Financial Times,* 24 April 2012. According to published forecasts, in June the recession seemed to be exceeding 6%, whereas in July it was certain that it would reach 7%.
2 *To Vima Tis Kyriakis*, 27 May 2012, p. A4.
3 See *Ta Nea*, 2 April 2012, p. 15.
4 See pp. 153ff.
5 The auditors of the Troika delivered in July, after the elections, an extensive list of problems that had not been settled. They stressed 'the inaction of previous months in implementing commitments, particularly in matters of structural changes and the failure to achieve targets in the domain of revenue and expenditure'. *Ta Nea*, 28–29 July 2012, p. 12.
6 *Kathimerini*, 6 April 2012, p. 4.
7 'Desperately seeking a bailout for Spain and its banks', *Financial Times*, ft.com, 9 May 2012.
8 'Europe's worst fear: Spain and Greece spiral down together', *New York Times*, www.nytimes.com, 20 May 2012.
9 'Sinking Dutchman haunts the Eurozone', *Financial Times*, ft.com, 24 April 2012.
10 'Cyprus scrambles to avoid Greek contagion', *Financial Times*, ft.com, 4 June 2012.
11 For example, the Purchasing Managers Index (PMI) on economic activity for the whole of the Eurozone was particularly disappointing in April 2012. This index represents expectations for the near future and is composed on the basis of production, employment, purchases and orders. If the index is over 50 it shows an expansion of economic activity, whereas if it is under 50 it denotes contraction. In April 2012 the index for manufacturing activity fell to 45.9, whereas it was expected to rise to 48.1, from 47.7 a month earlier. Similarly, the index for services fell to 46.9, whereas analysts had expected a small improvement, to 49.3, from 49.2 a month earlier. See Bloomberg, Eco Calendar, at www.bloomberg.com/markets/economic-calendar.
12 *IHT*, 20 April 2012, p. 1.
13 Martin Wolf, 'The riddle of German self-interest', *Financial Times*, 29 May 2012.
14 In 2013 a new political party, Alternative für Deutschland, was created in Germany. It proposed the exit of Germany from the EU. See *FAZ*, 16 June 2003.
15 See p. 213.
16 Martin Wolf, 'What Hollande must tell Germany', *Financial Times*, 4 May 2012.
17 Wolf, 'The riddle of German self-interest'.
18 The governor of the Bundesbank said, with regard to bonds: 'You don't trust someone with your credit card when you are unable to control his expenses.' 'Economie', *Le Monde*, 26 May 2012, p. 12.
19 *Global Financial Stability Report*, IMF, April 2012, p. 6.
20 See p. 128, note 38.

# Part V
# Elections of 6 May and 17 June 2012

# 24

# The election of 6 May: euro or drachma?

The results of the Greek parliamentary elections on 6 May provoked surprise, both nationally and across Europe.[1] What had been a comfortable government majority for PASOK and New Democracy crumbled, with the two parties barely securing a third of the vote between them (32.15%). The parties fiercely critical of the Memorandum and the policy of austerity that accompanied it secured a staggeringly large share of the vote (approximately 41%).

The vote was an unprecedented rejection the political status quo and the handling of the crisis by the major parties. The electorate had expressed its fury and frustration. SYRIZA, a party that premised its entire campaign on rejection of the Memorandum, saw the largest gains. Protest and anger were not directed exclusively against the Memorandum, but against all those responsible for the fall in income, the rise in unemployment and the loss of hope. Voters wanted to publicly condemn the leadership that had driven the country into the circumstances in which it found itself. Public opinion expressed a paradox of preferences: it wanted to retain membership of the EMU, but escape the reforms of the Memorandum, while retaining the financial support. Many citizens believed the assertions of SYRIZA, that such contradictory aims could actually be secured.

Indicative of growing public fury was the ascendancy of the extreme-right Golden Dawn party. It gained influence through the provision of 'protection' to impoverished communities against the growing 'risk' posed by illegal aliens. Desperate voters sought conviction and authority; neither was being provided by the hesitant state. The vote for Golden Dawn was also a conscious expression of contempt for the political system. Citizens voted for the extreme right to indicate the scale of their rejection of the status quo and the parties that sustained it.

New Democracy experienced the most losses in the elections. Throughout the campaign, its belief that it would secure an outright majority indicated not only how detached it was from public sentiment, but also how complacent the party had become. It not only failed to replicate its returns in the 2009 elections,[2] but failed even to approach a comparable figure. This was the result of its ambiguous policies. Instead of constructing and articulating a comprehensive platform opposing PASOK, it focused on rejection of the Memorandum, but without offering any alternative. Such campaigning did not provide the electoral gains it sought, but did legitimise the arguments of nationalist and far-right circles within its ranks. When the party's leader, Antonis Samaras, made his u-turn in favour of the Memorandum, many of his former supporters either abandoned him or kept their distance. To regain the lost ground and consolidate his position at the helm of the party, he insisted on a new general election, hoping to force those who had argued against him, both within the party and across society, to follow him. It was a major political miscalculation. The majority of the disillusioned, weary and anxious voters rejected Samaras and his political gamesmanship.[3]

PASOK's defeat came as little surprise. However, the extent of the defeat – a loss of 30% of its share of the total vote (from around 43% to 13%) – exceeded even the most pessimistic predictions of a drop of between 15% and 20%. In PASOK's case, again the loss of public confidence stemmed from its contradictory stances and its role in overseeing the waves of austerity. Public opinion had lost faith in PASOK's principles, as it had witnessed a massive cut in public expenditure and a reduction in the state apparatus. The party at the same time had striven to maintain the status quo where it could. The party's message remained vague and lacked conviction.

In the public mind, the pro-European parties had lost and the 'anti-Memorandum' factions had won. The impression stemmed from the spectacular decline of the two main parties. However, a holistic evaluation of the results indicates that the electorate itself lacked certainty. New Democracy secured 19%, SYRIZA 17% and PASOK just 13%; that is, none of the three most successful parties had sufficiently convinced the electorate of the accuracy of its arguments so as to play a decisive role in the formation of the new government.[4] New Democracy and PASOK needed the support of DIMAR to form a government, but DIMAR was not ready to collaborate. Moreover, all parties considered that in a new election they would achieve a better result and were consequently reluctant to join a government. A further general election duly followed on 17 June. In the campaign, SYRIZA claimed that, thanks to its own position, all the parties had accepted that a renegotiation of the Memorandum was necessary. This claim was not true. It was not SYRIZA that provoked the change in views. Long before the May election, a broad section of society believed that it was imperative that various terms of the Memorandum be re-examined. The majority of public opinion in Greece believed that an extension of the time scale for the reduction of the deficit was imperative, so as to make the cuts in welfare expenditure and the increases in taxation more manageable. There was a growing realisation of the dire need for investment as well, but the terms of the Memorandum made this a virtual impossibility.[5]

SYRIZA's position provoked a race in the run-up to the June election in terms of what the parties claimed could be achieved through renegotiation.

In order to secure votes, parties made more and more ambitious demands in their manifestos and public statements, each asserting they could and would achieve more than their counterparts. This competition and electioneering did nothing to promote a reasoned debate of the challenges. Greece's European neighbours would not engage with ultimatums from Athens the parties were indicating they would make. Furthermore, any renegotiations implied a coherent and operable plan; no party possessed such a plan. Equally, Greece did not command any European political backing or significant allies willing to support its case. Even France, the most sympathetic continental partner, was urging Greece to fulfil its obligations.

The results of the May election indicated that Greece's selection of the European path and integration were not widely questioned. However, the management of relations with the EU, the actions of the national government and those of the Troika were the cause of widespread dissent, dissent that now reached such a level as to call into question the future of Greece as part of the European project. This hostility to the established parties was not a demand for a new political order, or a call for the modernisation; rather, it was a regressive vote to preserve the social status quo, to guarantee the entrenched systems of patronage and to protect the social compromises that were now under threat. It was actually a vote in defence of all that had led Greece into the crisis it now found itself in. The 'punishing radicalism' was in all honesty 'desperate conservatism'.[6]

Criticism of the Memorandum was voiced at both ends of the political spectrum. While framed in terms of the defence of national sovereignty, or the rejection of neoliberal capitalism, isolationism was advocated at both poles. The 'drachma front', those who sought an exit from the euro to recapture national control of both economic and political power, was gathering support across electorate. Greece was a nation torn between the desire to return to a 'blessed past' and hopes of a revitalised European future; it was a nation in a state of utter confusion.

Under such circumstances, it was impossible to bridge the gap between the diametrically opposed factions and construct any alternative to the Memorandum. Cooperation and consensus were demonised. Intolerance, rhetoric and polemic were cultivated by all sides. New Democracy maintained the belief that new elections would return many of its lost supporters. SYRIZA believed that fresh elections would allow it to make further gains and take the largest share of the vote. PASOK and DIMAR believed elections would allow them to reverse something of the disintegration in their vote, stemming from their support of the Memorandum. All the parties sought a new decisive battle.

Both May and June election campaigns helped to obscure any genuine discussion of the country's future course. Traditional negative electioneering dominated, riddled with personal attacks, simplistic rhetoric and continual platitudes. The politics of reason, supported by research and data, were as absent as any coherent view for the future.

PASOK presented various proposals for the economy and highlighted six points:[7]

1  no cuts in income and the gradual removal of extra taxes, contributions and levies that had been imposed owing to the crisis;
2  the autonomy of the trade unions and the institution of collective bargaining agreements to be protected so that the labour market can function in accordance with European standards;
3  a drastic injection of liquidity through increases in the EU Structural Funds for programmes to promote job creation;
4  public and private investments in infrastructure, calculated at around €55 billion, to be released immediately;
5  the European Council's commitment to provide help for growth in Greece;
6  all programmes dealing with youth unemployment to be supported by funds from the European Social Fund.

PASOK had also included in its election campaign promises relating to the construction of a stable taxation system based on 10-year cycles and no further cuts in either incomes or pensions.

New Democracy announced that its modest goal was 'to change everything … the growth model and the system of government'.[8] In terms of foreign policy, its priority was to establish a Greek Exclusive Economic Zone. In order to reduce the deficit it promised 'to cut public squandering of funds'. It believed it would be possible to save €2.5 billion annually through the introduction of new electronic management systems in the public sector and the application of international accounting standards. Loss-making public utility companies 'should be privatised immediately'; at the same time, 'measures for recovery' would be implemented, such as 'developing the public sector's real estate' and absorbing the funds available from EU programmes. New Democracy asserted 'the recessionary measures are wrong. And we are asking for this mistake to be corrected.' The party promised to retract cuts in the lowest pensions and allowances for families with three or more children; it would also provide regulatory relief for those who had taken out loans, under which 'repayments must not exceed 30% of monthly income'. 'No more new taxes, no more reductions in salaries, no more across the board cuts in pensions', 'reduction in the corporate tax rate to 15%'. A clear timetable would follow, which would specify the framework for the 'reduction of the tax rates for all individuals, so that the highest rate will not exceed 32%'. 'A conclusive settlement of arbitrary constructions without building permits through urban planning.... We are talking of over 600,000 buildings, which can yield at least 9 billion over four years.' 'We shall strike down bureaucracy' and create a more business-friendly environment. 'We believe in the Greek – in his tenacity and the boundless forces hidden inside him.' 'Greece will not just start simply advancing, but it will start running ahead.'[9]

Samaras later indicated his targets were:

1 'to create new jobs, 150,000, within 2013';
2 'to extend the unemployment benefit by another year';
3 'to retain the level of salaries in the private sector';
4 'the gradual increase in the tax-free bracket from €5,000 to €8,000, and after that to €12,000.

He would 'negotiate these goals with the Troika', while also securing the extension of 'the Memorandum's time for adjustment by two years, up to 2016'.[10]

No cost estimates for these measures were presented; neither were their effects on the adjustment programme mentioned. New Democracy's major priority was 'to ensure Greece's place in the euro'. It justified its former position against the Memorandum by asserting: 'We saw the country's interest when we voted against the Memorandum, and we saw the country's interests again when we voted in favour of the debt haircut.'[11]

During the campaign for the 6 May elections, various members of SYRIZA made public its inherent contradictions. The party leader, Alexis Tsipras, said that 'the clear goal was for Greece to remain in the euro, without the destructive austerity policies'. Other members of the party supported a 'left-wing exit from the euro, in an all-encompassing collision with the European Union and its totalitarianism'.[12] As a result of these all-too-evident inconsistencies, the party devised a new programme for the upcoming June elections, presented on 1 June. The revised programme consisted of a series of slogans and grandiose claims. With regard to the critical matter of the Memorandum, the party stated:

> the first act of a left-wing government, as soon as the new Parliament convenes, will be to cancel the Memorandum and the laws deriving from it.... The new government will denounce the odious conditions and will request that the loan agreement be renegotiated.... In particular, with regard to dealing with the country's sovereign debt crisis in a sustainable way, it will request a European solution. Without a European solution ... Greece cannot simultaneously achieve fiscal adjustment and a primary surplus, manage the payment of interest on accumulated debt, and finance public investments and public policies.[13]

SYRIZA's National Reconstruction Plan provided for a series of new expenditure, the imposition of new taxes and other measures, without any reference to the financial data which would permit calculation of the cost of its policies.

SYRIZA's principal intention was clear: the rejection of the Memorandum. But what would happen thereafter remained wholly unclear. Non-compliance with the Memorandum would inevitably result in the suspension of the loan agreement and the loss of any further funding from the Troika. What would almost certainly follow would be the collapse of the Greek economy and a return to the drachma, a subject on which SYRIZA remained completely silent. It was therefore unfathomable how it could claim that a 'European solution' would be sought. If Greece refused to adhere to the rules stipulated by the EU, its continental neighbours would not entertain any further discussion of the conditions or terms of support.

Common to all election manifestos was a failure to engage with the underlying causes of the Greek crisis: low competitiveness, dwindling productivity, delays or failure in the uptake of EU funds and inefficient administration. They did not refer to these matters because their authors did not consider them important or salient to the challenges Greece faced. It was evident that the various parties had not learnt from the mistakes of the past; they still believed grandiose proclamations and platitudes were all the country needed. Statements and promises were motivated by concern for how many votes they could return; there was no genuine focus on ending the recession and returning to growth. It was indicative of the fact that no party wished to be 'out-promised' by another. Many of New Democracy's list of 18 proposals for the 17 June elections were virtually identical to points in the SYRIZA manifesto.

Abroad, frustration and fatigue at the results of the Greek elections were evident. In a commentary, the *Financial Times* wrote:

> The European Union has gone as far as it can in seeking to help Greece. If there is not the political will in Athens to do what is necessary to preserve membership of the euro it is pointless to continue.... Greece alone must decide its fate.[14]

*Le Monde* noted, a few days later: 'Euro or drachma? The Greeks must decide.'[15] The interest rate on Greek sovereign bonds, which at the end of April had been at a massive 20.18%, reached a staggering 30.8% by the end of May.

Europe's political elite were no less impatient. Angela Merkel underlined the need to continue strictly implementing the agreed reform programme. The German Minister of Finance stated that the Memorandum 'is not negotiable'. No one 'wants Greece to exit the Eurozone', but 'the choice between the parties is a choice between staying in the Eurozone or leaving it'.[16] The President of the Eurogroup, Claude Juncker, appeared mildly more conciliatory in the meeting of the ministers of finance in Brussels on 15 May. He declared that 'the Eurogroup will not refuse to discuss a change in the time limits for the reduction of the deficit if there are dramatic changes in conditions'. However, the Eurogroup demanded that Greece comply absolutely with the reform programme. Both the IMF and the European Commission made it publicly known that pending financial support would not be released as long as political uncertainty continued in Greece. However, it was made clear that the next instalment would be made available at the end of June, provided relative political stability returned.

The causes of the results in the Greek elections did not receive any substantive discussion abroad. The failure of the first Memorandum, the recession, and the fall in income and standards of living were not considered. It was widely felt that the Greek electorate fundamentally failed to appreciate the efforts made to support their economy. Debate focused on the social and political fallout of the Memorandum was little to non-existent. Even where subsequent initiatives implicitly recognised the existing failings, the mistakes in planning were never explicitly acknowledged. This was due in part to matters of prestige, but also the fear of fallout affecting either the markets or the policies of austerity being followed in other peripheral nations. However, these concerns did impede the prospects for any reappraisal of the suitability and value of the adjustment programmes.

The Greek constitution has provisions for the formation of a coalition government in the event that no party wins an absolute majority. However, the efforts by the President of the Republic to arrange the formation of a government proved fruitless after the May election. An agreement on the aims of a coalition between the two main parties could not be achieved. Throughout the negotiations, each party attributed the failure to form a government to the other. Proposals were made for coalitions that stood no chance of success, or demands were made that were known to be unacceptable. The focus remained on popular support in future elections, rather than on efforts at compromise and consensus. Even the proposal for a government of 'technocrats', comparable to the Monti administration in Italy, was rejected as the 'death of politics' or as a 'compromise with policies that have been rejected by voters'. The increasing likelihood of an obligatory exit from the Eurozone did not seem to concern Greece's political parties. The interim government that assumed temporary responsibility set 17 June as the date for a re-run of the elections.

As soon as it became known that there would be a fresh round of elections, discussions regarding the management of a Greek exit[17] from the Eurozone received coverage the world over. Member states across the EU made it evident that it would not be possible for Greece to remain in the Eurozone if it refused to comply with either the reforms of the Memorandum or the regulatory framework of the EMU. Financial support would be withdrawn immediately in response to non-compliance. Greece should follow the examples of Portugal and Ireland and adhere to the adjustment programme. There was no more time for displays of democratic indecision, or flippant changes in the Greek administration. The entire EU was felt to be put at risk by Greek instability and the possibility of a default. A collapse in Greece risked contagion that could affect Spanish and Italian banks, and provoke turmoil throughout the Eurozone. There was no time to procrastinate: it was time to act.

Certain commentators considered that a Grexit was inevitable. They argued that the current instability made any investment impossible. A return to the drachma would encourage the acquisition of Greek businesses by foreign capital upon very favourable terms. The value of labour would tumble, returning a competitive edge to Greece. Conditions conducive to recovery could be created. Major devaluations in South Korea, Indonesia and Russia had gradually fostered recovery and a return to growth.[18] A Grexit would also send a clear message to the other ailing peripheral nations of the single-currency area as to the stakes at risk and encourage rigid adherence to programmes of reform. It would indicate that the EU would neither be pressured nor be manipulated;

compliance was non-negotiable.[19] If this example were not set, the total debt of the Eurozone might grow, driving investors away from the euro and ultimately leading to the collapse of the EMU. Analysts advocating a Grexit denied the risk of a domino effect pulling other nations out of the single-currency area. As a result of the restructuring of Greek debt and the duration of the crisis, exposure to Greek liabilities across the European banking sector was limited. There would be instability and significant fallout, but it could be managed. The ESM would give to the Eurozone sufficient capital to overcome the consequences of a Grexit.

The official line throughout the Eurozone remained that no one wanted to lose Greece. The preference was that it remained within the Eurozone, provided that it fulfilled its obligations.[20] The EU had already invested €150 billion in supporting Greece, and there were Structural Funds available to Athens to drive a return to growth.

What exactly a Grexit and a return to the drachma would mean remained unclear inside Greece. Many believed any change would be of limited severity, not dissimilar to devaluation of a sovereign currency.[21] They asserted that a post-euro Greece could at least reclaim its freedom.

A report by the National Bank of Greece in May[22] dispelled any optimistic analysis comparing an exit to a conventional devaluation. It indicated that a Grexit would lead to a significant fall in citizens' standard of living. Per capita income would fall by at least 55%. The brunt of the pain would be shouldered by the economically weaker section of the population. They would be hurt by the scale of the devaluation of the new currency against the euro,[23] the consequent extended recession and the significant rise in unemployment. Even though recession had already reached a level of −22%, it would increase by a further −14%, and unemployment would climb to 34% from the current 21%. The competitive advantage Greece would acquire through devaluation would disappear through inflation. Inflation would begin at approximately 30% but then rise much higher. These factors would all compound falling living standards. Foreign currency, notably the euro and the dollar, would become incredibly scarce; exceptionally strict restrictions and controls on its use would affect trade, travel and, again, living standards. The country would be in no position to meet its commitments to its lenders abroad. It is unlikely the Troika would provide any further financial support; equally, Greece would no longer have access to any European Structural Funds. ECB financing of Greek banks would be suspended. Access to basic goods such as fuel, medicines and raw materials, all of which Greece is dependent upon imports for, would be incredibly difficult. Finally, the report noted that, under such circumstances, the budget deficit and sovereign debt would grow as percentages of GDP, resulting in a marked deterioration of the economy's credibility for a very long time. Thus, a Grexit would result in a deteriorating recession, with no end in sight.

The collapse of the economy would also inevitably result in social breakdown, with a rise in crime, in part through the looting of shops by desperate citizens, which almost certainly would be tolerated by a fatigued and under-paid police force: 'There would be chaos'.[24]

A return to the drachma, it is clear, would pose a great risk to the country and its citizens. Public anxiety and collapsing confidence were already evident in mass withdrawals from Greek banks and the transfer of savings abroad. It was calculated that after 6 May, the day of the elections, €3 billion was withdrawn from Greek banks. Any negative development risked sparking a mass run on the banks and the complete collapse of the Greek banking sector. Aside from merely domestic concerns, Greece remained exposed to externalities, such as a crisis in Italy or direct conflict with European authorities, which could force a disorderly default and a return to the drachma. In such a case, the consequences would be far graver than the orderly default considered by the National Bank of Greece report discussed above.

A return to the drachma would entail reinstating a regime of controls and restrictions which are not compatible with the basic principles of the EU, a point that critics of the Memorandum seemed to remain silent on. There would be no free movement of capital or of goods; inevitably, restrictions on the movement of people would follow. Greece would no longer have access to any of the benefits or institutions of the single market. At the same time, the population would suffocate under the regime of a state of emergency, which would most likely not last for weeks but years. Rights, freedoms and other possibilities taken for granted today would be subject to an assault of grave proportions; it is impossible to tell how far such regression could go. Failure to comply with the rules of the EU would lead, sooner or later, not just to an exit from the single market, but from the EU as well. Continued social breakdown as result of severe poverty would put democracy and the very rule of law itself to the test. Authoritarian attitudes and practices would prevail in order to restore order and security.

Whatever form it took, a return to the drachma, even an organised one, would mark a major political defeat for the country and would have exceptionally painful consequences across Greek society. Greece's ability to participate in European and global affairs would be enormously reduced. To a great extent, Greece would lose the capacity to defend its national interests. The country's participation in the European project helped also to ensure a political and cultural environment conducive to development and stability. After the exit, Greece would slide back to the status of a 'third world country'. It was not simply out of spite that certain foreign commentators argued that Greece was gradually returning to its traditional environment, the Balkans.[25]

The inevitable consequences of a Grexit were more or less known to a section of the left 'anti-Memorandum' camp. However, it advocated immediate cancellation without an exit from the euro. Numerous critics of the Memorandum cited the absence of any clauses in the Treaties permitting the exclusion of any member state from the Union, as evidence that no one could force Greece to leave the EU. Many on the left of Greek politics asserted that the economic and political damage to the EU itself of a Grexit would be far greater than the cost of ceding to Athens' demands.

These arguments pay no consideration to strongly held beliefs regarding the functioning of the single-currency area. Despite growing criticism and a loss of confidence, the Eurozone does not act without consideration and awareness of the need for uniform regulation. It weighs the risks arising from any deviation from its macroeconomic targets and decides accordingly. Greece accounts for just 2% approximately of the Eurozone's GDP. Its economic weight is insignificant. The damage it would cause, however, through non-compliance and the precedent it set would be of much greater significance. Such action would question the rules of the game. The cohesion of the EU is based on the ethics of mutuality. Each member state must fulfil its obligations and comply with the regulations; any violation of this premise undermines the entire European project. A unilateral cancellation of the Memorandum by Greece would fly in the face of the ethics of mutual respect and responsibility upon which both the EMU and the EU are constructed; it could risk sparking their collapse, and therefore could under no circumstances be tolerated.

The EU would have the power to ensure the rapid closure of the matter of Greek non-compliance through the complete suspension of all financial support, not only of the assistance foreseen in the Memorandum, but also of access to the ECB. With no money, Greece would no longer be able to service the interest it owes. More pressing in terms of domestic demands, it would no longer have the capital to manage state operations; it would be obliged to stop the payment of salaries, pensions and social security provisions. The banks would no longer have the necessary liquidity to finance businesses or to honour savings. In the market, the official currency would start being replaced by ad hoc currencies such as IOUs and company bonds. Any government would soon be obliged to issue a new currency; this would usher in the return of the drachma, in an effort to stem the tide of social and economic disintegration. Greece would exit the Eurozone of its own accord, without any discussion of how this would relate to the Treaty framework.[26]

The question had indeed been posed in the international press that if Greece were to 'fall', would this exacerbate the turmoil in Europe, or even act as a catalyst for a chain reaction of defaults? Most commentators thought this highly unlikely. Through the restructuring of its banks and the ESM, the Eurozone had already taken the necessary measures to support the exposed nations. Equally, with regard to the risk of any major run on the banks of the Periphery, the ECB had the ability to make unlimited injections of liquidity, while purchasing the sovereign bonds of such nations on the secondary market to ensure no exponential rise in the interest rates available to them.

In mid-May 2012 there was widespread indignation across Greece when the Commissioner responsible for trade said in an interview that the European Commission was studying the possible effects of a Grexit. The necessary denial by the Commission followed so as to placate Greek anger. Nevertheless, for an international organisation, such as the European Commission, comprised of developed nations as it is, it is inconceivable not to make preparations for an event that was looking increasingly likely with the passage of every day. A high-ranking European official said what was already evident: 'The whole world is examining what is a possibility. It would be irresponsible not to deal with the matter.'[27]

Various proposals regarding how Athens might avoid a return to the drachma, despite a refusal to adhere to the programme of the Memorandum, emerged in the press. It was proposed that the euro should continue to be used in everyday transactions in the country, while the official currency (the drachma) would be used only in extraordinary circumstances, as is the case in Montenegro, which is not a member of the EU but which has the euro as its currency. A selection of analysts argued in favour of 'stabilisation loans' so as to ensure the necessary funds for Greece's economy to function and the provision of essential produce – oil, medicines, food and so on. German economists proposed the implementation of a parallel currency, the Geuro, to cover the internal needs of the country.[28]

These ideas fail to take into account the fact that the creation of a special regime for Greece would risk setting a dangerous precedent. It would indicate that the Eurozone is not uniform, stable or in a position to control conditions; rather, it would have begun to come apart at the seams. Its leadership would avoid such a precedent at all costs.

At this point, it must be stressed that a Grexit from the single-currency area, or even an exit from the EU itself, would be no easy matter.[29] Despite the economic benefits which might arise for the developed countries of the Core, it would mark a historical defeat. It would highlight Europe's inability to ensure a common course for its countries. It would signify that the structure that had been constructed with such effort was not capable of saving its weakest member; consequently, what faith could be held in the capacity of the EU to overcome greater shocks? It would sow doubts over its future and act as a brake on any further integration. All member states would begin to question the value of growing losses of sovereign competence if the common model could lead them down the path Greece had followed.

### Notes

1 The results were: New Democracy, 18.93%, 108 seats; SYRIZA, 16.75%, 52 seats; PASOK, 13.22%, 41 seats; Independent Greeks, 10.58%, 33 seats; KKE, 6.87%, 26 seats; Golden Dawn, 6.88%, 21 seats; DIMAR, 6.09%, 19 seats. The parties that had been in the Papademos coalition government – New Democracy and PASOK – therefore now had between them 149 seats. The parties wishing to revoke the Memorandum – SYRIZA, Independent Greeks and KKE – had 111 seats. DIMAR – which supported the country remaining in the euro and a renegotiation of the Memorandum, and had not been willing to work with the previous coalition government – had 19 seats. The extreme-right Golden Dawn, with 21 seats, was not

considered an acceptable government partner by the other parties. It was, therefore, unclear and doubtful whether a governing majority could be formed. For the elections of 6 May and 17 June, see Y. Pretenteris, *The Cold Civil War, the People, the Events that Destroyed the Country*, Patakis, 2012, p. 132.

2  In 2009 New Democracy had received 38.48% of the vote.

3  See Fotis Georgeles, *Athens Voice*, 10–11 May 2012, p. 4.

4  T. Yannitsis, *Ta Nea*, 20 May 2012, p. A12.

5  See for example an interview with C. Simitis in *Vima tis Kyriakis*, 17 April 2011, and C. Simitis, 'Doubts requiring convincing answers', *Kathimerini*, 7 April 2011.

6  G. Voulgaris, 'Greece is not playing poker', *Ta Nea*, 26 May 2012, p. 10.

7  See *Ta Nea*, 28–29 April 2012, p. 26, and *Ta Nea*, 26 September 2012, p. 12.

8  Zappeion, Presentation of the programme for the economy, Elections 2012, New Democracy.

9  Ibid.

10  See *Kathimerini*, 1 June 2012, p. 5.

11  Ibid.

12  Panayiotis Lafazanis, election campaign speech in Lamia, 29 April 2012, reported in *Ta Nea*, 25 May 2012, p. A16.

13  News 247, June 2012.

14  *Financial Times*, ft.com, 8 May 2012.

15  *Le Monde*, 23 May 2012, p. 1. With regard to the consequences of a prolonged stalemate in the Greek party political scene, the President of the Bundesbank, Jens Weidmann, was clearer: 'We shall examine whether the agreements on which solidarity between states is based are being adhered to. If not, then financial assistance must stop.' 'Economie', *Le Monde*, 26 May 2012, p. 12.

16  *FAZ*, 16 May 2012, p. 12.

17  'Grexit' is the abbreviation used by the international press.

18  A. Subramania, 'Greece's exit may become Europe's envy', *Financial Times*, ft.com, 14 May 2012.

19  'Abschied Euro', *Der Spiegel*, issue 20, 2012, pp. 22, 24, 27. For similar views in the UK see 'Senior Tory MP calls for Greece to quit euro', *Financial Times*, ft.com, 5 June 2012.

20  Statements by the President of the EU, Herman Van Rompuy, on 24 May 2012, EUCO 93/12, Presse 215.

21  A. Theopeftatou, 'So, what would it matter? What would it matter if we paid in drachma?', *To Vima*, 20 May 2012, p. A16.

22  *Greek Economy*, special edition, May 2012.

23  It would have been approximately 65%.

24  M. Wolf, 'A permanent precedent', *Financial Times*, ft.com, 17 May 2007.

25  Tim Judah, 'Greece turns Balkan', Bloomberg.com.news, 14 May 2012.

26  On the various questions concerning Greece's inability to meet its liabilities, and moving to a new currency, see an article by 11 Greek economists, 'Yesterday and today of the Greek crisis', *Kathimerini*, 3 June 2012; 'Eurozone: if Greece goes...', *Financial Times*, ft.com, 13 May 2012; *Ta Nea*, 19–20 May 2012, p. 22; 'Catching up with a frenzied Eurozone', *IHT*, 29 May 2012, p. 17; and 'Leaders contemplate the best course if Greece pulls out of the Eurozone', *IHT*, 25 May 2012, p. 1.

27  *Le Monde*, 20–21 May 2011, p. 3. Indeed, more and more messages began arriving from various sources that the member states as well as the ECB and the other

central banks were preparing for an escalation of the Greek crisis and were studying the country's exit from the Eurozone. See *Kathimerini*, 24 May 2012, p. 3.

28 See L. Barber, *Financial Times*, 16 May 2012, p. 8; Deutsche Bank, 'The Geuro', *Global Economic Perspectives*, 18 May 2012; 'Petit Guide Pratique pour sortir de l'euro (vu par la city)', *Le Monde*, 19 June 2012; P. Bofinger, *Zurück zur D-Mark?*, Droemer HC, 2012, p. 144.

29 In 2012 a leading British businessman offered a prize for the best analysis of how a country could leave the euro while causing the least damage. See D. Lascelles, 'What a Eurozone break-up might look like', *Debating Europe Schools*, 18 April 2013.

# 25

# Cracks in the euro

The effects of the Greek crisis on the Eurozone became more and more visible during the Greek election campaigns in May and June 2012. Anxiety over the cohesion of the EMU grew. The *Financial Times* published a commentary entitled the 'Euro starts to crack'.[1] Various central banks and investors had become increasingly wary, no longer purchasing securities in euros as they had done. By the end of May, the exchange rate of the euro against the dollar fell below the level it had been on 30 June 2010, when the Greek crisis began.[2]

The markets predicted further falls. This was beneficial for the EU's export sector but it marked the deterioration of the crisis in the peripheral countries and a fall in the rate of growth across the entirety of the Eurozone. In May, unemployment across the Eurozone had reached 11.2%, the highest level since the euro had been established.[3] The inability of the member states to find a convincing solution to their problems served only to compound such anxieties.[4]

The deterioration of the situation in Spain was also significantly affecting the fall of the value of the euro. The rate of interest at which it was able to borrow was approaching levels that were no longer sustainable, levels which would require major European intervention. Even though Spain's sovereign debt was low, it was steadily growing year by year. Spain's banks were in- curring greater and greater losses. At the beginning of June, these losses were estimated to stand at €200 billion. As a result the banks would need for their recapitalisation a sum the Spanish government could not borrow. In Brussels it was increasingly felt that Spain should request the EU's support, a view the Spanish government staunchly disagreed with, due to its aversion EU oversight.[5]

The Spanish crisis rekindled fears of a run on the banks. The ECB would then be obliged to provide major injections of liquidity to prevent the collapse of the banking sector. The amounts necessary for any such operation would be far in excess of all the support so far provided to the peripheral nations. In the case of Spain alone, any such injection would reach approximately €1.5 trillion. The Core nations of the EU, such as Germany, refused to accept the risk of supporting the ECB in the event of such an operation, under any circumstances.[6]

The European Commission and the ECB advanced the idea of a 'banking union' which would complement the monetary union, to help deal with the problem. Four kinds of reforms to the banking sector would be needed for a banking union to be established on a European level:

1  a system protecting depositors, which would indemnify them should their bank go bankrupt;
2  a common mechanism for dealing with banking crises, which would transfer responsibility for the necessary regulation to the EU, restricting the power of member states;
3  the supervision of banks operating across the borders of every member state, by a single authority;
4  the establishment of common rules for the operation of banks within the EU.

As was rightly observed after these proposals were presented, 'a common source of financing would have to be created if they were to be implemented, either from the Union's budget or from a common organisation. In any case, a banking union entails new steps towards unification.'[7] The spreading of the crisis in the Eurozone and the unending recession in Greece indicated that case-by-case measures were not adequate. The member states needed to find a solution to safeguard the entire EU from current and future risks.

The President of the ECB, Mario Draghi, called on the member states to 'dissolve the fog'. He stressed that the structure of the EMU could no longer be preserved in its current form. The leaders of the EU would have to finally take major decision regarding the future of the European project. Neither the European Parliament nor the European Commission had the authority required by the times, while the ECB did not have the necessary competences to intervene. The way the crisis had unfolded had made clear that the framework of the EMU and the EU was not capable of managing the crises that it currently faced.[8]

At the same time, the President of the European Commission was calling for a firm strategy to strengthen European integration. 'We will support an ambitious and structural approach which should include a road map and a timetable for a full economic and monetary union in the euro area.'[9]

The various measures that had already been proposed needed comprehensive examination: eurobonds, initiatives for growth, the banking union, an extension of the timetable for the reduction of deficits and debt, and the restructuring of the debt of ailing member states. Major questions regarding the vision for the future of Europe required answering. Would there be genuine federal financing for weak or struggling states, similar to that which exists in the USA or the Federal Republic of Germany? How would the differences in competitiveness and levels of growth that cause the crises be overcome? Would a rate of growth of at least 4%, resulting from an actual rate of growth of 2% and inflation of 2%, be ensured so that restrictions on expenditure and income could be partially lifted? Could Germany and other members of the Core be persuaded to stimulate domestic demand, so the stringent terms of austerity could be relaxed in the peripheral nations?[10]

It was obvious that the EU would have to improve its operations and efficiency. But the main obstacle was, and remains, ever-growing public mistrust. The Greeks begrudged the austerity imposed by the Eurozone, even though they were granted unprecedented support in return. The Germans were increasingly angry at the costs they were expected to bear for the indiscretions of their southern neighbours, despite the evident benefits the EMU had had for the German economy. Compromise would need time; however, time was something that was not on the EU's side. The President of the European Council convened an informal summit on 23 May, for a preliminary exchange of views, including the newly elected French President, as a precursor to the regular summit scheduled for June. The focus of the informal meeting was growth; it sought to establish possibilities and proposals for future negotiation. As it was known that no binding decisions would be taken, it was an environment conducive to a more frank and open expression of preferences. After the meeting, Herman Van Rompuy stated that the talks had focused on the completion of the Europe 2020 programme, which laid the emphasis on investment and employment.[11] Various initiatives were already under way, such as European patents and financing for small to medium-size businesses.

These declarations indicated that substantive progress had not been realised. Repetitions of previous statements were of little value. The much-awaited summit demonstrated the difficulties that remained in securing compromise acceptable to all. Reports in the international media indicated the European leaders had postponed their decisions until the end of June; however, they instructed the principal institutions of the EU to consider proposals for closer fiscal cooperation, the guarantee of bank deposits, and project bonds.

The subject of Greece still dominated talks across European member states and institutions. Italy and France continued to make calls for the re-examination of the Greek crisis, with regard to the need for increased flexibility in the targets prescribed. However, the European Commission and the Bundesbank would not entertain any such calls; they felt any retreat might risk jeopardising the fiscal discipline of the whole Eurozone.

Their statements indicated there was still a place for Athens in the EMU, dependent on compliance:

> We want Greece to stay in the Eurozone, provided it sticks to its obligations....
> Continuation of vital reforms, pushing ahead with private investments and the enhancement of the Eurozone's institutions are the best guarantors of a prosperous future. We expect that the new Greek government ... shall agree with these choices.[12]

However, widespread anxiety still dominated. Officials of the European Commission requested the ministries of finance in all member states to make preparations to manage the exit of Greece from the single-currency area. This was an indirect recognition that the Greek crisis had now peaked.

## Notes

1 *Financial Times*, ft.com, 16 May 2012.
2 The exchange rate of €1 was $1.25. Its usual exchange rate throughout 2011 was between $1.40 and $1.30.
3 See www. Finfacts.ie/irish_financenews/European/article 1024698. For recent developments in unemployment at a European and a member state level see epp.eurostat.ec. europa.eu/statistics unemployment, 31 December 2013.
4 See *Le Monde*, 27 28 December 2012, p. 13.
5 See *Le Monde*, 1 June 2012, p. 6.
6 G. Davies, 'The anatomy of the Eurozone bank run', *Financial Times*, ft.com, 20 May 2012.
7 'La Commision europeenne soutient officielment l'idee d'une "union banquaire"', *Le Monde*, 1 June 2012, p. 6.
8 *IHT*, 1 June 2012.
9 'Fears in EU spur calls for systemic overhaul', *IHT*, 30 May 2012, p. 12.
10 See M. Wolf, 'A fragile Europe must change fast', *Financial Times*, ft.com, 25 May 2012; 'Europe fails again to quell the crisis', *IHT*, 26–27 May 2012; H. Dixon, 'Preserving euro and sovereignty', *IHT*, 21 May 2012; M. Wolf, 'The riddle of German self-interest', *Financial Times*, 29 May 2012.
11 European Council, The President, 24 May 2012, EUCO 93/12, Presse 215, PR PCE 78.
12 'EU leaders groping for a way out of the crisis', *IHT*, 24 May 2012, p. 1. See also 'Les Europeenes, testent un euro sans la Grece', *Le Monde*, 25 May 2012, p. 3; 'EU struggles to agree hard line on Greece', *Financial Times*, ft.com, 23 May 2012.

# 26

# The Union at a dead end: change of course on 29 June

Both Greece and the EU appeared to have reached a dead end at the beginning of June. It was looking increasingly unlikely that a compromise would be found by 29 June, when the next summit of the European Council was due to be held. In Greece, there was a growing cynicism that upcoming elections on 17 June would restore anything resembling political normality or stability. The pessimism was verging on the tangible.

The request from the Spanish Prime Minister for financial support for the ailing banking sector, at the beginning of June,[1] sounded further alarm bells across the Eurozone. The Iberian nation's preference was for direct support from either the EFSF or the ECB for its banks. Germany, however, favoured an official request from Spain, which would entail conditionality, comparable to the adjustment programmes in Greece, Portugal and Ireland.

This time the EU moved decisively. On 9 June the Eurogroup decided to grant direct funding from the EFSF and the ESM totalling €100 billion for the recapitalisation of the Spanish banks.[2] The loan would be taken up, on behalf of the Spanish state, by the newly created Organisation for the Restructuring of Spanish Banks, which would distribute the funds to the banks. 'However, the Spanish government will retain the full responsibility for the financial assistance and will sign the MOU [Memorandum of Understanding]. The policy of conditionality ... should be focused on specific reforms targeting the financial sector, including restrictive measures.' The IMF, which was party to the negotiations, was charged with the responsibility of 'supporting the implementation and the monitoring the financial assistance with regular reporting'. It was agreed that the specific conditions for the whole project would be stipulated at subsequent meetings. Spain was now the fourth country (after Greece, Ireland and Portugal) to have recourse to the EU for support. On 25 June 2012 Cyprus submitted an official request for support to the President of the European Council. This assistance would be used to recapitalise the banking sector (approximately €6 billion), as well as to cover the requirements of its deficit and bond redemption (approximately €3.5 billion). Cyprus thus became the fifth country of the Eurozone in need of external assistance.

At the beginning of June, the ECB did not reduce its basic interest rate; neither did it take any measures to increase liquidity. Its President repeated once again that while developments across the EMU were concerning, there were no magic solutions. The ECB alluded to the need for a reappraisal of approaches, in light of all the negative developments – the fall in the value of the euro, the capital flight from the single-currency area, the growing difficulties afflicting trade with the peripheral countries, the deteriorating recession in Italy, the ever-growing unemployment and the economic stagnation across the continent. Increasingly, officials throughout the Eurozone began to doubt the German prescription of strict fiscal discipline, and to seek instead less restrictive solutions – a more holistic remedy that included growth.

*Le Monde* posited a four-pronged approach to addressing the crisis:

1 *The establishment of a 'banking union'.* This would entail far greater supervision of the major banks, bank deposit guarantees by the EU and mechanisms for the recapitalisation of the banking sector.
2 *The Fiscal Compact and related fiscal control mechanisms to deter economic mismanagement and ensure stability.*[3] Most controversial in this debate was the institution of eurobonds, a system of mutual solidarity for repayment of debts. According to German analysis, the Treaties forbid burdening one country with the debts of another member state. Eurobonds could be discussed only within a framework of religious adherence to the Fiscal Compact and stringent control of every member states' expenditure.
3 *Mechanisms for the promotion of European growth.* This was the matter tabled by the recently elected French President Françoise Hollande. Germany maintained its insistence that structural reforms, coordinating regulations for the labour market, social security measures and changes in the form of corporation tax would be sufficient to stimulate growth. However, France believed that 'targeted investments' supported by the EU were required, along with an increase in the European Investment Bank's capital funding (through project bonds) to finance infrastructure development.
4 *The completion of the long-discussed model for economic governance.* This would require institutional reform to manage such periods of instability as the EU was currently witnessing, and would inevitably entail the transfer of further competences to the central institutions of the EU, including, in all likelihood, the creation of a permanent European Minister for Finance, and also the unification of taxation regimes.[4]

The fourth matter was crucial. In their efforts so far, the EU and the EMU had overcome challenges when compromise had not proved too elusive, whereas the more crucial, and inevitably more testing, challenges had been shelved, for discussion in the indefinite future. Such a practice is entirely understandable for a union of 27 member states, all with competing preferences and objections. However, the EU was reaching the juncture where major questions could no longer be eternally deferred because of the difficulties they entailed.

Such delays now posed a genuine threat to the stability of the EU and the future of the European project. The need to act decisively in the face of crisis required significant moves towards further integration and centralisation. To address the challenges facing the single currency, divergence in levels of development, the surpluses of the North and the deficits of the South, and the risks posed by a sovereign default, it was clear that Europe required unified financial governance and leadership capable of decisive action.

Any further transfer of power to the supranational institutions of the EU was met with distrust. Public opinion across member states was opposed to the idea of ceding more power to Brussels.[5] Strong opposition existed to proposals suggesting centralised control of pensions, working conditions or taxation; these were not the remit of the EU, but of national parliaments. Competences and relations between the national and the supranational go way beyond issues of administrative efficiency but pose much harder questions regarding the practice of democracy itself.

Germany felt that enhanced central authority for the management of the euro and fiscal policy was necessary. Berlin's preference was not simply for the creation of a European Ministry of Finance, but also for a significant expansion and reform of the competences of the Commission and the European Parliament, to address the perennial questions of democratic legitimacy. It was proposed that the President of the Commission be elected on the basis of pan-European universal suffrage. The quid pro quo for such reform to the structure of the EU would be the relaxing of German resistance to proposals regarding mutual solidarity and capital transfers to promote economic convergence. At the beginning of June, Angela Merkel emphatically stressed that 'we do not only need monetary union, but a fiscal union, and chiefly a political union'.[6] At the same time, however, she maintained that progress must be achieved 'step by step'. Such changes require meticulous preparation and care. The Chancellor added: 'If, however, certain members do not wish to follow, we must not stop.'[7] This suffix to German aspirations was perceived by many as an indication of the emerging reality of a two-speed Europe.

At the beginning of June, France and Italy as well as other nations were still to express a clear preference for the future of the EU. France had once been at the vanguard of pro-integration forces; in recent years, however, following the public rejection of the European constitution in 2005, France's tendency had been to prioritise national sovereignty. The crisis marked a change in this tendency in French European policy. In preparations for the upcoming summit of the European Council, both Italy and France indicated their support for further political integration. However, they asserted that this would be possible only if it was undertaken in parallel with efforts to drive a return to growth, so as to redress the economic divergence the continent was now witnessing. Once again, the focus of discussions returned to the mutualisation of liabilities to reverse these imbalances: 'Eurobonds are a way to lead the whole process to a conclusion'.[8]

Germany remained resistant to such calls. On 22 June, the Italian Prime Minister, Mario Monti, invited Hollande, along with the German Chancellor and the Spanish Prime Minister, to Rome, to try to find a compromise. They put forward proposals for a pact for growth, which would have at its disposal 1% of European GDP (€130 billion). It was hoped this pact could be endorsed and ratified at the European Council of 28–29 June. They also agreed on instituting a financial transactions tax. However, disagreement remained over how best to improve the way the EMU functioned. Even though all four agreed on the need for a 'banking union' and a 'fiscal union', they were unable to determine on what terms these could be established. According to Merkel's analysis, the direct recapitalisation of banks through EU support mechanisms, as favoured by Monti, was in direct violation of the Treaties.

Subsequently, hidden differences of opinion leaked out. The German Chancellor was fundamentally opposed to mutual responsibility regarding sovereign debt. She maintained that such a development would be possible only after political unification, to ensure the effective control of member states' economic policies. Hollande asserted that the transfer of further competences to a supranational authority could occur only in an environment of enhanced solidarity. Merkel indicated in unequivocal terms that, as long as she lived, there would be no eurobonds. France had no further leverage. Berlin felt that the financial assistance that had already been provided to five of the Eurozone's member states was indicative of sufficient solidarity. The IMF weighed into the conflict. The head of the Fund stated that without measures to establish the mutualisation of the debt of the EMU the sustainability of the euro was at risk. The leaders of the Eurozone needed to make sacrifices and reach sufficient compromise to guarantee the future of the single-currency area.[9] Many well known commentators expressed comparable views in the international media. The German preference for strict fiscal control needed to be moderated by a policy matrix directed at ensuring a return to European growth. Without this dimension to European economic policy, there was a very strong chance of a 'recurrence of political and economic crisis, even if the Eurozone survives.... The crisis of the Eurozone is likely to be a very long-running soap-opera – if it does not end in tragedy.'[10]

Just how dynamic and unstable the situation remained was indicated by the market response to the recapitalisation of the Spanish banking sector. The initial optimism on the international market regarding the expedient response of the Eurozone was short-lived. Assessment in the media was comparable; the intervention was viewed favourably, but it was noted that it had done little more than to buy Spain time. The underlying challenges had not been resolved. Madrid would increase its sovereign debt by approximately 20% with this loan. Repayment would inevitably pose challenges to Spain's future annual deficit. The bailout had transferred exposure from the banking sector to Spain's mounting sovereign debt. Proposals were suggested regarding the restructuring of the banks' debts or even a transfer of the banks' debts into shares, to permit direct oversight and control by the government. It was becoming quickly apparent to both the Spanish government and the Spanish public that the €100 billion package, initially presented as a victory, required substantive reappraisal, as it might risk fuelling further crisis on the Iberian peninsula. This reappraisal was to happen at the summit of the European Council on 29 June.

The turmoil in Spain was being felt in Italy too. Its rate of interest on borrowing again exceeded 6%; Italian debt appeared unsustainable. Public displeasure was mounting at Monti's technocratic government and there were calls for fresh elections. Across the EU there was growing concern that Italy might be dragged into the 'devil's trap' of austerity, recession and exponential rises in sovereign debt. Once again it was evident that drastic action was imperative.

The remaining concerns regarding the Greek crisis were an indication of the Eurozone's inability to deal with a matter effectively; it had let the problem stumble on for two years without resolution. Even the US President, Barack Obama, in a public address at the beginning of June, underlined the need for Europe to take immediate measures to restore confidence in the international markets. He enumerated the spectrum of possible negative consequences of a Grexit and called on the EU to provide substantive further assistance if the Greek people voted to remain in the single-currency area at the upcoming elections.[11] He would not have intervened in such a public fashion if the American administration did not have major concerns regarding the deterioration of the crisis in Greece and Europe and its possible ramifications for the US economy.[12]

Under these circumstances the Council Summit of 29 June acted as a catalyst. Across not only the continent but across the globe eyes were focused on the Eurozone. The tension between various member states had not reached such levels for years. National publics were again asking whether their leaders would finally be able to negotiate an agreement sufficient to ensure an end of this ongoing spectacle and to stem the downward spiral of the Eurozone and save the euro.

Two distinct camps were evident: on one side, the French–Italian–Spanish alliance; and the other the alliance of the Northern nations, led by Germany. Monti and Hollande were calling for immediate measures, such as the use of EFSF funds to purchase sovereign bonds on the secondary market, along with direct recapitalisation of any major banks that were exposed. Both believed that the matter of eurobonds required comprehensive examination. Merkel and her allies disagreed with these proposals intensely and with any kind of debt mutualisation whatsoever. She favoured further extensions of targets, along with moves towards enhanced political integration. Monti insisted he would not be a signatory to an agreement he deemed insufficient. He was adamant that more substantive discussions were imperative, 'even if it results in hell'. Merkel expressed her concern that 'much time will be spent talking about all kinds of ideas for a common sharing of debt, and far too little about improved controls and structures'. The various debt mutualisation measures proposed were 'economically misguided and counterproductive'.[13]

The matter of Greece was not even discussed at the summit. The whole of the Eurozone had made it clear that any further consideration of the Hellenic crisis would be undertaken only after the Troika's most recent report. Owing to the instability caused by the two general elections in Greece, the Troika had chosen not to return to Greece until the installation of a new government. In relation to matters of further political and economic integration, Athens expressed no interest in the debate aside from measures related to growth. Greece made no effort to involve itself even in the dispute about eurobonds, despite its evident relevance for the Greek crisis. It merely expressed the fantastical preference for bonds without conditions or restrictions.

Inevitably at European summits, each member state has its own preferences and strives to direct focus towards its principal concerns. Decisions on each matter are taken under the proviso that, at the end of the cumulative discussions, the member states will give their approval to the entire agenda. On the afternoon of 28 June, measures for growth were discussed. The outcome of the discussions regarding growth was announced by the President of the Council. Italy, France and Spain remained divided from Germany and its allies regarding the issues of bank recapitalisation and support for the economies of the peripheral nations. Monti indicated that if a satisfactory solution were not found for these matters, he would endorse neither the 'growth package' nor any of the other measures agreed at the summit. Merkel was faced with the realisation that the summit could conclude with absolutely no agreement being reached whatsoever. This would result in the collapse of the euro on global stock exchanges when they opened the following morning, in no small part the result of German refusal to finance the bank rescue. Heated negotiations carried on all night. In the early hours of the morning there was a shift in Merkel's position. She was obliged to take on board the views of her southern counterparts and accept a partial mutualisation of responsibility for debt repayment. She succeeded, however, in preserving the principle of strict control over the use of loans granted. Media reports spoke of a victory for the Italian technocrat in spite of the dogmatic position of Germany. The Germans spoke of Merkel being entrapped by Monti's underhand tactics. Such tactics, however, have been evident in heated negotiations throughout the history of the EU, especially when the allocation of funds is under discussion. Upon her return to Germany, Merkel presented the results of the summit as satisfactory, as the outcome still ensured stringent control mechanisms.

These outcomes stipulated three principal conditions for the provision of financial support to any ailing member state:

1 The ESM 'could, following a Community decision, have the possibility to recapitalise banks directly', provided that an 'effective single supervisory mechanism' for the banks of the Eurozone involving the ECB was established

by the end of 2012. Recapitalisation would be tailored to the specificities of each 'institution, sector or economy' and would be formalised in a 'memorandum agreement'. The Eurogroup would examine the possibility of implementing this regulatory framework in Ireland. 'Similar cases will be treated equally.'

2 Financial assistance to Spain would be effected by the EFSF and, when established, the ESM. They would assume the execution of the programme. In the case of bankruptcy or restructuring, the claims of the ESM would not have precedence over those of other lenders. This arrangement would ensure equal treatment for private lenders, so that they would continue providing loans.

3 The existing instruments of the EFSF and the ESM would be used 'in a flexible and efficient manner in order to stabilise markets for member states respecting their country-specific recommendations and other commitments.... These conditions should be reflected in a Memorandum of Understanding.' The ECB would 'serve as an agent to EFSF/ESM in conducting market operations in an effective and efficient manner'.[14]

These arrangements marked a break with the preceding regime. From now on, capital could be provided directly to the banking sector of a member state or indirectly to a state through the purchase of sovereign bonds on the secondary market. Lending to the state itself, as had happened in the cases of Greece, Portugal and Ireland, was no longer absolutely necessary. This meant that future assistance would not increase a member state's sovereign debt; consequently, there would be no negative effects on interest rates in the international bond market.

Even though the new framework clearly stipulated that any such indirect financial support would require a Memorandum of Understanding, there was no provision for direct oversight, as had been undertaken by the Troika in the case of Greece. However, it is stated in unequivocal terms that any member state seeking support must adhere to all fiscal regulations. There was no provision for special adjustment programmes or supervision by the IMF. The supervisory regime decided for Spain and Italy was far less intrusive than that in Greece, so as to avoid a major populist backlash. It is uncertain whether the same regime will apply to other countries in future. It also of significance that all member states were to be represented on the boards of directors of the EFSF and ESM, and that decisions would be taken, in general, on the basis of unanimity, with exceptional cases requiring a majority of 85%. The mechanisms aimed to ensure compliance and fiscal diligence. Furthermore, nations, such as Germany, France and Italy, would have the right to veto decisions with which they did not agree.

The decisions were considered a step towards a banking union and ensured far stricter supervision of banks. The Eurozone should now have the capacity for expedient action and more effective intervention in the markets when faced with a crisis. The agreement reached at the summit was received positively by the markets. The euro rose in value, as did stock markets the continent over. Rates of interest available to Italy, Spain and Ireland on the international bond markets fell. An air of optimism returned to Europe.[15]

However, the agreement remained vague on a range of issues and led to questions. Would the stabilisation mechanisms require guarantees from the banks prior to recapitalisation? If so, what would these be? Would member states be required to make guarantees on behalf of their banking sectors? Throughout the discussions, the Finns and the Dutch made it clear that they would not provide capital for the stabilisation mechanisms if there were no guarantees.

The capital available to the EFSF and the ESM was to amount to approximately €500 billion. Questions rapidly emerged about the adequacy of this amount to cover existing and future risks, and to realise the purchase of Italian bonds and the recapitalisation of Spanish banks. Discussions regarding the strengthening of the ESM indicated that at least another €300 billion was required.[16] Moreover, various analysts asserted that the ESM should have a minimum of €1 trillion at its disposal.

Many members of the Eurozone considered it imperative to assign a central role to the ECB, in preparation for its supervisory role in any future banking union. In Germany, however, questions were raised about how this might be reconciled with the ECB's current mandate.[17] The ECB has a statutory responsibility to ensure price stability. The extensive provision of financial assistance, under pressure from Spain or Italy, could significantly affect inflation. The bank would therefore find itself in the middle of a conflict of interests. After all, it would be impossible for the ECB, in its present structure and with its existing staff, to monitor 6,000 banks, over which there was to be supervision, while maintaining a focus on price stability.[18]

The summit of 29 June clearly indicated a shift in the form of intra-European relations. Previous summits had been dominated by the preferences of the Franco-German axis. This time Hollande did not synchronise his step with that of Germany, but cooperated with Italy and Spain. He in fact publicly acknowledged that he was aware of their intentions prior to the summit. After the summit he presented his own role as that of a mediator seeking to ensure that all participants would derive some benefit from any agreement. In reality, he contributed decisively to the change in course by not formulating a common position with Berlin. He brought back the matter of growth and highlighted the need for solidarity. Through steady pressure from Italy and Spain, with France's support, a front was formed that had the strength and conviction to challenge German policy preferences.

Behind this confrontation rests a broader challenge, which has yet to be clearly defined. It is the matter of the ultimate goal of European integration. Will it be a union of states that share certain common policies and permit the loss of limited competence to a supranational body, or will it be a federation of states with a strong central authority, a United States of Europe? Developments prior to the crisis very much indicated that a solution based on limited central authority and intergovernmental cooperation was correct. However, as always in times of crisis, integration can take major steps forwards. There are few, in light of the crisis, who would argue that Europe does not need a major reappraisal of its form, function and direction; but there remains huge disagreement as to what the objectives should be and how best to achieve them. The risks to Europe were still growing. The European Council of 29 June did not provide conclusive solutions.

What followed demonstrated one of the serious afflictions of the Eurozone: the indecision and delays even in the face of great risk. Various member states demanded caveats with regard to the capacity of the EFSF to lend directly to struggling banks. The Eurogroup convened on 9 July and reiterated the security and suitability of the agreed procedures.[19] German MPs who opposed the decisions of the summit made recourse to the Federal Constitutional Court, and requested that it rule on whether financing the EFSF by Germany was constitutional.[20] Even though the German government requested a rapid decision, the Court postponed judgement on the matter to September. The European Commission indicated that the establishment of a supervisory mechanism for the European banking sector, a precondition for any recapitalisation, would prove complex and take a long time to implement. Such statements led the markets to the realisation that further assistance to Spain would be significantly delayed. At the beginning of August there were renewed discussions regarding a crisis of the euro. The French newspaper *Le Monde* claimed 'the members of the Eurozone are not capable of creating a climate of confidence'; they were not in a position to speak with one voice, and so a cacophony prevailed, just when decisive guidance was needed.[21]

The President of the ECB, Mario Draghi, tried to placate international anxiety. He made an assurance that 'the ECB would do whatever it takes to defend the euro ... and what it will do, will be enough'.[22] However, he was not without criticism for the institutions of the EU, and indicated that their inertia and indecision posed major risks. Following this statement, everyone expected he would be announcing a series of initiatives at the meeting of the ECB's board of directors on 2 August. Measures, however, were not announced. The widely held impression was one of a disorderly retreat.[23] Once again, anxiety and uncertainty were on the rise.

In response to the fdisappointment over its lack of action, the ECB was obliged to announce stabilising measures. It proceeded with intense negotiations with the member states. The ECB is autonomous – it has the ability to act without consensus, or even support – but contact with countries like Germany or France is necessary if policies are to be coordinated and endorsed.[24] Draghi indicated on 6 September that, henceforth, the ECB would buy an unlimited amount of member states' bonds,[25] under certain conditions, on the secondary bond market.[26] The most important conditions for this were that:

1  that the state whose bonds were being bought must have accepted an adjustment programme (memorandum) worked out by the European stability
   mechanisms (EFSF/ESM), and these mechanisms must have already proceeded to buy bonds directly, in accordance with the decision of the
   European Council of 29 June;
2  the state must not have been excluded from the financial markets, as was the
   case with Greece, but must have retained its capacity to borrow;
3  the maturity of the bonds bought must not exceed three years.

Three key features are evident in this ECB proposal. The first is the *un-limited* ability to buy bonds. Therefore any fears that the programme might be suspended owing to lack of funds would be unfounded. The second is that the intervention *depends* on a memorandum being signed. States to which support was to be provided had to comply with an adjustment programme. If they did not, then support would come to an end. The third is that the *creditworthiness* of the country being granted support had to be recognised by the markets. If the state could borrow from the markets, then the memorandum would not need to be as stringent as was the case with Greece or Portugal. It would entail 'supervision', of a nature acceptable to countries like Spain and Italy.

The goal of the ECB programme was to reduce the risk for those buying bonds from states facing difficulties. A reduction in risk entails a reduction in the rate of interest. If Spain and Italy were to enter the programme, then it would ensure more favourable (and sustainable) interest rates on the inter-national bond market.

The markets welcomed Draghi's announcement with enthusiasm. But the German press was critical. The papers pointed out that, in assuming the support of policies that had failed to 'save Europe', the ECB had become involved in a process which was not compatible with its statutory mission, the stability of the currency.[27] In Italy and Spain scepticism was equally evident. Both countries were trying to avoid being bound by a memorandum. The terms specified by Draghi entailed a programme of adjustment. Any benefits to Greece resulting from the ECB decision would be only indirect. If Spain and Italy were to avoid an extensive crisis, thanks to the ECB's intervention, then the EU would be more able to support Greece.

The ECB's new policy provided countries threatened by a debt crisis with the necessary time to stabilise their economies and implement structural changes. It did not, however, solve broader, more fundamental challenges af-flicting ailing nations in the single-currency area – essentially, those stemming from a lack of competitiveness. If these were not addressed, and the ECB continued to buy the bonds of struggling member states indefinitely, there was a real risk of fuelling dangerous levels of inflation.

At the time of writing, it remains unclear who will have the right to stop the recapitalisation of banks or the purchasing of bonds on the secondary market, and when. If the ECB is the sole arbiter of any such judgements, its power is immense. This raises an entirely new dimension to questions regarding the democratic legitimacy of the EU.[28] The prospects for a comprehensive framework for 'economic governance' will also have been greatly undermined.

## Notes

1 Spain's official request for financial assistance was submitted later, on 25 June 2012.
2 Eurogroup statement on Spain, 9 June 2012.
3 See W. Münchau, 'How to build union to save the eurozone', *Financial Times*, ft.com, 27 May 2012.
4 'Les vingt sept intensifient leurs efforts pour sauver la monnaie unique', *Le Monde*, 3 June 2012.
5 See *Le Monde*, 27–28 May 2012, p. 3.
6 'Merkel urges of ceding power step by step within the EU', *IHT*, 8 June 2012.
7 Ibid.
8 'Merkel refuse de soutenir l'euro sans contre-partie', *Le Monde*, 9 June 2012, p. 3.
9 'Leaders vow to save the euro, but question is still how', *IHT*, 23–24 June 2012, p. 1.
10 M. Wolf, 'A bitter fall-out from a hasty union', *Financial Times*, ft.com, 19 June 2012.
11 *Kathimerini*, 9 June 2012, p. 5.
12 'American officials' were worried that a Greek exit from the Eurozone, before the date of the US presidential elections on 6 November, would hinder the re-election of the American President. See *Kathimerini*, 25 August 2012, p. 3.
13 See 'Heading for a moment of truth in Brussels', *IHT*, 28 June 2012.
14 See Eurozone summit statement, 29 June 2012.
15 For the evaluation of the decisions of the summit, see *FAZ*, 30 June 2012, pp. 1ff.; *Le Monde*, 1–2 July 2012, p. 3; *Kathimerini*, 30 June 2012, p. 1; *Ta Nea*, 30 June 2012, p. 12; *IHT*, 30 June–1 July 2012, p. 1, and 2 July 2012, p. 6, 18; 'European answers after summit crisis fighting measures', *Financial Times*, ft.com, 29 June 2012; 'The real victor in Brussels was Merkel', *Financial Times*, ft.com, 1 July 2012.
16 See pp. 167ff.
17 See *FAZ*, 30 May 2012, pp. 1, 11.
18 See *IHT*, 12 September 2012, pp. 1, 17.
19 Eurogroup statement on the follow-up of the 29 June Euro summit, 9 July 2012.
20 The subsequent decision of the Constitutional Court, on 12 September 2012, deemed that the operation of the ESM was compatible with the German constitution and, consequently, Germany could participate in its activities. See *Kathimerini*, 13 September 2012, p. 23; *Le Monde*, 13 September 2012, pp. 1, 3.
21 *Le Monde*, 27 July 2012, p. 1.
22 See *Le Monde*, 28 July 2012, p. 10; *Der Spiegel*, issue 31, 2012, p. 16.
23 *IHT*, 3 August 2012, p. 1; *Le Monde*, 4 August 2012, pp. 1, 10.
24 An indication of the negotiations were the public statements of the President of the German central bank, Jens Weidmann, and a member (also German) of the board of directors of the ECB, Jörg Asmussen. The former denounced the purchase of Italian and Spanish bonds planned by the ECB. See *Der Spiegel*, issue 35, 2012, pp. 66 , 75. The latter defended this. See *IHT*, 28 August 2012, p. 12; *Kathimerini*, 28 August 2012, p. 24.

25 See related *Kathimerini*, 7 September 2012, p. 3; *FAZ*, 7 September 2012, p. 1; *Financial Times*, 2 September 2012, p. 1; *IHT*, 7 September 2012, p. 1; *Le Monde*, 8 September 2012, p. 1, 13; *IHT*, 8–9 September 2012, p. 1. This new ECB instrument was named 'Outright Monetary Transaction' (OMT). According to P. Bofinger, *Zurück zur D. Mark*, Droemer, 2012, pp. 124ff., the ECB was dealing correctly with the risk of a bond run from collective panic which would lead investors in sovereign bonds to sell them off as quickly as possible.

26 That is, the bond market where private individuals buy and sell bonds.

27 See for example 'Kennt Not kein Gebot?', *FAZ*, 7 September 2012, p. 1.

28 *Le Monde*, 8 September 2012, p. 1. See also 'ECB bazooka faces peripheral tests', *Financial Times*, 8–9 September 2012, p. 12. The dangers from the power the ECB will acquire when, in accordance with the decision of the Union concerning control of banking institutions, it is assigned also the control of financing states or banks are stressed by the *IHT*, 10 September 2012.

# 27

# The election of 17 June: a new beginning?

The electoral uncertainty in Greece continued to undermine any prospects for economic recovery. Capital flight continued at an alarming rate, funds were being withdrawn to 'hide under the mattress', and at the same time state revenue fell dramatically as a result of the ongoing recession, which was continuing to grow despite forecasts anticipating a return to nominal growth.[1] The stock exchange index fluctuated round 480 points, levels not seen since 1990. Pensions and incomes continued to fall.

The fall in revenue by the end of the year would probably exceed €1.2 billion; such a drop would in all likelihood provoke further increases in taxation. The Troika delayed payment of the pending €1 billion, which resulted in a shortage of medicines among other essential goods and services. It was announced that there would be energy shortages across the country throughout the summer; the public electricity company threatened to ration electricity. Bookings in Greek hotels fell by 30–50%, according various sources, in the immediate fallout of the May general election. The real estate market saw its most significant fall in three decades.[2]

The only positive news was that the Hellenic Financial Stability Fund[3] had paid €18 billion to four large banks. These banks were thus eligible for financing from the ECB. However, even this faced various bureaucratic challenges and delays before capital could be secured. In terms of reforms, progress remained incremental, if it was made at all. Ministers and civil servants charged with responsibility for overseeing the adjustment programmes were increasingly intimidated by the risk of a populist backlash or the risk of reprisals from 'anti-Memorandum' forces.

There was a growing realisation abroad that, following the Greek elections, the whole situation might need reappraisal. Extending the timetable for the adjustment programme no longer looked sufficient to return any notion of normality to Greece. Furthermore, continual extensions would only sustain the period for which Greece was running a deficit, limit any prospects for a return to the markets and require the sourcing of yet further revenue to service liabilities and cover expenditure. There was no provision for such funds in the adjustment programme. The only solutions would lie in further loans or increased taxation, both of which posed inherent challenges. Growing numbers of economists were indicating that the only operable remedy lay in another restructuring of Greek debt. To date, the haircuts had not ensured a reduction of Greek debt below 120% of GDP. The most optimistic analysis forecast a reduction to 117% by 2020; however, this did not ensure debt would be placed on a sustainable footing; nor would it guarantee a return to the international bond markets and the cessation of the need for external support. Commentators suggested that Greece's liabilities to the ECB and other EMU member states that had not yet been subject to restructuring would also have to submit to a 'haircut'.[4] However, the members of the Eurozone were adamantly opposed to any such calls,[5] though restructuring made sense. The majority of Greece's liabilities were now to fellow member states of the single-currency area. These liabilities had primarily arisen as a result of the provision of financial support to service debt to the private sector. Banks now held only approximately 17% of Greek debt. In a circle contrary to logic Greece was led to borrow money from the member states and the IMF to pay debts to member states and the IMF.

Speculation mounted regarding Greece's inability to meet its liabilities and the inevitability of subsequent Grexit: 'The debate in Europe about Greece's exit from the Eurozone is increasingly moving from "if" to "how"'.[6] The institutions and member states of the EMU continued to assert that no one wanted a Greek exit; however, such assertions were always conditioned by a statement that the tenability of Greece's position was dependent on compliance. The tone was more often than not both critical and pejorative. Widely read German newspapers demanded that Greece 'vote correctly' so as to ensure that the country was not excluded from the single-currency area.

The deterioration in intra-European relations and continued failure to produce any closure regarding the crisis fuelled growing popular Euroscepticism across the continent. Domestically, Greece and the Greeks were presented as victims of a dogmatic and unjustifiable policy; many citizens lost faith in the EU as the guardian of progress and increasingly viewed the Union as a totalitarian supranational entity and defender of globalisation. They ceased to realise the risks of marginalisation and introversion. They felt it was time for Greece to return to an independent model of governance.

These calls were relayed, by foreign correspondents, across the member states of the Eurozone. Taken in conjunction with the ongoing electoral stalemate in Greece, such reports only compounded populist and political anti-Greek sentiment across the EMU. Greece was increasingly viewed as nation lacking leadership, direction or resolve, a permanent troublemaker, posing a genuine threat to the stability of the EU.

Astoundingly, the Greek political parties remained indifferent to the country's precarious position and the frustration such an attitude caused across the continent. They made no effort to promote an environment conducive to dialogue. Domestically, it was widely acknowledged that no single party would secure an outright majority; yet all acted as if they were the masters of Greece's future and would be in a position to dictate terms to the rest of Europe. Such delusion was rivalled only by the aversion to realistically engage with any of the challenges that Athens faced. Questions regarding the reduction of the deficit, the reconstruction of the public sector and the promotion of investment were given little attention. The debate conducted in the run-up to the first election was simply rehashed and repeated, partisan hostilities intensified and the arguments further simplified, to terms that completely failed to engage with the challenges on any meaningful level.

After a month of electioneering, uncertainty over the country's future had only grown. SYRIZA's initial vision of 'paradise lost' was clarified, a little, with a list of proposals, each more fantastical and detached from reality than the last; in its entirety it was evidence of the complete absence of a coherent plan.

New Democracy abandoned its impossible pursuit of an outright overall majority. In an effort to cater to populist sentiment, it adopted ever-more nationalistic tones. The party expressed its intention to assert Greece's needs and terms upon the European stage, increasing the likelihood of an inevitable clash with other members of the Eurozone.

PASOK redirected its efforts towards planning for the management of the post-election landscape, talking of a 'government of national co-responsibility'. However, its discussion of the need to compromise, talk of a 'vote of toleration' and the 're-establishment of a functioning democracy' were interpreted by public opinion as an indication of its resignation to the fact that the party was now a marginal political force.

Such was the state of confusion and widespread indifference to the risks posed by yet another unstable Parliament that the possibility of a complete collapse of the Greek economic and political structure grew with each passing day. Any domestic or external spark could act as a catalyst to the disintegration of the whole system: a crisis in Italy, government instability following the election, or the redirection of European support following a loss of patience with Athens. The country really was on the brink of the abyss, not only in the build-up to the election, but for as long disagreement between the Eurozone and Greece continued regarding sustainable procedures for repayment of debt.

SYRIZA's electoral success on 6 May represented the largest shift in the Greek political landscape and indicated that the party was in the ascendancy. More than all the other parties, it capitalised on the wave of popular anti-Memorandum sentiment. Its arguments were simple and well received; furthermore, the party was not tainted with responsibility for overseeing any of the policies of the Memorandum. These developments resulted in a new two-party standoff, between New Democracy and SYRIZA. New Democracy gradually absorbed a large number of voters from smaller associated parties, while SYRIZA capitalised on disillusioned left-wing voters and the broader anti-Memorandum sentiment. Much of the inter-party competition was premised on preferences regarding Greece's future inside the EMU. SYRIZA later 'clarified' its position, in response to opinion polls indicating that an overwhelming majority of citizens did not want to leave the Eurozone and rejected a return to the drachma. It asserted that it was not arguing in favour of a Grexit, but it supported the retraction of the conditions attached to the Memorandum and all domestic legislation stemming from it. Despite these last-minute 'clarifications', public opinion now viewed the June election as a referendum on the future of Greece's membership of the Eurozone.

The focus on these lines of cleavage masked the ever-pressing substantive concerns that Greece still faced the need for major modernisation and structural reform to permit convergence with its continental counterparts. In concealing these problems, those who continued to benefit from the systems of patronage and corruption could divert attention away from reforms that risked harming their interests. The need for the establishment of a modern state, no longer directed by these regressive forces, but focused on the needs of every citizen, was imperative to the country's progress. However, neither SYRIZA nor New Democracy paid any consideration to these concerns.[7]

The European project and the ever-increasingly interconnected nature of global relations gave Greece an unprecedented opportunity to overcome introspective and nationalistic tendencies. At a time when the country needed to develop the concept of a modern Greece in a modern world, the election campaign was being fought on terms that encouraged hostility, regression and isolation. The prospects for any renegotiation of terms or further support, while each party was striving to frame Greece's European allies in more derogatory terms than the other, were looking increasingly slim.

In the week before the June election, parties might have been expected to offer some specific proposals regarding how they aimed to lift Greece out of the crisis. Then, on 18 June, whichever parties were to form a government would have something verging on a plan to take to the Troika, regarding what the immediate and medium-term domestic policy matrix for Athens would entail. Above all else, measures to ensure economic stability and the promotion of growth were absolutely paramount, to rebuild confidence in Greece's ability to bring about its own economic recovery. Only then would any request for a relaxation of the 'debilitating' Memorandum measures be entertained by the Troika. Next, reform of the inefficient state, the complex and stifling tax structure and the regressive system of patronage needed swift action.

However, no measures were proposed. No realistic programme for the modernisation of Greek society was offered. The singular focus remained on the collection of prospective votes in a zero-sum game of electioneering. No action that risked angering any section of the electorate was entertained; no reference was made to restrictive measures, painful reforms or the genuine severity of the challenges that Greece faced.

The growth and normalisation of violence and conflict in everyday life was indicative of how far Greek society had imploded. In the week prior to the

June election, this became evident on a nation television programme when a member of Golden Dawn threw a glass of water at a member of SYRIZA before physically assaulting a female member of the Communist Party.[8] It required this shocking display of contempt for law and order on national television before public opinion rallied against political violence. Until then, the nooses of the *Indignados*, the attempts to occupy Parliament, burning buildings, deaths, arson with complete indifference to human life, and street battles with Molotov cocktails, rocks, slabs of marble and crow bars had been allowed to grow in frequency and severity, understood as a justifiable reaction to the 'injustice' of the Memorandum. Various forces sought to capitalise on this breakdown in law and order. Very little resistance or criticism was voiced. Violence had increasingly become a 'legitimate' means to settle differences, despite the evident threat it posed to any form of social order.

The election of 17 June drew a clearer picture of the preferences and hopes of the electorate.[9] The way the election campaign had been focused on 'the euro versus the drachma', 'New Democracy versus SYRIZA' led to the enhancement of the two parties 'capable' of achieving substantive change. A vote for the former was a vote to stay in the Eurozone, while a vote for the latter was a vote against the Memorandum and everything it represented.[10]

The 6 May election had been dominated by the protest against the parties in power, protests against the 'deconstruction' of the system. In the June election the electorate sought an end to the fragmentation of politics, an end to the absence of a capable government. These aspirations were only partially satisfied. Parliamentary parties were still numerous; there was no single dominant faction. However, it was now evident that the majority of the electorate wished the crisis to be managed within the context of the EU; public opinion had indicated it was opposed to a Grexit.[11]

Cooperation among all those parties in favour of a European solution was imperative. A government led by New Democracy's Antonis Samaras in coalition with PASOK and the Democratic Left was quickly formed. This did undoubtedly have some markedly positive consequences; it prevented further degradation of relations with frustrated members of the Eurozone and limited a major run on Greek banks, as deposits withdrawn earlier began to return.

The framework agreement for the three parties of government contained extensive references to the challenges Greece faced and how it would seek to overcome them.[12] While some specific measures, mostly related to the renegotiation of the Memorandum, were detailed, the majority of its content was an unsatisfactory combination of slogans and grandiose objectives. It was a list of fine aspirations, to which very few citizens would ever object: 'An overall strategy to strike a blow at bureaucracy; an overall strategy to strike a blow at tax evasion; the reconstruction of the public administration; formulation of a national plan for the reconstruction of the country with a new model for growth and production'. The programme did not designate priorities, deadlines or specific proposals for the achievement of these. As such, it risked very little in the way of a negative public reaction; neither did it commit the government to any sensitive reforms. As a result, it was not hard to ascertain that the progress of the administration's work would be heavily influenced by circumstantial factors and party political aims.

An evident priority was the renegotiation of the terms of support from the Troika. 'Matters pertaining to the revision of the loan contract' were to be raised with Greece's European partners and the IMF in an expedient fashion. These matters would include: an extension in the time frame for the reduction of the deficit; extending unemployment benefits to non-salary earners; and 'no further firings from the public sector'. The party leaders' agreement did not, however, designate when these matters would be discussed. It thus permitted a flexible and gradual approach to the problems. To raise all sensitive matters immediately, as had been promised in the election campaign, would inevitably result in major conflict and very little progress with the other members of the Eurozone.

In a letter from the Prime Minister to his European counterparts at the June Council summit, he stated briefly that 'there is the matter of certain necessary amendments to the programme in order to stem the unprecedented unemploy-ment and to check the destructive recession in which Greece finds itself for the fifth year running'. He also noted that 'implementation of the programme with emphasis on privatisation measures will be accelerated'. The letter was a careful formulation that avoided making any specific temporal commitments or promises that would tie Greece to any particular action.

On 21 June the Eurogroup convened in Luxembourg to discuss, among other things, recent political and economic developments in Greece. Those attending appeared willing to accept an extension of the time for adjust-ment with regard to deficits. However, they insisted that structural changes should proceed swiftly and continuing compliance with the Memorandum's regulations was necessary, without exception. The President of the Eurogroup stressed that substantial amendments to the programme were not possible. However, the President of the Eurozone's Working Group indicated that 'the programme is no longer valid'; 'we must seriously renegotiate the way in which we can return to the targets'. The Eurogroup decided to release the €1 billion that had been withheld from the last instalment.[13]

The statements and proposals from the Greek administration concerning re-negotiation were met with staunch rebuttal in the EU, most notably Germany. The German Foreign Minister stated, a little before the summit of 29 June, when quizzed on the Greek question: 'one thing is clear. We cannot allow a renegotiation of all matters. We can also not allow discounts. What has been agreed stands.'[14] Greece had to honour the promises it had made.

The Greek government's expectation that a discussion of the matters could begin at the summit of 29 June was quickly countered. Across the Eurozone, it was widely felt that any reappraisal of the Memorandum could be undertaken only after a Troika report had been issued on the current state of affairs in

Greece following such a period of political instability. Greece had no leverage, while the Troika and the Eurozone could simply refuse to release any further funds. Calculations by the Greek Finance Ministry indicated the country would not be able to meet its liabilities in August without further support; Greece would be insolvent.[15]

The ECB reminded Greece that it needed to be both cautious and conciliatory during intra-government discussions, regarding when and how renegotiations would be held, in July. On 20 July the ECB indicated it would provide no further capital to the Greek banking sector; instead, it should seek any necessary support in the form of ELA from the domestic central bank.[16] Borrowing from ELA is not only difficult, as capital is granted only in an emergency, but is also more expensive.[17] This cost inevitably filters down to the cost of credit granted by Greek banks, making them less competitive than foreign banks. Furthermore, such an increase in the price of credit inevitably stifles economic activity. The ECB had imposed a restrictive policy on the country, when, given the gravity of the recession, it might have been wiser to encourage business. However, this was not a simply miscalculation: it was a clear warning of the consequences of any unilateral Greek action; it indicated Greece had little choice but to follow the measures prescribed.

Renegotiation, therefore, would not be matter done between equal parties, as had been implied throughout the election campaign. The Troika and the member states of the EMU held all the cards. Greece needed to be able to clearly demonstrate the benefits of any proposed changes to have any possibility of securing European support for a reappraisal of terms.

Greece's request for a two-year extension on the adjustment of the deficit, for example, would require extra funding, of €20–40 billion. Greece would need to justify in unequivocal terms the benefit of this extra cost.[18] However, Athens was not forthcoming with any such explanations. Various member states of the Eurozone asked where Greece expected to source such capital, as they were fundamentally opposed to providing any further funding.[19] Greece also failed to provide any explanation regarding the failure to address its current-account deficit. With the ongoing recession, the deficit remained high.[20] It had to be covered by ECB support of the Greek banking sector. If this financing were to be restricted, Greece would again have to seek additional funds.

Various reports had already concluded that Greece was now a 'failed state'.[21] Accordingly, it was widely believed that Greece would fail to comply with its existing commitments. Athens was taking no serious measures to address the challenges and it was highly unlikely Greece would be able to pay back its existing debts. As such, why should any further effort or assistance be offered? Public opinion across the major countries of the EU, according to opinion polls, was now in favour of an exclusion of Greece from both the EMU and the EU. There was absolutely no sympathy for the country, nor any support for a relaxation of the terms of the Memorandum. The Spanish, the Italians and the Portuguese reacted in the strongest terms when any comparisons were drawn between them and Greece, despite their comparable difficulties. The only way to reverse such sentiment was to provide clear evidence of both effort and progress: merging or abolishing certain public organisations, the implementation of the privatisation programme, or comprehensive deregulation of the markets.

Furthermore, any renegotiation was at the discretion not simply of the Troika, but also of various member states, which would require parliamentary endorsement of any further funds for Greece; this would be no small feat, given the extent of popular anti-Hellenic sentiment. All negotiation is subject to the logic of 'give and take'. There was no evidence of any 'give' on the part of Athens, just 'take'.

After the European Council and the European Area summit of 29 June,[22] Greece made claims of inequality of treatment when compared with other struggling peripheral nations. As a result of the decisions taken by the European Council, loans to the Spanish and Italian banking sectors could be sourced directly from the European support mechanisms (the EFSF and ESM), avoiding any addition to the national sovereign debt. It had been indicated that Ireland might also be able to apply for such support on the basis of its extensive efforts: 'the sustainability of the programme is a proof of the good progress in reform to date'. Under the terms of the summit agreement, 'similar cases shall be dealt with accordingly'. The Greek government asserted that such terms should entitle Greece to comparable support; access to these mechanisms would contribute to a significant reduction in Greek sovereign debt. If Greece could source approximately €50 billion for the direct recapitalisation of its banking sector, Greece could ensure sovereign debt would fall below 100% of GDP by 2020. Beyond any doubt, debt would be then sustainable. Greece's return to the markets could be accelerated.

The European Commission indicated that such support was available only to countries in which the crisis was as a result of shortcomings in the banking sector, not to nations afflicted by a sovereign debt crisis already in receipt of major support from either fellow member states or the EFSF.[23]

The political posturing and gamesmanship of the parties of the coalition regarding efforts at renegotiations led to the first major intra-government clash towards the end of July 2012. The initial aspiration to expedite all matters for discussion at the summit of 29 June was abandoned after the staunch refusal of the presidency of the European Council. PASOK and DIMAR then raised the matter of a strategy for negotiations. They insisted that Greece immediately have the adjustment programme extended by two years and would not proceed with the agreed cuts of €11.5 billion until this extension had been secured.

In the meeting of the party leaders that followed, the Prime Minister (New Democracy's Antonis Samaras) indicated that the government would continue with the programme of €11.5 billion in cuts, ensuring its implementation during 2013. Samaras was aware that failure to do so would not only harm any prospects for an extension of terms but would in all probability result in a default and a Grexit. The leader of PASOK publicly stated that he was 'forced' to accept the Prime Minister's decision. In his opinion, however, this decision would lead to a further deterioration of the situation.

Public opinion was increasingly anxious as to what such attitudes would mean for the future of the government and the country.[24] Internal division was not compatible with a coherent and decisive government needed to pull Greece out of the crisis. The Prime Minister and the Minister of Finance, Yannis Stournaras, showed determination and an understanding of the need for immediate and sustained action. By September a little optimism had begun to return, despite much remaining anxiety over what the future held for Greece.

## Notes

1  The IMF had calculated the fall in GDP for 2012 at –4.8%. See *Greece First and Second Reviews*, IMF 13/20, IMF, January 2013. In the first quarter alone of that year it had shrunk by 6.5%.

2  See 'A breath before the crash in Greece', *Kathimerini*, 10 June 2013.

3  See Chapter 13, note 38, p. 128.

4  According to Reuters at the end of July 2012 'Community officials are working on a plan for a haircut of Greek debt by €70 to €100 billion, which will bring the country's aggregate debt down to a manageable level'. *Ta Nea*, 28–29 July 2012. See also *Le Monde*, 1 August 2012, p. 10. The views of the experts of various banking organisations concurred that Greek debt needed a new restructuring. They differed, however, over its extent. They either maintained that a haircut of 25% was needed, or else they deemed that the bigger the haircut the better: 'The country is insolvent and there is no other way to solve its problems.'

5  See *Le Monde*, 24–25 June 2012, p. 4.

6  *IHT*, 25 May 2012, p. 1.

7  See G. Voulgaris, 'Which Greece is voting tomorrow', *Ta Nea*, 5–6 May 2012.

8  On 'ANT1 morning' television, 7 June 2012.

9  The results were: New Democracy, 29.66% of votes, 129 seats; SYRIZA, 26.89%, 71 seats; PASOK, 12.28%, 33 seats; Independent Greeks, 7.51%, 20 seats; Golden Dawn, 6.92%, 18 seats; Democratic Left, 6.25%, 17 seats; KKE, 4.5%, 12 seats.

10  See for an evaluation of the electoral result G. Voulgaris, *Ta Nea*, 23–24 June 2012, p. 10.

11  The parties supporting the European policy won 48.19% of votes, whereas those against won 45.82%. Despite this relatively small difference in votes, the actual distance between the two was much greater. Parties of the left and the extreme right with completely incompatible agendas belonged to the 'anti-Memorandum' faction. Its political strength was therefore much more limited than the number of votes might suggest.

12  The 'immediate political priorities' were 'the revision of the terms of the loan agreement, growth, reconstruction and social protection, immediate economic priorities, changes in the political system and the state, safety for citizens, illegal immigration and, finally, foreign policy'. *Ethnos*, 2 June 2012, pp. 18–19.

13  See *Le Monde*, 22 June 2012, p. 3; *Imerisia*, 22 June 2012; 'Eurogroup overview of the situation in the eurozone', www.consiliumeuropa.eu, 3 July 2012.

14  *Kathimerini*, 26 June 2012.
15  See P. Ioakimides, 'How do we negotiate in the EU?', *Ta Nea*, 20 July 2012; V. Zeras, *Kathimerini,* 1 July 2012, p. 9. The critical matter in August was the payment of €3.2 billion in maturing bonds held by the ECB. The matter was settled by the ECB itself, but in a particularly expensive way for the Greek state. See 'An expensive breath of life worth €3.5 billion from the ECB', *Ta Nea*, 6 August 2012.
16  Emergency Liquidity Assistance. See Chapter 13, note 38.
17  Approximately 2% more expensive than ECB rates.
18  Financing should cover the deficits of the two years as well as extraordinary needs. Originally, approximately €10 billion had been considered sufficient. Meanwhile, it became apparent that the banks had larger losses than had been calculated during planning for recapitalisation. The new Greek bonds had already lost more than 80% of their face value. The continuing crisis had generated large-scale bad debts for Greek banks. It was therefore calculated that the shortfall of the banks would require additional financing of €30 billion. See V. Zeras, *Kathimerini*, 22 July 2012, p. 6.
19  At the Ecofin of 10 June, Ireland was granted an extension of one year, up to 2014, to reduce its budget deficit to less than 3%. It was the second extension it had requested and been granted. However, it did not request additional financing, either the first time or the second.
20  On 20 June 2012 it was 7.3% of GDP, that is, twice that of Portugal.
21  See Xenia Kounalaki, 'Greece isolated in Europe', *Kathimerini*, 1 July 2012.
22  European Council, 28–29 June 2012, Conclusions, EUCO 7–6/12, CO Eur 4, Concl. 2; Euro Area summit statement, 29 June 2012.
23  The Eurogroup extended in November 2012 the time in which the budget deficit was to be reduced. See Chapter 28.
24  See G. Voulgaris, *Ta Nea*, 4–5 August 2012, p. 9.

# 28

# Provisional solutions, October–June 2013

The initial efforts of the new coalition government to re-establish positive relations with the governments of the Eurozone were bearing fruit. Samaras's focus on the implementation of outstanding reforms was helping improve the climate for a return to the negotiating table. At a meeting of the Eurogroup on 14 September, held in Nicosia, the ministers around the table registered the concerns of the Greek minister, but also reiterated their calls for sustained adherence to the adjustment programme and indicated that further discussion of the matters could take place only after the publication of the Troika's progress report in October.[1] The Greek minister indicated his government's desire to find an 'all-encompassing solution' between the meeting of the Eurogroup on 8 October and the European Council summit on 18–19 October. Such a solution would not confine itself to an extension of the terms available, but also address further funding that the adjustment programme might require and guarantee the sustainability of Greek debt in the long term.[2] 'All-encompassing solutions' for Greece had been sought before, without success; they had been rendered redundant by negative externalities, inaccurate forecasting and the Greek administration's fundamental inability to adhere to commitments. The recession continued to deepen and the challenges remained severe. By the end of June 2012, both the Troika and the Greek government had upgraded their forecasts for the level of recession at the end of the year, initially predicted to be 4.7%. Both now anticipated a far higher contraction of GDP in 2012. By the autumn, unemployment had reached 25% and was growing. Turnover in many sectors continued to fall. The decline would inevitably affect tax revenues. There was a great risk that Greece would once again not achieve its designated targets and that, for the umpteenth time, unsuccessful efforts would result in demands for further restrictive measures from the Troika. Such demands would fuel further populist backlashes as well as resistance to government measures from MPs, resulting in further delays and deadlocks. The European Commission indicated the risks faced by Greece: 'By mid-June most observers wondered whether Greece would be able to avoid a default or an ejection from the euro area, or would even decide to quit itself at obviously significant costs.'[3]

In the autumn of 2012 there were two different views of the dangers now posed to the Eurozone. The first highlighted the growing risk of a Grexit and an ensuing chain reaction.[4] It would inevitably negatively affect growth and employment across the single-currency area, as a result of exposure to Greek default. Germany's prospective losses were calculated at €62 billion. It was clear that a Grexit would serve no one's interests and should be avoided at all costs.[5] This did not of course mean that Greece did not face the risk of being 'removed' from the Eurozone if it failed to comply with its commitments. Non-compliance would pose equal risks to the governance structure and stability of the EMU.

The second assessment perceived that the threat to the stability of the single-currency area would come from the crises in Spain and Italy, due to their size.[6] The funds available to the ECB and the EFSF/ESM were not adequate to provide liquidity to both these major economies, should these crises become even more acute and lead to capital flight from their banking sectors. Greece, as a minor economy within the Eurozone, did not constitute a substantive threat. It was simply a bad example for other countries, such as Portugal and Ireland; the case of Greece might lead to demands for comparable privileged treatment from these ailing nations. A Grexit, in its own right, would not destabilise the EMU. Greece absorbed barely 0.18% of the Eurozone's exports, a negligible figure. The European banking sector had limited exposure, as most liabilities were now held by member states or the ECB. European businesses actively engaged in Greece had, to a large extent, already left the country or were in the process of withdrawal; losses would be limited.

Political elites, the public and the media across the EU were, overall, of the opinion that the capacity and the opportunity existed to put an end to the Greek crisis. If Greece failed to comply with the stipulated conditions, then support should be withdrawn. Various analysts highlighted that such a move would free capital to address the far greater risk posed by instability in Spain and Italy; it would also permit more expedient reform towards a comprehensive framework for the long-discussed model for 'economic governance' and fiscal union.[7]

This harsh appraisal of Greece's place in Europe was detailed in the 'Iphigenia scenario'[8] – a proposal by the British Chancellor of the Exchequer. According to this, Greece would have to be sacrificed so the 'tail winds' could return to the EU. The sacrifice of Greece was to take the form of a voluntary exit from the Eurozone, following a limited further restructuring of Greek sovereign debt or a minor final bailout package to permit Athens to go it alone, on a mildly improved financial footing. The advocates of this proposal cited several advantages for the Core nations of the Union, now so opposed to the provision of any further support. With one final injection of capital, they would free the Eurozone of Greece and its problems; focus could then be directed towards larger economies within the EMU now at risk (Spain and Italy) and reform of the single-currency area, with the creation of a fiscal and banking union; furthermore, Greece could 'acquire some competitiveness' when it was free of the restrictions of the common currency.

The situation in the EU could not justify complacency. Spain had delayed in submitting a request to the EFSF/ESM for the recapitalisation of its banking sector. It was still negotiating the terms.[9] The question of whether the Spanish government would also need financial support remained open. Italy publicly declared that it would not sign any Memorandum restricting its scope for action. It was, however, doubtful that Italy's interest rates would remain low without any support from the ECB, which required some kind of a memorandum. The next parliamentary elections in Germany were to be held in September 2013. Given that German voters would negatively react to the provision of any further financial support to any country whatsoever, and particularly to Greece, no party would risk engagement with another bailout until the elections had passed. The IMF was also calling into question the benefit of any further support for Greece in the current context.

The Eurogroup meeting held on 8 October 2012 and the summit on 18–19 October did not result in the 'all-encompassing solution' that Greece had sought. Hopes had dwindled during negotiations with the Troika, whose principal concerns were still directed towards periodical assessment reports on the Greek economy. The difficulties in finding sufficient additional measures to achieve the targeted reduction in the deficits for 2013 and 2014, as stipulated by the Troika, had made evident just how many obstacles Greece still faced. However, talks did conclude on a positive note. Positions were clarified by all parties and Greece accepted additional obligations. By the end of the summit the climate between the Eurozone and Greece had improved significantly.

In a joint statement by the leaders of the countries of the Eurozone made on 18 October,[10] there was recognition of 'the notable efforts of the Greek people'. This was conditioned by the indication that the Eurozone expected the speedy implementation of the 'fiscal and structural changes' which 'will allow Greece to achieve growth again and ensure its future in the Eurozone'. The critical matters that had received so much domestic coverage in the election campaign in Greece were not discussed. There was no discussion of the request for a two-year extension for the reduction of the deficit or of the disbursement of €31 billion that remained unreleased. Despite the good words they had to say about Greece's efforts, the heads of state or government were not yet willing to engage in any substantive reappraisal of the Greek crisis.

The deferral of any major decision was justified on the basis of the forthcoming Troika report, not yet completed, even though it had been scheduled for the beginning of October. This was little more than a guise: the real cause of delay was the conflict of views of the various parties over how to handle the Greek problem. The IMF did not consider Greek debt sustainable and was advocating a further haircut. This analysis was not accepted by the EU. The IMF was advocating flexibility in the policy of austerity, so as not to compound the already grave recession in both Greece and across the continent;

it accepted calls for an extension of the Greek adjustment programme by two years. Member states, however, pointed out that the extension agreement was not possible without agreement over how to finance Greece during these two years. Those arguing against restrictive measures had their assessment supported by forecasts indicating that investment would fall and economic activity would shrink throughout the EU in the last quarter of 2012.[11] Even Angela Merkel conceded that 'it is our duty to do something for there to be a recovery in the economy of Europe'.[12] However, what that 'something' was remained very unclear.

An 'all-encompassing solution' to the Greek problem was not possible, nor would it be for many years to come. It required consensus and a comprehensive plan to address the crisis at a European level. There remained, however, great divergence in the assessments and policy preferences of the member states. The limited progress with regard to the supervision of the banking sector at the summit was indicative of this.[13] Though unified supervision was a precondition for direct recapitalisation of the sector and the financing of Spanish banks, the summit was yet not ready to take final decisions. It agreed to complete the necessary legal frameworks by the end of 2013.

Just a few hours after the end of the summit, it was clear that Hollande and Merkel interpreted the conclusion of the discussions differently. According to Hollande, the deadlines provided were binding. Merkel, however, was of the view that good work takes time, and hence implementation of the decisions would depend on whether the necessary preparatory work had been completed. At the same time, she refused to support any recapitalisation of Spanish banks in a form that would not add the amount granted to Spanish sovereign debt. Merkel asserted that the framework for the recapitalisation of the banking sector agreed in June was applicable only for future debts: it did not cover debt accrued prior to the completion of the mechanism for supervising the sector.[14] It was now being widely reported in the international press that the Council had managed an agreement so riddled with gaps as to be completely meaningless; it was simply a 'façade to cover the problems'.[15]

The summit once more confirmed, therefore, that there are no easy solutions to complex problems. Fine intentions and beautiful rhetoric are no substitute for a comprehensive and coherent plan.

After the summit, the Greek government sought a rapid release of funds. Greece had not received money since June 2012. Approximately €44 billion would be outstanding by the end of the year; without these funds Greece risked insolvency. Greece had adhered to the programme of adjustment and measures specified by the Troika; ongoing delays in the release of funds were no longer justified. However, concerns other than Greek compliance were now affecting the actions of the parties involved. The IMF had already informed the Eurozone that it would not continue financing Greece, because the country's debt was unsustainable. Its statute prevented it from supporting countries with unsustainable debt. Various Asian and Latin American nations within the IMF were protesting at the help being granted to Greece. It was most likely that they would vote against any decision to continue to provide support for Greece if immediate measures were not taken to restore the sustainability of the debt. The IMF considered the most appropriate way to secure this would be through a haircut of the Greek bonds held by the Eurozone states and the ECB,[16] so as to ensure that the sovereign debt was below 120% by 2020.

German preferences remained determined by the upcoming national elections of September 2013. The majority of the German electorate was fundamentally opposed to any further support for Athens and was not willing to incur any further costs; Greece was responsible for the situation the country was in and must manage its difficulties independently. Yet another restructuring of its debt was not acceptable. At the same time, however, they felt that the German government should avoid any action leading to a Greek exit from the Eurozone, for the fallout it would have on the single-currency area and the German economy. These conflicting preferences meant it was in Germany's interest to find a transitional solution, which would ensure stability until after the election. However, Germany would not entertain a haircut or any other substantive measures that would guarantee the long-term sustainability of Greek debt. Berlin's continual refusals risked leading negotiations into a deadlock.

A group of EMU member states led by France complained that the IMF and Germany were ignoring the primary concern: the need to release pending loans so as to stabilise the situation in Greece economically and politically. They favoured the provision of temporary support to Greece through a reduction of interest rates and a purchase of bonds on the secondary market. Any further measures could be considered at a later juncture.

The government in Athens was looking increasingly unstable; it appeared to be losing control of its parliamentary majority and was looking like it was unable to implement agreed reforms. The legislation relating to the negotiations with the Troika over limiting expenses and reducing deficits proved very difficult to pass through Parliament; the total number of government MPs had fallen to 176, and of these only 153 voted for that legislation on 7 November, against a background of mounting public protests and demonstrations.

Inside the Eurozone there was growing tension between Spain, Italy and the rest of the member states. These two countries wanted support from the EFSF/ESM to recapitalise their banks, and wanted that funding not to be included in their sovereign debt. Germany and the other countries insisted that this was not possible without the prior construction of a supervisory authority for the banking sector.[17] This tension diverted the focus from any consideration of the Greek question.

Following a teleconference on 14 November, which ended in deadlock, the Eurogroup convened on 19 and 27 November before it managed to reach a decision after approximately 23 hours of talks. It was a marathon negotiation, even by EU standards. The Greek government did not take a position on the dispute between the IMF and Germany; it simply sought to redirect the focus towards the question of its pending instalment and an improvement of the terms of the loans. In Greece, various commentators and sections of public opinion were still advocating the ambitious aim of a conclusive solution; in such a climate Greek demands bore no relation to reality.

The negotiations[18] resulted in a compromise that did go some way to satisfying all the parties involved:

1 The Eurogroup gave 'its political approval' for the disbursement of the outstanding tranches, totalling €43.7 billion. Of this, €34.4 billion would be paid during December 2012, and the balance in three instalments in the first four months of 2013, which would be considered in light of progress in implementing the Memorandum.

2 The Eurogroup also approved the extension of the time frame for the reduction of the budget deficit to 3% of GDP by two years, now to be achieved by 2016 and not 2014. Despite this, austerity would remain stringent. In 2013 and 2014 reductions of €13.5 billion must be made and further fiscal adjustments must be made totalling €4 billion over the 2015–16 period.

3 The Eurogroup designated new conditions to ensure the sustainability of Greek debt. Debt must be limited to 124% of GDP by 2020, as opposed to the 120% originally stipulated. This must be further reduced to 110% by 2022 and continue to fall at an accelerated rate over the following years.

4 In order to improve the sustainability of its debt, Greece would examine the possibility of buying back its bonds held by the private sector.[19] This arrangement was based on the fact that the new bonds that had been issued to replace the old ones submitted during the haircut had lost a large part of their value. In the market they were priced at 15% approximately of their original value. Holders were therefore likely to want to sell them to the Greek state, provided they were offered a price of up to approximately 30% of their nominal value. The state would therefore reduce its outstanding debt to bondholders whose bonds it bought back by roughly 70%. Some €10 billion would be made available for the buy-back. This amount would be granted from the available funds of the existing package of the EFSF.[20]

5 The Eurogroup also decided to improve the sustainability of debt in various ways: the further reduction in interest rates on the loans which had been granted by the member states during the period of the first Memorandum; limiting the commission Greece paid for the loans granted by the EFSF; extension of the maturity on all loans granted to Greece by 15 years and postponement of payment of interest on loans by 10 years; payment to be made to Greece of the profits made on Greek bonds held by the central banks of the Eurozone, in accordance with the existing arrangements of the ECB.

This bond buy-back and the new arrangements for loans were the result of significant compromise between the IMF and the Germany. With these measures it was expected that Greek debt would be reduced by approximately €40 billion, not as much as the IMF wanted but a significant reduction. While the sustainability of the debt might have been enhanced, questions remained as to whether these measures were sufficient.[21] For this reason the IMF reserved its conclusive approval of the decision.[22]

The decision of the Eurogroup went some way to clarifying EMU policy towards Greece from now on. If Greece did not achieve the targets that had been set in the agreement with the Troika, measures would be imposed to ensure compliance. The member states would continue to support Greece until it could secure access to the markets on sustainable terms, provided Greece stuck to its obligations.

A brief summary of the debt situation of Greece by the end of 2012 is presented in Box 28.1.

The agreement reached by the Eurogroup was positive for Greece. If the differences of opinion between lenders and failure to release pending instalments had continued, this would have led to a rapid and severe deterioration of the political and economic situation of the country that would have been extremely difficult to reverse.[23] The reduction in debt of approximately €40 billion might not have been in line with IMF preferences, but it did significantly reduce the burden on Greece. However, it was the release of €43.7 billion that allowed the country to gain a breathing space and prevented a complete collapse.

In Greece, the arguments continued to be simplified and presented as something of a false dichotomy. The Prime Minister asserted that 'the sacrifices of

---

**Box 28.1** Summary of Greek debt, as of December 2012

- First Memorandum. By December 2011 the members of the Eurozone had paid €52.9 billion and the IMF €20.1 billion, a total of €73.0 billion.
- Second Memorandum. By the end of December 2012, the EFSF/ESM had paid €108.3 billion and the IMF €1.6 billion, a total of €109.9 billion.
- Total payments based on both Memoranda therefore amounted to €182.9 billion. In the first four months of 2013, a further €14.8 billion was due to be paid.
- In addition, the ECB had financed the Greek banking sector with funds totalling approximately €130 billion. The EFSF had provided guarantees to the ECB on behalf of Greece amounting to €35 billion, to ensure that Greek bonds could be used as collateral to secure capital. According to the Bank of Greece the total foreign debt of Greece by the third quarter of 2012 was €413.667 billion.

See p. 193; see also *European Economy: The Second Economic Adjustment Programme for Greece, First Review, December 2012*, Occasional Paper 123, European Commission, December 2012, p. 58.

the Greek people have been rewarded and the road to growth has now opened'. New Democracy's partners in the governing coalition, PASOK and DIMAR, stressed the positive features of the agreement and how it contributed to 'the country remaining in the euro'. Those in opposition dismissed its value entirely: 'the solution did not contain a sustainable plan for Greece and that is why it is not a solution at all'.[24]

International political opinion and media coverage questioned the adequacy of the agreement.[25] Very few drew attention to what was now self-evident: the Greek government had begun to implement an exceptionally harsh adjustment programme resulting from the demands of Troika. Only the French newspaper *Le Monde* argued that the agreement was of significant value: 'It was not only useful for the Greeks, but for Europe as well'.[26]

It was widely acknowledged that the Eurozone had failed to come up with the only solution that was adequate to ensure the sustainability of Greek debt – a complete restructuring of all debt held by the ECB and EMU member states (by the official sector). It formulated a solution in two phases without expressly specifying it. In the short term, the agreement ensured the provision and regulation of further support for Athens, as well as the continued involvement of the IMF. It thus prevented a resurgence of the Greek crisis before the German elections. In 2014, after the German elections, discussion could return to a more conclusive solution and the broader challenges of a complete framework for 'economic governance' to manage risks across the single-currency area; this would permit an assessment of the Greek crisis under a universal framework.

The use of unspoken agreements to postpone discussion of a difficult matter or to expedite a favourable regulation is common practice in the EU. Governments attempt to assist one another in this way, especially in the event of elections. Such behaviour has prompted justified criticism when important matters are left unresolved and silence on them has misled voters.[27] Chancellor Merkel used this tactic to prevent both the crisis and the future of European integration from becoming topics of discussion in the German elections. But increasingly common tactical postponements have made it more difficult to arrive at solutions and have heightened the dangers for European integration.

Numerous critics indicated that any postponement of the Greek question by a further 18 months failed to recognise the severity and dynamic nature of the situation and consequently entailed significant risk. According to the Eurogroup, Greek debt would be at 175% of GDP by 2016 but would fall to 124% by 2020; a reduction of a staggering 51 percentage points in GDP in four years. Such a target would prove extremely difficult. In previous analyses, the Troika had stipulated reduction at a much lower rate. Now it changed its mind, maintaining that, due to recent Greek efforts, the imminent return of growth would make this expedient return to a sustainable level of debt 'possible'.

Whether such forecasts will be proved correct is highly questionable. Recession was expected to extend probably to at least 2013 and 2014 as a result of continued restrictive measures. Even if this were not to happen, experience indicates that recovery following four years of severe recession is likely to take much longer than predicted by the Eurogroup. Reports in the press indicated that the Eurogroup had attempted to overcome the problem through 'tinkering' with figures, that the agreement was premised on 'unreal hypotheses' and that the 'package agreed is not the last one'.[28] Another haircut was inevitable. The public sector would be called upon to bridge these gaps between the projections and reality.[29]

In Germany both Angela Merkel and Minister of Finance Wolfgang Schäuble toned down their comments, for fear of jeopardising their electoral success. They said re-examination of the sustainability of Greek debt and the possibility of a new haircut after 2014–15 could be possible 'provided everything proceeds according to projections'.[30] This was confirmation that further efforts at a European level would follow only after the German elections.

The existence of a tacit agreement between Germany and its partners was indirectly confirmed in May 2013. The French President, Hollande, announced a series of initiatives that would pull 'the Eurozone out of its "langeur"'.[31] These included the establishment of economic governance, combating youth unemployment and the formulation of a common investment strategy. According to media reports, both the timing and the nature of the announcement indicated preparation was underway for further negotiations following the German elections to be held on 22 September.[32]

Despite these measures and announcements, anxiety over whether the temporary measures would prove sufficient even for the short term remained high. Even the European Commission expressed its doubts publicly. In its report on the progress of the adjustment programme[33] it noted that the political instability, the struggling economy, the contestation of measures in court and subsequent delays in reform might postpone economic recovery in Greece. Implementation of what has been agreed within the timeframe specified, it stressed, was vital for the success of the programme; only such compliance would ensure the sustainability of Greek debt. The IMF made comparable remarks.

Greece proceeded immediately with the bond buy-back programme agreed by the Eurogroup on 27 November. The Greek state bought back bonds of a nominal value of €32 billion for approximately €11 billion.[34] While the programme was successful, if it had had more capital at its disposal it could have ensured a far more substantial reduction in debt.[35]

Following the conclusion of the buy-back, the Eurogroup maintained its distinction between a short-term strategy and a later formulation of a conclusive solution – a management strategy in 'two phases'. In a meeting on 13 December 2012 it approved the payment of €49.1 billion in instalments.[36] The first instalment (€43 billion) would be paid in December 2012, with the balance to be paid over the first four months of 2013, 'dependent on the progress in implementing the Memorandum'. The second phase, the period after 2014, was designed to produce the conclusive solution. The Eurogroup reiterated that it would take the necessary measures to achieve the reduction of Greek debt to 124% of GDP by 2020 and that debt at that level would be sustainable.

The IMF did not take a position in the discussion of Greek debt at the Eurogroup. It indicated that it would probably approve the release of the €3 billion pending before the end of the year; Greece would then receive a total of €52.1 billion for 2012.[37]

Media coverage did not pay particular attention to the decision to release the instalments of the Greek loan. In Greece there was an expression of understandable relief. The Prime Minister, Samaras, stated 'that today the rumours, the blackmail and the pressure for the country to exit the euro have ended'.[38]

After release of the €34 billion to Greece,[39] it appeared the country was experiencing something of a recovery in terms of its international standing. The ratings agency Standard & Poors upgraded Greece's credit rating. Subsequently, the ECB began accepting Greek bonds again as collateral for loans granted to Greek banks. Various European officials stated that the first signs of growth would appear in 2014.[40]

The Greek case was not on the agenda of Ecofin or the European summit of 13–14 December 2012. The Eurogroup's decision was considered sufficient for the meantime. The primary concern of the two meetings was the reform of the EMU and the completion of the Single Supervisory Mechanism to oversee financial institutions. It was agreed that the ECB, in conjunction with competent national authorities, would undertake this supervision.[41] The task would entail oversight of the largest 100–200 banks in the Eurozone, especially those whose balance sheet exceeded 20% of their country's GDP and in any case the largest three banks in every member state. The ECB could decide to carry out an audit whenever it wanted, on whichever banks it deemed necessary. The supervisory powers of the ECB would be exercised by a special supervisory council and would be entirely separate from its monetary responsibilities. The ECB was due to begin to exercise its supervisory duties on 1 May 2014.

Following this, the summit dealt with proposals submitted by the President of the Council in June 2012 to improve the functioning of the EMU.[42] The members of the Union limited themselves to an exchange of views and decided to continue discussions at subsequent summits. This postponement confirmed that member states were not yet ready for any major reform of the Treaties; their differences remained great.[43] Germany reiterated that any substantive reform could only follow its domestic elections. It supported calls for every member state to open channels of communication 'with the European institutions relating to the cost of labour, the level of public expenses, the promotion of efficiency of public administration' and other matters relating to competitiveness.[44] The summit concluded with statements indicating the priority of working towards proposals detailing common commitments and interests.[45]

The agreement of the European Council regarding supervision of the banking sector was hailed by the international media as a 'historic agreement' and indicative of 'substantial progress'.[46] However, it was noted that 'successful progress towards banking union requires a combination of short-term action, including the establishment of a temporary resolution authority [i.e. an institution] to identify undercapitalised banks and to restructure them'.[47] Progress proved difficult. The principal features of a framework for direct bank re-capitalisation were agreed in June 2013.[48] The Eurogroup indicated the measures, limits and contributions required to facilitate this framework for bank recapitalisation: a burden-sharing scheme would determine the contributions of the various member states and the ESM; €60 billion would be the limit on the volume of direct bank recapitalisations; and potential retroactive application of the instrument would have to be decided on a case-by-case basis.

Further decisions were taken by Ecofin in June.[49] Member states had to establish a resolution fund to tackle bank crises. It was agreed that shareholders and some creditors must accept losses before any direct support would be available to struggling banks. Governments could independently decide whether to compensate for any such losses. The media reports remarked that such a framework was open to significant divergence across member states with regard to its application and would undermine prospects for uniform economic governance.[50] The compromise was considered 'messy', but 'still a mark of progress'.[51]

The European Commission confirmed in its report of May 2013 on Greece that 'a moderate recovery led by investment and exports is projected for the beginning of 2014 leading to annual growth in 2014 of 0.6%, accelerating in 2015 and beyond'.[52] Public finances, according to the Commission, were steadily improving and important structural reforms were being implemented. But the Commission cautioned that 'the fiscal outlook beyond 2014 remains inherently uncertain' and 'the risks during the programme of implementation remain formidable'.[53]

In its review of Greece's performance the IMF was also of the opinion that the Greek authorities had made 'commendable progress in reducing fiscal and external imbalances and in restoring competitiveness'.[54] It stressed, however, that public debt was projected to remain high well into the next decade. It welcomed therefore 'the assurances from Greece's European partners that they will consider further measures of assistance, if necessary, to reduce debt to substantially below 110 percent of GDP by 2022'.[55]

This assertion of the IMF was contested by the Europeans. The German Finance Minister repeatedly denied the existence of such an agreement.[56] This dispute was further proof of continued anxiety among the creditors and of doubts regarding the success of the programme.

The Greek government functioned for quite some time without significant friction among the coalition partners. But cooperation among the three parties became increasingly difficult. The implementation of the measures agreed with the Troika so as to set limits on the public sector and reduce the number of civil servants was the main point of discord. DIMAR opposed the dismissal of civil servants and delayed the fulfilment of the engagements by various means. PASOK and New Democracy ministers insisted on supporting trade unions, retaining privileged provisions and postponing reforms. Democratic Left withdrew from the government and the coalition on 20 June 2013, when the Prime Minister shut down the state radio and television broadcaster for reorganisation and staff layoffs.

A new coalition government of New Democracy and PASOK was formed on 25 June.[57] The new administration acted decisively on some of the Troika's recommendations and in July 2013 received the outstanding payment of bailout funds. In spite of this, a sense of political instability pervaded public opinion. Many believed the government might experience another crisis if one of the coalition parties perceived that collaboration was having a negative impact on its popularity.

In July 2013 the European Commission and the IMF published their reports on the state of the Greek economy. Both organisations recommended that financial aid to Greece be continued.

The Commission appeared optimistic about developments in its July 2013 report, but the manner in which it expressed that optimism also revealed some misgivings: 'Greece continues to make overall, albeit often slow, progress ... with several important actions being delayed'.[58] On the one hand, annual GDP growth remained negative, as a result of the high negative carry-over from 2012 and the strong contraction of domestic demand. On the other hand, 'leading, conjectural and financial market indicators show improving confidence in the recovery prospects of Greece'.[59]

It is obvious that the European Commission did not wish to take a stand on what would happen to Greece in the years to come. This was largely because it did not deem it proper to initiate a discussion in July 2013 on whether Greek debt was sustainable. It wanted compliance with the informal agreement to tackle the debt problem of countries of the Periphery within a broader discussion after autumn 2013.

The IMF report was considerably more critical.[60] It pointed out that 'the ongoing correction of imbalances has come at a very high cost. The high adjustment cost reflects in important part the delayed, hesitant and piecemeal implementation of structural reforms.'[61] As did the Commission in its report, the IMF referred to the risks arising from the recurrent domestic political crises and the vested interests opposed to reforms. It underlined that 'reforms have fallen well short of the critical mass needed to transform the investment climate'.[62]

The IMF report differed in one significant respect, however, from that of the Commission. It observed that Greece had not secured the financing it required for 2014 and 2015, and that it needed ongoing support. Hence it believed that 'the commitment of Greece's European partners to provide debt relief as needed to keep debt on the programmed path remains a critical part of the program'.[63] As for the evolution of the debt, the report noted that 'after reaching around 176 percent of GDP in 2013, debt is expected to decline to

124 percent in 2020'.[64] The prerequisite for this would be additional contingent relief measures of about 4% of GDP, or approximately €8 billion, from Greece's European partners to be determined in 2014–15.[65]

As soon as the IMF report was published, the German government reiterated its view that there would be no new restructuring of Greek debt. Further provision of aid could be discussed only after the support programme had been completed.[66]

At the time of writing, despite optimistic assessments prevalent in Athens, Greece is expected to face extremely difficult negotiations at the beginning of 2014. The prospects of the euro area will be of crucial importance. Commenting on them in August 2013, ECB President Mario Draghi said: 'The picture seems to be better from all angles than it was a year ago'.[67] But Jörg Asmussen, a German member of the ECB board of directors, predicted that it would take '10 years of hard, painstaking adjustment'. The way out of the crisis for the Eurozone looks as if it will be a long journey through a dark tunnel.[68]

Most crucial to Greece's recovery is the continuation of membership of the Eurozone. The funds Greece has received will avert bankruptcy for at least another year, but that is hardly conclusive. The challenges and tasks Greece had to overcome remained severe and numerous as of summer 2013:

- *The level of debt.* Whether Greece manages to bring it down to 124% of GDP by 2020 or not, it will remain very high and will pose a threat to economic stability. It must be brought to a level below 100% of GDP, so as to prevent the risk of regression. A further haircut of debt held by the ECB and EMU member states is still necessary to achieve this, but such a proposal is unlikely to be accepted by the creditors.
- *Continued low confidence in the markets and among investors.* Recent measures have improved relations between Greece and its continental partners, as well as the perceptions of the market. However, investors and the market judge a country on the basis of its long-term economic performance, compliance and the speed of any recovery. Since the problems remain, rates of interest will remain high. Investment will take a long time to return.
- *The low competitiveness of the Greek economy.* It will remain the cause of a deficit in the balance of payments and it will oblige the country to continue to borrow. Reducing income is not the only measure to bolster competitiveness. Efforts must be made in other directions (administrative costs, business practices, quality control, etc.).
- *The enormous difficulties in achieving satisfactory rates of growth.* This, similarly, depends on securing the return of investment in the country. A strategic approach to public investment and reform efforts is necessary to ensure the efficient and coherent management of state expenditure.[69]
- *Administrative and structural deficiencies.* Greece remains a long way behind its European partners in terms of development. Comprehensive and painful reform remains an imperative.

- *Social inequality.* The danger of socio-political clashes owing to the extended policy of austerity continues to pose a genuine risk to stability in Greece.
- *Securing additional funding for Greece if extension of the adjustment time is approved.* The country's pending liabilities must be covered during the period of extension.
- *Adherence to the agreements with the Eurozone so as to ensure regular payment of the loan instalments.* At the same time, however, there must be renegotiation where necessary.
- *Greece's participation in the negotiations over economic governance and the changes in the structure of the EU.*

The country has the opportunity now to construct a realistic strategy for recovery; while this will not be without further pain, the opportunity needs to be seized.[70] It must look to reform the restrictions of the Memorandum, but equally be sensitive to the risks of further turbulence in the markets and the international economic and political situation. The plan must be developed by relevant experts, not only by the 'leaders' and their political advisers.[71] It must work out a road map for future negotiations with the members of the Eurozone and any reform of the Memorandum. At the same time, it must strive to deliver painful but vital reform to Greece. This is the only way Greece's slide towards a Grexit can be reversed.

Greece must take an active part in formulating the new architecture of the EU. At this moment the country has neither the prestige nor the conviction; it has become marginalised. Greece has lost much of the advantage it held as a result of its historical and cultural affinity with the continent. It must direct focused and unrelenting effort to redressing the deterioration in both its international status and its intra-European relations. This needs a systematic approach, consistency and insistence.[72]

## Notes

1 See Greek newspapers of 15 September 2012, and *IHT*, 15 September 2012, p. 12.
2 See V. Zeras, *Kathimerini*, 9 September 2011.
3 See *European Economy: The Second Economic Adjustment Programme for Greece, First Review, December 2012*, Occasional Paper 123, European Commission, December 2012, p. 1.
4 This view was called the 'domino theory'.
5 According to a *Financial Times Deutschland* article, at the end of August 2012, the German Finance Ministry was examining 'whether a domino effect spreading the crisis to the rest of the Eurozone countries could be avoided', should Greece exit the Eurozone. See *Kathimerini*, 25 August 2012, p. 3. This was confirmed by the spokesman of the Ministry, who clarified that a government is obliged to be prepared for every contingency.

6    See G. Chardouvelis, 'The Iphigenia scenario may be avoided', *To Vima*, 5 August 2012, p. 3; V. Zeras, 'IMF pressure and an uncertain future', *Kathimerini*, 12 August 2012, p. 3; H. W. Sinn, 'Germany and the crisis', *Ta Nea*, 14 August 2012.

7    For the proposed form of this planned new governance, see Chapter 32, under 'Economic governance'.

8    See G. Pagoulatos, 'The toxic discussion over an exit from the euro', *Kathimerini*, 19 August 2012.

9    In the international press, reports dealt mainly with the differences in the French and German views over the Spanish matter. See for instance *Le Monde*, 16–17 October 2012, p. 13.

10   European Council, 19 October 2012, EUCO 156/12, CO Eur 15, Concl. 3; State-ment by the euro area heads of state or government on Greece, 18 October 2012.

11   See Floyd Norris, *IHT*, 13–14 October 2012, p. 11.

12   See *Le Monde*, 13 October 2012.

13   See *Le Monde*, 20 October 2012, p. 7; *IHT*, 20–21 October 2012, p. 9; *Financial Times*, 20 October 2012.

14   See *FAZ*, 20 October 2012, pp. 1, 2, 13.

15   *Le Monde*, 20 October 2012, p. 1; *Financial Times*, 20–21 October 2012, pp. 1, 8.

16   This would concern the official and not the private sector, which is why it was called OSI (official sector involvement). See *Kathimerini*, 26 August 2012, p. 11; *Imerisia*, 1–2 September 2012, p. 7.

17   On various views of the Spanish matter, see *Le Monde*, 16–17 September 2012, p. 13.

18   See Eurogroup statement, 27 November 2012.

19   It is calculated that in November 2012 the private sector held bonds worth approxi-mately €62 billion.

20   In its meeting held in November 2012, the Eurogroup approved the buy-back plan. It was calculated that bonds worth approximately €30 billion would be bought back and the reduction in debt was calculated to reach approximately €20 billion.

21   According to calculations presented at the Eurogroup, the measures would reduce debt by 2020 to 126.6% of GDP and not 124%. See P. Spiegel, *Financial Times*, ft.com, 28 November 2012.

22   See *Le Monde*, 28 November 2012, p. 15; *Financial Times*, 28 November 2012, p. 3.

23   V. Zeras, 'What the decision means for Greece', *Kathimerini*, 2 December 2011, p. 8.

24   *Kathimerini*, 28 November 2012, p. 4.

25   *Financial Times*, 28 November 2012, pp. 1, 3, 8, 12, 13; *FAZ*, 28 November 2012, pp. 1, 2, 9, 10; *Le Monde*, 28 November 2012, pp. 1, 3; *IHT*, 28 November 2012, pp. 1, 3, 12.

26   *Le Monde*, 28 November 2012, p. 1.

27   J. Habermas, 'Ein Fall von Elitenversagen', *Der Spiegel*, issue 32, 2013, p. 26.

28   'Bricolages', *Le Monde,* 28 November 2012, p. 1.

29   *Financial Times*, 28 November 2012, p. 8. According to Z. Darvas, corrective measures are still necessary. See Z. Darvas, *The Greek Debt Trap: An Escape Plan*, Policy Contribution 19/2012, Bruegel, November 2012.

  •  'A credible resolution should involve the reduction of the official lending rate to zero until 2020, an extension of the maturing of all official lending, and indexing the notional amount of all official loans to Greek GDP. Thereby, the debt ratio would fall below 100 percent of GDP by 2020, even if the economy deteriorates further. But if growth is better than expected, official creditors will also benefit.

- In exchange for such help, the fiscal sovereignty of Greece should be curtailed further. An extended privatization plan and future budget surpluses may also be used to pay back the debt relief.'

30 See *Le Monde,* 4 December 2012, pp. 1, 16; *IHT*, 28 November 2011, p. 3.
31 Languidness.
32 See *Le Monde,* 18 May 2013, pp. 1, 6; A. Leparmentier, 'Hollande vote Merkel', *Le Monde,* 4 July 2013, p. 20.
33 See *European Economy*, Occasional Paper 123, December 2012, p. 5.
34 For details see *Kathimerini*, 13 December 2012, p. 18. It is calculated that, through the buy-back, the debt would fall by 9.5% of GDP by 2020.
35 According to *IHT*, 24–25 December 2012, pp. 1, 16, under pressure from its European partners the Greek government did not use all the possibilities at its disposal to reduce its debts and the profits gained by the hedge funds.
36 See Eurogroup statement on Greece, 13 December 2012. The €49.1 billion was more than the amount owed, of €44 billion, because €5.1 billion approximately was added since it had been loaned to Greece for the buy-back. According to EU cadres, the €5.1 billion would be withheld from future instalments of the loan Greece was entitled to receive.
37 See *Kathimerini*, 14 December 2012, p. 13.
38 *Kathimerini*, 14 December 2012, p. 1.
39 See for disbursements under the adjustment programme, *European Economy: The Second Economic Adjustment Programme for Greece, Third Review, July 2013*, Occasional Paper 159, European Commission, July 2013, p. 47. Total disbursements to the end of June 2013 (under both the first and second programmes) reached €183.5 billion from the European member states and EFSF, and €26 billion from the IMF.
40 See *Kathimerini*, 22/23 December 2012, p. 1; 'Greece, the lost cause turns into hope', *Le Monde*, 24/25 December 2012, pp. 1, 15.
41 See Council of European Union, 13 December 2012, EUCO 17739/12, CO Eur, Concl. 13; EUCO 205/12, CO Eur 19, Concl. 5; Remarks of the President Van Rompuy, 19 December 2012, EUCO 236/12, Presse 532. For Ecofin's proposal see European Council conclusion on completing EMU adopted on 14 December 2012.
42 See p. 331; see also European Council conclusions on completing the EMU adopted on December 2012.
43 See *Le Monde*, 14 December 2012, p. 2.
44 See *FAZ*, 14 December 2012, p. 2; *Le Monde,* 14 December 2012, p. 8.
45 See European Council, conclusions on completing the EMU adopted on December 2012, p. 4, para. 12.
46 *Le Monde,* 14 December 2012, pp. 1, 2; *Financial Times*, 14 December 2012, p. 5.
47 *Financial Times*, 14 December 2012, p. 4. See also N. Véron, *Banking Union: Short-Term Aspects*, Policy Contribution 2012/18, Bruegel, 2012, p. 1.
48 Eurogroup meeting, Luxembourg, 20 June 2013. See 'ESM direct bank recapitalisation instrument. Main features of the operational framework and way forward', Eurozone Portal, 11 June 2013.
49 Council of the European Union, Economic and Financial Affairs, Brussels, 27 June 2013, EUCO 1128/13, Presse 270, EUCO 11646/13, Presse 300.
50 *Financial Times*, 1 July 2013, p. 10.
51 Ibid. See also *Financial Times*, 28 June 2013, p. 12; *IHT*, 28 June 2013, p. 4, and 8 July 2013, p. 8; *FAZ*, 28 June 2013, pp. 1, 11; *Le Monde,* 28 June 2013, p. 4. Further

important decisions concerning the institutional framework of the banking union were taken by the European Council on 25 October 2013 (see EUCO 169/3, CO Eur 13, Concl. 7) and Ecofin on 18 December 2013 (see Council, 18 December 2013, EUCO 17983/13, Presse 596). A Single Supervisory Mechanism was adopted and a common position on the Single Resolution Mechanism (SRM) – which will consist of a Resolution Authority (Board) and a Single Resolution Fund – was agreed.

52  *European Economy: The Second Adjustment Programme for Greece, Second Review, May 2013*, Occasional Paper 148, European Commission, May 2013. The Eurogroup noted in its session of 13 May 2013 that Greece had made further substantial progress and approved the payment of the next EFSF instalment.

53  Ibid.

54  IMF, press release 13/195, 31 May 2013.

55  Ibid.

56  *Kathimerini*, 9 June 2013, p. 6.

57  The President of New Democracy, A. Samaras, remained Prime Minister; E. Venizelos, the President of PASOK, was named Vice Prime Minister and Minister of Foreign Affairs. The Ministry of Finance was entrusted to Yanni Stournaras, a member of the team that had negotiated and realised Greece's entry into the EMU.

58  *European Economy*, Occasional Paper 159, July 2013.

59  Ibid, p. 1.

60  Country Report No. 13/241, IMF, July 2013.

61  Ibid., p. 4. See also 'Greece faces cash gap, IMF says', *IHT*, 2 August 2013, p. 13.

62  Country Report No. 13/241, IMF.

63  Ibid.

64  Ibid.

65  The GDP at market prices was in 2013 €183 billion. See table B1, p. 9, of the Commission's report, *European Economy*, Occasional Paper 159, July 2013.

66  See 'IMF: Griechenland wird weitere Milliarden benötigen', *FAZ*, 1 August 2013, p. 10; *Kathimerini*, 1 August 2013, p. 18.

67  *IHT*, 2 August 2013, p. 13.

68  Ph. Pickert, 'Blasse Hoffnungsschimmer am Ende des Tunnels', *FAZ* online, www.faz.net, 25 July 2013.

69  See G. Lachmann, *Smart Choices for Growth*, Policy Contribution 2012/21, Bruegel, November 2012.

70  T. Yannititsis, *Ethnos*, 1 July 2012, p. 20: 'We will remain at zero point if we expect to exit the crisis only with foreign assistance, without a strategy of our own. Every now and again we ask to renegotiate our refusals of what we have already agreed to, while we remain indifferent to drawing up a convincing programme to achieve the targets.' See also pp. 315–16.

71  Plans such as those that achieved the stabilisation of the Greek economy and were elaborated by Gonticas, Spraos and Garganas in 1985, and by Papantoniou, Chritodoulakis, Yannitsis, Rapanos, Stournaras and Spraos in 1996.

72  See also for the Greek crisis: S. Kalyvas, G. Pagoulatos and H. Tsoukas, *From Stagnation to Force Adjustment: Reforms in Greece 1974–2010*, Hurst, 2012; O. Anastasakis and D. Singh (eds), *Reforming Greece: Sisyphean Task or Herculean Challenge?*, South East European Studies at Oxford (SEESOX), European Studies Centre, St Antony's College, University of Oxford, 2012.

# 29

# Evaluations of the assistance programme to Greece

In May 2013, the Bruegel think-tank[1] published an analysis of the reform programmes in Greece, Ireland and Portugal;[2] to date, this is the most comprehensive evaluation of the funding packages and associated reforms in the Eurozone. According to the report, the predictions of the first Memorandum with regard to growth, unemployment, the debt to GDP ratio and scope for a return to the bond markets (in Greece by 2013) were 'unambiguously dashed by events'. While the restructuring of Greek debt was not considered seriously in the spring of 2010, it was accepted as necessary by 2012.[3] Significant economic and political setbacks continued throughout the second programme of adjustment; however, it was not derailed entirely. Following the June 2012 election in Greece, the formation of the coalition and the renewed commitment to the reforms ensured the release of pending funds. Despite these efforts, the 'short-term economic outlook remains grim',[4] and 'the ultimate outcome is uncertain'.[5]

A range of factors have negatively affected efforts at ending the crisis in Greece:

> the external environment was more adverse than expected, euro-area policies were inconsistent, implementation by the Greek authorities was inadequate or insufficient, debt restructuring should have been front loaded, fiscal austerity has been excessive, and finally, not enough weight was given to the structural reform and competitiveness objectives.[6]

The report stressed that the impact of austerity was difficult to assess. Greece was already in recession when the programme was first implemented. However, 'it was evidently hazardous to impose a 10 percent GDP shock to a leveraged and uncompetitive private economy'.[7] Private demand could hardly replace public demand while the banking sector was increasingly conservative in its provision of credit. It must be noted that a European-wide focus on austerity without any expansionary measures to balance its effects, in a climate of falling confidence, was likely to hinder the optimistic forecasts of a return to growth.[8]

According to the report, 'Troika members are adamant that the major cause of the setbacks was lack of implementation on the Greek side. More precisely, they claim that the commitment of the Greek authorities started to waver towards the end of 2010, and stalled in late spring 2011'.[9] It has already been noted that the implementation of the adjustment programme was indeed deficient.[10] The authors of the Memorandum constructed the adjustment programme on the premise that Greece was a developed country, with the state infrastructure and social structure comparable to those in its Western European neighbours. This is not the case. As the Bruegel report indicates: 'the Troika overestimated the effectiveness of the Greek government machinery and its ability to follow through on agreed priorities'.[11] Equally, it fundamentally underestimated the scale of popular resistance that the programme would face. The report notes that the architects of the Memorandum were misguided in their forecast of how the reforms would affect employment: 'A final failure of the programmes is the level of unemployment, which is far greater than anticipated and which jeopardises the sustainability of the adjustment'.[12] The despair and disillusionment that inevitably followed from the high levels of unemployment resulted in the widespread rejection of the reforms; they were considered both oppressive and unjust. The Greek governments were neither prepared nor able to fight for a policy that was rejected by a vast majority of its citizens. A policy capable of success in the long run requires both public confidence and hope; austerity in Greece fuelled cynicism and despair. The report asserted 'that the Troika could have made more effort at an earlier stage to build capacity and to tailor the programme in such a way that its implementation could be assured'.[13] 'Instead of formulating a robust programme capable of withstanding adverse economic, political and financial developments, they did just the opposite. It is no surprise that these optimistic assumptions were not vindicated by events.'[14]

In its conclusion the report remarks 'The judgement of success or failure ... cannot be based only on a comparison between forecasts and outcomes, as the latter were affected by unforeseen developments in the euro-area environment'. If, though, such 'a simplistic judgement' of the programme's effectiveness is applied in the case of Greece, 'the programme was unsuccessful', the Irish programme 'seems to have been successful' and the Portuguese programme 'could also prove successful'.[15] However, this 'simplistic' interpretation is dismissed by the report as unsatisfactory. It prefers a more nuanced assessment: 'The programmes have been successful in some respects and unsuccessful in others'.[16] This broad appraisal, however, does not help with formulation of measures and reforms suitable to the idiosyncrasies of individual member states. That is to say, the report does not detail what was, and is, necessary for the successful provision of support to ailing nations by the EU.

In June 2013, the IMF published an 'ex post evaluation' of its 2010 stand-by arrangement (SBA) support programme for Greece.[17] The IMF indicated that, thanks to the programme, strong fiscal consolidation was achieved and 'Greece remained in the euro-area, which was its stated political preference'.[18] It underlines, however, that there were also notable failures:

> The recession has been deep with exceptionally high unemployment. The programme did not restore growth and regain market access as it had set out to do. Major contributory factors to this lack of success were the poor implementation of reform by the authorities, adverse political developments and inconsistent policy signals by euro leaders.[19]

In its main part the report examined the design of the programme, in order to ascertain the causes of the failures. In order to summarise its findings, a simple question-and-answer format was used. The replies contained in the report reveal that the IMF had misjudged the economic situation in Greece. Yet its authors maintained that under the circumstances in which the programme was designed, the IMF's policy was the only available option. The following extracts are revealing:

Q 'Should the larger economic downturn have been expected?'

A 'There were a number of reasons why the actual decline in GDP was so much greater than anticipated: ... The program initially assumed a multiplier of only 0.5 despite staff's recognition that Greece's relatively closed economy and lack of an exchange rate toll would concentrate the fiscal shock. Recent iterations of the Greek program have assumed a multiplier of twice the size.... Confidence was also badly affected by domestic social and political turmoil and talk of a Greek exit from the euro by European policymakers. On the other hand, the offset to the fiscal contraction from higher private sector growth that was assumed during the program period appears to have been optimistic.'

Q 'Should debt restructuring have been attempted at the outset?'

A 'The program was based on a number of ambitious assumptions.... Varying these assumptions would have materially affected the outlook for debt sustainability. The risks were explicitly flagged.... One way to make the debt outlook more sustainable would have been to attempt to restructure the debt from the beginning.... In fact, debt restructuring had been considered by the parties to the negotiations but had been ruled out by the euro area.'[20]

According to the report the programme served 'as a holding operation'. It gave the EMU time 'to build a firewall to protect other vulnerable members'.[21] However, by not tackling the public debt problem decisively at the outset, it created uncertainty about the Eurozone's capacity to resolve the crisis and aggravated the recession in Greece.

The Greek press saluted the report and the self-criticism of the IMF.[22] The Greek Prime Minister, Antonis Samaras, who took office after the second Memorandum following the elections in 2012, noted that his previous position against the Memoranda had been vindicated.[23] Expectations of policy change on the part of the Troika were high.[24] A new agreement with the Eurozone was suggested, one which would include measures for growth, attainable fiscal targets and efficient structural changes.

The Commission's reaction was fast. Olli Rehn, the Commissioner who was responsible for the management of the crisis, commented: 'I don't think it's fair or just for the IMF to wash its hands and throw the dirty water on the Europeans'.[25] The spokesman for the Commission made clear that 'we fundamentally disagree' with the IMF's opinion that an upfront restructuring of Greek debt in 2010 would have been desirable. 'Private debt restructuring would have certainly risked systematic contagion at that stage.'[26]

Mario Draghi, the President of the ECB, was conciliatory. He admitted that market tensions and the risk of contagion had been much higher three years previously. However, he stressed that 'often … you judge what happened yesterday with today's eyes. It's always very hard to make post judgments.'[27]

Comments in the international press differed. The *Financial Times* viewed as a 'disarming and admirable quality of the IMF that it has the self-regard and self-confidence to believe that things might have turned out better if it had acted differently or more decisively'.[28] The *Frankfurter Allgemeine Zeitung* judged the actions of the Fund rather differently: 'The IMF is a political organization where governments and not economists decide. If the same situation would arise in future the same decisions would be taken and the analysis would be adapted accordingly.'[29] *Le Monde* suggested that the 'self-flagellation' of the IMF was driven by a desire to re-examine the premises of future programmes.[30] Indeed, the chief of the IMF's Greek mission, Paul Thomsen, remarked at a conference immediately after the publication of the report:

> What really is important is looking forward…. As you know, we now have a framework on the table for reducing Greece's debt. We have a commitment on part of the Europeans to provide additional debt relief, if needed to keep the debt on the path in the programme. This will kick in, at the beginning of next year.[31]

The IMF, under pressure from its non-European members, did not want to continue its involvement in the Greek crisis and favoured an expedient and conclusive solution. However, the German government was fundamentally opposed to any action that would allow the Greek question to become the principal issue in its domestic elections in September 2013. Wolfgang Schäuble, Minister of Finance, therefore assured the Bundestag that the statement from the IMF representative did not indicate agreement on, or support for, a new 'haircut'.[32]

Both the Bruegel and the IMF reports examined the degree of cooperation between the members of the Troika. Bruegel indicated that the three institutions had different mandates and roles.[33] They cooperated in 2010 as the Commission lacked the necessary experience to handle the Greek case. 'But there is reason to question such an approach now.' The rules of each institution were not easy to reconcile with the constraints of the others. IMF participation remained advisable as long as Eurozone governance was incomplete, but not indispensable. The IMF had to have 'the possibility to disagree and walk away'. The ECB, if it continues to participate, 'should be mostly silent' because it is the Eurozone's central bank and negotiations regarding the programme 'cover a scope that extends far beyond the remit of a central bank'.

The IMF report was not as severe in its judgement. It underlined the need for 'more streamlining in the Troika processes'.[34] However, it noted that a clear division of responsibilities between the three members was 'difficult to achieve', given the overlapping mandates of the institutions. The Fund's presence was considered useful, but its policies and framework for lending to members of the Eurozone needed to be examined carefully.

## Notes

1  Bruegel is a European think-tank specializing in economics. Its membership includes EU member state governments, international corporations and institutions.
2  Jean Pisani-Ferry, André Sapir and Guntram Wolff, *EU–IMF Assistance to the Euro-Area Countries: An Early Assessment*, Bruegel, May 2013.
3  Ibid., pp. 44, 54.
4  Ibid., p. 60.
5  Ibid., p. 51.
6  Ibid., p. 51.
7  Ibid., p. 56.
8  Ibid., p. 93.
9  Ibid., p. 65.
10  See pp. 61, 196ff.
11  Pisani-Ferry *et al.*, *EU–IMF Assistance to Euro-Area Countries*, p. 53.
12  Ibid., p. 118.
13  Ibid., p. 65.
14  Ibid., p. 75.
15  Ibid., pp. 116, 117.
16  Ibid.
17  *Greece: Ex Post Evaluation of Exceptional Access Under the 2010 Stand-by Arrangement*, Country Report No. 13/156, IMF, June 2013.
18  Ibid., p. 1.
19  Ibid., pp. 32–33.
20  Ibid.
21  Ibid.
22  See *Kathimerini*, 9 June 2013, pp. 7–8.
23  *IHT*, 7 June 2013, p. 17; *Financial Times*, 7 June 2013, p. 3.
24  See *To Vima*, 9 June 2013, pp. 7–8, 10.
25  *Financial Times*, 8–9 June 2013, p. 4.
26  *Financial Times*, 7 June 2013, p. 3. K. Regling, the chief of the ESM, in an interview in the *FAZ*, 14 June 2013, maintained that the report of the IMF was unfortunate. 'The IMF made fun of the Stability Pact', he argued.

27  *Financial Times*, 7 June 2013.
28  Ibid., p. 12.
29  P. Welter, 'Politische IWF Kredite', *FAZ*, 7 June 2013, p. 11.
30  *Le Monde*, 7 June 2013, p. 6.
31  IMF, transcript of a conference call on Greece Article IV Consultation, with IWF Mission Chief Paul Thomsen, Washington, DC, 5 June 2013.
32  *Kathimerini*, 9 June 2013, p. 6.
33  Pisani-Ferry *et al.*, *EU–IMF Assistance to Euro-Area Countries*, pp. 103–119. See also Jean Pisani Ferry, 'Europe's Troika should grow up', 28 May 2013, at www.project-syndicate.org/commentary/the-legacy-of-the-troika-in-the-eurozone-and-beyond-by-jean-pisani-ferry.
34  *Greece: Ex Post Evaluation*, p. 34.

# 30

# Cyprus

The temporary improvement of the situation did not ensure peace in the Eurozone throughout the whole of 2013, as the Eurogroup, the European Commission and the IMF had hoped. In March, developments in Cyprus provoked unforeseeable and severe turmoil, indicating that the measures constructed to guard against future risk in the single-currency area were not sufficient.

The risk of an economic crisis erupting in Cyprus had grown steadily following the restructuring of Greek debt in the spring of 2012. Owing to the haircut of Greek sovereign bonds, the Cypriot banks lost approximately €5 billion. Bad management, speculation and failed investments cost these banks many more billion euro. Subsequently, the ECB stopped financing them. Cypriot economic policy had led to a significant rise in its budget deficit over a period of some years and the national government lacked the liquidity to re-capitalise the banks.[1] The shortfall stemming from rising national debt and the struggling banking sector was calculated at approximately €16 billion. On 25 June 2012, the government of Cyprus officially submitted a request for support to the EFSF.[2] However, negotiations were slow as the Cypriot administration did not favour ceding economic control to the Troika; Russia provided a loan of €2.5 billion.

The climate deteriorated significantly during the long-drawn-out negotiations with the EU. There was widespread public aversion to the provision of ESM support to Cyprus, most pronounced in Germany. It was widely cited that much of the capital held in Cypriot banks was that of Russian oligarchs and was of questionable legality; European public opinion did not favour recapitalising a banking sector designed to offer the wealthy a tax haven.

On 16 March 2013, the Eurogroup decided to lend Cyprus €10 billion. To ensure there was sufficient capital to secure the banking sector (approximately €6 billion) it was deemed necessary to tax bank deposits. The Cypriot government objected to the original idea of taxing all deposits over €100,000, for fear of a run on the banks by foreign holders. The Eurogroup accepted a tax on all deposits. Anger grew, across the country and the Eurozone, over the precedent that would be set by taking punitive measures against the holders of smaller savings accounts. Various members of the EMU pointed out that, in the past, deposits under €100,000 were safe even when the banks were in trouble. The Cyprus Parliament refused to ratify Eurogroup's decisions. The government of Cyprus again turned to Russia for help. Russia refused to grant any further funding. The ECB announced, meanwhile, that it would not provide liquidity to the banks of Cyprus after 25 March, if no agreement could be reached with the European Commission, the IMF and the ECB over a solution to the problem. The banks remained closed for a week in Cyprus; the country was on the brink of bankruptcy.

In an extraordinary meeting of the Eurogroup on 24–25 March, the government of Cyprus agreed that not all deposits should be taxed, and that, of the two largest banks in the country, one would be liquidated and the other would be reconstructed. For this to be successful, deposits in excess of €100,000 held in both of these banks would have to be taxed to source sufficient capital to overcome the shortfall; depositors would lose a large percentage, possibly even all, of their savings. The banking sector in Cyprus was being cut to approximately half its size. Furthermore, the Eurogroup decided that the economy of Cyprus would be restored to health through supervision by the Troika on the basis of an adjustment programme (a memorandum).

The decision aroused new protests in Cyprus. Analysts forecast a double-digit recession. Cypriot public opinion felt that the Eurozone had not shown the necessary solidarity, and that it imposed a punitive settlement disproportionate to the indiscretions of the country. However, Christine Lagarde, head of the IMF, indicated that the decisions of the Eurozone and the IMF constituted a comprehensive and credible plan for handling the crisis the island faced.[3] Media coverage inside the single-currency area agreed with Lagarde's analysis: 'The Eurozone did the right thing in the end. Other alternatives would only have been possible if a degree of solidarity, that is now absent, existed between member states.'[4] However, the solution did indicate the trend towards 'the making of a German Europe'.[5]

The conclusions drawn from the Cyprus crisis may be summed up as follows.

In the cases of Spain and Ireland, assistance from the EFSF/ESM to save their banks from bankruptcy was considered vital. Following the Cypriot crisis, the chairman of the Eurogroup, Jeroen Dijsselbloem, asserted that the funds were indicative of a continued commitment to the Eurozone. However, the investors and the depositors had to share the costs. They should bear the burden of bank failures rather than the taxpayer. According to the *Financial Times*, the Cyprus deal set a healthy precedent. 'Broke banks can be restructured, not kept alive by taxpayers on their own.'[6] However, in the countries of the European Periphery, there was intense criticism of this analysis. They felt that this principle would be applied by Germany and its allies only to nations of the Periphery, not members of the Core.

The ECB had to enforce rules on the basis of uniform regulations; banking supervision and a banking union were to be realised as soon as possible.

The 'value of ... bank liabilities depends on the solvency of the government standing behind the bank'.[7] A country cannot have a banking sector valued greatly in excess of its GDP. A country with a banking sector disproportionate to GDP poses a major risk.

The Cypriot government introduced temporary controls to prevent the collapse of its banking system. These controls indeed had to be temporary as 'a currency union with internal exchange controls is a contradiction in terms'.[8]

The crises in the Eurozone fuelled anti-establishment and Eurosceptic protest, compounded tensions in intra-European relations and doubts regarding the suitability of European policy. Public opinion was increasingly calling into doubt European solidarity and the compatibility of the structure of the EMU with the vision of a united Europe.

The delay of approximately two years in dealing with the Cypriot crisis indicated that the European strategy for managing risk was still far from satisfactory. It remained defensive and permitted risks to grow without adequate control. The reform of European institutions had become more urgent than ever before.[9]

## Notes

1 See Council Recommendations on the National Reform Programme 2011 and 2012 for Cyprus, 7.6.2011 SEC (2011) 803 final, Com(2012) 308 final.
2 See pp. 228, 252.
3 *Le Monde*, 26 March 2013, p. 12. For the decisions of the Eurogroup and the comments they aroused see: *Le Monde*, 27 March 2013, p. 12; *IHT,* 26 March 2013, pp. 1, 15; *Financial Times*, 26 March 2013, pp. 1, 3; *FAZ*, 25 March 2013, and 26 March 2013; *Vima*, 24 March 2013; *Ethnos*, 28–29 March 2013.
4 M. Wolf, 'Cyprus adds to Europe's confusion', *Financial Times*, 27 March 2013, p. 9.
5 G. Rachman, *Financial Times*, 26 March 2013, p. 9; 'Une victoire pour le FMI et l'Allemagne', *Le Monde*, 26 March 2013, p. 12.
6 'Europe gets real not before time', *Financial Times*, 26 March 2013, p. 8.
7 Wolf, 'Cyprus adds to Europe's confusion'.
8 Ibid.
9 'ECO & Enterprise', *Le Monde*, 26 March 2013, pp. 4–5.

Part VI
The future of Greece and
the European Union

# 31

# The causes of the crisis were not only economic

There was a plethora of divergent views across Greek society regarding the cause of and responsibility for the crisis. Political cleavages and affiliations had a salient and tangible effect upon how blame was ascribed. Common along this spectrum of interpretations was a belief in foreign causes: the EU, the EMU, German loan sharks, foreign and domestic capital were all held responsible. As such, Greece's redemption lay in the ability to rid itself of the debt or to exit the EMU and return to the drachma. The proponents of this view came to the conclusion that what was needed was a new patriotism, that of an 'independent Greece', and a new economic/political system to accompany it. According to another widespread opinion, responsibility for the crisis rested with the politicians, the parties and the associated corruption. In a growing sector of Greek society there was a belief that the debt (totalling approximately €300 billion) 'was devoured by the political elite'.

Such interpretations lie in the sphere of the absurd and lead to proposed solutions that are dangerous for the country. Corruption in political life is also found in Italy. Corruption exists in economic transactions in Germany, demonstrated in the examples of procurement contracts between Greek public companies and Ferrostahl or Siemens. Careless spending marks local government similarly in Spain, while inadequate public administration exists also in Portugal and in many of the new member states. Unfavourable economic and social conditions are a feature of many countries. Nationalism, fascism and individuals who aim to overturn the socio-political system can be found in all European countries. It is misguided to seek a single cause for these developments. The causes are as complex as they are numerous: backwardness in many sectors; ingrained practices and views; inadequate institutional frameworks; absence of social conscience; degree of adaptation to the modern era; even historic causes, such as the Civil War and the rule of the military junta in Greece.

Over five decades from the 1950s, Greece gradually unburdened itself of the plethora of controls and restrictions on economic and social life. And then the EMU brought unprecedented economic freedoms and possibilities. An example was individual access to low-interest credit, without the previously crucial intervention of politicians or 'important people'. The stabilisation of the economy, from 1994 onwards reduced social inequality, improved pension regimes and provided better health services. This positive and sustained development raised expectations and demands that bore no relation to the country's actual economic capacity. For example, there were large pay demands by civil servants and teachers the day after Greece entered the EMU. Resistance to this pressure provoked intense reactions, the occupation of ministries, strikes and protests. During the period 2002–04, the Minister of Finance faced criticism and threats, far more severe than his predecessor had experienced during the stabilisation period (1994–02).

Gradually, and especially since 2004, populist forces came (again) to prevail in politics. Pressure was brought to bear by the self-employed, the thousands of small businesses, the public sector employees and all those constituting the 'molecularly fragmented Greek society'.[1] Intensity grew in the 'clash over distribution', the battle for hand-outs, demands for higher salaries and clientelistic operations. To keep the discontent under control, the New Democracy government did not resist the collective improvidence. It ignored the economic constraints. Indeed, from 2007, when the first ripples of the financial crisis came to be felt in Greece, the government ignored, to the point of irresponsibility, the consequences of the hand-outs through which it sought to retain power.[2] The deficit and debt shot up to an unprecedented level. It is indicative of the role played by the political clientelistic system that the borrowing which provoked the flood of debt was to a great extent public, and not private, unlike in Ireland or Spain.

In 2009, the new PASOK government was also guided by a false picture of the country's position. It was felt that pedestrian economic constraints could be overcome thanks to networks of international connections, from Qatar to Washington. Priority was given to green economic growth and to transparency, truth and sincere dialogue with the electorate. In the same vein as the New Democracy administrations, once in power, the leadership of PASOK did not want to acknowledge the meaning of Greece's participation in the EMU, the Stability Pact, the restriction of deficits and debt imposed by the Treaties, globalisation and broader economic constraints. The PASOK administration believed that, in a club of developed states, everything could be settled amicably and without pressure. Economic and social matters played second fiddle to political and public relations activity designed to enhance the party's hold on power. Within a few months, the new government realised that the economic problems were far more severe than it had anticipated. It was then that the agonising effort to avert the country's default began, an effort for which it was unprepared, despite the warning signs.

What followed was disheartening. For three whole years of intense economic crisis, the dominant political forces did not manage to discuss, let alone formulate, a plan which did not obey the logic of the party leaders' one-way streets.

They, together with the EU, failed to produce a serious examination of how to combine fiscal rehabilitation with a development effort, or of cooperation with Greece's lenders in a flexible framework which allowed for adjustments in response to developments. Nor were they in a position to agree on a common course for the duration of a four-year term of office, so as to create the political stability needed to engage in the required structural changes. Each leader claimed that only he could do it. Papandreou pushed aside those with experience of service in previous PASOK governments who could have assisted him in his efforts but were not to his liking. Samaras, from the other side, maintained a high level of denial, viewing the crisis as a fantasy, since the deficit could be brought down to zero very rapidly and since the renegotiation, with himself at the helm, could very quickly return the country to normality. The two of them and the other parties cultivated head-on partisan collisions in order to convince the Greek public that they alone had the true solution. They should, instead, have instilled in the public the notion that economic solutions are complex, that cooperation is crucial and that, in the face of enormous national difficulties, leadership pursuits and egoisms have no place, that collective action is an imperative.

For most citizens, living under a constant storm of promises and reassurances, and having to endure systematic references to incomprehensible statistics and a barrage of slogans, the problem of sovereign debt was not something they could understand. For them, what was tangible was the pressing reality of the fall in income and the rise in unemployment, and the certainty that they had hardly any capacity to influence the situation or to avoid its consequences. Their fury turned on the political system and the politicians. They believed that the politicians' demagogy, their inadequacy, their pursuit of their own personal interests and the party state had led to the exacerbation of the crisis. An overwhelming majority of public opinion believed that the parties had failed to live up to the challenges of the times. Their miserable management had dragged the country down into humiliation, poverty and dependence on its lenders. At the same time, however, the deep-seated conviction remained that a serious effort was required for the country's recovery. Intense doubts were expressed over its European prospects.

The causes of the crisis are rooted in the country's backwardness. After the War of Independence in the early nineteenth century, the Greek state was constructed by the central government at a time when no integrated Greek society existed; there were essentially only small, isolated, scattered local communities. For over a century, the central state was the instrument that connected and shaped society and also drove economic and political development. This was different to the countries of Western and Central Europe, where societies had their own dynamic, and state intervention was not, right from the beginning, the decisive formative force. Even after the dictatorship fell in 1974, the Greek state closely controlled economic activity. 'Statism' was the consequence of this development and constituted the dominant ideology across society, in fact, much more so in the business class than in the working class. The suffocating presence of the state, after the civil war of the late 1940s, ensured 'law and order'. Even the labour unions were controlled by government. Today's wailing over the 'socialist' experiments, which from 1981 onwards supposedly led to the domination of the state, lacks any sense of history. It was the Conservative government following the fall of the dictatorship in 1974 which was accused of being 'socialist' because it nationalised the second biggest bank, the Commercial Bank, in keeping with the long-established tradition of Greek governments controlling the 'levers of the economy'.

The causes of the crisis in Greece are not, therefore, only economic. They are also related to Greek particularities: the dominant role of the state; the extensive presence of self-employed people and very small businesses; the guild-oriented social structure; and the clientelistic political system.[3]

State authority cannot, and must not, dominate economic and social activity. It cannot engage, as it had done in Greece, in the production of potters' clay for artisans, or in the nickel business or in assigning academic studies on immigration to the Ministry of the Interior. The problems of immigration can be studied better by an independent academic institution, the industrial processing of nickel can prove more profitable in the hands of a private company and the responsibility for producing potters' clay can be assumed by the artisans who use it. The presence of the state where it is not necessary creates significant distortions, at a cost to society as a whole. The 'problematic enterprises' that were 'socialised' in the 1980s, with the consent of the bankrupt owners, continued to operate for years, incessantly producing losses for the state. In the long period of state ownership of Olympic Airways, it was permanently overstaffed. In DEH (the national electricity company), OTE (the national telecommunications company) and all the other publicly owned enterprises, there was an abundance of clients appointed by every party. The state as 'saviour and guide' was stronger than society. It did not come up against the formal and informal checks and balances placed by civil society in the developed nations of Western Europe. It became a tyrant serving the interests of entrenched social groups.

The dominant feature of the Greek political system was clientelism. This system, serving as a channel for the expression of social discontent but also as an instrument for controlling it, intervened to curb protests and restore social peace. The main devices for successful mediation with various social groups were the state hand-outs, ad hoc provisions, state recognition of social privileges, beneficial exceptions to equality before the law and, of course, state jobs.

The public sector had always been the largest employer in the country and the clientelistic mentality has been a feature of the Greek state ever since its inception.[4] After 2004, when it returned to power, New Democracy claimed that clientelistic practices had developed after 1981, under PASOK, and that the public sector had then gradually turned into the major employer and driving force of the economy, through the clientelistic system. This is a view outrageously lacking any sense of history. The clientelistic logic prevailed throughout Europe in the nineteenth century, but was gradually overcome. In Greece, its continued prevalence after the end of World War II was an anachronism. The post-war conservative regime became a basic player in the clientelistic system. It strongly resisted any efforts to infuse objectivity into public appointments. It wanted to safeguard the public services from infiltration by people of different opinions and to sustain one of the strongest tools at its disposal for keeping voters. It is indicative that, while appointment of public servants through meritocratic examinations was established in Britain in the middle of the nineteenth century, in Greece this did not happen till almost one and a half centuries later, in 1995. It was established by PASOK, institutionalised through the introduction of examinations and evaluation by an independent body (ASEP, the Supreme Council for the Selection of Personnel).

Social stability, secured through clientelistic hand-outs, is welcome to a large section of society. The parties expand their power by the provision of protection and cash. The citizens demand and obtain something that falls within a framework common in their dealings with authority. The public administration, habituated in making sectoral, trade or special arrangements, goes about its business in the traditional and well understood fashion. Accustomed to being served in this way, public opinion does not react. In fact, the public debate gives priority to confrontations between the state and social groups and shows a marked sympathy for the protesters. The broader social consequences of the various favourable arrangements are played down. There is a general silent agreement: state hand-outs are a necessary precondition for social equilibrium.

How these benefits are financed does not concern society as a whole. A party in power that makes promises is responsible for the financing. When the government states 'rural wardens are needed', citizens have no reason to dispute it, or to reject the state jobs the government offers. Citizens are not conscious that, as taxpayers, they will ultimately foot the bill or that each act of largesse is at the expense of other, broader aims. It is enough for them that they collect the cash. As a consequence of the prevalent attitude, 'hand-outs, here and now', any gains achieved in the process of convergence with the more advanced European economists are easily reversed. A short term in government suffices to raise the budget deficit and sovereign debt, through reductions in taxation, thousands of appointments to the public sector and selective hand-outs to social groups. Public sector salaries increased from €18 billion at the end of 2003 to €31 billion by the end of 2009.[5]

The scope for clientelistic policies was enhanced by the fact that the most numerous social group in Greece were the self-employed,[6] comprising, among others, farmers, artisans, professionals, trades people and those in small business. These subgroups do not have the same perceptions or targets. Each attempts to protect its own members, exclusively, against competition, market risks and adverse economic developments, through direct dialogue with the state. They solicit special arrangements, special taxation regimes and favourable borrowing terms.

The state, therefore, did not find itself facing strong representation from a significant productive sector and having to pay attention to its broad demands, as happens in developed countries. The demands of various social groups were micro-manageable. It was easy to placate them within the framework of long-established horse-trading, without any planning. It did not require hard thinking and led to no serious political confrontation.

The guilds of sectoral interests, whether doctors, employees of the public power corporation or supermarket entrepreneurs, have established, in conjunction with the state, their own conditions of work, activity and earnings. What has been agreed is deemed 'acquired rights' and therefore irreversible, even if conditions change drastically. Every attempt at modification arouses intense reactions, strikes, demonstrations, the principal pressure lever being the hardship thus deliberately inflicted on the mass of citizens.

A typical example of this was associated with the attempt to turn the port of Piraeus into an international centre for transport to the Balkans with the concession of a port segment to the largest Chinese transport company, COSCO. Piraeus was thus to become the gateway for trade to and from Eastern Europe. The port workers mobilised against the concession by the then New Democracy administration, and forcibly occupied the port. They were supported by the local PASOK MPs, with the party's backing. When PASOK came to power in 2009, the roles reversed. New Democracy, now in opposition, supported the continuing protests by workers against the new administration. The PASOK MPs of Piraeus, modifying their line, tried to calm the protesting port workers. The dispute showed that the dockers' earnings, the product of decisions by both New Democracy and PASOK administrations, had grown significantly higher than prevailing levels for manual and other workers. In the political life of Piraeus, the port workers' unions constituted the electoral vanguard of all three major parties, with direct influence on the mobilisation of ballot preferences within each party's candidate list. Despite their differences, the party-tolerated guild mentality determined the parties' stand. The COSCO investment went ahead eventually, but under conditions that caused the Chinese company to abandon a large part of its plans and to seek instead another Mediterranean port.

Did the dock workers protest because plans to develop the port of Piraeus had been abandoned? Did they fight for a reduction in public debt or in the budget deficit? No, of course not. They wanted to defend the benefits of clientelism they had been reaping for years, seeking the continuation of the mixture of guild corporatism, localism and exploitation of their privileged position, which they had come to enjoy with governmental consent.

The crisis highlighted the element which had been overshadowed by developments such as entry to the EMU, high rates of growth, the transfers from the EU, the public works and the gains in prestige obtained by the half year of the rotating presidency of the EU, as well as the Olympic Games held in Athens in the summer of 2004. It brought back populism, the defence of clientelistic privileges, the politics of demonising opponents and the assignment of guilt to anyone who supported different views.[7] It revealed that the country continues to act in accordance with structures and practices of the previous century.

This nexus between state, political parties and society, shaped by clientelism, is still resisting change. It wants to retain the reins of power and sources of income, the socio-political compromise that secures the gains accruing to guild interests and the interests of those 'on our side'. It defends everything that caused excess borrowing and senseless spending.[8] And in this effort, it rolls over as much of the burden onto the faceless crowd as it possibly can. That crowd also protests, but its voice is drowned by the shouts, and the violence, of those who can activate the pressure levers.

The state administration obstructed Greek society's adjustment to the environment of the Eurozone owing to: its deficient organisation; its conservative attitudes; its resistance to change; its poor relation with the citizen; and the corruption permitted by an absence of scrutiny and accountability. In 2012, two cases highlighted the typical state weaknesses but also the exploitation of them by public employees and citizens alike.

First, the mayor of Zakynthos, in the Ionian Sea, mapped the island by aerial photography and discovered that 15,000 buildings had not been connected to the electricity network. This meant that the real acreage of hotels, businesses and residences had not been registered. The owners paid much less in municipal taxes than was due. When the council held a meeting to discuss the imposition of the correct taxes, the reaction was immediate. The meeting was interrupted by 'indignant' citizens who flung yoghurt at the mayor. He was 'punished' because he did something absolutely reasonable, which, however, previous mayors and the municipal services had either not wanted to do or avoided doing in their quest for electoral support.

Second, at the beginning of 2012, a census of pensioners who were entitled to social welfare allowances was completed. The picture that emerged was evidence of a system of clientelistic relationships, illegal enrichment and corruption in the administration. Some 150,000 non-pensioners collected a pension; 17,000 farmers' pensions had been granted without supporting documents; and 40,000 people claiming disability allowances did not show up to be checked. At the same time, it was discovered that employees of the social security (IKA) office in the Athens suburb of Kallithea and elsewhere were granting welfare and disability allowances, for a fee. The social security organisation had misallocated millions of euros. The checks also showed that the kinds of disability recorded for allowances varied from region to region and were much higher than average in certain electoral districts. Rumours that MPs or candidates for Parliament 'served' their voters with certificates of non-existent ailments were thus confirmed. The 'welfare state had been replaced by the clientelistic state'.[9]

The answer to why such flagrant abuses had not been detected earlier is simple. The development of an information technology (IT) infrastructure, which made scrutiny possible, only began, with pains and strains, in 2000. It materialised thanks to the Community Support Framework, that is to say, funds from the EU. The ministries lacked the relevant expertise and people of standing and experience to guide the effort. In 2001 the state was compelled to set up a special company, the Information Society S.A., to assist the planning and installation of the IT equipment.[10]

An absence of expertise and experience in the Ministry of Finance also plagued the introduction of the electronic system TAXIS, resulting in years of work before a satisfactory level of performance was achieved.[11] A lack of expertise, complex regulations, which obstruct quick and effective action, and a culture of mistrust of what is not already accepted or is not subject to multiple checks all lead to the backwardness of the public administration.

The regulatory system in Greece is extraordinarily complex: laws tend to specify everything in such minute detail that it excludes recourse to judgement or reason; orders cross-refer to other orders that also need interpretation with the help of other regulations; amendments are attached to unrelated legislation; and new laws always seem to contain exceptions. The labyrinthine whole serves two purposes: it relieves from responsibility but also allows for irresponsible and bullying behaviour. It underpins the large-scale bureaucracy and leads to the needless harassment of citizens, with refusals and delays. The state machine works at snail's pace, oppressively, and resists initiative. It breeds a culture of corruption by creating opportunities for bribery, to speed things up; often, bribing is the only recourse to overcome official obstruction. At the beginning of 2012, the entire Department of Investments of the Ministry of Development was dismantled following revelations that its employees systematically demanded money to advance investments projects.

The reform this nightmarish labyrinth of legislation is pursued with codifications that emerge as work on the side by professors and judges, operating through commissions that change as the administration does. The effectiveness of this process is minimal. What is needed is continuous and direct intervention in the drafting and enactment of legislation. The hundreds of amendments submitted prior to the May 2012 elections, a number of which became law, were warning bells of the difficulties encountered by any prior intervention. The clientelistic and guilt mentality is at odds with a rational approach.

The reason for Greece's backwardness in this area is the inability of the political leaderships to transcend personal pursuits. The guild set-up and the clientelistic mentality make political success dependent on the ability to distribute jobs and hand-outs. That is what politicians are interested in: providing services to their clients and satisfying their demands. The prospect of programmes, ideas, modernisation plans, shaking the establishment leaves them more or less indifferent. Cooperation or political compromises are not deemed expedient.[12] On the contrary, expediency is deemed extreme confrontation, the battle for absolute control that secures for clients the anticipated reward. The more extreme the conflict and the rhetoric, the more it reassures and encourages supporters, affirming that the prey will be theirs.[13]

The climate of combat magnifies the tension, defames and loads guilt on to opponents, burns bridges. Extreme confrontation costs the country dearly.[14] It does not allow for understandings, for convergence, for the search for widely acceptable solutions. Elections, parliamentary procedures, governance and the public debate are downgraded to scene-setting for confrontation and battle. Even in the run-up to the elections on 6 May 2012 – when the central problem was the economic direction of the country and the crisis made a common effort more imperative than ever – New Democracy's electoral advertising trumpeted that it 'assign guilt' for the subjection of Greece to the Troika Memorandum. Such relentless political conflict narrows drastically the scope for solutions and closes the door to a common effort and to necessary reforms. When even crucial structural changes, such as the reform of the social security system, encounter resistance from inside the camps of the respective governments, stagnation is the inevitable outcome.

Confrontation aimed at belittling or writing off the other opinion causes confusion as to what is essential and what is not; it leads to the inability to formulate any long-term plan; the continual overturning of decisions leads to opportunistic solutions. The victim is institutional continuity. Every change in government entails the reversal, as far as possible, of the policies adopted by the previous government, as well as a complete change in personnel at various levels of the administration. The new government acts as the castigator of the previous one. Responsibility for any negative development is shifted to the government's predecessors or its rivals. According to New Democracy, the fiscal collapse of the years 2008–09 was caused by the preceding PASOK governments and not by its own policy from 2004 onwards. PASOK's favourite argument while in government in 2010–12 was that the post-dictatorship period 'proved catastrophic down the decades', and therefore George Papandreou bore no responsibility for recent developments. The post-dictatorship period, however, succeeded in providing over 30 years of political stability, an unprecedented achievement in Greek history. Certain sections of society were disgruntled by the fact that from 1974 onwards, political and social discrimination was gradually but drastically restricted, as was state arbitrariness.

Both New Democracy and PASOK have claimed at times that the previous governments of 1996–2004 achieved growth through borrowing and the growth was a 'bubble' due to consumption. However, as the EU statistics show, sovereign debt over 1996–2003 was lower than 100% of GDP on average; from the end of 2005 it was consistently over 100% of GDP. Therefore, borrowing during 1996–2003, was much less than that in the following period.

In the four years of PASOK government 1996–99, the average rate of growth was 3.2% of GDP; in the four years 2000–03, it was 4.2%, higher than the EU average. This development was not the result of consumption; spending on infrastructure was higher than during any period before and, needless to say, the period after. Projects included: the airport at Spata; the Rio–Antirio bridge; the Athens Metro; the 519 kilometres of the Egnatia highway and the 482 kilometres of the Patras–Thessaloniki highway; 14 new hospitals; the development of the National Centre for Emergency Help (EKAV); the institution of a social security system for farmers; the 1,200 'help in the home' units; the industrial plants established by private enterprise (e.g. at Almyros and Grevena); the natural gas grid; and the operation of the DEH electricity plant at Lavrion. This programme showed that, with systematic monitoring and coherent effort, growth in Greece is possible. When all this is described as a 'bubble', it is inevitable that public opinion will lose its ability to judge, and will focus instead on the hand-outs, the guild-focused demands and on protests against any contribution that is being asked for. Public relations gain the upper hand and politics ceases to engage with changing social conditions. Politics exhausts itself in games of images and impressions.

The way the crisis was handled alienated a large section of the Greek public from the EU. The original measures were considered excessive, as in fact they were, and the restrictions on incomes and the extraordinary taxes were considered unfair. Despite later corrections, such as the cutting down of lenders' claims and the reduction in interest rates, the view prevailed that the sole purpose of the financing programme by Greece's partners was to serve their own interests. In this way, a new kind of nationalism appeared, calling on Greeks to liberate themselves, to refuse to cooperate with Europe, to go back to the drachma, having shaken off the yoke of the euro.[15] The new patriotism urged the return to the past of independence, under the slogan 'Greece for the Greeks'. It projected unrealistic and idealised images of the heroic country, which overcomes alone artificial difficulties deliberately created by foreigners.[16] This wave of nationalism, in its various forms, from the left to the right of the political spectrum, constituted an additional obstacle to solving the crisis. It created an environment of intense confrontation and fear that affected citizens. It cultivated doubt and hesitation.

The crisis and how it was dealt with by the Eurozone and the Greek government affected political developments dramatically. PASOK lost the majority of its voters. New Democracy managed a better electoral performance than PASOK, but its own strength fell drastically. Both far left and far right, in various guises, acquired a role in shaping public opinion. The dissatisfaction with politics and politicians was – and is – almost universal. The results of the elections confirmed this. The public reaction to the policy that was being pursued was – and will remain – negative. The scope for rational debate had shrunk to a minimum. The only plan for the future that public opinion was aware of was that of Greece's creditors. Counter-proposals were not convincing, as they were unclear and dealt only in generalities.

In this climate of confusion, any sense of the problems, of what caused them and of rational ways of dealing with them was lost. Utopian fantasies competed with extremist views from right and left, in an exaltation of paranoid perceptions, according to which Greece had the economic and political might to disregard the constraints of globalisation. The risk of a political deadlock was lurking and, with it, the possibility of economic catastrophe through a return to the drachma. Greece had known situations in the past where the sense of the international environment, of the reasonable and the necessary, had been lost. These led to tragic outcomes: the military dictatorship of 1967–74; the Civil War of 1946; the catastrophe of Asia Minor in 1922.

Close to the 'new nationalism', a new anti-parliamentarianism emerged, a conception that sought solutions to the country's problems by means fit for a totalitarian regime. The political system was considered a 'kleptocracy', a 'dictatorship of those serving foreign interests'. The *Indignados* of Syntagma Square displayed gallows and demanded that those responsible for the crisis be 'sent to Goudi', that is, to be executed. They themselves, as pure representatives of the popular, would decide who exactly was responsible. The rhetoric of 'disobedience' and 'resistance' also contributed to the promotion of totalitarian solutions. By disseminating arbitrariness and lawlessness, they created the conditions for the appearance of 'saviours', ready to establish their own oppressive system – and call it the law. The legitimacy of the post-dictatorship democracy was openly contested, not only with the manhandling of politicians and a refusal to accept the law, but also through the rise of political formations advocating a new order. What this would be was always unclear, but the common goal of the extremists was to 'overturn' the society of today, which would allow them to determine the society of tomorrow, in disregard of democratic procedures.[17]

Cooperation with the EU and the country's adaptation to the constraints that derive from its economic situation is a hard undertaking. Every Greek government will find itself faced with a public opinion that doubts, contests and disputes European proposals for an exit from the crisis. At the time of writing, the Eurozone's understanding of the Greek problem and its willingness to give further support had reached a minimum. The room for Greek manoeuvre is exceptionally limited. Whatever public opinion may favour is rejected by Greece's European partners. Whatever the partners recommend is considered just one more unjustifiable imposition by the public. To transcend this dilemma, whichever government happens to be in power must shoulder the solution, in its entirely, must assume complete responsibility for the necessary actions, defend them without hesitation and fight for their success.

The way Greek society has split is the result of choices made by the opposition on the right and the left. In essence, that political contestation, which was a perennially dominant feature of the country's political life, has been transferred to the issue of Greece's relations with the EU. The intense discontent of public opinion ensures a broad audience for anti-European rhetoric. Through its particularly aggressive stand, the opposition acquires the ability to extend its political influence. An anti-European sentiment is already dominant in public opinion. Routine comments of the European Commission, or by the President of the European Council, about 'sticking to commitments' are construed as derogatory. Observations in foreign newspapers concerning the deterioration of the economic situation in Greece are considered to be preparations to expel the country from the EMU or indeed the EU.

The political goal of those inciting extreme antagonism was power. The continual tension they cultivated was a tactical choice to split the government majority. Their street mobilisations were a means of invalidating negotiation with the Eurozone and of driving efforts for economic recovery to failure. In the ongoing confrontation, the government parties hesitated, made excuses for their policies. They took into consideration the political cost. However, hesitation and u-turns on the part of government make a situation worse. What is needed is an open mind and decisiveness.

The opposition routine in Greek political life, with its excesses, its clashes, the efforts to obstruct every government project, was not befitting of Greece's participation in the Eurozone, an international union of states aiming to shape common binding policies to implement common pursuits. The oppositional extremism obstructed negotiations with the EU, intensified inwardness and opposed the continuous broadening of relations with other countries that would give a role to Greece and enable it to participate in the European and the international community.

The cross-opposition hostility, together with the delays, the backtracking and the weaknesses of the official Greek side, sowed mistrust of the country, distanced all those who wanted to help and marginalised Greece in the EU. 'Inevitably friends, partners and enemies doubt whether this country has the will to save itself, to adjust and to function as a reliable, equal and normal member of the Eurozone.'[18] The Greek government still needs to overturn this image, through its deeds.

For a solution to the Greek problem to be grasped, the view that the Greek crisis is due exclusively to unfortunate European interventions and the conviction that it is a symptom of a general crisis of financial capitalism in the Eurozone (and hence not amenable to domestic solution) must be overcome.

Both interpretations seek to transfer responsibility exclusively to third parties.[19] The causes of the crisis, and how it spiralled out of control in Greece, are not only attributable to 'outsiders'; they are also tied to the 'insiders'. If the European leaders had shown greater care, had they reacted earlier with a plan adjusted to the capacity of the Greek economy, had they understood the risks of recession and the need to encourage growth, things would have run a different course. However, they would also have run a different course if the leadership of political parties in Greece had not focused on garnering votes with unrealistic promises but, instead, had put aside their party and personal rivalries and worked together to elaborate serious plans and specific measures. Reforms were carried out only under pressure, which is why they were incomplete. Overcoming the crisis concerns both sides, and requires cooperation.

In their statements, those responsible in the Eurozone – who left open the matter of what was to happen with Greece – overlooked the fact that the uncertainty they cultivated had negative effects. Under such circumstances, capital flight from Greece continued, foreign investors remained unwilling to invest and it was difficult to find reputable buyers for the newly privatised enterprises.

> Without investments and a return of confidence, Greece is bound to remain trapped in a vicious circle of recession and it is unlikely to meet its creditors' demands.... If the Europeans accept that a Greek exit is not in their interest, they should recognise the effort made and give it [Greece] a real chance to adjust further and recover within the euro.[20]

In Greece, the hope was still being expressed that everything would end well, thanks to some development 'that cannot fail to occur'. Either the French government would support the country without hesitation or the German Social Democrats would be part of the German government in 2013 and would overturn the harsh adjustment programme, or else the European institutions themselves would sanction eurobonds, so that borrowing could continue without restriction. However, there are no magic solutions. Political changes in Europe may result in a better understanding of the Greek problem, and allow more time for adjustment. However, exceptions to Greece's financial and other commitments will not be allowed on any account. The Greeks are, and will remain, obliged to solve their problems themselves.

The first fundamental principle for the solution to the Greek problem is that national efforts are set in the framework of: active participation in the EU and the EMU, with a view to widening 'the European perspective'; European cooperation in confronting the imbalances between North and South; and broadening planning for growth throughout the EU.[21]

The second fundamental principle is the formulation of a plan for the medium-term and long-term handling of the crisis, so that Greece acquires the ability to engage in documented and targeted negotiations, and to argue better for the amelioration of the adjustment terms. The precondition for substantive discussions of the country's direction and renegotiation is the demonstration of Greek will and capacity to adjust, thus to regain the confidence of those working with Greece, through actions and not again through hollow promises.

The third fundamental principle must be to confront the multiple causes of Greek society's backwardness. Certain measures under way – privatisation, deregulation of markets – are necessary but are not enough. The widespread role of the state and the habit of accommodating special interests, groups, political parties and the state machinery calls for systematic treatment; it is equally necessary to reverse the current disdain for the political system and public administration, through rationalising behaviours, serving the public, pursuing the common interest. The usual measures, such as changing the electoral law and revising the constitution, which have been tried repeatedly, create the impression of change but have not achieved substantive results. Backwardness derives from mental attitudes and behaviours, and these must be confronted and prioritised.

Finally, a fundamental principle for determining policy aims must be social justice. Adjustment through austerity and recession has hurt those on the lowest incomes the worst. Their anger and protests are exploited by those seeking a return to the drachma, or who want to minimise the role of justice and democratic norms. The 'European perspective' and the 'democratic belief', however, need the support of citizens. That support will be forthcoming only if they have the sense that the state is really concerned about their fate.

The context for this whole effort must be a plan clarifying the basic aims, the means to achieve them, the probable time scales and the anticipated re-actions and the ways to overcome them. The basic aims of this plan must include a clear vision for: growth and productive development in the country; the centre of gravity of investment; the stabilisation of the economy; the constraints on fiscal policy; the containment of incomes with a simultaneous effort to reduce inequalities.[22]

Plans are proposed frequently in Greece. However, government policy has hardly ever followed a planned and carefully crafted course. Populism and clientelism are counter to planning because it binds and constrains, it makes the scattering of promises difficult, it forces sincerity on politicians and high-lights backtracking. The downward slide that began in 2004 could have been avoided if the political leaders had not followed the format of the traditional opportunistic politics encapsulated in 'everything for the sake of power'.[23]

In 2010 New Democracy followed the path of denouncing the Memoran-dum, without pointing at its weaknesses, the dangers it harboured or possible amendments. It was the old, well known recipe of denial. Later it was forced to accept loud nay-saying was a dead end. It veered towards condemning the government's weakness in negotiation, advocating the need for the country to stand up and assert itself. But at the critical moment of negotiations fol-lowing the European Council of October 2011, New Democracy was not in a position to present equivalent solutions which could have mitigated the burden on salaried employees and pensioners. During the election campaign of April–May 2012, with its Zappeion III programme, New Democracy con-tinued the tradition of empty reassurances and promises. In its claims to be able to avoid the imposition of new taxes, the party resorted to stock generalities such as to 'limit public expenditure', 'reduce the deficits of public enterprises', implement measures suggested by their 'analysis item by item, of the budget headings'. Its only specific commitment was 'a rise in the tax on electronic games, to generate money for pensioners'. Added to this were declarations, made a thousand times, about 'striking at tax evasion', 'develop-ment priorities', 'structural changes in the public administration' and others, which every party seeking power without exception also referred to. Its rhetoric clearly showed that its sole concern was the election result. Experience shows that, in such cases, turning from insubstantial waffle to specific, serious policy is exceptionally difficult. PASOK's electoral victory in 2009 was a tangible example of how reassurances and triumphant tones obstruct substantive preparation for dealing with problems, and so end in resounding failure.[24]

The parties of the left contributed to the deadlock. It would have been reasonable for them to point out the shortcomings of the Memorandum, and to propose other solutions in the context of European cooperation. However, they opted for the utopian claim that, while staying in the Eurozone and retaining the euro, they would pursue an anti-capitalist march for Europe, in the course of which Greece would impose its terms on the capitalist countries it was cooperating with. Such an exaggerated claim was made purposely and consciously; it served the same purpose, in a different way, as the nebulous promises made by the right, to gather together a front of all those opposed to the European course. It conveyed the message that any change in the EU's policy would be useless, since it was the system that was at fault. Till the system had been overturned, nothing already acquired would be questioned, no reform would 'be allowed to pass', as any change would be for the benefit of the capitalists and the foreign 'loan sharks'. The only thing to pursue was the total change of the system. On the critical issue which it raised, 'the return to the drachma in the event that we are compelled to exit the Eurozone', the left did not present any reasoned policy. It did not give any answer to how this exceptionally complex process might be undertaken, such that the country was not led to destitution. It thus confirmed that, in essence, it was not interested in the effects of a return to the drachma, the social misery it would entail, the enormous redistribution of wealth at the cost of workers. Nor did it appear to be concerned by the fact that it was of the same mind as all those million-aires – debtors to the state, speculators – who sought a return to the drachma in order to make a painless gain.

The conflict between those supporting the Memorandum and those against it was engineered by the extremes, to promote confrontation and to push the electorate into one of the two camps. As presented through this clash, the dilemma is misleading. Greece was on the brink of bankruptcy and it had no way out other than to borrow, as it always used to. Every loan comes with conditions, more or less harsh, according to the borrower's creditworthiness. In the case of the loan from the Eurozone and the IMF, the conditions set by the lenders might be questioned, as might the plans of the country or the intentions of the lenders. What cannot be questioned, however, is the fact that the actual loan was necessary or that any such intervention would have come with strings attached. There is also scope for discussion over changing the conditions attached to the loan or for additional financing (unless it is no longer needed).

Therefore, the true issue here is not about 'yes' or 'no' to the Memorandum, but about its contents, about the demands and the concessions Greece makes, about whether it is possible not to borrow at all or to borrow from sources other than the EU and the IMF. These are questions that are inextricably linked with the economic development of Greece and how to realise it. They concern as much the struggle against backwardness as the borrowing policy. A 'yes' or a 'no' to the Memorandum conceals the complexity of the subject; it overlooks the fact that critical questions cannot be answered with a simple 'yes' or 'no'. It blocks any thinking about how best to pursue the country's interests. Presenting a conflict in black and white deceives citizens. It lures them into a maelstrom of oversimplified reasoning that renders solutions impossible.

## Notes

1  See G. Voulgaris, 'Greece is not playing poker', *Ta Nea*, 26 May 2012, p. 10. See also note 1, Chapter 2, p. 20.
2  See Chapter 2.
3  See K. Featherstone, 'Why does Greek fail?', *Kathimerini*, 7 October 2012, p. 23. In *Greece of Oblivion and Truth: The Long Adolescence to a Forceful Adulthood*, Themelio (in Greek), 2012, C. Tsoukalas examines the development and structure of Greek society at the start of the crisis.
4  In his *History of the Greek State, 1830–1920* (5th revised edition), National Bank of Greece, 2004 (in Greek), p. 135, G. V. Dertilis, writes: 'After the 1864 Constitution and the establishment of parliamentarianism the totalitarian institutional power also sustained itself by indirect vote-buying, which was carried out on the one hand through the patronage network, and on the other through public expenditure. The new political classes sought to protect themselves from the novel electoral power of citizens and to buy it by distributing hand-outs and, in addition, making a show of their patriotism, in an auction of patriotic rhetoric during electoral campaigns (but that is another story). The clientelistic system was consolidated by electoral practice and spread rapidly; the granting of public sector appointments became an important weapon in the struggle of the political powers in their quest for votes and, ultimately, in the consolidation of centralised power.'
5  *General Government Data*, European Commission, spring 2012, table 39A.
6  In 1984, they were 50.9% of the total number in employment; in 2000, 42.0%; and in 2007, 35.9%.
7  See Y. Pretenteris, *The Cold Civil War, the People, the Events that Destroyed the Country*, Patakis, 2012, pp. 87, 99, 206.
8  The reasons for reform failure in Greece are examined by S. Kalyvas, G. Pagoula-tos and H. Tsoukas, *From Stagnation to Forced Adjustment: Reforms in Greece 1974–2010*, Hurst, 2012.
9  Ph. Georgeles, *Athens Voice*, 22–28 March 2012, p. 4.
10  See 'Decision of Ministers of Interior, Public Administration and Decentralisation, the National Economy and Finances', GG B 324, 27 March 2001.
11  The Tax Information System (TAXIS) constitutes the largest IT infrastructure project in Greece. It was implemented within the framework of European Structural Funds. Its purpose is to constitute a full IT system to monitor taxation, to counter tax evasion and to improve service for citizens.
12  'Compromise', which is the key word for the progress in European unification, is a 'dirty word' in Greece.

13 'The mentality of clashes, the ideology of no retreat in struggles, the culture of violence, the self-centred egoism of the political system, the lack of a democratic ethic, which would allow a national agreement to deal with the crisis, are to blame.' D. Psychogios, *To Vima*, 3 June 2012, p. A15.

14 T. Pappas, *To Vima*, 3 June 2012, p. 63, says: 'However, discussions over which of the two parties was a greater cheat did not go on within the national workshop with the audience made up of Greek citizens exclusively. The fallout and accusations they bandied about with regard to the deceit and inadequacies of the two parties of power, reached Europe, resulting in the establishment of the conviction of foreign governments that "the lazy, squandering and unstable Greeks tricked us into giving the green light for their inclusion in the EMU".'

15 A sample of statements: the country is 'under occupation'; the supporters of a European path represent 'the occupying powers'; 'In 2012 the struggle against the foreign invaders of World War II is being repeated'.

16 See *Ta Nea*, 9 March 2012, p. 7; I. Laliotis, *To Vima*, 25 March 2012, p. A25; S. Polymilis, *To Vima*, 22 April 2012, p. A7.

17 In an interview she gave to the Protagon website on 24 April 2012, the Secretary General of the Greek Communist Party (KKE) called for 'worker power', 'the dictatorship of the proletariat', 'social revolution, armed if need be', abolition of the current system of electing Members of Parliament and their replacement by 'people's MPs', who would represent 'the factory workers, students and pensioners'.

18 P. Ioakimides, *Ta Nea*, 17 August 2001, p. 9.

19 See V. P. Ioakimides, 'Greece's particularity', *Ta Nea* online, 24 August 2012.

20 J. Pisani-Ferry, 'Europe should choose whether it wants Greece in or out', *Financial Times*, ft.com, 22 August 2012.

21 See G. Voulgaris, *Ta Nea*, 5–6 November 2011, p. 11.

22 In *Ta Nea*, 30 December 2011, p. 9, G. Voulgaris stresses the need for such a plan, for there to be 'a common framework of agreement and long-term strategic goals'. See pp. 286–7 as well.

23 A. Papahelas. *Kathimerini*, 15 July 2012, p. 26: 'The parties in Greece and politicians have learnt to give everything to gain power, without ever preparing for it.'

24 For 'Zappeion III' see *Eleutheros Typos*, 23 April 2012, p. 7, and New Democracy's related text, 'Zappeion. Presentation of the plan for the economy', New Democracy, 2012.

# 32

# A new European policy is necessary

At the inception of the financial crisis of 2007 and after, and at the start of the public debt crisis of 2008, the conservative position was dominant; indeed, there was a widespread aversion of new initiatives across the EU. It was widely held that the Lisbon Treaty of 2007 contained all necessary changes to the EU's institutional framework and no further reform should be sought. The rejection of the draft European Constitution by France and the Netherlands in 2005 and the difficulties encountered by the recently joined member states in accepting the new Treaty showed that changes to the Treaties were a painful process that produced significant resistance. The President of the Commission, José Manuel Barroso, articulating the climate of the first decade of the new century in November 2004, stressed that he would not seek to change the existing situation, but to consolidate it, so that the institutional framework would function better.

Reform fatigue prevailed in the Union, contrary to the activism of the last decade of the twentieth century. There were various reasons for this. The accession of 10 new members in 2004 multiplied the difficulties in consultations and decision-making in the EU. These new member states, mostly formerly in the Soviet sphere, reacted (and still react) against unifying efforts and new rules: 'We did not become members of the Union to substitute Brussels for Moscow'. France and Germany had exerted pressure for the EU to be expanded, in the hope of acquiring new markets and new allies. However, the new countries felt that their supporter par excellence was the USA and they expressed doubts over and objections to European policy.

From 2001 onwards the composition of the European Council began to change. The social democratic majority was gradually replaced. Governments were elected in Germany, France and Italy that no longer nurtured the same interest in European affairs. Their focus shifted towards internal concerns. The European Commission underwent a shift in composition reflecting this trend, with conservative Commissioners becoming increasingly dominant. The line 'no more changes, there have been enough' increasingly expressed the position of both member states and Community institutions. During the era of Jacques Delors' presidency of the European Commission, decisive steps had been taken, with the accomplishment of the single market and the signing of the Maastricht Treaty. This was an era from the distant past and an example to be avoided. The idea of continually studying the EMU's operations and complementing the Treaties with new regulations to deal with the new problems was abandoned. The currency was a matter for the ministers of finance and the central banks, a technical matter, which prime ministers should not have to deal with.[1] There was no vision. The EU suffered from 'short termism'.[2]

Many matters which should have been dealt with in the context of European integration were victims of this development. These were demoted, forgotten or classified as utopian. The 'European ideal', the hope of overcoming the traumas of World War II, creating a community of states capable of dealing with common problems, was slipping into history. The goals of the current era were more technocratic – closer cooperation to achieve 'balanced economic growth', 'a competitive social market economy', 'social justice' – while the loftier aims of 'solidarity between member states'[3] were relegated to rhetoric. European integration aimed at 'growth', a 'social' Europe beyond the common market, the single currency and a vague notion of a common foreign policy.

The political and economic conditions prevailing after 2004 expedited this trend, turning attention exclusively to the problems of the single market, and the single currency. Policies for growth and initiatives to reduce the imbalances between member states were considered unsuitable. The increase in funds for the EU budget so that new projects could be launched met with intense resistance. The view that convergence should be sought by every member state through its own means and not through new tangled interventions by the EU dominated. The financial crisis that began in 2007 furthered this sentiment.

In a climate hostile to initiatives, the European Commission lost its leading role in shaping policy. It was replaced by the French President, the German Chancellor, the European Council and EMU-related institutions. The choice of a permanent President of the European Council, in accordance with the Treaties, contributed to this development. The first office holder, Herman Van Rompuy, a former Belgian Prime Minister, had been distinguished for his ability to achieve compromises between the different parties of his country. He worked intensively and successfully to these ends at a European level. Inevitably, the promotion of Europe-wide initiatives in this general climate slipped down the pecking order. The Franco-German axis established its own order, of which the dominant policy concern was fiscal discipline and its expression, the Fiscal Compact. When the crisis began, the Union's inclination was towards maintaining the status quo, avoiding interventions, projecting the view that automatic stabilisers would solve any problem. The climate was hostile to 'agitators' sowing doubts over the EU edifice with the troubles they were provoking. The fault lay with them and not the Union.

Soon, economic developments revealed a truth that the pro-Europe language of all participants concealed. The road towards European integration was and will remain inevitably incremental, as the complexity of the project and the diversity of its participants are not conducive to a coherent and structured vision of the end game for Europe. Every step towards integration entails disagreements and a struggle between various ideologies, pursuits and interests. The compromises and opt-outs permitted for each wave of changes and the maintenance of the status quo mean that progress comes to a halt. European integration presupposes motion, changes and the inescapable disputes that accompany them.

Greece triggered the crisis in the Eurozone, but was not the cause of it. The cause is inherent in the fact that the Eurozone is a full monetary union but an imperfect economic and fiscal union of member states with different structural features; the mature economies of the European North differ significantly from the less mature economies of the South. The current crisis is a public debt crisis only to a small degree, and in that dimension it largely concerns only Greece and Portugal. The causes of the overall crisis are far more complex and varied: the frenzy of construction activity and the resulting artificial price rises in Spain and Ireland; the over-borrowing by enterprises in Italy; Germany's refusal to increase domestic demand so as to facilitate exports from the South; and the deterioration of competitiveness of the peripheral countries. The causes of the crisis lay also in the private sector of the economy, in the banking systems of a number of member states and in the inadequate oversight and control by the fiscal and monetary authorities in the Eurozone. The EU has still not designed a rounded policy of economic governance, a new way of dealing with imbalances between the developed Core and the less developed Periphery. It has not formulated procedures for the systematic promotion of economic growth, which would distribute the benefits to all members in as balanced a way as possible.[4]

The absence of a general consensus on the direction of the EU, and differences provoked by this absence of clarity, together with the ineffective efforts to control the crisis, have affected European public opinion negatively; the European project has come to be viewed as problematic. In the countries of the South, a large proportion of citizens considered the stabilisation programme being applied as oppressive and a dead end. In Germany, by contrast, public opinion approved it. Three-quarters of its population did not wish for any more concessions to Greece and rejected any new financing.[5] In the countries which had not been dragged into the maelstrom of the crisis, mistrust prevailed over the efforts to renew the European project. The feeling was common that any changes to the Treaties would restrict further the already imperceptible role of the small member states of the EU.

The absence of a policy that would render the European project convincing means not just a delay in shaping the European edifice; it is the cause of the continuous anxiety and the instability of the markets. The markets highlighted the weakness in solving the Greek problem and the deterioration of the situation of Spain and Italy, the delays in creating a common, efficient stabilisation mechanism, and the doubts related to the ECB. The markets realised that, under these conditions, bondholders are at risk, and that their loans may not be paid back. They demand deeper unification and more effective governance. However, the member states were hesitant, and their hesitancy provoked further turmoil and adverse reactions in the markets.

It is a principle of the Treaties that, in the context of the EMU, every country is responsible only for its own liabilities, and not obliged to cover the liabilities of other states. In any economic and monetary union, however, the action of each member state influences the actions of the others. Therefore, strict non-responsibility is impossible. The crisis compelled the members of the Eurozone to engage creatively in weakening the rules of the Treaties, under pressure from the developments and the risks deriving from the inability of the peripheral states to meet their obligations. In the case of Greece, they devised financing through bilateral loans; in the case of Portugal and Ireland, they established a provisional stabilisation mechanism. The provisional mechanism later became permanent. The obfuscation, the disagreements, the partial solutions, the reconsiderations were continual. The decisions over supporting Spanish banks were revised twice. The Fiscal Compact does guarantee an efficient pre-emption of crises, but it does not ensure that an existing crisis can be overcome. The decisions of 29 June 2012 showed that it is necessary to settle many problems beyond the observance of fiscal discipline. A plan for the future is needed, one that will allow faster and more decisive decision-taking in the EMU, and that will grant means and options that, while necessary, do not exist today.[6] The divergent levels of competitiveness, administrative capacity and education cannot be overcome simply by debt reduction, or the recapitalisation of banks. The underlying problems have been known for a long time. There is an evident lack of central guidance and the absence of a truly inclusive way for setting all member states to pull in the same direction. The development of a coherent policy that will confront the causes of grave imbalances and will unify partial and fragmented efforts in a common direction towards economic growth is imperative. This requires a step to be taken towards much closer economic and political cooperation, for which the members of the Eurozone are not yet ready, whether ideologically, politically or technically.

Those responsible for the management of the Eurozone and the EU showcase their efforts in ensuring fiscal discipline and monitoring the economies of the member states. This has indeed been extensive. But, as Jacques Delors observed, given the overlapping complexity of the European Semester, the Six Pack, the Two Pack, the Fiscal Pact, the European Pact, the Growth Pact, the 'rescue' mechanisms and the regulations of the ECB, 'who is in a position to understand, let alone administer the system?' Who can deduce with any certainty where it will finally lead the EU?[7]

The conditions prevailing up to 2004, when the EU was enlarged, have changed. The Union is in a 'process of transition'. The following are the features of this new period: changes in the international environment and

China's leading role in the global economy; the international financial crisis and the sovereign debt crisis that destabilised the banking system, with no end to the anxiety and uncertainty in sight; the omissions and imperfections present in the EMU system; the yawning gap between the Core and the Periphery; the enlargement of the EU to 28 member states, which do not possess the homogeneity of the original group of members; and the emergence of Germany as the major political and economic power of the Union. The new conditions created new dynamics and tendencies in the European structure. The efforts to introduce new rules, especially with regard to economic cooperation, led to increasingly hostile reactions against the transfer of power from member states to the centre. Political unification is questioned.[8] The roles of the European Commission and the Council of Ministers for General Affairs have been watered down. The European Council has emerged as the central player and the European Parliament has acquired a more pronounced presence. As a consequence, the balance in the institutional triangle of the Commission–Council–Parliament has been altered. The Franco-German axis has become the lever for European policy formation and, despite the obvious disagreements between the two countries, it will continue to have a decisive influence. Informal groupings of member states with special interests have materialised. Nevertheless, despite increasing Euroscepticism and the reactions against austerity policies being implemented by the Union, the conviction that there is a need for a unified, strong and effective authority has prevailed.

The conviction that the European project is not just about the achievement of a single monetary and economic area also remains strong. United Europe constitutes a much broader project. It is framed by the coexistence of the peoples of Europe over centuries, their common experiences and the interaction of their cultures, their related ways of life and the organisation of their societies. It derives from their common values and established practices of cooperation, but also from the painful experience of wars and obscurantism. It is connected to a nexus of principles where democracy, personal liberty, respect for the individual, education and widening knowledge play a primary role. This project concerns the need for common action and the inevitability of a shared future, in an ever-changing globalised world in which new possibilities have an increasingly determining presence.

The euro is not, therefore, the result only of economic assessment; nor was it imposed by the markets to subjugate people to their designs. It was a politically necessary step to expand common activity, to abolish constraints and national boundaries, to create economic stability and growth. It was a goal of the predecessors of the EU long before discussions over the purpose and the form the monetary union had begun.[9]

European unification is all the more necessary because of globalisation, which has greatly expanded the ability of markets to guide and determine policy. The balance of power between markets and politics has tipped steadily in favour of markets. The Greek crisis is a classic example. The markets forced the euro area to bail out Greece by continually raising interest rates so that it could no longer borrow from the banks. Greece received funding of €110 billion, precisely the sum it owed to the Eurozone banks. Once that was done, the Eurogroup was extremely slow to act on the European debt crisis. It then believed that the basic problem, that of Greece, had been resolved and there was no pressing need for further decisions.

The current global climate necessitates mechanisms for monitoring the international markets, rules to clamp down on international speculation and central political authorities that are in a position to impose on the markets behaviour that will protect the shared interests of the public. Political union is imperative.

Dealing with the economic problems of the EU is, for this reason, integrally linked to the understanding of the political logic that underpins it. The measures to control the crisis, the common fiscal rules and the common framework for drawing up budgets must be understood and implemented in conjunction with the broader pursuit of a common course. The obligations every member state assumed through its participation, as well as the rights it acquired, are tied to the commitment for mutual solidarity, and the pursuit of the Union's common interest. The EU is neither a club where only the select have a say, nor an amalgamation of states governed by orders from an authority with superpowers.[10] It is a collective project espousing liberty, growth and adjustment to the new international conditions.

The Cyprus crisis, in March 2013, rekindled doubts over whether the Eurozone can survive in its present form. It showed that the way it operates continues to pose a risk to its cohesion and its orderly operation, despite all the measures that have been taken.[11]

The first feature to note is that the currency union increases the danger of a credit crisis. The less competitive economies of the South incur external deficits. In order to maintain their standards of living and levels of employment, these states are obliged to resort to excessive spending, through both their private and their public sectors. To acquire the necessary funds, they borrow from the international markets. The markets cease lending as soon as they ascertain that they risk not being paid back the loans they grant. The consequence is a crisis in state finances, as was the case in Greece and Portugal, or a crisis in the banking sector, as in Spain or Cyprus.

The second feature to note is that, as already mentioned in the case of Greece, the common interest rate of the Eurozone was far lower than the interest rate existing previously in the South. The historically low interest rate and the abundant supply of money triggered asset price bubbles and credit booms in peripheral economies. The Eurozone structure encourages the North to lend excessively to the South. This phenomenon, together with the South's reduced competitiveness, contributes to a widening of the gap between them.

The third feature to note is that, had the countries currently finding themselves in crisis maintained their own currency they would have been able to devalue it in order to restore competitiveness and growth within a few years. This is not possible any more. States in crisis must implement a strict austerity policy and extensive structural changes for a very long time. It must, however, be noted that devaluation does not prevent a growth-reducing fiscal tightening. Without tightening, inflation will erode the devaluation. Up till now, this has resulted in recession, social unrest, the growth of support for political forces rebelling against participation in the Eurozone, a loss of credibility and the possibility of a decade of economic stagnation. The deepening economic contraction in southern Europe has not been addressed in a persuasive way. Major policy measures concerning southern member states are not yet on the agenda. The tackling of the root causes of the crisis is still necessary. The difference in levels of growth between the Centre and the Periphery of the Union 'threatens the integrity and perhaps the existence of the euro'.[12] The Eurozone is an achievement which, for economic, social and political reasons, cannot be reversed. A return to different currencies is neither useful nor possible.

The fourth feature to note, as the international press highlights, is that the 'Eurozone remains stuck in a horrific mess'.[13] The case of Cyprus certified the 'unbelievable difficulty, not to say the impossibility of managing a currency zone in which economies as diverse as Germany and Cyprus belong'.[14]

> If austerity in the South had at least been compensated by fiscal expansion in the North, the overall fiscal stance of the Eurozone would have been, in macro-economic terms, neutral. But since the North joined the drive for austerity instead, the Eurozone ended up in recession.[15]

The view has gained ground that there will be new crises in the Eurozone; the Eurozone will limp through crisis after crisis.[16] The reasons for this are: the lack of stability which is caused by divergent levels of development; the absence of a common fiscal policy; the failure to implement strong centralised supervision of banks; the absence of a central bank as lender of last resort; and the continual recourse to provisional solutions, stop-gap measures that delay the necessary comprehensive solution. The continual eruption of crises has eroded confidence. Investments are not realised; capital flights occur. Incentives for higher spending and production have become meaningless. The preconditions for a swift recovery do not exist. The European Commission insists on one-sided contractionary adjustment. The possibility of an export-led solution is limited because all countries are imposing a policy of austerity simultaneously. The competitiveness of economic drivers such as Italy and France is eroding.

The fifth feature to note is the increasing difficulty in adapting the existing EU structure to the new realities. A series of innovations and new rules were decided in response to the crisis. The members of the Eurozone accepted more governance, a stricter coordination of national and EU policies, as a form of crisis management. The initiatives they took changed the existing euro regime but did not replace it with a new one that was easier to manage. It became increasingly complex and difficult to handle. There is lack of clarity. The 'rebuilding of Europe' proved 'messy'. Moreover, the main characteristic of the new situation is 'an increasing legal, institutional and policy divide between euro-area and non-euro-area member states', with rules that vary from case to case.[17]

Finally, it should be noted that, while economic maladies dominate the debate, the problem facing the Eurozone is primarily a political one. At the same time, the steps towards unification that have been made so far have created new conditions, new dynamics and new problems which require novel solutions. The countries of the EU at present seem unable to overcome their differences; they try to postpone solutions, or else they proceed with limited adjustments. The tension between national policies and European international economic and political interdependence has increased. A clear vision must be developed of the desired course of the EU and the EMU, and a plan for their renewal must be articulated and implemented without hesitation or delay.[18] Otherwise, the current system will become more and more dysfunctional, increasing the risk of a meltdown.[19]

What is needed is a new way for the Union to function. The primary issues requiring a solution are twofold. The first – over which there has been extensive debate – concerns the governance of the EMU, commonly referred to as 'economic governance'. The second concerns how to deal with the imbalances across the Union, so that the EU can also function for the benefit of the weaker states, sharing prosperity among its various regions. This has not aroused the same extensive interest as the first. Its key challenges are summarised below under the heading 'Inclusion and participation'.

## A. Economic governance

In the statement issued after the Eurozone summit in July 2011, a chapter on 'economic and fiscal coordination' was included. Various measures were mentioned related to drawing up the budgets of member states, observing the rules imposed by the EU and the supervision which must be exercised over fiscal matters by the European Commission. It was also announced that the economic pillar of the EMU would be enhanced, especially the coordination of macro- and microeconomic policies. Finally, one paragraph was devoted to the 'structure of the Eurozone's governance'. Its main points were the institutionalisation of regular summits and how the presidency of the Eurozone and its auxiliary organs should function. This was a noteworthy event: such a detailed reference to matters of the Eurozone's governance had never appeared in earlier texts.

References to the need for economic governance at a European level, and how to organise it, were the exception at the beginning of 2009. The term 'economic governance', proposed by France, was not liked because it implied intervention in the markets.[20] Gradually, however, with the measures the Union had started to take in order to deal with the financial crisis, the term 'economic governance' came to be increasingly used. The first decisions regarding direct state support for the banking sector, after the financial crisis of 2007, were presented as steps towards economic governance. The term was attractive because it denoted that the members of the EMU were abandoning the perception that interventions in the economy were not needed and they were taking the necessary initiatives to confront the crisis.

From the texts of the European Council, the European Parliament and the Eurozone summits, it appears that 'economic governance' constitutes a descriptive umbrella term for the regulation of primarily fiscal matters and the implementation of commitments made by the member states to fiscal discipline. It does not describe a governance structure, its powers and its objectives. It does not refer to a design for handling the Union's economic matters. Although the texts hint at the existence of such a design, they desist from describing it. They continually underline the need for cooperation, for collective effort in fighting the crisis and for fiscal discipline. The measures proposed, however, appear as exceptional interventions. Genuine economic governance cannot be reactive, a temporary or forced response in the face of difficulty. Its implementation presumes sufficient political will for a new structure of governance which will complement – even modify – existing structures. It also presumes clarification of the issues over which it will expand its mandate, beyond fiscal discipline, to growth and social policy.

Since July 2011, various proposals for the establishment of a new structure to handle economic and political matters have been made. The President of the ECB, Jean-Claude Trichet, proposed that the European Council should have the right to veto decisions of member states, should they endanger the Eurozone's economic stability. He also proposed establishing a 'European Finance Ministry'.[21] Its remit would be to track economic developments and to impose decisions deemed necessary, to oversee the financial sector and, lastly, to represent the Eurozone in international institutions.

Close to Trichet's proposals, but less demanding in terms of Treaty reform, is the view that the ECB should undertake the role of lender of last resort when banks cease to lend to a member state. The ECB should have comparable powers to those of the Bank of England and the US Federal Reserve in being able to judge and decide whether and when to adjust liquidity flows. This would make it easier to handle crises. However, the Treaties have ruled out ceding such extensive powers to the ECB. Their authors believed that such a regulation would very probably fuel inflation, and push the ECB to an accumulation of losses, which the member states would be called upon to pay in the end.

The Spinelli Group, a federalist network of senior Europeans, presented a plan for economic governance in October 2011 and a revised version in June 2012. The main points of this plan included a restructuring of the European Commission and the designation of one of its members as Minister for the Economy in the Eurozone, to head a group of Commissioners responsible for governance in the Eurozone'.[22] Current practice – in which the member states of the Eurozone handle various matters principally through the Eurogroup, on the basis of intergovernmental cooperation – is, according to the Spinelli Group, the source of indecision and delay. If it becomes possible for a single centre to deal with all facets of economic governance, within the context of the European Commission, quick reactions and continuity will be achieved. The success in promoting the single market in the 1980s was due, according to the Spinelli Group, to the Commission functioning as a single centre of decision-making.

The need for single leadership should be stressed. However, a precondition for assigning to the Commission such a position of leadership is a change of attitudes of the major member states of the EU, which see the Commission as a subordinate organ. They downgrade its role and restrict its participation in shaping the Union's policy. A consequence of this stand is that they usually propose as Commissioners people who have neither the vision nor the ability to lead European cooperation. They are politicians who, in their countries, have either completed the cycle of their careers or have only limited prospects for assuming government positions. When the leading powers have such a stand vis-à-vis the European Commission, economic governance will encounter difficulties very quickly.

In a study undertaken by J. Arthuis, commissioned by the French government,[23] the solution to the Union's problem of economic governance was understood to lie in a concentration of powers. This would put an end to the phenomenon of different decision-making centres which concur in neither their announcements nor their policies. It proposes the establishment of the office of President of Europe, who will be President of the European Council and President of the European Commission at the same time. It is argued that this will achieve better guidance and coordination between the two circles that shape European policy, the Council and the Commission. At the same time, there must be a Finance Minister for the Eurozone, who will chair the Eurogroup, the Council of finance ministers of the 28 states (Ecofin), and who will be the Commissioner responsible for economic and monetary matters across the entire Union, as well as all issues relating to the euro. The Euro Working Group, which consists of the representatives of the Eurozone's finance ministers, must acquire a stable infrastructure, with its own experts and its own departments, so as to exercise the management controls at its disposal, such as the European Semester. It will constitute the Secretariat General of the Minister of Finance, headed by a Secretary who will chair the Euro Working Group. The decisions of the institutions of the EU and the Eurozone will be debated and voted on in national parliaments only if they concern the general context of policy. Partial measures, such as those established to control each country's budget, will not be examined by national parliaments.

The European Parliament has a limited policy role. This leads to the perennial questions concerning democratic legitimacy. The European Parliament decided that regular sessions be held of the chairs of economic committees of the national parliaments and the corresponding chairs of the European Parliament, as a way to confront the problem. The establishment of a 'Commission to supervise the Euro',[24] in which approximately 100 members of national parliaments and an equal number of members of the European Parliament would take part, has also been proposed. This Commission would have an oversight remit and serve as a record for proposals and reactions relating to the policies of European institutions. However, it would not have legislative powers. There are also more radical proposals. Among others,[25] the Spinelli Group proposes that the competence of the European Parliament should be greater, commensurate with that of the parliaments of member states, so that the policy matrix can be constructed and legitimated, in the model of electoral democracy found within the member states.

The Chancellor of Germany, Angela Merkel, in repeated statements, maintained that the mission of her generation is to complete the EMU. In her view, the path to a political union also determines the necessary initiatives for shaping economic governance. Fiscal discipline, compliance of every state's fiscal policy with common rules and the related controls over the members' budgets are not an end in themselves but preconditions for economic stability and the efficient functioning of the EMU's policy, free of problems. She herself described her goal as follows:

> In the course of a long process we shall transfer more and more competences to the European Commission, which will become the government of the Union. It shall exercise the powers assigned to it. This arrangement requires a strong Parliament. The European Council, made up of Heads of State and Prime Ministers will constitute the Upper House. Lastly, the European Court will be the Supreme Court.[26]

This schematic description presents the structure of the institutions of a European federation. The main problem is not, however, what institutions will exist in the political union. The main problems are the causes of the crisis: the difference in levels of growth; the functioning of the EMU to the benefit of certain countries; and the lack of democratic legitimacy in decisions made by the central authority. It comes down to the inclusion and participation of all members in a common effort, without overlooking their particularities, while at the same time implementing common goals.

At the beginning of August 2012, the German Social Democrats presented an approach which differed from that proposed by Merkel.[27] They deemed that the crisis did not come about because of wrong behaviour at the national level, but that it was mainly due to problems with the European economic/monetary system. Coping with it was not, therefore, possible by member states, each acting within its own jurisdiction. A systemic answer was necessary. From the development of the crisis so far, it appears that the only appropriate way of dealing with it is through the 'mutualisation of responsibility for the repayment of bonds of the Eurozone countries'. This is the way, they argued, to overcome or significantly restrict the risk of a member state not being able to meet its obligations. Collective responsibility must be accompanied by strict EU control of national budgets and fiscal policy. The supervision of fiscal policy is to be carried out by supranational institutions, not by individual national governments on the basis of pre-agreed rules. The *collective* responsibility will extend only to the portion of the debt that does not exceed 60% of GDP, that is to say, the maximum ratio stipulated in the Treaties. Germany must assume the initiative of setting up a European Constitutional Convention, which will propose the necessary amendments to the Treaties. Its findings must be approved by referenda in the member states: 'The peoples of Europe must unite their forces, if they want to continue influencing global developments. Abandoning European unification would mean exiting world history.'

Two observations are useful in evaluating this proposal. Mutualisation of responsibility does not in itself constitute a solution. The proposed mutualisation is not a sufficient measure in its own right unless it is combined with other policies that will prevent the explosion of the public deficit debt and will provide for timely control.[28] However, the proposal on the table is not open-ended. It is not the same as the eurobonds without any limitations that Greece had asked for. The setting up of a European Constitutional Convention has also been proposed by parties of the European Parliament. However, the follow-up – holding referenda in all the countries of the Eurozone – presents problems which emanate from the crisis. As shown by long experience, citizens would not express their view of the plan for a new Treaty in the referendum, but their view on their government's current overall policy. The new Treaty would most likely be rejected, especially by the countries of the North, where many begrudge their commitment to financing the South. Other paths must be constructed if unification is to advance.

At the European summit of 29 June 2012, the President presented a report entitled 'Towards a genuine economic and monetary union'.[29] Its main focus was how to deal with the problems of economic governance. The review presented 'a vision for a stable and prosperous EMU based on four essential building blocks'.[30]

The first of these four blocks is an 'integrated financial framework'. The crisis brought to the fore serious deficiencies in the way the EU functions, and the banking system was at the core of these. In certain countries, such as Spain and Ireland, the banks did not exercise due diligence in their transactions. The risk of bankruptcy obliged their governments to support them, which, in turn, affected the solvency of those states. To avoid repeating such phenomena, the 'current architecture should evolve as soon as possible towards a single European banking supervision system with a European and a national level'.[31] At the same time, a European system of guaranteeing deposits must be established. The credibility of any deposits system requires the establishment of a mechanism capable of restoring banks to health and protecting depositors.

Lastly, the ESM must constitute the lender of last resort for the support of the financial system.

The second building block of the new system is an 'integrated budgetary framework': common rules for the fiscal policy of all the member states of the Eurozone so as to constitute a fiscal union. This would serve to ensure a consistent structural environment, through a system of mutual guarantees. The report proposes, among other things, setting limits on budget deficits and debt. In the event of a breach of the agreed limit, a state's borrowing through the issue of bonds 'must be supported by a reasoned case and be subject to prior approval'. In the medium term, the issue of eurobonds could be examined. This goal must be achieved through a gradual process. It requires a strong framework for fiscal discipline, common guidelines for drawing up budgets and a framework of collectively acceptable conditions for the mutualisation of risks.

The third building block is a unified framework for economic policy. The report notes that stronger economic integration is required. However, no proposals are presented on this. It refers to principles set out in previous decisions made by the EU, in the form of the Euro Plus Pact and in the European Semester.

The last building block in the report touches on the issue of democratic legitimacy and accountability. It notes – correctly – that it is of particular importance to achieve 'public support for European-wide decisions with a far-reaching impact on the everyday lives of citizens'. It does not, however, mention ways in which this can be achieved. It states only that 'Close involvement of the European parliament and national parliaments will be central'.[32]

The report concludes with the observation that 'Further work is necessary to develop a specific and time-bound road map for the achievement of the genuine Economic and Monetary Union'. The authors said they would continue to consult with the member states and the institutions of the EU.[33]

The report adopts the tenets of German policy to a great extent. It accepts the Fiscal Compact, the need for fiscal discipline and the application of a more or less uniform fiscal policy throughout the Eurozone. At the same time, however, it goes in step with the French view that, up to a point, the member states must share responsibility in securing funds and it tentatively suggests 'eurobonds'. This is an attempt to reach a compromise, which aroused intense reactions in Germany. On the matter of how economic governance should be exercised, the authors of the report did not commit themselves, evidently because they did not want to upset the existing balance between the European Council and the European Commission. The continuation of consultations, which they proposed themselves, was inevitable.

A different approach to the problem of 'the single supranational currency and the simultaneous existence of economic policies determined by each state' was presented in the report of the Tommaso Padoa-Schioppa Group.[34] That report proposed political initiatives in four areas:

1  The single-market project must continue, and be advanced, so as to minimise price divergence across the EU. The single rate of interest will therefore cease to function as a factor fuelling inflation and increasing debt levels in less competitive areas.

2  The second initiative bears on the way to deal with the consequences of a single monetary policy and, in particular, with the fact that member states do not have the option of devaluing their currency. The establishment of an insurance fund would be useful. It would help in dealing with the effects of crises – especially with the inevitable internal devaluation – with supplementary income support, where income had fallen and unemployment risen. The insurance fund's revenue would derive from contributions made by states when their rate of growth exceeds the average rate in the Eurozone.

3  The third initiative concerns stricter supervision of the member states' fiscal policy. States that no longer have access to the markets must lose some autonomy. The establishment of a European Debt Authority is proposed, which would ensure financing for states facing debt problems, in exchange for control of their economic policies. The extent of financing would determine the degree of autonomy surrendered. If debt exceeds 60% of GDP, as in the case of Greece, the Authority would control the budget and public spending.

4  The fourth initiative is aimed at a banking union, and the establishment of central supervision over the Eurozone's banks.

The review concluded that these changes require a 'new institutional and legal structure'.

In May 2013, the French President, François Hollande, presented his 'initiative for Europe'.[35] His first aim, he stated, was to enhance the economic governance of the Eurozone 'through the appointment of a real President with a long term of office'. The element of 'economic governance' here concerned 'the main decisions of the member states' economic policies'; the President's office 'shall seek to promote social cohesion and shall implement a plan to combat tax evasion'. Hollande included youth unemployment, energy policy, investments and a rise in the EU budget in the matters he stated needed to be dealt with. This statement of vague generalities was construed as an invitation to Germany for discussions, without rejecting out of hand German views on an extensive change of the Treaties and the establishment of a political union.

From the various proposals, it emerges beyond doubt that change in the functioning of the EMU is imperative. There is agreement in certain directions, such as the need for a banking union. But there are serious disagreements over other matters, such as eurobonds. A new way of exercising economic governance is deemed desirable, but views differ on what is to be done. It is generally agreed that results will be slow to emerge, but action is urgent.

At the end of August 2012, the finance ministers of Germany and France set up a task force to formulate common views on the Union's response to these serious challenges.[36] This move was considered the first step towards a common effort in designing the necessary reforms.

The discussion of economic governance has brought the matter of the legitimacy of the European authorities to the fore again. Currently, European policy-makers are selected by the governments of the member states in procedures where neither the European Parliament nor citizens have any say. Those selected are answerable only to the European Council and through it to the governments of the member states. The selection and accountability of those responsible are therefore undertaken by a small, closed circle. However, an economic government whose decisions determine the lives of citizens should be selected in open, democratic procedures and be answerable to the representatives of the EU's citizens. This will ensure greater acceptance of policies and help counter the public indifference which is observable today.

Certain of the above proposals for the establishment of economic governance would provide for a more representative European Parliament, and one that would exert more control over policy-making. However, the idea of granting the Parliament powers commensurate with those enjoyed by national parliaments has yet to mature. The member states are not yet prepared to cede a substantial part of their sovereignty to European organs. Furthermore, the citizens of each state do not wish to take on additional commitments so as to make the EU function better or to help other states.

## B. Inclusion and participation

The dominant view in the EMU is that the remedy to the problems of growth and of the narrowing of the gap between North and South rests upon market (particularly labour market) reform and structural adjustment. The market will then be able to restore the necessary equilibria on its own. When it comes to tackling backwardness in certain areas, such as infrastructure and small and medium-size enterprises, the Union has instituted the financing of certain activities on the basis of programmes submitted by the member states themselves.

The policy of using the automatic mechanisms of the market to even out levels of development across the EMU has not had the expected results. It is generally accepted that, from 2000 onwards, Europe has been in a state of stagnation. It was not in a position to achieve rates of growth that would ensure employment and prosperity in both the North and the South.

At an earlier stage, the European Commission had supported the view[37] that programmes are needed to promote the development of European infrastructure, such as transport and energy grids, so as to enhance economic activity, in both the Core of the Union and the Periphery. The matter of finance could be solved in various ways, either through taxing financial transactions, or through the issue of bonds. The newly elected President of France, Hollande, supported the view that, beyond a pillar for stability, the Union's economic policy also required a pillar for growth.[38]

This view was not acceptable to the European Commission and various countries. They maintained that the cost of common development programmes for the whole of the Union would be excessive. Each country would have to decide for itself, on the basis of market conditions, what development action it required. The European Commission also rejected plans for a steady increase in financing for research and development, and the allocation of research activity to more countries, with collective coordination. It was 2010 before a programme (Europe 2020), of questionable value, was formulated with the aim of improving competitiveness.[39]

A third way to combat economic disparities is to enhance demand in the markets of North Europe, so that exports from the South can grow. Such a move will lead to a slight increase in the rate of inflation in the North, perhaps to 3%, but such a side-effect is preferable to continual recession in the South.

The ECB and the countries of the North expressed strong objections to increasing demand in the North through inflation. They felt that such a solution would constitute a violation of the Treaties. The founding agreement of the ECB determined that the bank should keep inflation below 2%. Even a small exception could lead to all hell breaking loose.

Research shows, however, that the current model of a steady low rate of inflation in the North and a restrictive policy in the South is of no value in terms of improving the health of the South.[40] When the debt of a country of the South exceeds a certain level, the situation fails to improve – it deteriorates, as exemplified by the case of Greece. Monetary policy must therefore seek to contain debt, by creating a favourable environment for the exports of the South and the services it has to offer. The acceptance of a higher rate of inflation in the North would be a powerful means for strengthening the South. Inflation increases demand in the North, and extends to the goods and services of the South.[41] Fears over dangerous rates of inflation returning, should deflationary policy be even slightly relaxed, are, as the latest developments have shown, unfounded.[42]

It has been demonstrated that neither deflation nor inflation immediately follows changes in economic policy. This delay has various causes, including a temporal cycle of business estimates concerning economic prospects and monetary policy. The delay permits a more flexible policy to be adopted. The ECB can risk a reduction in contractionary policy without running the danger of immediate inflation. It is also possible 'to aim for the highest levels of economic activity consistent with stable inflation'.

A different approach to overcoming the problem of different levels of development was presented by M. Wolf, the well known *Financial Times* columnist.[43] He proposed the coordination of two activities. The first would consist of a supranational insurance for the member states. Its funds would derive from premiums paid in by the member states themselves. The organisation responsible for managing the system would provide targeted support for countries that have suffered a severe economic blow, provided certain conditions were satisfied. The second initiative would aim at ensuring conditions for the member states that would restrict the possibility of crises occurring and would control their consequences. Every country of the Eurozone would be obliged, according to economic circumstances, either to take stabilisation measures, such as cutting state expenses, or to increase demand, and thus exports from the ailing countries. The combination of these two policies would ensure a more permanent control of recession in vulnerable countries.

The European Council held on 29 June 2012 decided, following efforts by the French President,[44] to mobilise approximately €120 billion for immediate growth initiatives. Of this, €10 billion would be new funding. This would be used to increase the European Investment Bank's capital. The rest of the funds would come from: Structural Funds which were stagnant (€55 billion); the floating of project-related bonds for the construction of infrastructure projects (€5 billion); and from loans to the European Investment Bank (€50 billion). This was a careful step completing the ongoing policy, but not a striking turn. The comments from the press were negative; the verdict was 'much ado about nothing'.[45] The same applied to the Growth and Employment Pact, which was presented and approved at the summit in order to counterbalance the negative impression made by the Fiscal Compact. It contains generalities and repetitions. The media did not pay any attention to it.

An apparently simple solution to combat regional disparities in the EU would be a change in the Treaty that would provide for permanent financial transfers to member states. A common euro-area budget could provide a significant transfer of resources to 'countries that are affected by severe recession for a number of years; or in order to help combat unemployment or to finance important investment projects'.[46] However, the experience of the crisis years suggests that even small transfers presuppose long debates. The decision-making process will not be able to deliver results under existing circumstances. The necessary condition for such a system to work is federal decision-making with political union.

In any case, the procedures followed in deciding and applying the stabilisation policy have to change. The stabilisation policy was shaped by continuous negotiations involving the European Commission, the Eurozone and a series of decisions taken by national parliaments. These negotiations inevitably sparked friction between donor and recipient countries, mutual accusations and a climate of intense nationalism. In Greece, hostility towards Germans rose sharply, while in Germany friendliness towards Greeks turned into disdain. Any post-Memorandum stabilisation efforts in the countries of the Periphery will have to be implemented by different means. Transfers of EU funds must be part of a broader policy designed to limit direct negotiations and clashes among the member states.

In Greece and other countries there is support, mainly from the left, for a different European structure, which would allow every state to implement the policy it chooses. Detail about how this can happen is lacking. This is a revival of the ideology of the absolute autonomy of the nation state. Every country would be in a position to implement the socio-economic system of its choice.

In today's globalised world, economic, social and political ties between states have become irrevocably entwined; a return to complete autonomy is no longer possible for any country of the Union. Symbiosis, cooperation, policy coordination and common targets are a pressing necessity. In the EU's current context the problem is not one of regaining lost autonomy but the formulation of a common European policy fit for modern boundary-transcending conditions and which at the same time responds to the needs and particularities of the peoples of the Union. This is about devising ways to cooperate on a European level: making it possible to adjust to the demands and values of citizens, to combine efficiency with market control, growth with greater equity and the democratic set-up with meaningful participation. What is being sought is a policy for the European polity, in the supranational era, which will both take account of the particularities of every member state and secure the attainment of common goals.[47]

Economic governance and permanent measures to deal with crises require, in any case, amendment of the Treaties. However, the political will to effect such a change does not exist on the part of either politicians or citizens. The last major reform was the Lisbon Treaty, finalised in 2009. It was the result of long negotiations, involved the rejection of a European constitution and produced ferocious confrontations over almost a decade. The transfer of powers by member states to the Union's institutions is inevitable, but comes up against intense reactions, especially in the smaller countries and those that do not belong to the Eurozone. Even though citizens want economic unification to proceed, they do not accept a supranational economic authority that would decide on matters for their country, ignoring the views of their own governments and parliaments. They take the view that European policy restricts member states in their efforts to respond to the needs of their citizens. It focuses on the free functioning of the market and not on correcting the consequences of market failure. Social justice consequently suffers. Democracy also suffers. Moreover, the complex decision-making process and the large number of participants in policy-making limit the possibility of state intervention or of effecting a change of policy.

To overcome the current distancing of the public from European problems, the banking union or the European Parliament's participation in decision-making are not enough. Jacques Delors used to say 'people do not fall in love with a single market'.[48] Ideas and proposals are needed that will generate a broader mobilisation for European unification in every country. We must determine and explain what future we are aiming at.[49] We must convince the citizens that in the era of globalisation we will not be able to face competition from the USA, China and other states with populations of hundreds of millions if we insist on fragmentation, mini-states, national egocentrism and a solitary course on the part of every state. Our continent's history, with its continual wars, hegemonic aspirations and nationalist excess clouds an understanding of 'a common narrative for the future'.[50] But, without it, we will be unable to maintain and improve our common way of life, with its liberties, opportunities and values.

In seeking a new framework for the functioning of the EU, we must not begin by asking whether we aim at a federation, or confederation, or some other model of common action.[51] European unification will not be achieved by adopting historic examples of federation, such as Germany or the USA. The post-national reality of the EU has already drafted a multilayered, supra-national structure of governance. However, the current form does not constitute the final framework. Under circumstantial pressure, member states continue to cede sovereignty and to adopt new rules affecting autonomy and cooperation. The most striking example of this constantly evolving situation is the system of assistance to members facing an economic crisis. It was constructed as a succession of decisions made over a period of three years, despite the silence of the Treaties on the relevant issues and despite the principle that every state is responsible only for its own debt.

Political union can be achieved only gradually. Economic governance is a step towards enhancing cooperation, testing ways of resolving differences over policies to be implemented and broadening the democratic accountability of Eurozone institutions by strengthening the role and decision-making powers of the European Parliament.[52] The experiences acquired in the process will make it possible to design the next step with a far greater degree of success.

Many commentators on recent developments of the EU have supported a gradualist approach to new forms of cooperation.[53] Despite the differences in their reasoning, they agree that exiting the crisis will involve 'escaping forwards', that is, in the direction of stronger economic governance and political union. That is the goal we must pursue seriously and insistently. The Greek problem was not an unfortunate happening in the forward march of the Union, not a deviation that overturned a well designed project. It was the catalyst that showed up the weaknesses of how the EU had been functioning, that showed up the need to remodel its institutions, so that it does not fall short of the broader role it is being called upon to assume.

**Notes**

1  J. Pisani-Fery, *The Known Unknowns and Unknowns Unknowns of the EMU*, Policy Contribution 2012/18, Bruegel, October 2012, p. 64.

2  G. Serman, 'Courtermisme', *Le Monde*, 13 July 2012.

3  See article of the European Union Treaty of 12 December 2007.

4  See N. Karamouzis, 'The Eurozone crisis, causes and prospects', *Kathimerini*, 27 November 2011, p. 7. The German Sachverständigenrat (Council of Economic Experts) has reviewed the causes of the crisis from the German point of view. See 'Euroraum in der Krise', in *Jahresgutachten 2011–2012*, Sachverständigenrat, 2012.

5  *IHT*, 25–26 August 2012, p. 12.

6  See P. Lamy, 'Setting up and governing the euro', *Notre Europe*, 10 July 2012.

7  See J. Delors, 'Fear not, we will get there!', *Notre Europe*, 28 June 2013, p. 2, available at www.eng.notre-europe.eu/011-16309-Fear-not-we-will-get-there.html.

8  The existing tensions in the Eurozone are due to two problems that have not yet been resolved. First, what is the price that Core countries are willing to pay to save the euro? That price will reflect the degree to which governments can reconcile external expectations and pressures with domestic sensitivities. Second, how much adjustment are countries of the Periphery willing or able to make in a short space of time? The EU needs answers to those questions that are consistent with each other. L. Tsoukalis, 'We need a new grand bargain in Europe', *Zeitschrift für internationale Beziehungen*, vol. 20, issue 1, June 2013, pp. 125–32.

9  See M. Walser, 'Das richtige Europa', *FAZ*, 21 August 2012, p. 25.

10  Ibid.

11  See M. Wolf, 'Cyprus adds to European confusion', *Financial Times*, 27 March 2013; M. Wolf, 'Why the Irish crisis is such a huge test for the Eurozone', *Financial Times*, ft.com, 30 November 2012; H. Dixon, 'A union that exists in name only', *IHT*, 1 April 2013; W. Munchau, 'The break-up of the Eurozone is even closer', *Financial Times*, 25 March 2013; 'Chypre, le sauvetage qui fragilise la zone euro', *Le Monde*, 19 March 2013; P. Krugman, 'Treasure island trauma', *IHT*, 23/24 March 2013.

12  Z. Darvas, *The Euro Crisis: Ten Roots, But Fewer Solutions*, Policy Contribution 2012/17, Bruegel, 2012, p. 11.

13  M. Wolf, *Financial Times*, 27 March 2013.

14  *Le Monde*, 26 March 2013.

15  W. Munchau, *Financial Times*, 25 March 2013.

16  See M. Wolf, *Financial Times*, 27 March 2013; M. Wolf, 'Why the euro crisis is not yet over', *Financial Times*, ft.com, 19 February 2013.

17  See Jean Pisani-Ferry, André Sapir and Guntram Wolff, *The Messy Rebuilding of Europe*, Policy Brief 2012/01, Bruegel, 2012.

18  The President of the Eurogroup, J. Dijsselbloom, the Vice President of the European Commission, O. Rehn, an executive board member of the European Central Bank, J. Asmussen, the managing director of the European Stability Mechanism, K. Regling, and the President of the European Investment Bank, W. Hoyer, in a common article ('Europe is responding', *New York Times*, nytimes.com, 18 April 2013) maintained that 'the Eurozone has shown a degree of resilience and problem-solving capacity that many observers and policy makers would not have predicted a year ago'. Five major reforms are under way. (1) The Eurozone finance ministers 'are undertaking major adjustments to consolidate national budgets and improve competitiveness'. (2) New economic policy rules to strengthen the foundations of the EMU have been agreed. (3) The ECB 'has taken successful actions to address the fragmentation of financial markets'. (4) Europe has created effective financial backstops that can be deployed to support countries under intense market pressure, the EFSF and the ESM. (5) All EU countries participated in a €10 billion capital increase of the European Investment Bank, which will significantly increase its lending activities. 'Europe has responded to adversity by moving closer together and deepening integration.'

19  P. Bofinger, *Zurück zur D-Mark?*, Droemer HC, 2012, p. 170.

20 The announcement of the European Commission of 12 May 2010 (COM/2010, 250 final) contains, under the title 'Enhancement of coordination of economic policy', a review of measures for coordination and control that were then in use. The term 'economic governance' was not used.

21 See Bofinger, *Zurück zur D-Mark?*, p. 141.

22 The plans may be found at www.spinelligroup.eu.

23 J. Arthuis, *Rapport, Avenir de la Zone Euro: L'intégration politique ou le chaos*, Premier ministre, March 2012.

24 Ibid., p. 62, 'Euro Supervision Commission'.

25 See K. Guerot and R. Menasse, 'Es lebe die europäische Republik', *FAZ*, 28 March 2003.

26 See 'Le grand dessin de Angela Merkel', *Le Monde*, 8–9 July 2012, p. 13. For the German conservative view on the matter of European unification see: K. Wilhelm, *FAZ*, 7 July 2012; P. Kirchhof, 'Verfassungsnot', *FAZ*, 12 July 2012; O. Hoffe, 'Souverän ist wer über Verstand verfügt', *FAZ*, 10 August 2012.

27 S. Gabriel, J. Habermas, J. Nida-Rumelin and P. Bofinger, 'Einspruch gegen die Fassadendemokratie', *FAZ*, 4 August 2012, p. 33. Gabriel is the President of the German Social Democratic Party; the other authors are among the best-known German intellectuals. See also K. Bursch, C. Hermann, K. Hinrichs and Th. Schulten, *Euro Crisis, Austerity Policy and the European Social Model*, Friedrich Ebert Stiftung, February 2013.

28 See the section 'Inclusion and participation' in this chapter.

29 EUCO 120/12, Presse 296, 26 June 2012. The report had been drawn up by the President of the European Commission, the President of the Eurogroup and the President of the ECB, on orders from the Council.

30 Ibid., p. 3.

31 Ibid., p. 4.

32 Ibid., pp. 6, 7.

33 Ibid., p. 7. An updated report by H. Van Rompuy, J. M. Barroso, J. C. Juncker and M. Draghi was presented at the summit of December 2012. See N. Veron, *The Challenges of Europe's Fourfold Union*, Policy Contribution 2012/13, Bruegel, August 2012. According to Veron, 'the only way to resolve the crisis successfully is a sustainable effort to achieve a fourfold Union: banking union, fiscal union, competitiveness union and political union. Progress must be made in parallel on each of the four components.'

34 *Notre Europe,* June 2012. The report was drawn up on the initiative of J. Delors and H. Schmidt. See also 'EMU: long-term matters are urgent matters', *Notre Europe*, 13 September 2012.

35 See *Le Monde*, 18 May 2013, pp. 1, 6.

36 See *Financial Times*, 28 August 2012, p. 4.

37 See the Delors plan set out in the white paper 'Growth, Competitiveness, Employment: The Challenges and Ways Forward into the 21st Century', COM(93) 700, December 1993. For other programmes for growth see Guido Montani and George Irvin, 'Transforming economic governance of the Eurozone', 18 May 2010, at www.europa-union. de/dachverband/news/transforming-economic-governance-of-the-eurozone.

38 *Le Monde*, 15 June 2012, p. 3.

39 In the spring of 2010 the European Council ratified a new 10-year programme to enhance competitiveness and the performance of the EU under the title 'Europe

2020'. The initiatives planned mainly concerned an increase in employment, investment in research, improvement in the level of education, and so on. However, and despite efforts for closer monitoring of the plans of member states, coordination remains slack, and implementation of the measures depends on national governments. It is thus almost certain that the plan will not work. See Yannos Papantoniou, *The Lessons of the Eurozone Crisis*, Friends of Europe, spring 2011, pp. 91ff.

40  See Silvia Merfer and Jean Pisani-Ferry, *The Simple Macroeconomics of North and South EMU*, Working Paper, Bruegel, July 2012; Z. Darvas, *The Greek Debt Trap: An Escape Plan*, Contribution 19/2012, Bruegel, November 2012, p. 10.

41  According to P. Krugman, *IHT*, 31 July 2012, p. 9: 'What could turn this dangerous situation around? The answer is fairly clear: policy makers would have to (a) do something to bring southern Europe's borrowing costs down and (b) give Europe's debtors the same kind of opportunity to export their way out of trouble that Germany received during the good years – that is, create a boom in Germany that mirrors the boom in southern Europe between 1999 and 2007. (And yes, that would mean a temporary rise in German inflation.) The trouble is that Europe's policy makers seem reluctant to do (a) and completely unwilling to do (b).'

42  See M. Wolf, 'How central banks beat deflation', *Financial Times,* ft.com, 16 April 2013.

43  M. Wolf, 'A new form of European Union', *Financial Times*, ft.com, 12 June 2012.

44  See European Council, President, EUCO 127/12, Presse 13, 28 June 2012; European Council, 28–29 June 2012, Euro 76/12, Concl., p. 11.

45  See H. Dixon, *IHT*, 2 July 2012, p. 18.

46  See G. Wolff, *A Budget for Europe's Monetary Union*, Policy Contribution 2012/22, Bruegel, December 2012.

47  See O. Cramme, *The Power of European Integration: Choice and Purpose for Centre-Left Politics, After the Third Way*, Policy Network, 2012, pp. 157ff. After observing that the Union has now become a nightmare, Leonard and Zielonka propose a 'Union of incentives', where there will be clear incentives for states and societies, to induce them to participate in the European project. Their proposals, however, are neither clear nor complete. M. Leonard and J. Zielonka, *A Europe of Incentives: How to Regain the Trust of Citizens and the Markets*, European Council of Foreign Relations, 2012.

48  See Lamy, 'Setting up and governing the euro', *Notre Europe*, 10 July 2012, p. 4.

49  See J. Delors, 'Rules, but a vision above all', *Notre Europe*, 11 September 2012.

50  Lamy, 'Setting up and governing the euro', p. 6.

51  The President of the European Commission, José Manuel Barroso, in a speech he gave in the European Parliament, said that the common goal was the creation of 'a federation of nation states, which shall deal with common problems through the participation of all the members in exercising sovereignty'. See *IHT*, 14 September 2012, p. 9. His speech provoked the immediate reaction of the head of the Liberal Alliance of the European Parliament, Guy Verhofstadt, who pointed out that the Union needs Community institutions independent of the member states. In his comments (*Ta Nea*, 14 September 2012) J. Pisani-Ferry noted: 'It is impossible for a common European direction to arise from ... governments and parliaments that are uniquely answerable to their own voters. Europe must give an answer to the authentic, up to date, representation of the common interest.' See also a related

article by P. Ioakimides. 'The only solution is federation', *Ta Nea*, 28 September 2012, p. 9.

52  According to Veron, *The Challenges of Europe's Fourfold Union*, p. 1: 'Europe must overcome its tendency to jump to permanent solutions and acknowledge the need for pragmatic short-term actions that are tailored to the urgency of the crisis'.

53  Various views have been voiced on the process of completing the Treaties and formulating an institutional framework for the adjustment of existing regulations to new needs. See D. Cohn-Bendit and G. Verhofstadt, *Debout l' Europe! Manifeste pour une revolution postnationale en Europe 2012*, André Versaille, 2012; Jean-Claude Piris, *The Future of Europe: Towards a Two-Speed EU?*, Cambridge University Press, 2012; H. W. Platzer, *Vom Euro-Krisenmanagement zu einer neuen politschen Architektur EU?*, Friedrich-Ebert Stiftung, 2012. Gavin Hewitt, *The Lost Continent*, Hodder and Stoughton, 2013, p. 318, is far more pessimistic: 'Europe … had had its dream. It was flawed and proved dangerous. Its leaders were fearful of their currency breaking up with the risk of economic collapse and yet they lacked the confidence to push forward and redesign their continent…. They have held back, unsure of the assent of their citizens, who remain stubbornly committed to the nation state.'

# Appendix

## Key meetings and decisions of the institutions of the European Union relating to the financial crisis

A comprehensive listing of the meetings is provided; almost all are discussed in the text, and for these the relevant pages are indicated. Note that the decisions of the organs of the European Union, including those from the meetings listed below and discussed in the text, can be found on the Union's official website, http:// Europa.eu.

| Institutions | Date | Page |
|---|---|---|
| | **2009** | |
| **Eurogroup** Greece is called upon to take measures to reduce its budget deficit | 19 October | 24 |
| **Eurogroup, Ecofin** It is noted that Greece did not respond to the advice given from time to time with regard to the rules of fiscal discipline | 1–2 December | 27 |
| **European Council** The need to implement EU rules and the responsibility of every member state for the management of its problems is reiterated | 10–11 December | 28 |
| | **2010** | |
| **European Council** Energy and innovation | 4 February | |
| **Eurozone summit** Discussion of the Greek crisis but no decision taken | 11 February | 37 |
| **Ecofin** Assessing Greece's government debt and deficit | 16 February | 38 |
| **Ecofin** The Greek problem deferred to the next summit | 10 March | 40 |
| **Eurozone summit** Greece's efforts are acknowledged. Decision taken for bilateral loans to be contracted between member states, if this is deemed necessary | 25 March | 41 |

# Trajectory of the Greek financial crisis

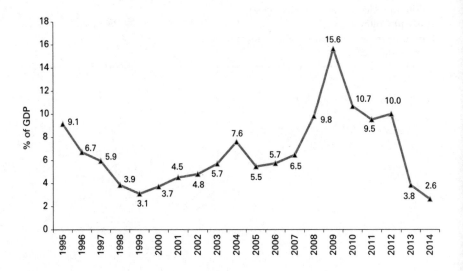

**Figure 1** Greece's deficit as a percentage of gross domestic product, 1995–2014.
Source: European Commission

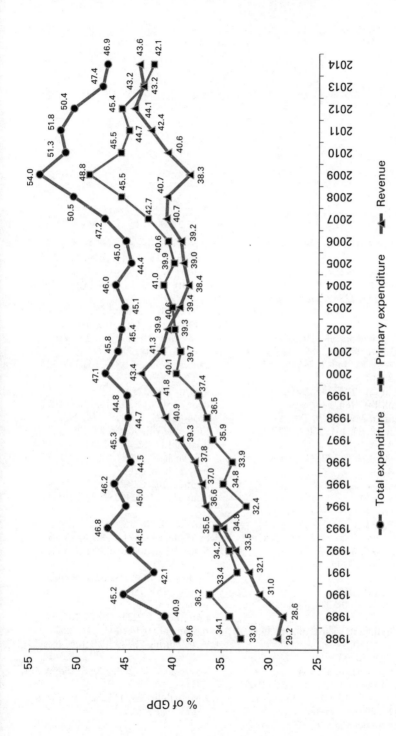

**Figure 2** Greece's expenditure and revenue, as a percentage of gross domestic product, 1988–2014 (total expenditure is primary expenditure plus debt repayment). Source: European Commission

349

# Index